# JOHN WESLEY
*A Theological Biography*

MARTIN SCHMIDT

# JOHN WESLEY:

## *A Theological Biography*

VOLUME II
John Wesley's Life Mission
PART II

*Translated by*
DENIS INMAN

ABINGDON PRESS
NASHVILLE     NEW YORK

12/1976
Rel.

PRINTED IN GREAT BRITAIN
BY EBENEZER BAYLIS AND SON LIMITED
THE TRINITY PRESS, WORCESTER, AND LONDON

# Contents

# Contents

# Translator's Preface

THIS translation consists of the final chapters in Volume II of the original German edition.

In his preface to Volume II, Part 1 (pp. 7–8), Norman Goldhawk has already reproduced in full what Dr Schmidt says in his author's preface about his method of procedure throughout the second volume of his theological biography of John Wesley. Doubtless anticipating a possible criticism of the fact that in this volume he does not devote a chapter specifically to Welsey as a theologian, however, Dr Schmidt also adds by way of self-justification some remarks which apply more immediately to this second part of the English translation. 'The author thought long and hard as to whether or not he should include a separate chapter on "John Wesley as a theologian", particularly bearing in mind the publication in recent years of major studies on specific doctrines – for example, David Lerch and Harald Lindström on sanctification and John Deschner on Christology. He finally decided against this course, on the grounds that it seemed to him so typical of Wesley that his utterances on matters of doctrine were made in sermons, in devotional writings and cautionary tracts, and in the cut and thrust of polemical and apologetic debate, in which he invariably spoke pungently, to the point and to the immediate situation. It would be misleading if a biographer were to diffuse this inherent concreteness by generalising abstractions.'

As in the earlier volumes, quotations from John Wesley's *Journal*, *Letters* and *Sermons* have been reproduced according to the text of the Standard Edition. In some instances I have corrected slips or misprints in the original text or notes, and in others added to the latter. In the case of John Whitehead's obituary address I have ventured to make a series of alterations to the page references in the notes, a liberty warranted, I believe, by direct cross-reference to the address itself.

TRANSLATOR'S PREFACE

The Bibliography includes several works which have appeared since the original German edition was published in 1966. Unlike the German original, the Index only relates to this final part-volume, as each of the earlier parts of the English translation has its own Index.

Finally, I wish to place on record my profound indebtedness to David Tripp, a former Circuit colleague, for his unstinting and inspired assistance in resolving countless linguistic problems.

CULLERCOATS
*1973*

# SIX

# *John Wesley as Preacher*

METHODISM first came into the public eye as a preaching movement, and retained this character as its determinative heritage. This
image was not, however, imprinted on it from its very inception, for
in the student circles at Oxford personal pastoral care had dominated
its initial way of life and governed its external activity. In his turning
to the work of preaching, John Wesley's distinctive idea of mission,
which had driven him to Georgia, finally found its proper expression.
Conversely, his missionary endeavour—that which was begun and
broken off there, and that which was begun afresh and so magni-
ficently pursued at home—was bound to entail a high evaluation of
preaching. He had hardly returned from the New World before he
was continually preaching, in the early Christian manner, the
message of repentance, new birth, justification, joy in salvation and
earnest pursuit of sanctification. Behind this lay a basic theological
decision. He elevated the questions which he repeatedly dealt with
in his sermons to the normative content of the whole Christian
proclamation. The very fact that he preferred to identify himself as a
man of one book[1] expressed his determination to confine himself to
what was essential, to the Bible itself. But even within these limits he
was still selective. Consequently, the limited scope of his preaching
themes seems to round off the picture—the picture of a single-minded
man who had made up his mind and was free from problems.

And yet this is not the whole story. One cannot but be amazed that
for all this concentration and within the confined framework which
he imposed upon himself by his method of work Wesley remained
concerned for a genuine theological culture. His sermons themselves
developed into doctrinal statements of principle. This was possible
only because he conceived of preaching as a theological task. In a
conversation which he had on 13th September 1739 with a serious
Anglican clergyman,[2] he said this in particularly clear terms. The
latter asked in what points the Methodists differed from the Church

of England. Wesley replied bluntly: In none. On the contrary, they were preaching the doctrines which the Church of England, in its official Book of Homilies—the Reformation sermons by Hugh Latimer, Nicholas Ridley and Thomas Cranmer—had not only approved of but laid down as normative standards. It is not the Methodists, therefore, who are the sectarians, but that section of the Anglican clergy which has abandoned these doctrines. Wesley, then, appealed exclusively to that evangelical strand within the Anglican tradition which ran directly from the Reformation. He then went straight on, however, to define the differences more precisely. All of them concerned one point—the relationship between justification and sanctification, or, to put it another way, the sequence of inward experience governing the separate phases of the life of faith. Wesley judged that those who were not of a Protestant mind normally took justification and sanctification to be one and the same thing. They thereby attributed too much to man's own activity. For them, to become holy meant to make oneself holy. On this basis, justification came out looking, at best, like a later, secondary act in the process of a Christian's growth, and not as what it should be—its permanently effective source. For the only and all-sufficient cause of justification was for him the death and the righteousness of Jesus: only thereby was there any possibility whatever of a Christian life, since our own inherited nature is incapable of good and unworthy of God. But what, then, does Christian life mean? His opponents among the Anglican theologians detected in it something external, as if it were a matter first of all of doing no harm, then of doing good in the conventional ways, namely, giving loyalty to the Church by attending worship and using the sacraments and helping one's neighbour. But for Wesley himself holiness meant a completely inward process for which only the strongest words were adequate, namely, the life of God in the soul of man. It meant participation in the divine nature. It meant genuine discipleship after the pattern of Jesus. In sum, it meant a new heart, in which the image of the Creator Himself was reflected. This is why for John Wesley everything depended on the new birth. This was for him much more than the transition from a manifestly evil to an apparently good life, more than a change from vice to virtue. New birth meant for him a complete transformation of one's inmost nature. Instead of love for created things, love for the Creator filled the Christian and instead of earthly affections, a desire for heaven and for God Himself. New Birth meant that the inherited natural image of the devil was replaced by the image of God, and the redeemed man had left behind the world of darkness. Now the light of salvation shone around him. He stood on new ground.

John Wesley never compromised on these basic convictions. Only half a year later, the opportunity again presented itself to assert this.[3] At Newgate the Ordinary had reproached him for having deserted his colours and gone over to the Nonconformists (Dissenters), the non-Anglicans. The bitter censure contained in such a comment was based on the still prevalent British notion that there could be only one Church in one country. The medieval axiom *Cuius regio, eius religio*[3a] survived here for a particularly long time, and only after bitter struggles lasting nearly a century had the Dissenters been able to win even a secondary place in the life of the nation. Wesley replied in the same vein as before, saying in effect: It is not I who have deviated, but the others, who do not stand by the Primitive Church and the Reformation. Admittedly, it was noteworthy that in saying this he thereby made no distinction between ethical and dogmatic criteria; for he also identified as Dissenters in the proper sense those who blasphemed their Lord by their godless way of life. Nevertheless, this only underlined the seriousness with which he regarded the whole question. As so often, he sharpened the formulation of the question and the way of thinking which was brought against him. For him, doctrinal decisions and practical decisions carried the same weight; in this respect he was of course in close affinity to German Pietism. Like the latter, he demanded that Holy Communion should only be administered to earnest Christians.[4] On closer examination, however, a notable difference comes to light. For the primacy of doctrine over life is ensured by Wesley's judgement that those who impugned the authority of the Bible and so robbed Jesus of His Crown Rights as Redeemer and generally denied the unique saving power of faith were Dissenters 'of a very high kind' because they struck at the very foundation of Christian existence.[5] Wesley continued: 'Were their principles universally to obtain, there could be no true Church upon earth.'

As a result, his sermons, in the form in which they have come down to posterity, give the impression of being theological treatises which develop, expound and prove the central statements in extremely simple terms, but at the same time in a strictly logical way, and also repeatedly draw out the practical consequences, and open out into exhortation or warning. They keep strictly to the subject, but without being slavishly bound to the text. Not infrequently they offer detailed exegesis of particular texts, in which not only the essential meaning of the words in question, for the most part in the original Greek, is closely examined and carefully brought out, but also text-critical considerations are taken up in the light of the history of the text. The sermons forego rhetorical embellishment, vivid imagery, startling turns of phrase. They use a wealth of biblical quotations, but otherwise settle for familiar phraseology. They make no detours, but move directly towards their goal.

This is the case in the first sermon, which may be regarded as a manifesto. Its title, 'Salvation by Faith', is derived from the text on which it is based: 'By grace are ye saved through faith' (Ephesians 2⁸). The very first sentence expresses the decisive truth. All the blessings which God has bestowed upon man are of His sheer grace and favour. His free grace has given everything; nothing has been earned. Man has no claim on God. This holds good from start to finish. It is true of the creaturely relationship, of the life which God has bestowed on man, but even more of His own divine image which He has stamped on the new creature. Such free grace continues to the present day. Everything that man does has been wrought in him by God, and God alone.

This principle of God's sole agency in itself prevents man from asserting his own achievements. Even if he did have any to offer, even if they were really impressive, they would have been produced by God in any case. They would not be his own, but God's. Man's very creatureliness, properly understood, denies man the path to self-glorification. How can he, a bad tree, whom original sin has corrupted, bring forth anything but evil fruit? If therefore sinful men find favour with God, then it is grace upon grace.

With this Wesley has reached his subject, and sets down the simple statement: 'Grace is the source, faith is the condition, of salvation.' Then he asks further after the nature of saving faith, and the nature of the salvation which is guaranteed to such faith. In discussing this in detail, he pursues the inner logic to its final conclusion and makes full and free use of the entire content of the New Testament. He says: the required true faith is not the faith of a heathen, nor is it the faith of a devil. In this context, his whole interest lies with the marked difference between the two. The faith of a devil goes significantly further and gains deeper insights than the faith of a heathen. Heathen faith comes to a halt in the Outer Court, demonic faith penetrates into the secret of the Holy Place. Heathen faith gets as far as a general presentiment of God, demonic faith knows that Jesus is the Son of God and is sufficiently conversant with the Bible to recognize its consistent testimony to this truth. But saving faith, the faith which really counts, true Christian faith, towers above this. It even surpasses a third stage, the faith which the Apostles had in Jesus' lifetime, although this faith was in a position to work miracles, to vanquish demons and—for Wesley the greatest thing of all—included the authority to proclaim God's lordship. With these preliminary discussions, Wesley has claimed for true faith a position of superlative eminence from which he can demonstrate its distinctive greatness in positive terms. Faith which conclusively saves man is first and foremost faith in Jesus Christ. It has Jesus Christ, and through Him God, as its proper object. In this respect it is distinguished clearly and finally from the kind of faith which ancient or modern heathens may possess. It contrasts with the faith of a devil, in that it does not state an intellectual opinion imposed by compelling arguments, but has to do with the heart just as much as with the head. Indeed, it brings in its train a definite disposition of the whole man. Man believes with the heart, and thereby he is justified (Romans 10¹⁰). As the Bible puts it: 'If thou shalt confess with thy mouth the Lord Jesus, and shalt believe with thy heart that God hath raised him from the dead, thou shalt be saved' (Romans 10⁹).

This in turn indicates in what way genuine full faith surpasses that of the apostles in Jesus' lifetime. Full faith is knowledge, perception and acknowledgement all in one, because it takes account of facts, submits to them, grasps them in their internal and mutual consistency, and translates them into its own life. It acknowledges, first of all, that the death of Jesus was necessary. It further acknowledges that the death of Jesus possesses atoning power. Finally, it knows that the resurrection of Jesus conceals in itself an unexampled power, becaue it gives man access to eternal life and immortality.

Wesley is now in a proper position to conclude his description and definition of faith, which is one of the most notoriously difficult tasks of Christian dogmatics. In the light of what has been said, Christian faith is not simply an assent to the Message brought to us in Jesus and declared by Him. On the contrary, Christian faith is a full reliance on the blood of Jesus, a trust in His merits. To put it another way: it rests entirely on the power of His life, His death, His resurrection. Consequently, Christian faith means that one relies absolutely on Jesus, who was offered up for us, and lives in us. When I really know this, then I stake my life on Him: I close with Him; I cleave to Him; I accept Him as the true wisdom, righteousness, sanctification and redemption (1 Corinthians 1³⁰). I ratify for myself the fundamental declarations of the New Testament, above all those of the Pauline epistles. Such faith cannot settle for anything less. There is nothing either forced or artificial about it.

With this, Wesley turns to the second section of the sermon, which is devoted to salvation. First of all he establishes that this salvation is a present blessing. It does not hang suspended in mid-air, nor is it in the first instance a goal for eternity, but rather a present reality. This is why the Apostle speaks of it in the perfect tense. This temporal definition is followed by a definition of content. Salvation is deliverance from sin. Here again Wesley achieves a sharper formulation by the distinctions he makes. Jesus saves from all sins: from past as well as from present sins, from individual sinful acts as well as from one's general state of guilt, from sins of the flesh as well as from sins of the spirit. There is no sin without a cure. But equally Jesus annuls the guilt of sin just as well as its power. In Wesley's view, guilt is the primary, indeed the most important, factor in sin. For, by basing itself on and drawing its nourishment from the Law, sin issues an unavoidable indictment against us. Jesus has quashed this indictment by nailing it to his cross (Colossians 2¹⁴). There is therefore no longer any condemnation for those who believe in Jesus Christ.[6]

Deliverance from guilt brings with it deliverance from fear, a fear which has two aspects. It is fear of the penalty and fear of the wrath of God. Christians have put behind them the fear of a slave; filial fear, which has love and trust as its foundation and essence, has replaced it. Therefore they have peace with God, and the love of God dwells in their hearts. They are firmly convinced, albeit not at every moment of their lives, that neither death nor life, neither things present nor things to come, neither height nor depth nor any other creature can separate them from the love of God which is in Christ Jesus their Lord (Romans 8³⁸⁻⁹).

Then follows the highest stage—deliverance from the power of sin. This consists in regeneration, the new birth from God (1 John 5[18]). Here again, Wesley strives after clarity. Anyone who is born of God through faith, he explains, no longer sins from any habit of sin, for this would mean that sin reigns in him. Further, he does not sin deliberately, for as long as he abides in faith his will is resolutely set against all sin. Indeed, he abhors it like deadly poison. Nor does he sin through any sinful desire, for his desire is constantly directed towards the good and perfect will of God, and nips in the bud any unholy desire. Lastly, he does not sin out of weakness, whether in thought, word or deed. Here, at this most difficult point, John Wesley offers an unconvincing argument. In his judgement, the weaknesses of the believer are in no serious competition with his will, as the latter is definitely directed towards constant, unbroken communion with God. Here it becomes clear how voluntarist Wesley's thinking is. In this respect he is in harmony with the general tenor of the Bible. But the Bible says more, always reckoning with the power of sin to override even the will of the believer.

For Wesley, faith reaches its zenith in the new birth, which bestows new life in God through Jesus Christ. His sermon on faith ends up by becoming a sermon on regeneration. In this respect he shows his true colours as a disciple of Pietism, and also as its friend and ally. The new life is certainly 'hid with Christ in God' (Colossians 3[3]). But the new-born man gladly and thankfully receives the pure milk of the Word. He grows by it and advances in the might of his God and Lord from faith to faith, from grace to grace, until he grows up to the complete man according to the measure and stature of the fullness of Jesus Christ his Exemplar (Ephesians 4[13]).[7]

Whereas the new life calls for the more biological metaphors of growth and maturity, the old life had been dominated by the imagery of battle. Here John Wesley finds the point of departure for his characteristic and highly controversial doctrine of Christian perfection. The life of Jesus Christ becomes the life of the Christian himself.

Having thus defined the meaning of saving faith, its presuppositions and its goal, in such a decisive and comprehensive way, he deals in the third section of the sermon with the objections which may be raised against it. The first that he takes up is the one against which Paul and the Reformers had to take issue. Does not the preaching of faith abrogate the requirement of good words? Does it not devalue love, and above all the Law? Wesley retorts, first of all, that in fact his preaching of faith is expressly aimed at producing precisely love and good works through creative faith. But then he adroitly turns the objection right round and says: Anyone who does not preach faith, devalues the Law. For according to the testimony of the Scriptures only faith is capable of fulfilling the Law, because it alone properly perceives the intention of the Law, and it alone creates love, which fulfils it. To put it more plainly, one may say that everyone who believes, obeys Jesus Christ completely: he follows Him alone, he binds himself to Him in trust and in his manner of life—and does not that mean satisfying the Law of God? Through such faith it becomes possible—and this is the proper context for a favourite phrase so constantly used by Wesley—for the new man to have in himself the very mind that was in Jesus Christ Himself.[8] Is there any greater demand or any higher expectation than this? He asks further: Does not the preaching of such faith lead man into pride? The answer: Not at all. The message of justification through faith, properly understood, is in fact precisely calculated to exclude pride. For only if man were to attain to righteousness before God on the basis of his own works would there be any occasion at all for self-preening. Grace, when experienced, makes one humble and awakens the endeavour to show oneself worthy of it.

This leads on to the next objection. Does not the message of grace and faith encourage men to persist in their sins? This abuse, answers Wesley, is admittedly possible. There may be transgressors who presume to continue in sin so that grace may automatically come their way. These people themselves must answer for their shameless conduct. However, those who hear the message of grace with a pure heart are far too preoccupied with grieving over their own failings to want to make capital out of them for the future. They simply take to themselves the miracle of the forgiveness of sins and, as the Acts of the Apostles shows (for example, in the case of the Philippian jailer) come to faith without delay.

But is there not the opposite danger? Cannot men, through the assurance that nothing whatever depends on their efforts, be driven to despair? True, such despair is unavoidable. It must be endured. Without it, there is no faith in salvation by grace. Indeed, it is the intrinsic and decisive presupposition for faith. Admittedly, this is an uncomfortable doctrine[9]—looked at from the human side. But behind this all too human judgement stands the Devil himself. In reality the message of sins forgiven is the most pleasant news that can be communicated to man. For when the Gospel announces: there is grace for Zacchaeus, a public robber, for Mary Magdalene, a prostitute, then many a man who might despair of himself will say: then there is grace probably even for me; there is still hope, even for me.

With this Wesley has refuted every objection. But what if he is advised not to proclaim this doctrine of saving faith indiscriminately to all and sundry? To this he counter-poses: Whom, then, should I exclude—the poor perhaps? According to the will of Jesus the good news is precisely for them. Or the unlearned? Precisely they are called to apprehend the mysteries of God. Or the young? Jesus rebuked His disciples when they wanted to send the children away from Him. Or, lastly, the sinners? It is precisely they who are addressed by the Gospel. Should one perhaps go the opposite way about? Should one except the rich, the learned, the reputable, the moral men? To be sure, they except themselves oft and enough from hearing the Gospel: but this is all the less reason why the preacher may spare them the message. The commission of Jesus reads: 'Go and preach the Gospel to every creature' (Mark 16[15]). With these observations— and they may look rhetorical, but they are not—Wesley protests against imputing a class-structure to the Gospel, in any shape or form and for whatever reason.

On the contrary, Wesley asserts, the doctrine of saving faith through grace was never more seasonable than it is today. Only with this doctrine can one resist the romanization which is insidiously taking root. By this doctrine England was freed from Popery. It was the corner-stone of the Reformation and is still therefore its immoveable rock.

The doctrine of saving faith through free grace is the sign of victory in the apocalyptic battle between God and Satan, which is why the Devil has deployed all the powers of hell against it. He strove through lies and calumnies to impede Martin Luther in his work of reviving it, and when that was impossible he sought by all means to destroy him. Armed with this doctrine a little child, holding a reed in his hand, will face up to a heavily armed warrior and prevail over him. Thus God has made His strength perfect in weakness. On this note of victory John Wesley concludes his sermon on saving faith.

In retrospect, one perceives the simple stylistic means, but at the same time the carefully calculated application of these devices, by which he achieved his ends. He works from first to last with the thrust of the Biblical declaration itself. This governs the sequence of thought. The outstanding formal characteristics are gradation, climax, antithesis and arresting question. By means of over-statement he leads the argument as developed on to a higher level and in this way gives it trenchancy and originality. The dignity and uniqueness of faith could hardly be made more readily understandable than by the climactic progression which ascends from heathen through demonic to apostolic faith and reaches its peak in Christian faith. Again, although the importance of salvation could perhaps have been brought out in a different way, both the progression of thought from faith through new birth to the new and perfect life of communion with God and the way in which salvation was developed as deliverance from the guilt, fear and power of sin must have brought home the doctrine itself just as effectively as the universal claim of this message. It still remains worthy of note how little space and energy John Wesley expends on polemic, which could well have been prompted by the altogether differently orientated eighteenth century with its moralistic self-reliance. For him, positive attestation of the early Christian, Pauline message was enough. Here he proceeded in a manner completely dissimilar to that of the German Franz Volkmar Reinhard (1753–1812), who two generations later in his famous Reformation Sunday sermon of 1800 reasserted Luther's doctrine of justification and sharply settled accounts with the moralism of the Enlightenment.[10] But John Wesley did not even attempt to establish or explain the authority of the Bible, particularly the New Testament. For him, it stood secure. He made it his starting-point, with an uncomplicated natural certainty.

We must now consider the second sermon. Taking up King Agrippa's ironic confession to Paul: 'Almost thou persuadest me to be a Christian' (Acts 26[28]), this sermon discusses in detail the question: What does it mean to be almost a Christian? It sharpens the question by asking further: What does it mean to be really a Christian?[11] It is not without its own fascination to establish that there were precedents in British tradition for the use of this text and theme. Just eighty years before, one of the most effective preachers of late Puritanism, Matthew Meade (1630–99), had delivered a famous series of sermons on this in London and by request had published

their substance as a treatise, which gained a wide readership.[12] It was
certainly no coincidence that Wesley again took up this tradition,
even if in the details of his performance he diverged widely from the
Puritan preacher and went his own way. As with Meade, one is
immediately struck by the force of the challenge. In the formula
'almost a Christian' is included for Wesley first of all the honesty
which prevails among the heathen. Part of this is that one has regard
for others, that one respects their property, that one does not oppress
the poor, that one does not defraud one's neighbour. All this comes
under the general idea of justice. A second group of duties and
patterns of behaviour among the heaven results from the demand
for truth. It was impossible to call upon God as one's witness if one
lied or if one falsely accused one's neighbour. Indeed, liars were
reckoned as a disgrace on mankind, as a plague on society. Further,
they expected from one another a certain degree of love and help,
such as food for the hungry or clothes for the naked.

But this is not enough. 'Being almost a Christian' demands a piety
which is at least outwardly identifiable. Anyone worthy of this name
does nothing that the Bible forbids. He does not take the name of
God in vain. He neither profanes the Lord's Day, nor suffers others
to profane it. He does not commit adultery. He does not make himself
guilty of any uncleanness in word or look. He abstains from all idle,
disparaging and frivolous gossip. He also desists from the fondness
for raillery, jesting and horse-play which were so much appreciated
by the heathen.[13] In all things he scrupulously conducts himself by
the Golden Rule: What you don't want other people to do to you,
don't do to them either. He by no means confines his good works to
such enterprises as do not cost him much. On the contrary, he really
puts himself out and sacrifices time, money and thought to help
others. He cares about them like a pastor: he reproves the wicked;
he instructs the ignorant; he strengthens the waverers; he comforts
the afflicted. He is at pains to arouse those who are asleep and to lead
them to their Saviour. It is hardly necessary to remark that he is a
regular church-goer and communicant. And this is a serious matter
to him, for it does not occur to him to appear in great finery so as to
be admired at least as much for his wealth as for his piety. Much less
still can it happen that he falls asleep during the sermon, or that,
leaning back comfortably, he is immersed in his own thoughts or
looks round with a bored stare. No, everything about him indicates

close attention and worthy deportment. He knows why he is there and lets others see that he knows it. If we further add to this picture that at home he constantly prays with his family and allows as well time for private prayer, then we certainly have in our mind's eye a man who visibly and convincingly offers the outward form of godliness. Only one more thing is needed to make him an Almost Christian. What is that? It is sincerity—taken here in the sense of a final governing principle—which conditions the man's very self and penetrates his whole life, so that a convincing figure emerges.

To be sincere means to have in oneself a real and effectual principle from which all that has been mentioned flows. For without this principle one would not yet have even the honesty to the lack of which the heathen were so sensitive. One would be a hypocrite. Sincerity includes in itself having only one aim in life, namely, to serve God with one's whole heart, to fulfil His will, to want to please Him.

But is this not carrying things too far? How on earth can all this describe, not a complete Christian, but only an almost Christian? Wesley counters this objection by saying that he himself had in fact thought this way for a long time. He had held what has been detailed to be the marks of a true Christian, but he had since learned to see things differently.

The real Christian has even deeper sources from which he receives his inner life. These are faith and love. Faith which is active in love (Galatians 5⁶), and love which springs from faith. Love of God—which is what characterizes real Christian perfection—a love which knows nothing whatever but God, no wish, no aim, no task, no desire, but Him; love which cries out with the Psalmist, 'Whom have I in heaven but thee? and there is none other on earth that I desire but thee' (Psalm 73²⁵). Such a man, who is filled with nothing but desire for God and the desire to become like Him, is crucified to the world and it to him. 'He that abideth in love abideth in God and God abideth in him' (1 John 4¹⁶). From such love flows spontaneously love of neighbour. The question, Who is my neighbour? answers itself. Every child of the heavenly Father, even one's enemy, indeed even God's enemy, is one's neighbour; nobody can be excepted. There is no other way to describe such love than the way Paul does in the 13th chapter of the first Epistle to the Corinthians. Such love grows only in the soil of faith. Without faith it is impossible to please God or to have any part or lot in Him. But faith gives man new life from God. It frees the believer from judgement and confers eternal life. Faith, which thus purifies the heart from pride, carnal desire and all unrighteousness, which completely fills the heart with true love for God and neighbour—a love which is stronger than death, which is consumed in the service of others, because it knows that this is service for God, a love which not only willingly endures contempt and ridicule as the reproach of Christ but can rejoice in it—such faith and such love characterize the true, real Christian. This is an entirely different faith from, say, an intellectual conviction or a convention into which we drift on the current of tradition.

Where, however, do we find the witnesses to such faith? Let every man ask himself whether he lacks something that is essential even to the status of an almost Christian. Let every man wake up to the demands. Let him confess and lament his sins and trust solely in the grace of God in Jesus Christ. Let every man then cry out in all humility with Peter: 'Lord, thou knowest all things; thou knowest that I love thee.'[14]

In retrospect, this sermon is seen to retain all the features observed in the first sermon: precision of thought, gradation, inexorable call to decision, seriousness and depth of demand. And yet new, different elements appear. Much as here, too, the fundamental doctrine of the Reformation—justification of the sinner by grace alone through faith alone—is maintained and set to work, it does not dominate the thrust of the argument. The theme and tenor have a different ring about them: they aim at the perfection of the Christian in love for God. It is to this all-consuming, all-conquering love that John Wesley's passion is devoted. The ethical rigorism which seems to predominate, especially in the first challenging, and formally speaking more effective part, has no more than an introductory function. The heart of the matter is love. The Wesley who speaks here is not the Wesley who bears the stamp of the Reformation, but the Wesley on whom Romanic mysticism has made the strongest impression. Here the picture of the perfect saint, whose perfection consists in the unaffected simplicity by which the creaturely world is transcended, has stood sponsor. It is the picture which he had received from his favourite book, the biography of the Marquis de Renty, the picture by which on first encounter he assessed and overrated Count Zinzendorf.

Both these sermons, then, are capable of expressing the motivating forces and mental range which were in Wesley. The third of his sermons, bearing the title 'Scriptural Christianity', adds a new note— that of mission. Its structure is as follows. Scriptural Christianity is to be presented first of all as it exists in the individual, then as it spreads from one to another, and lastly as it covers the whole earth. This time a factual statement from the Acts of the Apostles ($4^{31}$) forms the text: 'They all were filled with the Holy Ghost.'[15] Wesley begins historically. He alludes to the fact that the same assertion has already been made at the time of Peter's Pentecost sermon, and immediately draws attention to the fact that in the further scene which is mentioned here—the return of Peter and John to the infant Christian community—the Holy Spirit is received without any super-natural signs. This leads to a clear and emphatic call to sobriety. When God bestows His Spirit on men, His purpose is not directed towards some outward phenomenon which is experienced only by a few as a sign of distinction and which is gazed at in astonishment by the world, but rather towards something deeper, something better, something available to all, with which God equips Jesus' disciples. It is, as Wesley typically puts it, the mind which was in Jesus Christ Himself. It is the manifold fruit of the Spirit, which Paul describes as being first and foremost love, joy, patience, gentleness and goodness (Galatians $5^{22-23}$), to which are conjoined faithfulness, meekness and temperance.[16] It is not the extraordinary gifts of the Spirit, which have so often been the object of idle speculation and egotistic arro-gance in the history of the church, but the ordinary gifts which are valid for every generation, that are the decisive gifts. It is these which constitute Scriptural Christianity.

After this fundamental clarification John Wesley goes on to describe the course of church history, viewed from within. Through the preaching of the Apostles, first of all an individual was brought to faith. He was convicted of his sin, felt deeply repentant about it, and believed in Jesus. He therefore received the Spirit of God; hope in the world to come was kindled in him; he knew himself to be a child of God; he lived his further life in constant communion with Jesus. Indeed, this was the very essence of his life. Out of profound grati-tude for all this, love of God took possession of his heart, as did love of neighbour. Quite spontaneously, the corresponding deeds ensued. This was how the inner life of the early Christian was effected. In the very nature of the case the community life was commensurately transformed. A renunciation of possession of earthly goods was immediately taken for granted, for this is a direct manifestation of the fact that the first Christians were crucified to the world and the world to them.

Equally, they could not do other than feel compassion for those to whom this news was still unknown. It would have been unnatural if they had failed to spare any pains to win them for the new reality which determined their own life. And so they did good to all men (Galatians 6[10]), as John Wesley puts it in the all-embracing favourite formula of his days as a youth in the student circle at Oxford.[17] In doing so, they bore witness to the Gospel in a variety of ways. They threatened the unsuspecting sleepers who were indifferent to their salvation with the full force of God's wrath. They comforted the anxious by pointing them to the Advocate Jesus Christ who has borne the sins of every man and thereby reconciled men with God. They spurred on the faithful to love and to free and joyful obedience to God's will. They held up before them the high goal of holiness, which comprises one of the conditions of entry into eternal life (Hebrews 12[14]). The Word was their tool and their weapon. It was not without effect—not only in the faith of newly won adherents, but also in the enmity of opponents. The world felt itself assailed, and inevitably so, for its deeds were unmasked as ungodly. The religious leaders and authorities were stripped of their magnificence and dignity by the witness of the early Christians, for their pretension was contested by the matter and content of the message. The growth of Christianity and opposition by the non-Christian world went hand in hand. Both constantly increased in extent, depth and sharpness.[18] Thus John Wesley unfolds an extremely lively, animated picture of the history of the church which is far removed from the idyll which could have so easily followed from the initial sketch of the complete Christian.

Enmity from without led to a martyr-consciousness. The first Christians proved themselves servants of God in every situation of life, in all their conflicts, onslaughts, disappointments, calumnies and set-backs, as it is put in Paul's classical description in 2 Corinthians 6[4ff]. But this by no means meant—and here again John Wesley remains sober—that the inward effect of persecution had only been that of a salutary purifying process. Among the adherents of Jesus there was chaff as well as wheat, and almost from the very beginning the early Christian writers had occasion to bewail the decline of piety. But, asks John Wesley by way of preamble to the third part of his sermon, is that the whole truth? Do we not have to turn our attention to greater things, to higher aims, to wider horizons? Having only just spoken of the corruption of Christendom, at this decisive juncture he characteristically invokes the promise of God in order to redress the balance, and to provide a new point of departure. His most vigorous question is: Can Satan cause the truth of God to fail?[19]

With this rhetorical question Wesley strikes a positive note and introduces the special promise which is his real concern here. The time will come when Christianity will prevail over all, over men and institutions alike. The preacher summons his hearers to pause for a moment so as to let the picture of a Christian world sink in. The fact that it was Wesley who saw and passed on this vision takes on added significance in view of the fact that he had repeatedly quarrelled with his literary opponents as to whether or not England was a Christian country. He had categorically denied this assertion. Now he quotes the prophetic predictions, above all those of Isaiah, in order to represent the future kingdom of faith and righteousness according to the will of God as a reality.[20] With these predictions he directly links the expectation of Paul, which for him means a certainty that God will call home His ancient people the Jews to Himself and to salvation (Romans 11[1, 11, 12, 25, 26]). In portraying this kingdom of peace, Wesley becomes amazingly eloquent. No more war and destruction, nor yet strife between neighbours, no oppression of the weak, no exploitation of the poor, no robbery! Retaliation ceases; nobody commits evil; unkind words are no more to be heard; neither fraud nor guile now occur; candour and love govern men's dealings with one another. God is the undisputed Lord of all. Wesley ends this description of the eternal city by citing in full the 60th chapter of Isaiah, in which the world of light in its conquering power overcomes the darkness and transforms all things. Light is the symbol for complete knowledge of God.

After this magnificent vision of the future the preacher returns to the present. He asks trenchantly: Where does this Christianity exist today? Where do such Christians live now? Where do such circumstances prevail? Since this question is only capable of a negative answer, he now repeats with utmost emphasis his basic thesis that no

Christian country is to be found on this earth.[21] The significance of this judgement may be all the more strongly underlined by recalling Wesley's youthful dream of encountering primitive Christianity in the present at Herrnhut—even if this was six years previously.

Wesley knows what he is saying. On the one hand, like Paul he asks, nay adjures his hearers, if they should take him for a fool, to bear with him as a fool for God's sake. On the other hand, he explains the absolute necessity for someone to open up these home-truths to them. Let no man deceive himself or place his faith in any pleasantly familiar notions. Who knows whether the end of human history is not round the corner and whether this sermon is not the last warning which God will issue? After this appeal Wesley becomes quite specific and questions in turn all manner of persons in this city, both sexes, all age-groups, and constrains them to examine themselves unsparingly as to whether they match up to the picture of Scriptural Christianity which he has unveiled. He stands in the pulpit of the University Church of St Mary's, Oxford, and levels at the Professors and Fellows the question as to whether everything that they teach bears a genuine and real relation to the love of God. Are they really intent on making the students into soldiers of Christ, burning and shining lights of the Gospel? Indeed he goes so far as to touch on the seriousness with which they undertake their task—and this at a time when a certain laziness throughout the University life was all too well known. He emphatically secures himself against the misunderstanding that he might be addressing himself only to future clergymen. Not at all. He knows perfectly well that his hearers will be taking up every conceivable profession. He makes only one assumption: namely, that they intend to be Christians and to become better and better Christians. This holds good irrespective of profession. This is why he must put such pointed and personal questions. For if Christianity is not taken as seriously as he has presented it, then we shall deceive ourselves and profane the name of God. So he asks further, and with the same trenchancy, whether his hearers really intend to restore true Christianity and whether they are prepared to hold themselves available as instruments to this end. Indeed, he lifts his hand in the threatening gesture of the Old Testament prophets: Must God send hunger, pestilence or the sword, or the hordes of the Romish aliens, His apocalyptic horsemen, in order to bring England back to its first love such as signalized the early Church?

After such an appeal there is only one possible way for him to conclude—namely, with a prayer to God for His help. Any other, any renewed exhortation would only be an anticlimax. The eschatological and apocalyptic perspectives give to this thoroughly missionary sermon its special greatness. They protect it from sinking to the level of mere accusation or moralistic threat of hell. By putting this sermon in the setting of the dialectic of church history, he lifts it above its immediate, practical application, and yet correspondingly brings out the wider meanings of this application. Here again the formal and stylistic characteristics of his preaching recur: antithesis and gradation, together with the radical question demanding a decision. It is in the content, however, that the aforementioned new motifs make their appearance and give this sermon its distinctive character.

The three sermons discussed so far were preached in the University Church of St Mary's, Oxford, in the years 1738, 1741 and 1744. They were therefore suited to an academic audience. Their severely logical structure was calculated to make them attractive to this audience. To be sure, they were given universal application in their content; they had in mind Christian existence in general. Their simplicity conferred on them an almost lapidary character. The last of the three had a catastrophic consequence for him: the Vice-Chancellor, the real head of the university, demanded his manuscript and deprived him for the future from his right to the pulpit.[22]

We now turn to the group of sermons which has new birth as its subject. In the first of these, entitled 'The New Birth'[23] and based on Jesus' word to Nicodemus, 'Ye must be born again' (John 3[7]), Wesley in his usual manner plunges *in medias res*. The first sentence declares clearly and decisively that if it is proper to characterize any statements within the whole wide compass of Christian truth as fundamental, then only the following two come under consideration—justification and new birth. The former relates to the great work which God does for us when He forgives our sins. The latter has to do with the great work which God effects in us when He renews our life. Chronologically, neither of these takes place before or after the other. Conceptually, that is, in order of thinking, precedence must be given to justification, with which the new birth begins. Only when the wrath of God has been turned aside is His Spirit able to work in the hearts of those who believe. Wesley bluntly asks, Firstly: Why must we be born again? secondly: How must we be born again? finally: Where-to, for what ultimate purpose must this happen? He replies to the first question more fully than one expects. He does not begin by alluding to sin and man's sinful situation, but goes a step further back and begins with creation, which destined man to the divine likeness. Here, too, he proceeds with great precision. God created man as His image, but not primarily in terms of His immortal nature, although that is part of it; nor was His main concern man's dominant position within the total order of this world, real though this is. Rather, He willed to have in man an inner, moral likeness of Himself. What mattered to Him was righteousness and holiness (Ephesians 4[24]). God is love, so man should also become love. God is righteousness, so man should also exercise righteousness. God is mercy, so man should also be merciful. God is truth, so man should also speak the truth and live the truth. God is purity, so man should also keep himself pure. We see that Wesley takes up the strongest strategic position. His constructive interest in man dictates the order of the day. In accordance with the concise but rich doctrine of the original state, which has its centre of gravity not in the condition of man but in the intention of God, he moves on with the vigorous assertion that man was created in a mutable state. He had the ability to stand, but was equally exposed to the danger of falling. Disobedience to God's command, rebellion against his Lord, self-assertion and wilfulness brought misery upon him. So he sought his happiness not in God but in the world, in the works of God's hands. God had threatened him with death if he were to act against His prohibition, and in stepped death—not perhaps the death of the body, but a death of far greater terrors. He lost the life of God. Unselfconscious fellowship with God was forfeited; the child-like communion with the Father came to an end. He became an alien to the life which springs from God, and God became a stranger to him. Instead of seeking to be near Him, he fled from Him, and when he could no longer do this, he hid from Him. No longer confidence in God, but servile fear governed him. So he lost both the knowledge and love of God—the very thing which constituted the image of God in him. He became, as Wesley put it with another of his favourite expressions, unholy and unhappy.[24] The devil's image of pride and self-will impressed itself on him, and surrender to sensual appetites and desires allied him with the beasts. What happened to the first man happened to all men. His fate propagated itself in a continuous reproduction.

Only now does John Wesley introduce the concept of new birth. It is against the background of the hopeless situation into which humanity has brought itself that this concept begins to look convincing. If any deliverance is to come about, then it can only be by a completely new beginning.

How, then, is this new birth to take place? What is the peculiar nature of this process? Wesley recalls first of all, and in almost slavish dependence on the conversation with Nicodemus, that it is a mystery. 'The wind bloweth where it listeth, and thou hearest the sound thereof, but canst not tell whence it cometh and whither it goeth' (John 3⁸). The Holy Spirit and His work can be observed, but not explained. Therefore it is nonsensical to require a philosophical, logical analysis. The matter can, however, be made comprehensible by means of analogy. Here Wesley has recourse to the comparison between an embryo and a child which has grown to an independent existence. The embryo has every organ. It has eyes, ears, hands, feet, but they are as yet undeveloped. As soon as it is detached from the mother, these organs become active. Similarly with man. As soon as he is born of God, his unawakened spiritual organs become functional. God enlightens his eyes, that they may see the splendour of his calling. God opens his ears, so they hear His voice in His Word, which addresses to them the forgiveness of his sins. God permits him to attain a deep peace and to experience an inexpressible joy. The love of God is imparted to him, and he is completely transformed. And so a child of God is born. But this initial state is not the limit of his development, for it continues by a natural progression to bring him to full maturity. No other word is capable of expressing the nature of re-birth so aptly as the word 'change', and Wesley therefore uses it with repeated emphasis in the following sentences.[25] Everything has become different. Everything is changed into its complete opposite, and the man who makes this experience his own is confronted by a miracle.

What, then, is the final goal of the new birth? Its general direction has already been indicated: holiness. God wants saints. But holiness means that the original image of God in man is restored and that, as Wesley says yet again, the mind which was in Christ embeds itself in him. This is expressed in a continual love, a love which has now become one's higher nature and which embraces both God and one's fellow men. It knows no greater task in life than to offer every thought, word and deed as a continual sacrifice to God through Jesus Christ.[26]

At the same time such holiness imparts to man true fulfilment in life, what in popular parlance would be called happiness. For both belong inseparably together. Nobody can be permanently happy who does not lead a holy life. Only concord with God guarantees inward peace. The evidence of our own eyes confirms this: all unholy, ungodly tempers make man discontented and unhappy. They beget a hell in the heart—like malice, envy, jealousy, vindictiveness. But even softer passions create far more disquiet than pleasure—such as anxiety, pining, disillusion, hopeless expectation. Above all, however, this is true of the impulses which stem from egotism: pride, self-will and idolatry, abandonment to things which God has forbidden.

One notices that John Wesley commends new birth, rather than presenting it abruptly as a duty. His very recommendation has its own abruptness, for he testifies to it in such a way that one recognizes in it life in the truest sense. Probably the immeasurable success of his preaching was based on this very manner of expression. The very seriousness with which he called his hearers to decision pre-empted his preaching of any oppressiveness. In the last analysis, he was making an offer, he was revealing an immediate possibility, he was advising. Throughout all his exhortations the positive note of testimony, of invitation with no suggestion of imperious summons, is sustained. In any total picture of Wesley's personality it is hard to find a place for this trait, and the judgement may be justified that here the Gospel itself in its total structure has prevailed over Wesley's nature. Moreover, the passages in which he speaks of paradise lost and regained sound like an echo from the book that meant so much to him in his early days, Henry Scougal's *Life of God in the Soul of Man*.[27] In lines of thought such as these one detects the points of departure for the mystical leanings which stayed with him throughout his entire life.

Wesley could have ended his exposition here. Nevertheless, he adds a few further points which seem to him important as following on from what he has already said. First of all, he stresses that baptism is by no means new birth. With a characteristic emphasis he directs his attack against a sacramentalism which works on the assumption that everything decisive has happened with the reception of this sacrament. On the contrary, the truth is that baptism as a sign and re-birth as the content are to be clearly distinguished, as it expressly says in the Catechism of the Anglican Church. The one is an external, the other an internal thing. Wesley finds it necessary to stress that no ecclesial community in Britain teaches such a sacramentalism. It follows therefore that new birth does not necessarily accompany baptism. It is possible to conceive of baptism without regeneration and new birth without baptism. Wesley, then, reckons seriously with an ineffectual baptism.[28]

Wesley next turns his attention to the understanding of the new birth which his erstwhile teacher, William Law, advocated. In his book on the *Grounds and Reasons of Christian Regeneration* (1739)[29], Law had lumped sanctification and regeneration together and attributed gradual growth to both. Counter to this, Wesley teaches that the new birth is the entrance-gate to sanctification. Adhering closely to the strict logic of the analogy, he holds that the new birth is an event of short duration.

Whereas the last point deals with a less weighty objection, this is not the case with the final controversial point which he raises in connection with this sermon. The question at issue is whether or not a preacher acts insensitively if he tries to bring a notorious sinner of long standing to re-birth, that is, to complete conversion and complete newness of life. To the obvious answer of the sinner and his advocates, who are evidently to be sought within the Anglican Church and its theology, that he has been baptized, Wesley replies that this makes matters even worse, for this circumstance simply aggravates his guilt. For what does baptism mean? Does it not mean that at eight days old the child was dedicated to God and has since become consecrated to the Devil year after year and for decades? Yet the example of the sinner was only John Wesley's initial point. The same is true of the so-called good churchman, who attends worship regularly, receives Holy Communion every week and does as much good as he can. For him, too, the new birth in indispensable. Everyone, whoever and whatever he is, cannot and may not do other than pray to God: 'Let me be born again.'

In another sermon, Wesley deals with the marks of the new birth in connexion with the next verse of the Bible (John 3[8]).[30] As the text itself yields nothing, he has to turn to other statements of the New Testament, from among which Galatians 3[26] assumes pride of place: 'Ye are all the children of God through faith in Christ Jesus.' Wesley's preaching of faith proves itself to be a preaching of regeneration, in that it starts from the other side, from regeneration itself.[31] As elsewhere, he describes faith as a living, active conviction that in Jesus Christ God has forgiven sins. But despair about sin must precede this conviction. Among the fruits of such faith he lists power over sin, appealing for this first to the Pauline statements in Romans 6 (dead to sin, alive to God), but also and immediately to the First Epistle of John (1 John 3$^{1ff}$). Another fruit of such faith is peace, which according to Romans 5$^1$ takes possession of a man and leads him to accept all that God sends him. Linked with faith, which has undisputed primacy and which predominates in the life of the new-born man, is hope, which like faith was still known in the Pietist parlance as 'living' hope. For this Wesley appeals to 1 Peter 1$^3$. The inheritance, which is promised to the children of God in eternity, constitutes the object of hope. Its liveliness is attested in the awareness of being truly a child of God. The Biblical evidence for this train of thought is the 8th Chapter of the Epistle to the Romans. The third mark of the new birth is love, which brings Christian existence to its acme. This love is directed first of all towards God Himself and therefore at the same time to Jesus Christ the Saviour. It results directly in love of our neighbour. It is in these three—faith, hope, and love—but quite specially in love, that Christian perfection consists. These specified marks must become inwardly real to the Christian, who must have an immediate sense of their presence. It is not enough to refer to baptism. For what counts is not what once happened, but the very present. Wesley's concern is for a thoroughly dynamic, vibrant Christianity. Therefore he concludes, as so often, with a prayer, the substance of which is that God might again make His own those who have been made His children by baptism, but who have later come under the sway of Satan.

There is a direct, thematic connexion between this sermon and another sermon, that devoted to the great privilege of those who are born of God.[32] The text itself (1 John 3$^9$) declares that what is at issue here is victory over sin. Here again Wesley stresses that the new birth may not be confused with baptism, but must be conceived of as a complete change in one's whole existence.[33] Here again he uses the comparison between the foetus and the child in order to bring out as forcibly as possible the reality of this transformation. What is new, however, is that he sees a real problem in the victory over sin itself, and indeed one which is posed by the Bible itself. For David was unquestionably born of God and yet committed the dreadful sins of adultery and murder. The same was unquestionably true of Barnabas, and yet afterwards he managed to quarrel seriously with Paul, his companion in the missionary work from the beginning (Acts 15[39]). No less serious a case in point is that of Peter, who as a new-born disciple of Jesus denied having had fellowship with the Gentile Christians in Antioch before the authorities of the early Church (Galatians 2[12]). What Wesley has in mind in citing these striking examples is that faith is no secure, safe possession. When all these men fell into sin, then by the same token faith and love had been lost. For faith and sin cannot co-exist. Wesley takes quite seriously Paul's dictum that 'whatever is not of faith is sin' (Romans 14[23]). For him faith is God's ceaseless, active presence in man, which leads to genuine mutual openness between them.[34] He goes on to try to formulate a thesis: Some sin of omission, some inward sin precedes the loss of faith, but an outward sin follows it. His exposition culminates with a warning against making light of sin. It is more to be feared than death or hell.

Broadly speaking, all the sermons which have to do with the fruits of the Holy Spirit belong to this context. In the sermon on 'The First-Fruits of the Spirit', which according to Romans 8[1] are a direct consequence of assurance of justification,[35] Wesley underlines the fact that no condemnation on account of their sins, not even their secret sins, hangs over those who live in Jesus Christ. Consistently with all that he advocates elsewhere, he emphasizes that those who are born of God commit no sin, but rather keep God's commandments. Even so, the root of sin, the secret evil impulse, maintains its position in the heart as long as man lives on this earth.[36] Nonetheless, there does exist the condition of weakness in faith, in which sin can conceivably conquer by a surprise attack. In these circumstances no other course is then open but to ask God for His help, to implore Him to uphold and support in the hour of temptation. Another sermon, in accordance with Romans 8[15], contrasts the spirit of bondage with the Spirit of adoption.[37] In connexion with the related subject of the witness of the Spirit, which has the subsequent verse as its textual foundation,[38] the reverberations of John Wesley's famous conversation with Bishop Joseph Butler in Bristol[39] are readily detected. For even before beginning to handle the theme itself, the preacher speaks of the misunderstandings to which this very phrase has been exposed and subjected in Christian history. By this he means the all too frequently voiced claim to have received special revelations directly from God. What Wesley has in mind here is all the accusations of fanaticism and enthusiasm brought against the Methodists by their vociferous opponents, of whom Lavington and Warburton were the most distinguished. Wesley opens up for himself the right course by stating at the very outset the simple principle that it is not a question here of extraordinary gifts but of the normal and basic endowment of the Christian. In the discussion proper he demonstrates with philological minuteness that the Spirit of God and the spirit of the believing man work together. Neither of the two may be omitted. He equally emphasizes that the witness which the Spirit of God gives to the spirit of the unbeliever is only a witness for the latter himself. One may not, therefore, imagine the gifts of the Spirit to be generally visible ornaments which can be put on display to excite admiration. Admittedly Wesley advocates the view that man perceives his life with God just as much as he feels and knows his own moods and notices that he is content or oppressed with pain or tormented by ill-humour. Here he comes close to Schleiermacher's axiomatic notion of immediate self-consciousness.[40] But the believer is also able to supply information on the visible manifestations of God's Spirit. His conscience tells him day by day whether or not he has actually kept God's commandments. But the function of conscience is not only to accuse. It is equally—and this is in complete harmony with the medieval doctrine of the conscience,[41] which had been further maintained and developed in the conservative English tradition, particularly in Puritanism—man's instrument for converse with God. It testifies that God loves each and every man. It testifies that He wants saints. It testifies that He forgives the believer his sin. In every instance God Himself has the first and the decisive word in this conversation. What Wesley is offering and voicing here could be expressed with the modern concepts of assurance of salvation and certainty of faith. It is man himself who is in the line of vision and who is made the subject of reflection. Here we see anthropological self-reflection, which characterizes the modern age. Wesley belongs to this age. It is at this point that he clearly and decisively parts company with the Reformation. In the second section he discusses the pertinent question, How may this assurance on the part of a child of God be distinguished from the presumption of a natural man, not to say a man in love with himself? For his answer he refers to the clear statements of the Bible itself, which mentions features and developments inherent in the assurance of salvation: for example, repentance and conviction of sin, and the new birth in the sense of a radical, revolutionary change in the whole man. Both fundamentally contradict the natural man's self-understanding and sense of identity. Conversely, the Scriptures describe the redeemed man's joy in salvation as being a humble joy. Self-complacency and arrogance have no part in it. Genuine love of God manifests itself in obedience to His commandments, whereas the natural man would derive a false freedom for himself from belonging to God. By these means the Bible supplies enough signs to guide us to a sound decision.

The sermon on 'The Witness of our own spirit'[42] works with the concept of conscience in an entirely similar manner. Here it is of great importance to Wesley that this time-honoured, comprehensive term be preserved in preference to the new-fangled notion of 'moral sense' brought into currency by the Enlightenment, above all because the former is Scriptural. In his opinion it has been demonstrated that the numerous books which have been written on this subject, crammed full as they are of ancient and modern learning, have done more to obscure than to illuminate the phenomenon. Over against this, one must proceed from the simple fact that man is a creature endowed with consciousness, above all with self-consciousness. His consciousness is constantly making value-judgements. The conscience intensifies this process. It excuses or accuses; it approves or disapproves; it acquits or condemns. The good conscience which Wesley demands has its essence in the fact that it follows the Word of God as attested by the Old and the New Testament. Therefore a right understanding of God's Word, which is the expression of His will, is one of the basic prerequisites for a good conscience. The second requirement is true self-knowledge which relates to the whole of life—to our inward tempers as to our outward behaviour. In the third place, man must agree with the clearly comprehended Word of God and direct his whole life accordingly. Finally, he must perceive this concurrence as a stabilizing factor in himself. All this is integral to the 'good conscience'. It is man's initial response to God's gambit. Nevertheless, an essential difference from the Puritan doctrine of the conscience is discernible. The very fact that the principal Biblical passage (2 Corinthians 13[5]) cited on every hand in Puritanism occurs less frequently in Wesley, is in itself significant. Indeed, the whole order of thought is reversed. Conscience should not decide whether or not the Christian is in a state of faith; on the contrary, a good conscience, which is functioning properly, grows in the soil of faith. Faith comes first. But the conscience follows its lead almost of necessity. So there comes into being a way of life which obeys God's commandments in simplicity and sincerity and is able to reflect the will of God. But the idea that here it is primarily a question of a relationship of a legal character is wildly misleading. The good conscience centres on the joy which the redeemed and new-born man has in his communion with God. Such a man testifies with Paul that he no longer has his life in himself but in Him who died and rose for him. He knows that the eternal glory is his, even his.

In reflecting on these two sermons devoted to the distinguishing marks of the Spirit, one is struck by their great restraint. There is nothing affected or artificial about what is commended here. The end-product is sanctification of everyday life, and the means by which this result is achieved is a philosophical and logical neatness in the textual analysis as well as in the whole use of the Bible.

The previously mentioned sermon dealing with the great privilege of those who are born of God[43] may serve to round off this circle of ideas. Its text is 1 John 3[9]: 'Whoever is born of God committeth no sin.' Wesley again begins with logic. He sets his face against the frequently expressed opinion that justification and regeneration are one and the same thing. No doubt they cannot be separated from each other, but they can be distinguished. Justification, as Wesley concisely puts it, comprises only a change of relationship, regeneration, on the other hand, a change in condition. In justifying us, God does something *for* us; in begetting us again, He accomplishes His work *in* us. Justification changes our outward relation to God, so that from being His enemies we become His children. The new birth changes our inmost being, so that from being sinners we become saints. Justification restores us to God's favour; regeneration restores us to God's image. Justification takes away the guilt of sin; regeneration takes away the power of sin. Seldom has justification been delimited over against regeneration in such clear, sharp terms and at the same time without unworthy polemic.[44]

In what follows, Wesley proceeds to consider, first of all, what the expression 'born of God' means, and then turns to sinlessness. Regeneration cannot be equated with baptism without qualification, for it is a complete inward change which the Spirit of God brings about. It is, as Wesley says with a formula which already anticipates Sören Kierkegaard, 'a change in the whole manner of our existence'[45], for from the moment of re-birth onwards men live in a completely different way from before; they are in another world. The new birth itself closely resembles natural birth in many respects. The unborn child feels its life vaguely, if at all. It hears little, if anything. It sees nothing, for its eyes are still firmly closed, and therefore has no contact, no communication with the outside world, no conception of it whatever. Nevertheless, the very moment birth takes place, all this is instantly changed. It feels everything that surrounds it; it hears, it sees, it has a part to play in the external world. Similarly with a regenerate man. Although man, like the child in the womb, is surrounded on every side by God's presence and supported by Him, yet he is incapable of recognizing Him and of coming into a conscious, positive relationship with Him. Although he inhales the divine breath, without which he could not live for a single moment, he does not feel it and knows nothing of God's presence, which is so close to him. Just as the child has no notion of the external world, so the man who has not yet been born again has no presentiment of the eternal world of God. Nevertheless, as soon as the new birth has taken place, his soul becomes receptive to God and perceptive of His nearness. On the basis of experience he can confess with the 139th Psalm: 'Thou compassest my path and my lying down . . . Thou hast beset me behind and before, and laid thine hand upon me.' The breath of God which is received by faith, returns to Him in love, prayer and praise. In this way spiritual life intensifies day by day. Man increases in inner strength; all the faculties of his soul become alive and effective, and distinguish spiritual values and spiritual evils. The inward eye perceives God, who according to His essentially merciful nature offers His Son for the sins of the world. His inward ear is attuned to the voice of God, because it is the voice of the Good Shepherd. His faith, as it were his new intellect, fosters an unhindered familiarity with the invisible world. He now knows what the peace of God is, what joy in the Holy Ghost is, what love of God is. He dwells in God and God in him.

If one takes all this seriously, then one must not only ascribe sinlessness to the new-born man, but also completely deny that it is possible for him to commit sin. By sin Wesley means here a trans-

36

gression against God's command which is actual and voluntary in the true sense. But if this happens, as with the well-known Biblical figures David, Peter and Barnabas, then clearly this is because they did not remain true to their high calling. When temptation came upon them, they gave way to it, and God withdrew Himself. The new birth, then, is not something we possess. It is at once an imputation and an exhortation, an indicative and an imperative. Anyone who commits sin loses his faith. In saying this, Wesley concedes that some sin of omission may precede loss of faith, but insists that a previous loss of faith lies behind a sin of commission. Everything depends on unbroken communion with God. God must be continually present. His dealings with man must be met with a corresponding response by man. The current must flow ceaselessly this way and that. Which means that man offers up all his thoughts, his words, and his deeds, as a holy sacrifice to God. God does not continue His activity if our counter-activity ceases. Wesley ends with the challenge: Let us fear sin, more than death or hell! Take care always that you hear God's voice, then you will always believe and always love, and never commit sin!

Thirteen sermons are devoted to Jesus' Sermon on the Mount, which is thereby given a full hearing in an exhaustive and verse by verse exposition. The first three have to do with the Beatitudes. In the very first of them,[46] Wesley underlines the claim, the seriousness and the importance of this collection of sayings by emphasizing that they apply to all who desire to learn of Jesus, and not solely to the inner circle of His disciples. This discourse concerns all mankind to the end of the world. Then Wesley points out the difference between the mount of this sermon and the Old Testament mountain of revelation, Sinai-Horeb. There the mountain was the place of wrath; here it is the place of consolation. There God thundered forth threats; here He addresses us as 'blessed'. Thus in line with Paul and Luther Wesley makes the antithesis between Law and Gospel into the dominant viewpoint from which to treat the Sermon on the Mount. As he immediately replaced the word 'blessed' with the word 'happy', the first note he picks up from the Beatitudes is a Yes to life, an affirmation of the desire for life.[47] God wants to bring man to fulfilment. The note of joy permeates the whole discourse. In what follows Wesley offers for consideration the view put forward by some that the Beatitudes set down a deliberate, consequential succession of stages by which the life of the Christian progresses in a continuing pilgrimage. So the life of the Christian should progress from one stage to the next. It begins in the depths of spiritual poverty and it mounts to the commanding heights of triumphant self-denial, where one is able to be happy and thankful in the face of slander and persecution. The poor in spirit, says Wesley in interpreting this disputed phrase, are not those who are free from covetousness, but rather the humble, and in fact the whole fabric of the Christian life must be erected on the foundation of humility. For this, however, a native modesty which deprecates itself is not sufficient. On the contrary, it depends on repentance and contrition, which precede faith. Along with this admission of guilt must go a recognition that we are incapable of making amends. So Christianity begins at the very point where heathen morality has to stop. Significantly, the Latin language has no pre-Christian word available for genuine humility. Rather, a re-minting of the ancient expression for the insignificant *(humilitas)* had to be resorted to. Here Wesley makes a pertinent and profound linguistic observation.[48] The reward which is held out to such an attitude of Christian humility is not an outward blessing, but the greatest thing there is—in Wesley's famous turn of phrase, 'the life of God in the soul of man', the mind which was in Jesus Christ Himself, the image of God in man. This creates inward peace. It imparts calm and serenity. It produces filial fear and filial love. With all this it effects a true relationship to the heavenly Father.

The mourners, to whom he now turns, are the tempted from whom God has—temporarily—veiled His face. Their distress, their dejection will surely be turned into consolation and joy. Nevertheless, grief over their own sin and their own failures remains their constant companion.

In discussing the meek who shall inherit the promised land,[49] Wesley analyses the meaning of the word with particular exactitude. Christian meekness is neither weakness nor apathy. It in no way excludes zeal for God, but rather includes it. It knows, to be sure, how to avoid extremes. Vis-à-vis God one can best characterize it as 'resignation', in relation to man as contentedness and patience. In short, meekness is the kind of inward poise which man does not achieve by his own efforts. It is the ability to achieve a true balance between recollection and passion always and everywhere. It is the capacity to be in complete control of oneself without killing one's emotions. Thus meekness often manifests itself as self-control; and yet, because of its origin, its very nature and its scope, it is far wider than this. In all this the characteristically English predilection for the happy medium becomes perceptible, as it gains expression, for example, in the classic devotional book *The Whole Duty of Man* (1659 and many later editions). What is there advanced as the true attitude of the Christian under the term 'sobriety' is here called meekness. That men of this kind should inherit the earth is not as paradoxical as it sounds. It is precisely the man who has his goal in heaven who knows how to use the world aright. But the promise is far more comprehensive than this. It pledges us the eternal Kingdom, the new earth in which righteousness dwells.

In passing under review the first three Beatitudes, Wesley now makes the surprising observation that so far Jesus had had to remove the hindrances to a true faith—first, pride, which opposes poverty of spirit; then levity and thoughtlessness, which are combated by holy sorrow; finally, anger, impatience and dissatisfaction, which are healed by Christian meekness. In this way the preacher succeeds, by starting from the negative side, in making the promises of the Beatitudes really concrete. Now he passes on to a positive approach. Hungering and thirsting after righteousness is for him the first instance of a genuine turning to Christian faith. Here he interprets righteousness in the widest possible sense, using his well-known terminology of the image of God in man and the mind which was in Jesus Christ Himself. Man cannot be satisfied with anything less. How strongly this high aim contrasts with the typical understanding of the Christian life, in which it is reckoned that one has done enough and tried enough by avoiding the outward sins, by helping the poor and by claiming allegiance to the Church! But the man whose life is really derived from God not only receives fulfilment in his own being, but also as a merciful man feels the miseries and necessities of his fellow-men and shares with them what he has; in sum, he practises love. And so all the great statements which Paul associates with this virtue in 1 Corinthians 13 may be applied to him. Following this *locus classicus*, Wesley expounds these statements clearly and separately and thereby achieves a contemporization of the Beatitude, 'Blessed are the merciful, for they shall obtain mercy', a contemporization which is both practically relevant and true to the whole of the New Testament.

Purity of heart, which Wesley now analyses, really upsets his
structural arrangement, and in fact he is not in a position to carry it
through because purity of heart presupposes purification. Hence this
Beatitude belongs to the first group, whose subject is the hindrances
to true faith. Which is in fact how Wesley treats it. His sermon explains fully the stains from which man must be cleansed. By the
same token, it assumes a predominantly negative character. And yet
not entirely so. Wesley wrests from the promise, 'They shall see God',
an original meaning. He does not limit it to the after-life. No, here
on earth the pure shall constantly perceive the living God, whose
presence goes before them, the God who is near to them in all things
and in all events. The Christians are transformed into the disciples of
Emmaus whose eyes are opened. The man with the pure heart sees
the whole world full of God.[50] This has direct, practical consequences.
The Pharisees believed they could restrict the prohibition of oaths to
a lightly taken oath by God. But Jesus makes it clear that God is
everywhere, and therefore forbids every oath. Anyone who separates
God from any area of life perpetrates a practical atheism.[51]

At this point Wesley introduces a new principle of division. Up to
now, he says, Jesus has shown what a Christian is to be in his nature.
He now, in Wesley's view, proceeds to characterize him according to
his deeds. A Christian is a peacemaker. There is no limit to the
meaning of this. By it is meant not only that he has to settle strifes
and prevent them from breaking out. It means also the obligation to
do good wherever one can. Strictly speaking, doing good is the prerogative of God. He has the capacity to do it whenever He chooses.
Therefore this sharing in the work of God, when granted to man,
constitutes his highest dignity. God wills it to be so. The distinctive-
ness of God's activity consists in His helping man through his fellow-
man. There is a profound rightness about the fact that Jesus connects
sonship with God with precisely this.

One would imagine, Wesley continues, that a man who is thus disposed would be held in the highest esteem by his fellow-men and
would enjoy the greatest popularity. Far from it! Jesus knows the
realities of life better than that. He foresees that persecution awaits
the true Christian, and He links the promise of the eternal Kingdom
with the persecution which is suffered for righteousness' sake. For the
Christian himself the sole remaining question of importance is how
he is to behave in this situation. He must not bring persecution upon

himself; provocation is out of place here. Neither may he respond to it with anger or hatred. Nor may he despair and become weary or apathetic. On the contrary, it is a matter of proving love of one's enemy to be the distinctive Christian virtue. This virtue is what James calls the 'perfect law of freedom' (James 2[12]). With such love one attains to true holiness, which at the same time includes in itself the fulfilment of one's nature.

This concludes the Beatitudes. In the following sermons, which concern the imagery of the salt of the earth and the light of the world,[52] Wesley starts from what has been established and asks, What more should happen with those who are adorned with the beauty of holiness (Psalm 29[2]; 96[9]; 110[3]), and where will this holiness lead them? Clearly with half an eye on the Mystics as he had come across them in William Law and in the for him misguided Moravian commendation of 'stillness', he here underlines the truth that Christianity is a corporate affair. He goes so far as to say that anyone who conceives it to be a private matter, a solitary religion, destroys it.[53] Taking his stand on the Beatitudes, he stresses that all the dispositions and actions spoken of there relate to one's fellow-men, that they can only take effect in the cut and thrust of human relations. He rejects even the attenuated commendation of solitude which works on the assumption that one might achieve more through an undeclared, exemplary Christianity. He contrasts this view with the saying of Jesus that the city on the hill cannot remain hidden. It is indeed the Devil who, under the pretext of enhanced piety, would like to lead astray and into escape from the world the man who is dedicated to God. Even the dictum so much loved by Wesley, and cited by him again and again, that faith is a matter of the heart and has its roots in the inmost soul, may not be played off against external duties. Anyone who abuses love as the fulfilment of the Law in order to release himself conveniently from the Law, fundamentally misconstrues the intention of the Pauline text.

The following sermon[54] is organically connected with what has just been discussed, averting as it does the misunderstanding that the Law has been abolished. One of the many reproaches levelled against Jesus was that He introduced a new religion. To this He could confidently reply that He was only taking up the familiar religion with total seriousness and taking it to its logical conclusion. His religion is in fact as old as creation, as Wesley puts it, subtly latching on to the title of the deistic Bible, Matthew Tindal's *Christianity as old as the Creation* (1730). Thus in Wesley's judgement the Law and the Gospel do not contradict each other. There is no need for the Law to pass away in order to make way for the Gospel. On the contrary, both unfold one and the same thing from different points of view. The Law gives a cutting edge to the content of the Christian life in terms of a commandment; the Gospel reveals it in terms of a promise. The Law continually prepares the way for the Gospel; the Gospel leads to a fulfilment of the Law. Thus, for example, the Law requires that man love God and neighbour. It demands that man be meek, humble and holy. Man is acutely aware that he is not sufficient for all these things. Then the Gospel comes on the scene and gives him to know what he is able to achieve what is required, because God grants him the power to do it. No contradiction obtains, but a complete harmony between the two.[55]

Here Wesley goes so far as expressly to limit the doctrine of salvation by faith alone to the principle that only a faith which is active in love has redemptive power. He thereby comes astonishingly close to the classical Roman Catholic standpoint. Seemingly what matters in Christianity is love, that is, the achievement of man, albeit of regenerate man. The summons of the New Testament, 'Believe and thou shalt be saved', does not mean, Wesley explains, that one steps straight from sin to heaven. On the contrary, holiness must be inserted between the two as a connecting link. Faith is no substitute for holiness.[56] Far from being content with faith, Jesus presses the demand for righteousness to its final conclusion by comparing it with the highest ideal of His times and environment, that of the Pharisees. This ideal was aimed at external obedience to the ordinances. Jesus, however, challenges the whole inner man. The righteousness of the Pharisees means doing nothing evil, but always and only doing good. It means fulfilling the clear commandments of God. But this is still external. The demands of Jesus, in contrast, have as their object poverty of spirit, sorrow for sin, patience in tribulation, meekness, hunger and thirst for righteousness, and purity of heart; and these can only be realized and perfected in the inmost soul. In this connection Wesley lights upon a striking and memorable formula for the difference: 'The Pharisee laboured to present God with a good life, the Christian with a holy heart.'[57]

The next sermon,[58] the sixth devoted to the Sermon on the Mount, takes as its theme purity of intention in a Christian's activity. It follows exactly the Biblical text concerned with almsgiving and prayer, and discusses in detail things that do not ring true in a Christian's conduct. It is important for our total interpretation of Wesley that he relates prayer principally to man, to the one who prays. The purpose of praying is not to inform God of the needs and wants about which one is anxious; God already knows everything in any case. On the contrary, the one who prays must be taught, in the sense that he must learn to recognize in the light of his needs how absolutely dependent he is upon God. He has also to bear in mind that God is always ready to come to his aid. This is why requests for blessings should not really characterize prayer. On the contrary, prayer should lead us to receive God's rich bounty in the right way. It is not God who must be moved to do something, but the one who prays. Prayer thereby loses, one is bound to object, its fundamental character of conversation with God; it becomes a conversation with oneself. It loses its directness and spontaneity. It is virtually reduced to systematic reflection. Here a whiff of the Enlightenment hangs about Wesley's theology, although the basic aim of prayer—namely, communion with God—is still emphasized.

When he then goes on to expound the Lord's Prayer, he stresses first of all the encyclopaedic character of this model prayer. The Lord's Prayer omits none of the things for which, although we have no right to them, we depend on God, and which we may understandably and properly ask of Him. At the same time, however, it holds true that God Himself has the primacy; His purposes precede human ones. All His majestic attributes together are contained in His *Name*. Equally, however, He is, as the form of address puts it, the Father, and that both by virtue of His claims as Creator and by virtue of His claims as Redeemer. Wesley gives a concise paraphrase of the content, without making any particular comment on any phrase in it or placing an original emphasis on any particular aspect of it. At the most what strikes one is the fact that in his interpretation of the third petition, 'Thy will be done', the will of God is raised to the sum and substance of the life of Christians. Nothing else but God's will, nothing outside of His will, everything *as* He wills, everything for the sole reason that it is His will—these are the dominant themes for Christian conduct. To the obvious question, Where, then, is the will of God to be found? Wesley would have replied tersely: In holy

Scripture, the oracles of God. With this reply his legalistic understanding of the Bible, which stood out so startlingly in the preceding
sermon, would be re-endorsed. It also strikes one as distinctive that
the daily bread of the fourth petition is not restricted to the bodily
necessities of the one who prays, but also includes his spiritual
nourishment in the Sacrament of the Altar. Here Wesley aligns himself emphatically with the ancient Fathers of the Church who under
appeal to this petition stipulated daily reception of Holy Communion.
He concludes the sermon with a rhymed paraphrase of the Lord's
Prayer, possibly derived from his brother Charles.

The next sermon, which treats of fasting,[59] has as its title 'Outward
and inward piety'. Wesley introduces it in the following manner: It is
one of the wiles of the Devil to put asunder what God has joined together—faith and good works, end and means in the Christian life,
and also, by the same token, inward and outward piety. In this way
two parties have always arisen in church history, because each isolated one of the two poles—either faith or good works, either the
end or the means, either inward or outward piety. On a smaller scale
this recurs in the case of fasting. Some have extolled it as an activity
almost necessary to salvation; others have scorned it completely as
an out-dated superstition or a meaningless formality. Wesley himself
indicates his comparatively high valuation of it by the very fact that
he devoted the whole of the first part of his sermon to the forms and
the history of this practice from the Old Testament down to the early
period of the Christian Church. When he then proceeds to the motives,
he puts in first place sorrow over sin, that is, penitence and fear of
God's wrath. When a sense of one's own unworthiness overwhelms
the soul, there is no room left for earthly things, not even for the
elementary necessity to take nourishment. The example of the
Apostle Paul after his Damascus road crisis bears eloquent testimony
to this. This argument from the Bible has its parallel in church history. Wesley immediately refers to the Homily on Fasting from the
English Reformation—a fresh testimony to his Anglican sensitivity
to tradition which came to expression even on an apparently secondary issue. To this he adds—and this sequence, too, is indicative of his
English make-up—a thoroughly rational consideration deduced from
experience. Many have decided on fasting when they realize how
often they have sinned by immoderate eating, and sinned not only by
the misuse of God's gifts themselves but particularly because gluttony

and self-indulgence offered a fertile soil for other vices or at least for sinful desires. In this light abstinence has the appearance of a sheer counsel of prudence. Nevertheless, fasting is not in any way to be confused with the general principle of moderation, for it is always connected with particular occasions and evinces a heightened sense of reality. But perhaps the most weighty reason for fasting is that it is a valuable spiritual aid to prayer. For if the desire for earthly things no longer dominates a man, if he is capable of freeing himself even from the apparently obvious necessities of life, he becomes free for undivided devotion to God. In the very nature of things, an earnest composure then reigns in his heart. This is why the Bible ascribes notable results to fasting. It shows that by fasting one can avert God's wrath, even though no necessary connexion between human repentance, for which fasting vouches, and God's blessings, may be asserted. Yet Wesley sees the decisive motive in the fact that Jesus Himself summons us to it—not directly, but indirectly, and therefore all the more strongly—by giving directions on how one has to fast. Only after this detailed and cogent exposition does Wesley come back to the opening question: How are the inward content and the outward form of piety related to each other? Does not the maxim suffice that a Christian should fast from, i.e. abstain from, his sins—and not from food? The answer which Wesley gives has already been indicated by the previous discussion. If the greatest figures of faith found in the Bible, with Jesus Himself at their head, set an example of the inseparability of prayer and fasting, how can the present-day, simple Christian want to evade this binding model? From among them, and consistently with the missionary idea which is the lodestar of all Wesley's activity, special emphasis falls on the scene of Barnabas and Paul's commissioning, where the whole community in Antioch acted in this way. Here he does not hesitate to use the most pointed phrases. Had anyone at that time opted out of fasting and praying, the community for its part would have justifiably expelled him from its midst, for he would have caused nothing but confusion in the Church of God.[60] Once more restoration of primitive Christianity is shown to be John Wesley's real concern.

With the following sermon on Matthew ($6^{19-23}$),[61] the warning against laying up of treasure, there begins according to Wesley a new set of themes. Up to now it was a question of the Christian's direct relations with God; now it is a question of his being put to the proof in the world. Not only prayer, fasting and almsgiving, worship in the true sense, should become one's offering to God, but also the work of one's vocation. Here as there the same purity of intention must prevail. The eye is the light of the body, and this light must be single, artless, clear. The task of the eye is to furnish knowledge in moral behaviour; therefore knowledge of God has the primacy. It is followed by action as a total scheme of activity, that state of holiness which is well-pleasing to God. Such a state guarantees true fulfilment of life. Here again Wesley's pet phrase, that holiness includes happiness, gains convincing expression. At the same time he underlines the fact that Jesus challenges us to a straight choice. The absolute demands made of the eye are also to govern action. In the sphere of a deliberate action, too, there is no middle course. Either it is entirely pure or it is totally impure. If such action is not singly fixed on God, it is reprehensible. Even the slightest tarnishing by ulterior motives makes it quite impure. From this point of view the laying up of treasures on earth must be condemned, for it proves how seriously one's perception has been distorted.

At first glance what the heathen do corresponds exactly to the will of Jesus as it comes to expression here. The Indian tribes of North America, which Wesley was able to observe in their care-free existence, suddenly appear in his mind's eye. Is such a care-free day-to-day living what Jesus intends? Surely not. He would by no means wish to oppose responsible and regulated provision for our own future and for our family. No, He directs His attack against the inordinate desire for possessions which can never be sated, against the carking discontent which measures its own wants by the standards of excess. He condemns the whole frame of mind which thinks only of earthly possessions. Anyone who has lapsed into such a frame of mind has not only dissipated his time and squandered his energies, he has also murdered his soul. Compared with this, the happy-go-lucky attitude of the heathen is surely preferable. The true treasure is in heaven, and earthly riches are best used when they are used for charity.

The text of the next sermon (Matthew $6^{24-34}$)[62] pursues this further. Its thesis, 'No man can serve two masters', is tailor-made for Wesley. In an introduction underscoring the fact that decision cannot be evaded, he claims faith to be the basis for serving God. For him, love comes next in line, followed by imitation of God and then obedience to Him. It would seem noteworthy that only here does the latter establish its position, and not at the beginning. Wesley gives it a profound, comprehensive meaning. To obey God means to glorify Him with our body and soul. Wesley analyses worship of Mammon in exactly corresponding terms. Trusting in money, with which he begins, brings in its train love of the world. It leads to conformity to the world and culminates in obedience to it. The individual thereby becomes one of the herd, differing not one iota from his neighbour. This stark antithesis highlights the fact that only one of the two ways is open to us. This in turn determines Jesus' attitude to anxiety. What He forbids is the harassing anxiety of the worldly-minded person whose only thought is for earthly criteria. This anxiety poisons the blessings of today by fear of the dangers of tomorrow. It is not only a defect or a sickness but an affront against God, because it distrusts His providential government. Indeed, it maintains that He does not deal wisely with His children. Reliance on God is in fact only another expression for readiness to let God be God. This is why striving to realize God's sovereign will necessarily precedes every other thought. This is also what is meant by the righteousness of God. God's righteousness does not refer merely to the forgiveness of sins, though this describes its essence, but must be understood in the widest possible sense. It means holiness of heart and restoration of the divine image in man. Certainly anyone who imagines he can get by with his own external righteousness necessarily hardens himself against the righteousness of faith, and resistance to the latter is tantamount to resistance against true Christianity as a whole. Thus Wesley has established the connexion of this group of ideas concerning anxiety with the central message of justification. His train of thought shows a remarkable compactness. He adds practical exhortations and warnings: such as not making care about the future into an excuse for neglecting present duties. Or again: we should not let our relationship with God be based on temptation, when He hides His face, in the false hope of better times. Or again: we are not to torment ourselves with temptations that might come tomorrow. Over against Horacian superficiality, Wesley calls for a *carpe diem* ('snatch the passing moment') understood in Christian terms: for it is God who has apportioned to each day its own joys and its own burdens and who insists on being taken seriously in both.

In that the text of the following sermon (Matthew $7^{1-12}$)[63] begins by forbidding us to judge others and ends with the Golden Rule (treat others as you want to be treated), Wesley holds that here another new section of the Sermon on the Mount begins. This text is taken up with removing hindrances to true faith and the true life of a Christian. Wesley sees the first great adversary in the judgmental spirit, and immediately emphasizes that in the whole course of a Christian's development, from the first moment of repentance and of faithful acceptance of the Gospel onwards, there is no stage at which the warning against such a spirit does not apply. The desire to pass judgement on others, and the opportunity to do so, are never absent. The warning applies in the first instance to the children of the world who, instead of taking true Christians as models for their own way of life, find fault with them as off-beat, extremist, peculiar people, even though it is only a bad conscience that forces them to do so. The judging which is here forbidden is that attitude towards one's neighbour which runs counter to love.[64] On this basis Jesus discountenances every condemnation of others, be they innocent or even guilty, as offending against compassion, to which the Christian is committed. Love thinks no evil; it sees everything in the best possible light. It is significant that the text in question is used to the full by Wesley for purposes of his main concern—the exaltation of love as the substance of Christian perfection. The associated warning: 'Give not that which is holy unto the dogs', guards against irresponsibly extending love to all and sundry. It is undoubtedly an extremely difficult task to establish the worthiness or unworthiness of a person to receive the message of salvation. But here Jesus unequivocally summons us to resolve the matter. The love which Wesley preaches is not something effeminate and indulgent, but something stern and severe. Sentimentality is totally foreign to it. Wesley sees in this warning a clear instruction for the preacher. He feels that here his own and his proper work, the persistent ministry of preaching the message of salvation, is delineated. Hence he detects in the negative words the positive command: Do everything you can to bring men within sound of the Gospel of Jesus Christ! Leave nothing unventured, and if you fail, recognize and respect the limits which God Himself has clearly set for you in the ill-nature of the recipients! In the light of these considerations he interprets the next promise: 'Ask and you will receive', and everything that follows, as God's answer to those preachers who see no fruit for their labours. This promise means that even those whose minds are still closed will open their hearts

tomorrow or the day after. Wesley relates even the concluding
Golden Rule to judging and condemning others. He carries the main
thought through to the end and in this way attains a rounded-off,
self-contained circle of ideas: Love is the essence of the whole of
Christian conduct; faith is its presupposition. Therein lies the unity
of this sermon.

The following sermon[65] has as its textual basis the metaphor of the
narrow gate through which the Christian is to pass into life (Matthew
$7^{13-14}$). Consistently with his general line of interpretation—that at
this stage it is a question of the hindrances on the way of salvation—
Wesley elucidates this metaphor from the obverse side. True, he does
not describe the road to hell with the vividness of a John Bunyan, but
he does use all the force at his command. For when he looks around,
he discovers on every hand—in every walk of life, at every stage of
life, and among men and women alike—wanderers on the primrose
path. Here, too, he contests the mistaken idea that one lives in a
Christian country. For not only the notorious evildoers, but equally
the respectable people, the 'saints of the world', are children of perdition, an abomination to God, because they have only the outward
appearance of being pious, but are inwardly rotten. Here the word of
Jesus applies—that the despised often fare better before God than
the eminent. Men of wealth and influence, men who are the wonder of
their times, hear the call of the Devil luring them to the broad road
and follow his siren voice. The decision to enter in at the strait gate
and the narrow way thereby comes all the harder. Outstanding
examples are conspicuous by their absence. Humble, insignificant
people dominate the scene. This is why Jesus rightly says: Strive to
enter in at this gate! The battle which must precede the decision to
do this must be taken seriously in all its magnitude, and this means in
all its costliness. Conviction as to one's own sinfulness is integral to
this, as are also sorrow, shame, fear and incessant prayer. Wesley does
not hesitate to call it the mortal combat of the soul. He is equally
austere when he puts it in positive terms. It is not simply a matter of
avoiding the evil deed, but also of avoiding every appearance of evil.
It is a matter of doing all the good that lies in one's own power. It is
a matter of renewing one's self-denial and taking up one's cross daily.
Indeed, according to the stern words of Jesus, it is, if need be, a
matter of cutting off one's right hand and plucking out one's right
eye.

D

The next warning that Jesus issues is directed against false prophets.[66] Wesley links this warning with the preceding one by reflecting that if a large part of mankind takes the road to hell simply because they fall in with so many and such important fellow-travellers, the situation is made infinitely worse still if the accredited messengers of God misdirect them. Who, then, are these false prophets? Those who invite their hearers to the broad way must be classed among them without qualification. Anyone who makes things easy for people, anyone who would spare them the discipline of humility, suffering, self-denial for Jesus' sake, is a false prophet. But then one must class among them those who may well mouth all the right pious phrases, but who pay them mere lip-service. Again, this description even more obviously applies to those who teach the very opposite and commend the way of pride, levity, ungoverned passion, worldly desires, even self-indulgence. If one asks, Who, then, teaches this? Wesley answers, Tens of thousands of wise and honourable men, and that in all Churches and Christian congregations, large and small. These highly respected, esteemed contemporaries are in truth traitors to God and man, the first-born of Satan. They far outstrip ordinary cut-throats, for they go so far as to murder souls. What form, then, do they assume? Do they appear in all their terror, so that one can tell by looking at them how dangerous they are? Oh, no! They put on the cloak of harmlessness. They come as agents of what is useful and practical in life. But not only that. They present themselves as religious men and cloke their advice under zeal for God, saying that they want to defend the Church against its enemies. Above all they approach with an outward show of love which draws them to their hearers and would like to relieve these hearers of every burden.

How can one expose them, cunning as they are? Here it is a question of abiding by the rule recommended by Jesus Himself: 'Ye shall know them by their fruits.' One must check whether they are disciples of Jesus in their own lives. A good prophet does not bring forth good fruit just now and then; on the contrary, his whole being is impregnated with them. Ought one, then, to hear false prophets? Here everyone has to decide for himself. If attendance at their services of worship troubles one's soul, so that one perceives spiritual damage occurring to oneself, then one should stay away. Wesley ends this exceptionally pungent sermon by urgently exhorting the false prophets to realize what they are doing and to be converted, so that, as

Scripture has it, they as true teachers might shine in eternity like the brightness of the firmament (Daniel 12³).

The last of the sermons devoted to the Sermon on the Mount takes up its closing words (Matthew 7²¹⁻²⁷), with their imagery of the wise man who built his house on the rock.⁶⁷ Wesley stresses, first of all, that here Jesus declares Himself, in an exclusivist sense, for the way which He has pointed out. If we want to attain to salvation, we have no choice but to obey. All the high-sounding words in the world are to no avail; they can be mere lip-service. Indeed, one must go even further. The saying, 'Lord, Lord', may include doing no harm to any and being a burden to none. It may even include the fact that one does good works; that one not only goes to church, receives the Sacraments and thus cares for one's soul in the traditional sense, but also that one feeds the hungry, clothes the naked, shares one's bread with one's neighbour in his need. But what is this as compared with the perfect holiness, the inward kingdom of faith, which He has just revealed in all its magnitude in the Sermon on the Mount? Everything depends on whether one builds on the rock. But the rock is no other than Jesus Himself—not our fulfilment of our own duty, nor our personal piety, nor our personal orthodoxy. On the contrary, it means, to use Pauline and Franciscan terms: Learn to hang naked on the cross of Christ, to deem all that you have done but dung and dross (Philippians 3⁷⁻⁸). Cleave to Him like the thief on the cross and like the harlot with her seven devils; then, but only then, will you be able to live, as the Sermon on the Mount puts it, hungry and athirst for righteousness, comforted in sorrow, merciful, pure in heart, loving your neighbour as yourself, loving God with all your heart and with all your strength.

It is of the utmost significance that at this concluding point in this long series of sermons John Wesley upholds justification of the sinner by God's grace alone through faith alone as being fundamental and central. This reveals how much it means to him. Precisely the Sermon on the Mount could have led him to assign the dominant rôle to his favourite theme—the perfection of the Christian in undisturbed love of God. Here his conversion of 24th May 1738 is yet again confirmed in its essential import.

The sermon which is explicitly devoted to Christian perfection⁶⁸ therefore merits all the greater attention. In the ensuing discussion of this theme on the basis of Philippians 3¹², Wesley proceeds, according to the principle of litotes, from the negative side, asking first of all in what sense perfection is denied to the Christian, in order then to push forward to the positive exposition. In complete accord with the spirit of the Enlightenment, he begins with knowledge. Christians certainly know full well all the things relative to life in this world and in this respect are in no way different from their contemporaries. Moreover, they know the fundamental truths with regard to the other world. They know the manner of love with which the heavenly Father has loved them and the goal to which He has called them. They know the mighty working of the Holy Spirit in their hearts, as also the wisdom of God's providence. It is clear to them at every moment of their lives what the Lord requires of them and how they can keep a conscience void of offence towards Him and towards man.

All this they know. Nevertheless, there is an abundance of things which they do not know. Ignorance and error are part and parcel of the human condition, and by the same token also of the condition of Christians—this Wesley tosses in the face of the spirit of the Enlightenment in its cultural zeal and intellectual pride. Christians by no means completely succeed in fathoming God's nature and its mysterious ways. They are unable to fathom either the tri-unity of God or the manner of the incarnation of the Son of God. The time and place of God's future action—such as, say, the in-breaking of His final reign—remain as hidden from them as the reasons for His often incomprehensible dealings with man, including the experiences of their own lives. If the text, 'Ye have an unction from the Holy One and ye know all things' (1 John 2[20]), appears to contradict this, the correct interpretation of it reads: 'Ye know all things that are needful for your souls' health.'

But not only ignorance and error set a clear limit to Christian perfection. Christians are also not free from infirmities and temptations. To be sure, the word 'infirmity' may not be misused to condone real sins. If someone wanted to make excuses by remarking that every man has his infirmity, and mine is drunkenness, then one must refute this sharply. Rather, one must think here of slowness of understanding, inability to think things out, lack of imagination, or of the inability to draw logical conclusions, slowness of speech or gauche appearance. The Christian cannot imagine himself to be immune from temptations, seeing that Jesus Himself was exposed to them.

Christian perfection, then, is only another expression for holiness.

Anyone who is holy is perfect. This is also why the notion that there is a final stage in the process of sanctification must be rejected. However far someone may have attained, there is always yet more growth ahead of him.

In what, then, does the perfection of Christians consist? It manifests itself in the fact that they no longer commit sin. This pretentious assertion cannot be proved by statements made about themselves by individual Christians, perhaps least of all by Christians of high standing, but solely by the only competent authority—the Law and the testimony, i.e. the Bible. This is the right place to apply seriously the statements of Romans 6. How can we who have died to sin go on living in sin (Romans 6²)? We know that the old Adam has been crucified with Christ so that the body of sin is destroyed, so that henceforth we do not serve sin (Romans 6⁶). For now that you have been made free from sin, you have become slaves of righteousness (Romans 6¹⁸).[69] The least that these sentences say is to assert that the Christian has put outward sin behind him in the sense that he practises no sinful action. The First Letter of John clinches the matter. 'He that committeth sin is of the devil; for the devil sinneth from the beginning. For this purpose the Son of God was manifested, that he might destroy the works of the devil' (3⁸); and, 'We know that whosoever is born of God sinneth not; but he that is begotten of God keepeth himself, and that wicked one toucheth him not' (5¹⁸). But, someone will object, did not Abraham commit sin when he passed off his wife for his sister, and Moses, when he tempted God at the waters of Meriba, and above all David, the man after God's own heart who at one and the same time committed adultery and murder against Uriah? Wesley replies that these were all men of the old dispensation. Since Jesus came, the new order, as He Himself declared in manifesto form (Matthew 11¹¹), is in force. It will not do to fall back into the Jewish dispensation. On the contrary, it is all-important to uphold the difference between the Old and the New Testaments.[70] Indeed, Wesley goes so far as to declare, on the basis of John 7³⁸ff, that the disclosure of the new possibility of being purified from sin was the real mission of Jesus. And so the Christian is freed from sinful words, sinful thoughts, sinful impulses and sinful dispositions. The old Testament promise finds its fulfilment in the fact that God's intention is to circumcise the heart (Deuteronomy 30⁶). The desire for a clean heart (Psalm 51¹²) is gratified, and the outcome is the new race,

53

well-pleasing to God, which the prophet Ezekiel announced (Ezekiel $36^{25-36}$). The sermon concludes with an appeal to translate what has been said into life.

The bipartite sermon on the relation between faith and the Law points in the same direction. On the basis of Romans $3^{31}$, the surrounding argument that in truth faith establishes the Law is carefully developed. In the first of these sermons[71] Wesley restricts himself to negative matters and discusses the usual methods and arguments by which the Law is made void through the faith of the Christian. The very first and real purpose which the Law serves, namely, the task of convicting man of his sin, should preclude this. For no faith can originate without a profound awareness of sin. Anyone who is not overwhelmed by his own lost-ness, who does not tremble before the threatening judgement of God, cannot take Jesus Christ seriously. Wesley directs his attack against 'cheap grace'[72]—rather as Thomas Müntzer found in Luther only a preaching of a 'sweet' Christ and believed he had to impress upon him the bitter Christ.[73] A further way of dispensing with the Law through the faith of a Christian consists in putting faith higher than the obligation to strive for holiness. This is a falsely understood liberty. In reality, holiness requires obedience. The works of the Law, which admittedly are unable to bring man into a right standing before God, ensue upon faith as its first fruits. Faith gives no grounds for Antinomianism, declares Wesley roundly. There may well be an echo here of his painful experiences with that section of the Moravians headed by Philip Henry Molther. The third way he sees of eliciting liberation from the Law is unthinking licentiousness.

In the second of these sermons,[74] Wesley, after a short summary, closes directly with the crucial question: What kind of Law, then, is established by faith? It cannot be the ceremonial law of the Old Covenant, nor the whole Mosaic dispensation, but simply the moral Law—though without in any way implying that the fulfilment of all its requirements could be the condition for attaining righteousness before God. Wesley prefaces the discussion with these preliminary considerations, which are not as obvious as they may seem.

The Law is directly established, first of all, through teaching. That is to say, it is given the dignity of a permanent and a constituent part of the Christian proclamation, particularly in the Protestant countries, of which Britain is one. Such preaching may meet with resistance, but this very resistance proves how challenging it is. The 'religion of the heart' which the Methodists commend so vigorously may alienate many a person. But it does mean that the Law is interpreted in higher terms than those of outward observance of rules and that men seek after that better righteousness which is fundamentally different from that of the Pharisees. It is not right to extol all the blessings and all the promises of God without at the same time summoning people to obey all His commandments; for Jesus Christ is not only the High Priest who has reconciled the world to God, but also the Prophet who instructs men and urges them to keep the divine commands. He is the King who lays down the Law. This Law aims at the perfection of man, at the restoration of the divine image.

But this is not the whole story. Authentic proclamation of Christian truth also exalts the Law in indirect terms, namely, by the preaching of faith. For the Methodists do not urge faith upon their hearers with the intention that it overshadow or supersede the challenge to be holy, but rather with the intention that it should be directly productive of holiness. This is exhibited above all by the fact that faith pales into insignificance when compared with love; indeed, the superiority of love over faith is a direct extension of the principle of the superiority of the Gospel over the Law.[75] For all its excellence, faith has a purely supportive rôle in relation to love. It may sink to nothing in order to make way for love. The all-important thing is to put faith in its proper place. In God's purpose, its rôle consists in re-establishing the original Law of love. Angels do not need faith, because they continually behold the face of the heavenly Father. This is also why Jesus did not assume the nature of an angel, but that of a man—such are the speculative flights of fancy to which the prosaic Wesley soars! Love, on the other hand, existed from the beginning of time. Its *fons et origo* is in God, the ocean of love. Faith presupposes sin and God's declared wrath against the sinner; it thus becomes the means of restoring the loving union intended and created by God. Accordingly the inner meaning of the Law is true, undivided, undisturbed love of God himself, the appropriate response to His own prevenient love for man. Therefore all preaching, both the direct preaching of the Law and the indirect preaching of faith, aims at really establishing the Law at the deepest level—in men's hearts and lives. All theory— and preaching cannot but be theoretical—is sounding brass and

tinkling cymbal, as compared with reality. But how does this happen?
It happens through faith alone. Vital faith, faith that is verified in life,
establishes the Law, for it engenders the love which the Law intends.
Love is the fulfilling of the Law (Romans $13^{10}$). How could the man
whose sin has been forgiven, that is to say, taken away, start sinning
all over again? After justification, indeed through justification, must
not the Sun of righteousness shine in his heart? Wesley ends with an
appeal which is at the same time a promise: 'Now use all the knowledge, and love, and life, and power you have already attained; so
shall you continually go on from faith to faith; so shall you daily increase in holy love, till faith is swallowed up in sight, and the law of
love is established to all eternity.'

One leaves this double-barrelled sermon with mixed feelings.
Either the whole of Christianity is here brought under the dominant
concept of the Law, so that obedience is placed above the freedom of
the children of God which has become their higher nature, and even
eternity is represented as a kingdom governed by law. Or the stage
of legality has really been surmounted. This surmounting of legality,
however, is expressed in legal thought-forms, so that Wesley takes
the same kind of liberties with words as Paul does in Romans 8,
where he speaks of the Law of liberty. Wesley, however, probably
had the first of these two possibilities in mind.

In which case another sermon can serve as a corrective—namely,
the one which has original sin as its subject.[76] Its text is Genesis $6^5$:
'And God saw that the wickedness of man was great in the earth, and
that every imagination of the thoughts of his heart was only evil continually.' Wesley begins with an exclamation which must have been
painfully relevant to his own times: How this judgement contrasts
with the comforting pictures which men in every age have drawn of
man and his ways! How eloquently not just the heathen of antiquity
but also numerous Christians can extol the dignity of man, particularly in the present age! Is it any wonder that portrayals of this kind
are readily welcomed? But, Wesley goes on to ask, what in that case
must we do with our Bibles? For they just do not agree with this. To
his mind there can be no vacillation or concession. The Bible is right;
and in what follows he endeavours to vindicate the whole rigour of its
evidence, first of all in the context of the Biblical story of the Flood.
God, who saw everything, condemned everything. His judgement
was passed on all men, on all their inward fabrications, their words

and actions, all their aspirations and inspirations. Evil, he explains, means that which is contrary to God's nature, contrary to His will, contrary to His image, in which He had originally created man. Wesley rejects any watered-down version. Man's situation was certainly not a mingling of good and evil in his nature, nor just one in which his life was punctuated by periods of good action or moral sensitivity.

This is how things stood with man prior to the Flood. What is his position today? The Bible gives us no reason for thinking that things have changed. But this also corresponds to daily experience. Without being instructed by God, men are without God; they are atheists in the strictest sense of the word—just like children, who, thrown on their own resources, would acquire no real language but would only be able to utter inarticulate sounds. Natural religion, which has been abstracted from traditional religion and thereby detached from the influences of God, is such an inarticulate sound. Without knowledge of God there can be no love for Him, and no fear of Him either. Nevertheless, atheism of this kind does not protect us against idolatry. Man sets up his idols in his own heart, even if he does not worship graven images or offer sacrifices at man-made altars. Pride, which is the ascription of everything to oneself, is idolatry, no less than self-will, which knows no other law than the egotistic impulse or love of the world which sees in the world the be all and end all of things and expects from it complete satisfaction.

The doctrine of universal sinfulness, Wesley concludes, constitutes the fundamental difference between Christianity and Heathenism. For even though there is a great deal said against the vices of particular men in ancient literature, this condemnation is never so radical as to include all men. It is always a question of individuals or particular groups. But owing to this fundamental difference Christianity itself is something different. It is not a didactic system like those of antiquity, or ritual purification; in essence it is redemption, and brings healing of the soul. God heals the natural atheism of mankind by making Himself known. He heals by giving us faith, i.e. firm trust in His loving will and His loving act. Repentance and humility are the remedies for pride, submission to God's sovereign will the remedy for wilfulness, love of God the remedy for love of the world. Wesley sets such inward religion of the heart in sharp contrast with the conventional, outward religion, which contents itself with springs of action and purposes based on rational considerations. Anyone who takes the Bible seriously knows that what is required is complete renewal, the restoration of the divine image. Anything short of this would be a farce and an affront against God. And so Wesley appeals urgently for self-knowledge and refers his hearers to the second Adam, Jesus Christ, in whom the true life has appeared and through whom this life is appropriated by the believer. He ends with the exhortation: 'Now, go on "from faith to faith" until your whole sickness be healed, and all that "mind be in you which was also in Christ Jesus".'[77]

Rightly as the essence of the Christian message is hit upon here, nevertheless there is no gainsaying the fact that the whole line of argument is thin and unconvincing. It is curiously undeveloped; indeed, it rests entirely on the formal authority of the Bible. What is more, it rests fundamentally on this one Biblical text, instead of bringing into play the whole of the Bible—for instance, the Pauline theology. Perhaps Wesley's sole interest was in the clear-cut statement, with which, as with an insurmountable boulder, he intended to block the path which his contemporaries were taking with such superb confidence, to their Utopia. Perhaps his interest was confined to the radical juxtaposition of corruption and regeneration, so that he leaves out of consideration the repercussions and continued presence of sin in the regenerate. This is why this sermon on original sin in no way gives the lie to his view of the Law as being needed by the believer and as revealing the possibilities which his faith can realize. Its one-sided sharpening of the issue prevents it from really altering this view. Wesley did, however, explicitly make the mystery of iniquity which continues in the Christian Church[78] into the subject of a later sermon. But he confines its outward forms to such palpable facts as partisanship in Jerusalem[79] and the early Christian controversy over obedience to the Jewish Law.[80] Later on he uses by way of evidence the criticism which the letters of Cyprian in Carthage level against the North African congregations, and then proceeds to pillory the Constantinian volte-face in the fourth century as the great apostasy, on the grounds that Christianity suddenly gained wealth and influence and that conversion to it frequently took place in a merely external manner. This gives him the cue for his well-known fundamental assertion that the so-called Christian peoples of the eighteenth century were not Christian at all but were completely indistinguishable from the heathen—a fact which was corroborated by such countries as, say, America, where Christian and heathen live side by side.[81] Precisely at this point where he allows his own missionary experience in Georgia to speak so eloquently,[82] he should have pursued his line of thought further, to the point of asking sharply whether or not the combat between God and His adversary is continually taking place in the hearts of individual Christians themselves.

When one turns from the dogmatic sermons to the ethical ones, one immediately meets a new Wesley. Even in terms of its subject, his famous sermon on 'The Use of Money' occupies an exceptional position. It also has a peculiar style of preaching to match. The text (Luke 16[9]) is the conclusion drawn from the parable of the unjust steward—Jesus' summons to use unrighteous Mammon in order to win friends.[83] Wesley begins by comparing this parable with the preceding one about the prodigal son and by emphasizing that Jesus here turns to His disciples and the children of God, whereas He has just said what needed to be said to His adversaries, the Pharisees. He immediately seizes upon the decisive point. Jesus commends the behaviour of the steward because it is consistent, seen in the context of the world's own laws and purposes. By the same token, the behaviour of the Christian should be consistent, i.e. related to its end— namely, the everlasting habitations. Thus—purely by the logic of the matter and the analogy of the situation—money becomes the means of furthering the eternal destiny of the Christian.

This is the surprising conclusion to the first paragraph of this sermon. The second paragraph takes up the point decidedly and decisively, to the extent that, in sharp contrast to the customary disdain shown by the poets, orators and philosophers of antiquity, it emphasizes the positive value of money. The introduction of money is for Wesley one of the greatest examples of the wise government of divine providence. It is not money that is evil, as antiquity thought, but love of money, as Jesus says. Money itself serves as a universal means of commerce between the civilized nations. It is the best instrument for giving extensive help in every possible form. It would only be dispensable if and when mankind were living in a state of innocence. But since man is not in such a state, he needs it all the time. For this very reason everyone must know how he ought to handle valuable resources, how to turn them to the highest purposes. Three simple rules are offered: Gain as much as you can; save as much as you can; give as much as you can! The first of these rules of conduct is commended, according to Wesley, by the very fact that here we meet the world on its own familiar ground. Precisely in this way one can contain the world's apparently natural, but in reality exaggerated pursuit of profit. This comprises the proper task of the Christian.

The world must be told that we are not to be enslaved by acquisitiveness at the expense of health. Here Wesley does not hesitate to lay down quite specific regulations with regard to industrial hygiene. Thus he warns against being involved with arsenic or similar injurious substances, against breathing in lead fumes. Thus he emphasizes that an employment connected with a great deal of writing is injurious to health by virtue of people being constricted to a sedentary life. All this has to be taken into consideration precisely by Christians, to whom their Lord has said with due emphasis that life is more valuable than food and the body more than clothing. If this is true even with regard to bodily health, how much more so when it comes to spiritual health! Here the prime consideration is fraud and ruthlessness. This precludes sources of income which depend on the evasion of taxes, because such sources defraud the king of his lawful rights. Does he not deserve at least the same treatment and consideration as our fellow-subjects? No less may we gain our livelihood from businesses which aim at cheating our neighbour, even if this may be acceptable to the general code of honour of the time. Furthermore, the Christian has to abstain from those activities in the course of which, as a result of getting into bad company, he necessarily offends his conscience. Finally, there are various idiosyncrasies among men. One man can pursue an employment which does not overburden or endanger his soul in the slightest, whereas it spells ruin for another. Thus, interestingly enough, Wesley confesses concerning himself at the dawning of the age of modern mathematics and natural science, that he could not study mathematics without thereby becoming at least a Deist, if not an atheist, whereas another may be able to do so without any hesitation. A third viewpoint is essential to the restraints on acquisition—the welfare of one's neighbour. We may not feather our own nests at his expense. This also includes, for Wesley, unfair competition. He expressly directs his attacks just as much against the temptation to sell goods below the current market price as against the enticing away of good workmen.

Since we have also to respect our neighbour's physical welfare, we cannot sell anything injurious to health, above all strong alcoholic drinks. This is directed quite particularly against avaricious doctors and chemists who, on the pretext of healing, may do physical harm. But this prohibition applies even more to offering things for sale which hurt our neighbour spiritually. Here Wesley is thinking of vapid pictures, opera music, and frivolous diversion which appeals to time-wasting and sexual instincts. The first summons of the sermon: 'Gain as much as you can', must therefore be more closely defined: 'Gain all you can by honest industry. Use all possible diligence in your calling. Lose no time. . . . Let nothing in your business be left undone, if it can be done by labour or patience.' Wesley finds it amazing how many men make things easy for themselves in their daily work and follow the same dull track as their forefathers, instead of using to the full the improved state of present-day knowledge. In reality all work is a continual learning, from one's own and others' experiences, from intensified reflection. By this means it is now possible to discharge our daily responsibilities more effectively than was the case in the past.

But this bold and eloquent filling out of the first rule, 'Gain as much as you can', saturated as it is with experience of life and observation of life, is only a first stroke of the brush. The next rule reads: 'Save all you can.' Wesley develops what this means by use of contrast. Do not lay out your money on frivolous, empty, transient pleasure of the moment. And do not pander to a refined Epicureanism, for which pleasure still presents the real goal. No, be content with what nature makes readily available. Shades of Rousseau! 'Save' means be thrifty, be frugal! Here the classical Puritan, typically English ideal of sobriety, as put forth peerlessly in the widely used devotional book *The Whole Duty of Man* (1659) finds expression once again.[84] Here, too, Wesley goes into specific detail, advising against superfluous and expensive furniture, but also censuring with Puritan severity costly pictures and books and wanting to see beautifully landscaped gardens replaced by kitchen-gardens. How serious he is about all this is shown by the saying of Jesus to which he appeals: 'Let the dead bury their dead. Follow me.' This is one of the sharpest words handed down to posterity, and Wesley makes it even more severe by making an assertion reminiscent of Kant: 'Are you willing? Then you are able so to do!' Impressing people in this life by a proud appearance, being a much admired presence, is not at all the proper thing for a Christian to aim at. But let everyone closely examine himself as to whether or not this desire is unconsciously working in him. Once a person has become accustomed to this kind of thing, he sees his desire insatiably increased. How naturally he transmits it to his children! In his eyes nothing is good enough for them, and in the process he spoils them in a fatal way. The anxiety of many parents about not bequeathing enough to their children is in truth a delusion. Wesley asks provocatively: Can you not bequeath to them enough murder weapons, arrows and firebrands, in the shape of destructive desires? When you and yours are lifting up your eyes in hell, you will have enough both of 'the worm which never dieth' and of 'the fire that never shall be quenched'. But Wesley does not let matters rest with this massive threat. It could well be that someone with a considerable fortune to call his own might ask him personally: What would you do in my case? Wesley replies to this question, not without acidity, that he does not know what he *would* do, but he does know what he *ought* to do. If he had several children, he would deem it his indispensable duty to leave the bulk of his fortune to the child who best knew the value of money, but to leave the rest in such a way that they could continue living in the manner to which they were accustomed. But if they were all equally ignorant of the true use of money, then he would be duty bound to provide for them all in such a way that they did not suffer penury.

Yet even thrift has no merit in itself. Anyone who imagines his wealth best preserved by depositing it with the Bank of England might just as well throw it into the sea or bury it in the ground—so judges Wesley even in purely worldly and utilitarian terms. Why? Because the one is as far removed from the truth as the other, and both miss the real situation at its crucial point. They forget that the rightful Owner of heaven and earth did not place man on earth as proprietor, but as steward. Nothing that God entrusted to man really belongs to him. Everything is loaned to him for a season. This is also why God supplied him lavishly with goods in order to make his livelihood secure. But everything, if it is to fulfil its declared purpose, should be a holy sacrifice to God, acceptable and pleasing to Him through Jesus Christ. Therefore the truly Christian imperative reads: Give as much as you can! Here again Wesley is careful to avoid over-simplified advice. It would be wrong, for the sake of the Christian principle of cheerful giving, to neglect our own family, the domestic servants in our own household, and friends too, and thus to show love for those furthest away to the exclusion of our nearest and dearest. If doubts should arise in the mind of the individual as to how far he should go, Wesley's advice to him is to ask himself: Am I acting here as a proprietor or as a steward? Can I expect a reward at the resurrection of the just for what I am now doing? Immediately upon such self-examination we can turn to consider expenses for worldly purposes with a clear conscience.

With all this, and particularly with those detailed considerations which he brings under the general heading of Christian prudence, Wesley goes far beyond his text and the implications of the Biblical parable. At this very point, too, he takes up the message of Jesus in such deliberate detail, and in such a fully and logically developed manner, that one can readily see how such preaching was of immediate practical help. It is perhaps permissible to conjecture that when he expounded the message of salvation orally he was also able to relate it with equal pertinence to the situation of his hearers, whereas to be frank the printed text undoubtedly takes on a quite predominantly abstract, dogmatic form. Even so, this sermon, taken as a unity, leaves one dissatisfied. Fundamental defects remain. The construction itself is disproportionate. The contents of the second and third parts, on thriftiness and the duty of giving, are not nearly so carefully and closely argued as those of the first, on earning. Wesley evades a whole series of questions. He gives no directions for such genuinely problematic situations as how, say, personal thrift and national savings campaigns are related to each other as means for the increase of wealth. He evades the question, which is so pressing for the individual, of where the duty of saving ends and the duty of giving starts. If some wished to counter that such matters lie beyond the scope of preaching, the correct answer would be that here this sermon expressly concerns itself with the demands of everyday life and must therefore consider the difficulties which result from their conflicting obligations.

In the concluding section, which deals with giving, he brings home the sheer magnitude of the matter, and this in two ways. Firstly, he identifies clearly the one to whom we give. It is none other than God Himself. Secondly, he rejects 'the lore of nicely calculated less and more' in giving, even Old Testament, Jewish-Christian tithing. Everything belongs absolutely to God, who has not entrusted parts of the world to man, but the world in its entirety. By the same token, one can only offer Him the whole as a sacrifice—the whole of life, the whole of our possessions, the whole of the world's affairs. Wesley ends impressively with an appeal to the Christian's sense of identity, as this comes to expression in the paranesis of the New Testament Letters, but also in the first classical Christian apologetic writing, the *Letter to Diognetus*: We Christians are different from the heathen. Our kingdom, our wisdom is not of this world: heathen custom is not valid for us. We imitate our fellow-men only insofar as they themselves are followers of Jesus Christ. Therefore I entreat you: Walk worthy of your calling!

On another occasion John Wesley devotes his attention to distraction and dissipation.[85] He takes as his text 1 Corinthians 7³⁵: 'This I speak—that ye may attend upon the Lord without distraction.' The original Greek word, which Luther translated into German '*unverhindert*' ('unhindered'), met with a more precise rendering in the English of the King James' Bible, where it is translated 'without distraction'. Wesley, however, does not take this phrase as the basis for his exposition, but employs a cognate word, 'dissipation'—a term which can also connote wastefulness and frivolity. Obviously, for him it is a case of double-entendre. First of all, he refers to the frequency and newness of this particular word. According to common usage, this word seems to be almost a vogue word which has become current from the criticism of court life since the time of the unpopular Hanoverian kings. It is not only his conservative royalist attitude which Wesley is ventilating; strangely enough, this word had only then come into vogue, although the reign of Charles II, whom he injudiciously calls one of the most loathsome and superficial of men, had given cause for it.[86] Rather, he is here expressing his keen sense of justice. One must not blame a ruler who is at present unpopular with what an earlier one has already embraced cheerfully. In the treatment of the subject itself he endeavours to go deeper. In common parlance, dissipation, squandermania, frivolous dealings with time and money, with people and problems, is a matter of outward behaviour. But before things come to that, he emphasizes, an inward disorder has set in. First something takes place in the heart, then in outward appearances. What is the Apostle really driving at here? Wesley becomes specific and searches out the exact meaning of the opposite positive phrase in this sentence (πρὸς τὸ εὐπρόσεδρον τῷ κυρίῳ), which means literally 'sitting in a good posture before the Lord in order to listen to Him'. To be receptive to Him, all dissipation and superficiality should be banished. According to Wesley, Paul alludes with this phrase to Mary at Bethany, who on Jesus' arrival immediately realized what mattered, whereas the busy Martha, in her distraction, mistook her task. Wesley did not invent this analogy, but inferred it from the Greek word. In Luke 10[40] it is said expressly of Martha that she περιεσπᾶτο, that 'she was cumbered about much', as the King James' Bible has it. Martha is a model of contemporary man generally. The thousand and one things of daily life, the justified and the unjustified demands which crowd in upon him, pull him from his centre, from his origin, from his Creator. This happens all the more easily because, says Wesley bluntly and in decided contradiction to the spirit of the age, man is by nature an atheist. Behind his tendency to dissipation, his vacillating desire for outward things, his activist bent, is hidden his flight from God. How can things become any different? Not by mystical withdrawal, nor by systematic exertion of the will, but solely by the new birth from on high, by the miracle of the divine intervention in Jesus Christ. Here one notes yet again how Wesley reverts to the principal Pietist concern. His preaching of faith and his preaching of morals alike culminate in the preaching of regeneration. The dissipated, superficial, dissolute man is the man redeemed by God. Reconciliation with his Creator also ends his dissipation, which in truth is aimlessness. This is why it would be confining things far too much to look for characteristics of this kind solely among philanderers, receivers of stolen goods, spendthrifts and gossips. No; an honoured statesman, a respected aristocrat, a worthy businessman can come absolutely under this judgement. A whole age can be superficial—such an age being one in which God is generally forgotten. More than any other previous era, the present age must be so adjudged. And it is true of England that it is now a dissipated nation to a superlative degree, indeed, that in this respect it far outstrips the other nations of Europe. Obviously Wesley is thinking here of the deluge of Deistic literature and the ready reception which it has found. Superficiality, a tendency to dissipation, aimlessness then becomes—and this is what Wesley is getting at—synonymous with godlessness. Thank God this does not turn out to be true of everybody! There are more than 7,000, if not ten times as many in England today, who have not bowed the knee to the god of this world. They can bear testimony against the flood of unbelief and in so doing invite others to faith. Does not what he says agree with the recommendations of Thomas à Kempis? asks Wesley. For when he counsels simplicity of intention and purity of affection, this is nothing other than faith that works by love. Simplicity surely means that we constantly fix our eye on God, and purity surely means that we love Him without any ulterior motives. In requiring purity of intention, Jeremy Taylor, too, has the self-same thing in mind. It is noteworthy how here again in his mature years John Wesley allows the authorities of his youth to come to expression. He does so consciously. For in immediate connexion with this, he refers to the early history of his student circle in Oxford, which had taken all this seriously and thereby started a movement. Moreover, it merits notice that he does not allude to the massive, phenomenal activity of this movement, a thing to which, as is well known, he was by no means averse in his apologetic correspondence, but instead stresses self-examination as the nerve-centre of this circle. He also makes emphatic reference here to the Mystics with their summons to 'introversion'. The impulse to outward things spells disaster. The classical proof-text for Puritan examination of the conscience: 'Examine yourselves, whether ye be in the faith; prove your own selves. Know ye not your own selves, how that Jesus Christ is in you, except ye be reprobates?' (2 Corinthians 13⁵), must always be the touchstone of Christian existence. At the same time it becomes clear at this point why the Wesley who was absolutely bent on a decision of the will and authentication in life could be such a firm friend of Romanic mysticism. Thus this sermon, which ostensibly has to do with external superficialities, takes us right to the centre of the Christian life and exhibits its source. The *cri de combat* against the spirit of the age turns into an appeal to conscience which enjoins the one thing needful. This sermon can therefore rightly stand at the end of this representation of John Wesley the preacher.

# SEVEN

# John Wesley as Theological Writer

JOHN WESLEY was a man of action, and for him all the theological erudition which he had at his disposal in sufficient, perhaps even in high measure, and which he constantly enlarged by indefatigable reading, served the purpose of effectively opening up human life to the fundamental truth and the fundamental claim of God as attested by the Christian message. Thus for him thought was immediately transposed into life. And so it is not surprising that from the outset of his literary career we come across not only sermons, but also devotional and dogmatic works, extracts from documents of the Christian tradition, above all biographies and accounts which express his living relationship to history as the locus of experience.

In the year 1742 he published a pamphlet under the title, *The Character of a Methodist*.[1] Here he explains in the very opening words that it is by no means doctrinal opinions which constitute the Methodist's distinguishing mark—although for him the inviolable validity of the Bible as the rule of faith and practice, and the full revelation of God in Jesus Christ, stand secure as irrevocable truths. Neither may we identify a Methodist by certain modes of expression or such peculiar customs as, say, a special costume, unusual habits of eating or drinking, or even renunciation of marriage. Nor would it prove to be the case that he unduly emphasizes a particular point in Christianity, such as, say, justification by faith alone, although with this we should already be coming substantially nearer the truth. Only a definition which is as rounded, as comprehensive and above all as Biblical as possible can get to the heart of the matter. Consequently Wesley positively revels in Biblical phrases in order to describe the core of the Methodist's life and his behaviour. No soothing, pious phraseology, no mindless ecclesiastical jargon can serve the purpose here. On the contrary, it seems as if Wesley can only do justice to the Methodist by the closest possible adherence to the original statements of the New Testament itself. A Methodist is one in whose heart the

67

love of God has been shed abroad by the Holy Ghost; one who for his part loves God with all his heart, and with all his soul, and with all his strength. He confesses with the 73rd Psalm: 'Whom have I in heaven but thee? and there is none upon earth that I desire but thee.' He is happy in God, because he has in God a well of water springing up into everlasting life. Since perfect love casts out fear, instead of fear he knows only joy—joy over the amazing fact that through Jesus' sacrificial death he has obtained reconciliation with God, the forgiveness of all his sins, so that he can now know for sure that he is a child of God. As such he has confidence in the promised future which perfects him, the life everlasting where righteousness and freedom reign supreme. He lives in hope of an incorruptible inheritance. This makes him more than a match for all earthly vicissitudes. He has overcome anxious concern about daily life. It does not matter to him whether he is well or ill, rich or poor, respected or despised. His communion with God is never interrupted, and he realizes this by means of prayer. 'The loving eye of his mind', as Wesley puts it in the idiom of the Romanic mysticism so highly esteemed by him, is continually fixed upon God alone. Whether he sits or lies down, whether he eats or drinks, whether he works or rests, whether he speaks or is silent, his heart is ever with the Lord. But since love of God demonstrates its authenticity in love of one's brother, sacrificial compassion is due also to his neighbour. He embraces every fellow-man with his love, even the one whom he does not know at all, yes, and what is more, the one who persecutes him with hatred and shows himself ungrateful for kindnesses. Love of God has made him pure in heart, so that all evil passions like jealousy, malice, vindictiveness and wrath have become foreign to him, as also have pride, lust for power and contentiousness. Since he has no inordinate desire for worldly goods, but desires God Himself and God alone, whom no one can take away from him, all grounds for contention are simply removed. Instead, striving after holiness pleasing to the Lord in-dwells his soul—God reigns supreme in it. He keeps all the commandments, and does so freely and willingly. It is a joy for him to keep them. It is his glory so to do. His obedience, which is in exact proportion to his love, is its very source. Therefore he continually presents his soul and body as a living, holy and acceptable sacrifice to God. Everything he does is done to the glory of God, and the world around him cannot lead him astray. The world no longer holds any temptation for him. As opportunity affords, he does good to all men and in every possible way. He seeks to awaken those who sleep and to bring those who are awakened to the cross of Jesus Christ, so that there they may obtain reconciliation and as justified men have peace with God, so that they may all grow to the full stature of the mature Christian, to perfection.

If in the light of this description someone exclaims: Surely these are only the common, fundamental principles of Christianity, John Wesley can only acknowledge the truth of his view. These principles and nothing else are what he expects from his Methodists. He and his people do not want to be distinguished from the rest of men by anything but the distinctive characteristics of plain, ancient Christianity. The Spirit of Jesus Christ lives in them. They want to hold up to an unbelieving world, says Wesley in classical Pietist phraseology, the fruits of faith as something real. This is what matters, not opinions or turns of phrase. Therefore he can do no other than invite his readers and hearers to strive with him for this authentic Christianity. The unity of the Spirit in the bond of peace, the *one* calling to the *one* hope unites all men together, so that the great words of the Epistle to the Ephesians are fulfilled: 'One Lord, one faith, one baptism; one God and Father of us all, who is above all and through all and in you all'.[2]

Since this little pamphlet goes straight to the heart of the matter—primitive Christianity—it has no shades of emphasis. From beginning to end it stays on the same plane as has been set by the Biblical quotations. Even so, it does not come across in a stereotyped manner, because the passages have been carefully selected and each stands in its correct place according to the internal coherence. If we are to look for something analogous in church history, then very significantly it is the first rule of Francis of Assisi that comes to mind.

The style employed here is maintained throughout the whole of John Wesley's theological output, which, as is well known, he described as his spontaneous work, in sharp contradiction to the polemical and apologetic work which was forced upon him.[3] He stated his opinion as plainly as one can imagine, without any striving for effect, in very direct statements uniquely combining the styles of religious confession and of conversation, in a dependence on the Bible which had become his second nature and governed all that he said. By these means he invested his statements with an irresistibly aphoristic and peculiarly clear-cut character. It is a significant literary fact that twenty-three years later his short exposition on the character of a Methodist passed almost unchanged into his book on Christian perfection.[4] Nevertheless, he was by no means hidebound by this method. His next separate work, *An Earnest Appeal to Men of Reason and Religion*, from the year 1743,[5] is quite different in character. Here Wesley begins with the grievous assertion that when the Christian looks round him, he either sees men without any faith or discovers men who practise a lifeless, purely formal, conventional religion. However, he knows of a religion which is unique in being worthy of God: it is a loving disposition, love of God and mankind. Such love, he is convinced, is able to heal all the evils and all the miseries of a disordered and fevered world. It makes man happy, and spreads peace and joy all around it.

This religion of love is attainable by faith, which is ordered to things invisible and is completely certain of them. Since this faith is rooted in the eternal world, it knows itself to be superior to things earthly without despising them. Faith is the eye of the man who has been born again of God and for God. It puts to flight all listlessness, fear and anxiety. If someone asks why in view of such an alluring offer all men do not have this faith, the answer is that God Himself and God alone gives it. It is not immediately at man's beck and call. God bestows it as a free gift; and certainly not on those who prove or think themselves especially worthy, but on the contrary on the unholy and the sinful. Only one pre-condition must be met. The recipients of the gift must be seized of their failure and their remoteness from God. A sense of sin must precede faith.

Is not such a religion reasonable and sensible? Does it not commend itself to a right-thinking and deeply sensitive man? Does not the summons to love God and to love our neighbour and thus to do good in every conceivable way sound forth with imperious authority? Can more be packed into one life than that we should make it one continuous labour of love? Should we not lament with the Roman emperor Titus over every day in which we have not done good and cry out: 'I have lost a day'? With this the catch-word has been used which ran through John Wesley's youth and in particular his student circle in Oxford: doing good.[6] But doing good does not mean, as he and they understood it in their early days, to pile up individual achievements, but to save men from the fire, the fire of lust, anger, malice, revenge. Should this not be self-evident for those who can see only themselves as men whom God has saved—sheer gratitude for what they first received?

It may be that modern man is still able to agree with this, or at least to tolerate it. But will not his opposition be aroused when he hears that all this has to be brought about *by faith*? For does not faith stand despised in the wings as a meaningless, outdated thing? Over against this general opinion of the Age of the Enlightenment, Wesley now endeavours to vindicate the concept of faith in its full import and authenticity. Faith, he amplifies, is the constant communion between God and man, an uninterrupted communication which draws the whole of life into its sphere of influence. All things are possible to him who believes. Anyone who believes travels through this world as a citizen of heaven; he has citizen's rights in eternity. He loves the invisible God; he hears His voice; and God's Spirit bears witness with his spirit that he is a child of God. If this is how one views things, then one will, of course, find that there are only a few who champion this faith. To the objection that there are surely enough men who profess themselves Christians, Wesley replies: Yes, too many. For far too many give the lie to their profession of faith by their way of life. In this context he relates the following experience. A lady bewailed in a conversation the hopeless situation of the Christian missionaries to the Indians in North America, because the natives were so wicked that they resisted every improvement. John Wesley appointed himself advocate to the accused and stressed to the contrary their temperance, justice and veracity, with which he was acquainted partly from his own experience and partly from reports. Thereupon the lady in question asked: 'Why, if those Heathens are such men as these, what will they gain by being made Christians?' Wesley had to admit that if they went by the European Christianity of the time they could in fact only stand to lose. A further question arose. What else, then, did Wesley understand by Christianity besides the virtues already mentioned? Acquiescing in the lady's formulation of the question, he retorted by asking whether in her opinion good sense and sound judgement, good manners and proper behaviour, might not serve as a starting point. These qualities, according to which she in fact determined the worth of a man, are, says Wesley, contained in genuine Christianity, and that in their highest perfection. Nevertheless, they are only shadows of the Christian reality. Good sense and sound judgement can only feebly hint at what faith means. Good manners have only a remote resemblance to Christian love. Finally, good behaviour exhibits only a dead copy of that holiness in which the living image of God visibly manifests itself. All these, put together by the hand of God Himself, he calls Christianity. Astonished, the lady replied that if this was Christianity, then she had never yet met a Christian. Perhaps this is true, says John Wesley, pursuing the conversation, for many of his readers as well. If so, then they are only to be pitied, for he can only wish that they should not talk of Christians and Christianity until they have met a real, living personal witness. For what John Wesley has expounded is Scriptural Christianity,[7] genuine Christianity, as it emerges from its authoritative, original charter.[8]

If he thereby satisfies the historical mind, which insists on going back to original sources for proof, a further train of thought shows how far he enters into the Enlightenment's way of thinking. He declares himself in agreement with the wish of his interlocutor to have a religion founded on reason. But what does reason mean? The primary and proper meaning of this word can only signify objective reason, namely, the very nature of things, which is established as an eternal order—in this case the nature of God and man. Only so shall we do justice to both parties, each in his distinctive nature. Only so can we establish their mutual relations in a suitable and valid manner. For the phenomenon called 'religion' begins by teaching man to know God. This happens in faith. Religion continues its work by enabling man to love God, and of its very nature comes to the point where he also loves all mankind as well, since he cannot but follow by inward compulsion the admired and loved example of God. Christianity completes its task of properly representing the nature of God and the relationship of man to Him, by bringing man to faithful service of his Lord. The same thing comes to light when we look at man. Christianity mediates to him, first of all, self-knowledge: he perceives himself to be a sinner. It then goes on to lift him out of his condition of misery by offering him the only effective remedy by which the foolish man becomes wise, the wicked man virtuous, the unhappy man happy. It ends by restoring the proper relationship between God and man. The gracious Father and the grateful, obedient son become at one again.

But Christianity is reasonable not only in this objective sense, but also in the subjective sense. Being reasonable, making use of reason, means, surely, to prove with the aid of reason, to conduct rational debate. In the New Testament one finds Jesus and His apostles engaging in continual dispute with their opponents, adducing convincing argumentation with their associates. The Epistle to the Hebrews is a single, sustained exposition based on reasoning. Indeed, in this context John Wesley calls Jesus and Paul the strongest 'reasoners' that have ever lived and takes up energetically the Pauline admonition, 'In malice be ye children; but in understanding be ye men'.[9] Whereupon the exhortation goes out to all Christians to search out the truth as persistently and as incisively as possible, albeit from the correct point of departure, from carefully established positions. Further, since (a) all knowledge, as John Wesley the empiricist says in concurrence with John Locke, proceeds from the senses, and since (b) the bodily, earthly senses are unable to perceive supernatural things, this calls for spiritual powers of comprehension, spiritual senses, which can distinguish spiritual good from spiritual evil. Just as someone who is colour-blind cannot pass any judgement on colours, so one can certainly make no judgement of divine things if one has no conception of faith. Thus precisely a modern man who has absolute confidence in reason must submit to, and lay himself open to, the uniqueness of Biblical, supernatural truth. As a genuine, incorruptible person, who goes to the root of the matter, he cannot really contradict it at all. He must at least accord it formal respect: the right use of true reason requires this of him.

The very name of a Christian makes this even more of a duty. To be a Christian means not only to keep the classical ten commandments of God, but to acknowledge the truth of the Scriptures in all things, even and primarily in its judgement of damnation of the sinner.[10] It means to lead a responsible life, not to fritter away our days in superficial pastimes or in an empty busy-ness which precludes the state of recollection. No serious man could be satisfied with this. He achieves real satisfaction, abiding happiness, only through the religion which John Wesley and his people preach. For this alone says to him that he is a child of God, that he bears in himself the image of God as a privilege and responsibility.

The exposition now turns into a personal appeal. John Wesley asks his reader not to shut his eyes to reality any longer. He should, he must acknowledge that he himself lies dead in sin and is still

73

estranged from God by pride, vanity and self-will. Is victory over sin attainable? Is there, in this sense, such a thing as Christian perfection? John Wesley expressly affirms that there is, but emphasizes that it is not he who has invented this teaching but the New Testament itself, as Paul (Romans 6[1, 2]), Peter (1 Peter 4[1, 2]) and John (1 John 3[8]; 5[18]), the three arch-apostles, establish. It is precisely the same with the vexed question of justification by faith alone. Here, too, the Methodists must appeal to Paul himself. If, therefore, someone doubts whether he may ascribe or credit so much to faith, whether in particular faith includes assurance of salvation, then it must be pointed out to him that he thereby adopts the position of the Council of Trent. But how can this be reconciled with the Old and New Testaments? Job knows that his Redeemer lives. Thomas exclaims: 'My Lord and my God.' Paul confesses: 'The life I now live, I live by faith in the Son of God, who loved me and gave himself for me' (Galatians 2[20]). The same apostle writes to the Colossians: 'We give thanks unto the Father, who hath delivered us from the power of darkness, and hath translated us into the kingdom of his dear Son; in whom we have our redemption through his blood, even the forgiveness of our sins' (Colossians 1[12-14]). If with the early Christians we can speak in this way, then we also consider it possible that 'the dead shall hear the voice of the Son of God and live' (John 5[25]). For God has only to speak and it is done. His love is as great as his power, and neither knows measure nor end.

The Methodists have been forbidden the churches for preaching this message. But they cannot withhold the message and desist from preaching. With this message they go in early Christian fashion into the streets and market-places, by rivers and on mountain-sides. They are prepared to undergo persecution and know that Jesus' promises for the persecuted are true for them too. Does this conspire to undermine the Church of God or even just the Church of England? Is it not precisely calculated to support and establish it? What a pathetic picture is given if people try to blame the Methodists for breaking particular canonical laws when in the fundamentals and the essentials —preaching, administration of the Sacrament, and living faith—they are in complete accord with the Church! In point of fact, on closer examination even the alleged offences against church order dissolve into nothing. The popular allegation that the Methodists are deserting the Church will not hold water. The very reverse is true: they strive to be increasingly loyal churchmen. In what follows John Wesley defends himself against a whole series of allegations, in particular those of avarice and contempt for the Church. His description of the origins and development of the Methodist movement is given in broad outline, but with detailed examination of points which are controversial issues. Imperceptibly he turns into an apologist. His strongest argument is the change which has taken place in public morality within a matter of a few years as a result of the Methodists' activity, their preaching, their formation of societies. He insists on the fact that Christ has been preached with a new urgency, and sinners converted to God. The least that the Methodists may claim for their movement is compliance with the counsel of Gamaliel (Acts 5) that the onlookers bide their time so as to see whether the work is of God or of men. He ends in the assurance of the victory which the cause of Jesus has won in the past and which it continually wins afresh, and thereby makes himself independent of every human judgement.

Is this writing of a piece? At first sight, it does not appear to be, because exposition and vindication, argumentation in matters of principle and allusion to current events are intermingled. He moves from one subject to another apparently without system. Nevertheless, on closer examination the apologetic purpose stands revealed as the dominant and unifying feature of the work. This book is planned to this end. It is intended to engage in dialogue with the rationalists of the time. This is why here the testimony of the Bible is less prominent.

The wide-ranging book, *A Farther Appeal to Men of Reason and Religion*, from the year 1745,[11] pursues the same matter further. This detailed exposition combines in a unique and highly arresting way the features which up to now we have observed in isolation—personal identification with the Bible, logical argumentation and apologetics. This combination is achieved in the noteworthy sequence that this treatise begins with positive Biblical exposition, which is then followed by apologetic argument. By this very procedure Wesley tellingly frees himself from the thought-patterns and the literary style of the Enlightenment, which, particularly in the rational-supranaturalistic theology prevalent in official Anglicanism, at best arrived at the Biblical evidence as the final goal and thereby cast it, perhaps unintentionally, in a secondary rôle. At the same time Wesley let it be known from the subordinate apologetic that he shared the *essential* concern of the Enlightenment, i.e. a true definition of the relationship between revelation and reason. In his treatise he explains, first of all, the doctrines which were important to him and the Methodist movement and which the opposite camp had questioned and contested. At bottom there is one and one only: namely, justification—which, however, is covered in the whole range of its implications. In this connexion he starts from the literal meaning. In the New Testament justification sometimes denotes, it is true, the verdict at the final judgement (Matthew 12$^{37}$), but far more frequently the present forgiveness of sins which adoption demonstrates. This is how it has been understood in church tradition, as this tradition gains for Wesley normative and exemplary formulation in the Homilies of the Anglican Reformation. In this context Romans 3$^{25}$ and Hebrews 8$^{12}$ furnish New Testament proof-texts. Of these the second has special weight, because it presents a quotation from the Old Testament (Jeremiah 31$^{34}$). Clearly Wesley was concerned to bring out the unity of the Bible at this crucial point. The condition which must here be fulfilled on the human side is faith, as Romans 4$^{5}$ states. Nevertheless, Wesley is quick to pin down the meaning of the ambiguous term 'condition' by defining faith as the *event* in which justification takes place. Good works, understood as the entire process of sanctification, ensue from such faith; repentance, understood as conviction of sin and accompanied by a desire for amendment of life, precede it. All this he adduces from New Testament passages which he does not cull from any particular tradition but relates independently to the subject.[12] In this connexion it is a striking fact that in this range of ideas so central to Pauline thought he works exclusively with evidence from the first three Gospels. Here, once again, for Wesley the unity of the Bible is at stake. Justification and sanctification denote the process which takes place by virtue of God's closure with man. Its outcome is deliverance from sin, restoration to original health. Indeed, Wesley goes so far as to say that the outcome is recovery of the divine nature. The image of God, in which man was created, is to shine forth with renewed lustre, in justice, mercy, and truth.

As seen from man's side, everything depends on faith. Here Wesley reiterates his own conversion-experience by stressing with the Epistle of James (2$^{19}$) that faith as assent to objective propositions is not enough. On the contrary, everything devolves on personal appropriation: Christ died for *my* sin; He loved *me* and gave Himself *for me.* In underlining the fact that he can only conceive of such faith as happening in a flash, as an immediate, luminous perception of the decisive truth, Wesley further reflects his own experience. Nonetheless—and this, too, is noteworthy—he leaves other possibilities open.[13]

Faith of this kind and with this content is the beginning of the new life. It is, in a word, 'the new birth', which cannot be restricted to the moment of baptism. The very converse is true. If baptism does not produce any fruit, then it indicts the sinner, instead of guaranteeing his state of salvation. Indeed, everything hinges on the new birth which is effective here and now, on the present operation of the Holy Spirit, because God is a present God. He alone is the Author and Fashioner of the whole event of conversion and the whole gift of salvation. *How* He does this, whether He has recourse primarily to man's powers of understanding or to his affections or to his will, remains an open question.

Having developed this in as concise and simple terms as can be imagined, John Wesley seeks to authenticate his Biblically grounded interpretation by quoting the Protestant *Homilies* of the Anglican Church, and then proceeds to invalidate the objections to the Methodist movement which can be reduced to the well-known common denominator of 'enthusiasm', understood as a wilful misunderstanding of the work of the Holy Spirit. Here Wesley contends, first of all, for as close a scrutiny as possible of the facts: only that which is enthusiasm, frenzy, madness can be called such. Then he contends for the freedom of the Holy Spirit to work as He wills. Rigid rules do not apply here, and the 'Enlightened' man of the eighteenth century will have to learn to accept extraordinary testimonies as valid. Certainly John Wesley's whole primitive Christian interpretation is once again implicated. It came hard to people of that time to discern the hand of God in such strange utterances as, say, the speaking in tongues at Pentecost. Behind these popular misgivings, however, more serious objections loom up. In two polemical tracts the doctrine of justification itself had been described as unscriptural.[14] Wesley now thoroughly establishes that the understanding of justification developed by him from the New Testament is reproduced at various points in the Liturgy, significantly quoted first, in the *Articles of Religion* and in the *Homilies* of the Anglican Church. The last serious objection relates to the fact that by their field-preaching and their disputes with the church authorities, the Methodists are disturbing the public peace. In this matter John Wesley appeals to the experiences of Jesus and the apostles as the eminent and normative models, who in fact were even prepared to accept division within families as part of the price of the Gospel.

The seriousness which he has attained by this appeal determines the second part of the work, in which he holds up to the contemporary Church the fate of the Israelites of the Old Testament and warns England in particular against toying with God's offer of grace. Here identification with the Bible reaches its zenith: contemporary England should become a people of God in obedience and readiness for sacrifice, in order and discipline, and transcending all the formalism of the canon law fulfil the true task of the disciples of Jesus as the only proper stance.

This work would undoubtedly have been improved by presenting its train of thought along the lines drawn out here. The prolixity with which John Wesley proves the doctrine of justification from the foundation-documents of the Anglican Church and with which he discusses it point by point, spoils the effect and confers on the apologetic an importance which it cannot bear on its own. The reason for this diffusiveness is not hard to find. When it came to the doctrine of justification, its co-ordinates and correlates—faith, regeneration, sanctification—the whole of theology was at stake for Wesley. The *Farther Appeal* demonstrates afresh the central position which this doctrine held for him. To him it was the essence of the early Christian tradition. Just as one of his duties as a theological author was to defend the Methodists, so on the other hand he had to express his opinion on groups adopting a deviationist theology. Someone had asked for his judgement on 'the Friends', the Quakers. Wesley replied that for him there was an absolutely fundamental difference between them and true Christians.[15] For this, he takes as his basis the characterization of them by their eloquent, successful apologist, Robert Barclay (1648–90).[16] He acknowledged the authority of the Holy Spirit, who alone grants true knowledge of God, to be the common point of departure for them and himself, but immediately asserted that there is a parting of the ways when the Quakers refuse to subject the revelations of the Holy Spirit to the Bible. In this connexion he went as far as he could in allowing for shared beliefs. If by the sovereign authority of the Spirit be only meant that the Holy Scriptures are derived from the Holy Spirit, then he could agree, but not if the uncontrolled Spirit was superior to the Scriptures. In order to arrive at a clear mode of expression, he proposed to call the Holy Spirit the 'guide' and the Holy Scriptures the 'rule' of the Christian life.[17]

From the Holy Spirit he moved on to the subject of the 'inner light', thereby touching upon a favourite Quaker formula. When the 'Friends' maintained that the recipients of the 'inner light' experience a spiritual birth which brings forth in them holiness, righteousness, purity, and all other fruits, this was bound to sound familiar to him from German Pietism. But it is characteristic of his keen perception and his certainty of touch that here he immediately posed the question of justification. His judgement was: If the Quakers are convinced that this spiritual birth produces first sanctification and then justification, then they teach justification by works and set themselves in opposition to the Bible. Like the Roman Catholics they put sanctification in the position where justification belongs, and thereby canonize human achievement.

He then mounted his attack against the Quaker notion that we may only speak of God and pray to him if the Holy Spirit moves us to do so. Here Wesley issued a firm warning against confusing one's own inner compulsion with the prompting of the Holy Spirit. Far from manifesting Himself solely through impulses, feelings, personal wishes, pressing desires, the Holy Spirit equally issues stern commands which the recipient resists. This is why the Church does right to arrange regular times of worship. The silent worship offered by the Quakers is without Biblical foundation; it is self-willed conduct. All the Bible passages pressed into service on this question, e.g. the summons to wait upon the Lord (Psalms $27^{14}$; $37^{7,\ 34}$; Proverbs $20^{22}$) or the reports that the first Christians were gathered together with one accord in one place (Acts $2^1$), say something quite different. In these interpretations, it is not the Bible, but Jakob Böhme speaking. Similarly, on the question of the Sacraments there is a radical difference. The Quakers consider Baptism and the Lord's Supper to be outward signs, whereas Jesus Himself did not leave them at this low level, neither when He distinguished the baptism of John from His own and yet indicated a connexion between the two of them, nor, still less, when He urged on us the duty of continually celebrating the Lord's Supper in remembrance of Him. The doctrinal differences

79

between Lutherans, Calvinists and Papists on the Sacrament of the Altar, so eloquently brought out by Robert Barclay, can in no wise annul the express command of Jesus to keep the feast. Thus John Wesley sums up at this point: The difference between the Quakers and true Christians lies in their respective attitudes to the Scriptures, Justification, Baptism and Holy Communion.[18] Since these matters touch upon matters crucial to salvation, this is no meaningless trifle.

This judgement can be even more applicable to matters of outward conduct. In refusing to render honour to other men and in keeping their hats on in the presence of the king, as George Fox did, the Quakers can in no wise appeal to the Bible, for Paul honoured the Roman governor in the prescribed manner. To make form of address ('thou' or 'you' or 'ye') into a question of faith is a laughable non-sense. Here it is lawful to follow the local usage. In this connexion John Wesley showed himself well informed about France and Germany. Nor can the prohibition against taking the oath be in any way founded on the Bible. Although Jesus did not desire it from His followers, He nevertheless took the oath before the High Priest, in that He only replied to him when the latter had *adjured* Him in the Name of the living God (Matthew 26[63-64]). A man who goes over from mainstream Christianity to Quakerism behaves as a deserter: he is no longer intent on the primary and proper goals—love of God, holiness and righteousness—but on petty, capricious idiosyncrasies, on opinions and externals,[19] and thereby diverges from the will of Jesus.

Among the doctrinal treatises there are two in particular which capture a commanding position by virtue of their subject-matter, their compass and their thesis. The first of these treats of original sin, and was written in 1757 in a controversy with John Taylor; the second was devoted to Christian perfection, and belongs to the year 1766.[20] John Taylor was a noted Unitarian theologian, and this neo-humanist trend of thought, which rejected the doctrine of the Trinity as an expression of the mystery and richness of God, was at that time making massive advances in English intellectual life, particularly paving the way for the Enlightenment.[21] In 1757 Taylor, who to begin with worked as a minister in Norwich, became a tutor at the Dissenting Academy in Warrington, which had a certain reputation. With his usual bent for over-simplification Wesley adjudged that no one since Mohammed had inflicted such deep wounds on Christianity as

he had. Here he did not hesitate to use the most pungent terms, saying of his books that they had poisoned not only many of the clergy
but also the places of their education in England, Scotland, Holland
and Germany.[22] The reference to Mohammed was natural enough
because Islam had raised the most violent, passionate opposition to
the Christian doctrine of the Trinity and in the areas which it had
conquered had achieved the greatest successes known to the history
of the church in its campaign against Christianity. Wesley's annihi-
lating judgement was particularly related to Taylor's book on the
*Scripture Doctrine of Original Sin,* from the year 1735–36, an undeniably thorough work. This is precisely why Wesley considered
him to be a positive menace to faith and also said as much to his face
in a letter, by declaring that Taylor's view was naked heathenism
which was setting back the process of making Europe Christian.[23] He
established to his sorrow that every so often he met among his hearers
adherents of this man and could then accomplish nothing.[24] Between
himself and Taylor it was a straight Either/Or.[25] Nevertheless, in the
preface to his own treatise, and elsewhere too, he was thoroughly
prepared to give credit where credit was due to his adversary, and
not merely as a matter of form. He acknowledged that he was
equipped with understanding, erudition, imagination and a masterly
style; that he was motivated by love of humanity; yes, even that he
feared God. However, he placed his gifts at the service of a reprehensible cause.[26] What he had the effrontery to expound as being
according to Scripture was in actual fact contrary to the Scriptures;
it was crypto-Deism, crypto-atheism, to which overt Deism is to be
preferred, in which we know what we are up against. The harsh
words demonstrate how violently a theology of this kind provoked
him, because it violated what for him was the Holy of holies and
struck at the very foundation of things. At the same time, however,
he sought to regain his self-control. In the preface he expressed the
hope that he might succeed in pleading his cause in the right way,
not with contempt or disdain, but in such a way as to attest the truth
in love. The whole tenor of the work completely matches up to this
hope. In the exposition, polemic— the immediate reason for putting
pen to paper—is kept to a bare minimum, so that for whole stretches
the reader forgets it almost entirely. He rests content with bringing
to expression the view that he champions, and does so by adhering
very closely to the Bible. He asks first of all after the past and present

F

state of mankind and gives precedence to God's judgement prior to the Flood: 'The thoughts and inclinations of man were always evil from his youth up' (Genesis 6⁵). He attaches himself wholeheartedly to this judgement, aligning himself with the widely read Dialogue of his erstwhile friend, James Hervey, *Theron and Aspasio* (1755). He takes it to be an historical assertion about a time-span of at least 1,600 years. If we turn to the state of mankind after Noah, the first significant event is the Tower of Babel, which again can only be interpreted as a proof of man's wickedness. Then follow Sodom, with its depravity, and Egypt, the land of wisdom, which provoked God's indignation by resisting His purpose. The Israelites themselves, who as bearers of the promise and guarantors of the future were delivered from all these confusions, proved themselves godless, from their dancing round the golden calf at Sinai-Horeb down to their worship of Baal in Canaan. If this is true even of the Chosen People, who enjoyed a special relationship with God, who were in fact favoured with special revelations and who as a theocratically constituted community did not have any real possibility of disintegrating, how much more true of other nations! Roman writers attest this all too loud and clear. Virgil and Juvenal serve here as secondary witnesses. In addition to them, there are various accounts of sexual barbarism which even went as far as pederasty, bestiality reported without any sense of shame, and the cult of Preapus which the honourable Roman mothers practised as the natural thing to do. Wesley further cites infidelity, which made the breaking of promises and covenants into an everyday occurrence, cruelty towards one's own children, whom people were allowed to expose if they were unwanted, the absolute power which the Roman law granted to the paterfamilias by allowing him to kill his son with impunity. But first and foremost, how unmercifully the Romans treated their political enemies, the courageous Hannibal and the noble Vercingetorix of old! Wesley pursues his argument entirely in the style of Augustine in his work on the City of God, in which the much lauded Roman virtues were unmasked as splendid vices. But all this is in the service of a strict Biblicism. For him, what matters is to prove the Pauline and Apocalyptic judgements of the New Testament on paganism to be literally true.[27] Identification with primitive Christianity governs everything.

How, then, do matters stand with mankind at the present time? According to a computation of Edward Brerewood,[28] if one divides the inhabited world into 30 parts, 19 of them are heathen, and of the remaining 11, 6 are Muslim and only 5 Christian. Wesley focuses his attention first of all on genuine pagans, as they are to be met particularly in Africa, and finds that in their environment, in their everyday life, particularly eating, drinking, and relations with the opposite sex, they hardly rise above the beast; that they treat one another in the most inhuman way, having cut their fellow-men's throats for generations or at best sold them as slaves to their colonial masters,[29] and having developed no form of legal procedures but abandoned every man to the whim of the mighty, and having suppressed the truth at any price.

The position is scarcely any better with the Indians in North America. Their primitive forms of life, as evidenced by their miserable huts, their pitiful sustenance (e.g. maize, fish, deer and water) which is barely cooked and consumed almost without preparation, and their scanty clothing, hardly show a capacity for development. They can neither read nor write. They cannot formulate laws. Accordingly, they seem to have no desire whatever for anything different, but to be entirely satisfied with hunting and tribal warfare. In their religious cultus one notices a vast difference between the natives of the North and those of the South. The Indians of the North are devil-worshippers who pursue a cult of the grotesque, the revolting, the frightful. Those of the South, on the other hand, do not have the slightest conception of public worship. They, whom after all Wesley confronted for one and a half years and for whose evangelization he strove earnestly and ineffectively, could not be brought to an understanding of prayer. They just would not understand that God could hear and answer. Their objection was: 'He that sitteth in heaven is too high; he is too far away.' Consequently they do not turn to Him, and manage their affairs without any reference to Him whatever. They have no alphabet, no laws or traditions. They live carefreely from day to day; they steal and murder; they scalp their neighbour, deceive him by lying, cheat him; they get themselves drunk and practise unchastity. Above all they are unmerciful and implacable. Vindictive and inhuman, they seek only to satisfy their carnal appetites, their lust for power. They torture their prisoners of war. Grown sons kill their own fathers and mothers because they are no longer of any use. Men leave their wives when they have no further use for them; and conversely, out of disillusion and thirst for revenge

83

the women cut the throats of the children whom they have conceived by such a man. They also procure abortions or throw the newborn babes into the water. The dark picture of the Indians which John Wesley unfolds here looks very different from the one which filled his mind in the days of his youth, when every so often, in the mood which Rousseau later made into the common property of Europe, he was tempted to contrast the noble savages with the degenerate Europeans.[30] And yet even in those days he had not been completely blind and had been able to correct his preconceived ideas in the light of reality.

Even now he instances a major exception—the tribe of the Chicasaws. They alone betray some notion of a communion between man and a superior Being, by speaking of their 'beloved ones', whose instructions they carry out in such matters as eating and drinking to their hearts' content at any hour of day or night. Their 'beloved ones' also expressly command them to torture, indeed to burn, all their prisoners—which they do over a slow fire in the most gruesome way.

So much for America. In Asia the Chinese are reckoned to be the epitome of wisdom, culture and morals, not only on the authority of their self-estimate but also on the authority of numerous eulogies by many European travellers. We are in the eighteenth century, the classical age for holding China in high esteem, an esteem which gained its most eloquent expression in the great polymath of the age, Leibniz. Wesley does not let himself be dazzled by it. He points to this nation's unnatural custom of having the feet of little girls and women so crippled that they no longer bear any proper relation to the size of their bodies. Furthermore, what is one to think of the fact that their most aristocratic people, the Mandarins, too indolent to use their own hands, have their food put in their mouths by two slaves? Can their learning be all that marvellous when they actually went into raptures over the ability of the Jesuit missionaries from France to calculate ellipses? But first and foremost, their religion must be judged to be idolatry, in that they persisted in ancestor-worship with a stubborn tenacity. As for their social behaviour, the favourable accounts are certainly one-sided, if not prejudiced. Over against them are to be set very unfavourable ones, such as those of Admiral Lord Anson[31] and many Britons who have travelled in various parts of this immense country. In commerce they seek to cheat their associates by every expedient. The polite, considerate behaviour to which their laws bind them does not prevent but rather promotes a colossal hypocrisy. This is the way things are with the best and wisest of all the heathen in Asia.

When we reach Europe, we meet up with undisguised heathenism in the North: for example, among the Lapps and Samoyeds between Sweden and Russia. How savagely people behave there! What alarming forms of idolatry, what adoration of hideous, grotesque creatures are found there! There is probably nothing to choose between them and the Africans of the Cape of Good Hope.

A recently published, new translation of the Koran[32] touchingly went to great lengths to represent the Islamic prophet and his followers in as favourable a light as possible. But it proves impossible to whitewash the Moors. How many bizarre and perverse things the foundation-document of the Muslims contains! Wesley desists from citing details and underlines the fact that according to Islamic interpretation anyone who does not swallow everything in the Koran is condemned to the fires of hell. Not a trace of divine love or even sheer human love is found among these fanatics, who do not tolerate any alternative view; on the contrary, in Turkey and Persia a persecution-mania gave rise to widespread and fearful blood-baths, and this over differences of opinion on whether or not one must wear a round turban. The whole history of Islamic conquest and dominion is an unparalleled story written in blood. Nowhere has so much devastation of once flourishing countries and towns been perpetrated.

Finally, if we turn to the Christians themselves, we establish the fact that in Eastern Christianity not only the Orthodox Diaspora of the Ottoman Empire, but also vast hosts of people who live in closed communities, have passed their days in childish, superstitious ceremonies and inane logomachy about dogmatic formulae and must in consequence have presented a rock of offence to the Muslims. Perhaps at this point a Roman Catholic would interpose that such results are only to be expected if people depart from the one true Church. The heretics reap the harvest they deserve. This is to be answered with the counter-question: How do things stand, then, in the traditional Catholic countries—Italy, Spain and Portugal? The sole advantage which the Italians have over the Greek Orthodox Church is their 'Italianism', which they have taken over from their forefathers, i.e. their heathen Roman superstition which lives on, unshaken, down to the present day.[33] Over and above this, no other

European country produces as many Deists, if not atheists, as Italy, and from there this undermining of Christianity has spread far and wide, particularly to France, where the nobility for the most part still adhere to the Christian revelation, but only from worldly motives. Again, nowhere do so many assassinations occur as on the Apennine and Iberian peninsula, where no foreigner's life is really safe. Look at the visitation of Alva and his troups on Flanders! Look how His most Christian Majesty treated his Huguenot subjects! See how much Protestant blood the Dukes of Savoy shed among the Waldensians! Witness how many human lives the Inquisition, which gives itself the elegant title of the 'House of Mercy', has on its conscience! For purposes of insult the pyres bear the beautiful notation 'autodafé' —acts of faith. It is in such a fashion that the ennobling effect of the Christian Gospel is held up for display. But have the Protestants, who by virtue of the Reformation have been freed from such errors and corruptions, any cause for self-congratulation? Just consider closely how they conduct themselves, for example, in the administration of justice, where lawyers are readily found to support an unjust claim.

Over and above this, however, there is a massive, irrefutable indictment to be levelled against the Christians. War takes place among them, and it is justified by ostensibly good arguments. This is not only an offence against the fundamental principles and purposes of Christianity, but also an affront against reason. For what justification can there be for thousands of men shooting at one another because their lords and masters have a quarrel with one another? How on earth can a victory on the field of battle, won in such a primitive way, be a proof of justice in this quarrel? If every country, pagan and Christian alike, considers war to be a last resort and the final solution to their difficulties, this in itself is the surest sign of the utter degeneracy of the human race.[34]

Thus the fact of war serves as the strongest proof that the fundamental Christian assertion about original sin is true. John Wesley places it in telling contrast to the grandiose and arrogant talk of the age about the dignity of human nature in its present state. He thereby declares open war on the Enlightenment, as the German revival movement did a full generation later through Gottfried Mencken,[35] by repudiating their ideal; and in order to prick its pride, he alludes to an ancient poet like Ovid, who had already depicted the golden age as a kingdom of peace. But perhaps someone interjects, Wesley continues, that although this is true of other countries, it is certainly not true of Great Britain and Ireland, where educated persons live in freedom under a just government and enjoy the blessings of a true religion. Wesley replies: Just go to Ireland and the Scottish islands and see for yourselves how the native people live there, and what kind of knowledge they have! They have no notion of a genuine piety: they know nothing of the life of God in the soul of man. In England and in the much-vaunted, cosmopolitan seaport towns, things are no better. In fact the people there are highly accomplished in the arts of smuggling and robbery. And the soldiers and sailors? It is not without cause that the ships have been called floating hells. Let us go one step further, Wesley proposes. How do things stand with the customs officers in British ports? Are they judicious, wise, conscientious men who fear God and do the right? How many among them would sooner be torn in pieces than allow the lawful revenues of His Majesty to suffer loss? How many are totally incorruptible? What about the tradesmen? Certainly a number of them are an honour to the nation, but is this true of the rank and file? Wesley, too, once thought highly of the British merchants. But all too often he has been disillusioned. How must one judge the representatives of the law? Do they never defend a bad cause? Do they really so love their neighbours as to plead their cause without hope of personal gain? Do they always defend the poor against their oppressors? Do they not on occasion protract a lawsuit indefinitely and in the process reap their own advantage, instead of helping straight away? One can, however, depend on the nobility, many think. Wesley has to unmask this conviction, too, as a prejudice. He reiterates emphatically the saying of Jesus that it is hard for the rich to enter the kingdom of heaven and the assertion of Paul that not many noble and mighty of this world are called into a Christian community; for too many seductive serpents surround them for them always to be able to offer resistance. Indeed, we must really look upon it as the greatest of miracles if a few of them come to faith and hold on to faith. But even if we make more modest claims and expect of them not piety but merely good sense, such a quality will frequently be conspicuous by its absence. Great wealth is no guarantee whatever of high intelligence. In most cases it's the other way round.

Finally, Wesley turns his attention to the church leaders. Can we not at least speak good of those who as God's servants are the leaders of

God's cause? Are they all moved by the Holy Spirit? Are they true shepherds, who have entered by the door into the sheepfold? Is their eye single? Are their affections set on things above? Do they lead a holy life? These are the criteria he sets, in the classical imagery of the New Testament. In mentioning the entry through the door with a certain emphasis, he undoubtedly has in mind the traditional Anglican 'ladder of preferment', on which the minions of the Crown, the nobility, and perhaps even of Parliament, encompass their elevation to the episcopal bench.[36]

Nevertheless, this argument from a necessarily generalized survey is not sufficient, and he supplements it with a personal question which every individual is to put to himself and his milieu, thus making the question not only a pressing one but even inescapable. In the manner which had become a firm tradition, indeed a habit, through the Puritan examination of the conscience, he first asks every man to examine himself as to whether he is satisfied with himself. A list of more than a hundred questions[37] cascades from his lips and sets in motion a lively, passionate dialogue between him and his reader. The outcome of this uncontrived but penetratingly considered series of questions, so pertinently relevant to everyday life, is an admission of mistakes, failures and sins. Experience, not theory is the order of the day; observation, not the doctrinaire preconception. The questions ended, he does not cite, as might well be expected, Biblical judgements on humanity, but Ovid's lament over lost peace.[38] He concludes summarily: Universal misery is a consequence and a proof of universal corruption. Men are unhappy because they are unholy.[39] In this context he consciously omitted the gross vices and kept to the refined, invisible sins—pride, anger, self-will, foolish desires.[40] He emphasizes, yet again, and with the Epistle of James, that these inclinations in the individual human soul furnish the fertile soil for the great war between nations and kingdoms.[41]

This concludes the first part. He has put the case clearly and defended it against all attempts at denial or mitigation. Now the Biblical judgement on this matter comes into its own. One can criticize the sequence which Wesley follows here. Luther stressed that asserting the total depravity of human nature, in other words, original sin, cannot be the object of human perception, but must be believed from the Scriptures.[42] This axiom of the Reformer's, which a theological teacher of August Vilmar reiterated, made such an indelible impression on him as a student around 1820 that Vilmar adhered to it all his life. In the same vein Sören Kierkegaard enjoined that the doctrine of sin, and specifically original sin, is integral to the Kerygma and can only be understood from it. Sin must be authoritatively declared.[43] Here as so often John Wesley, deviating from the Reformation, proves himself to be a son and heir to Pietism. Philipp Jakob Spener, too, had evinced the sinfulness of modern Christendom in concrete terms by observing daily life, by inquiry into human behaviour.[44] In a debate with Taylor which goes into the minutiae of his train of thought and his Biblical proofs, John Wesley reaffirms the statements of the Story of the Fall and Paul's argument in Romans 5. Adam and Jesus Christ are not, as modern 'enlightened' man would have us believe, individual persons, but representatives of the whole progeny first of sinners, then of the redeemed. At this point in the argument, it is important to note that the true doctrine of justification which, as Taylor's opponent David Jennings had stressed, was the decisive content of the Epistle to the Romans, has already been set forth in two preceding chapters and can be assumed.[45] Understandably enough, Taylor did not acquiesce in this Biblicist reply but, to undermine it, directed against it the objection that God would be unjust if He let a vast host of people suffer for the guilt of a single individual. He wanted to rid himself of the difficulty by pronouncing death to be a benefit, so that it became a phenomenon of the biological cycle, but not a punishment for sin. John Wesley counters, with David Jennings,[46] that it is by no means experienced as such, but that its approach produces anxiety and anguish, indeed frequently causes men to cling like a grapnel to the perishable goods of this transitory world. The connexion between death and sin can no more be explained away than that between the death of Jesus and redemption. The virtue of Jesus and following Him in no way expiates the transgressions of the whole human race, as Taylor says, reiterating the words of the humanist Faustus Socinus, but only Jesus' death. It is a question of upholding the content and by the same token the gravity and emphasis of the Biblical message. Wesley does not choose to demonstrate this Biblical message, but rather to protect it from being sold short or falsified. In this connexion his main line of thought is that original sin does not turn out to be the sum of single transgressions, but precedes them as their starting point.[47] Outward wickedness results from inward wickedness, as above all Psalm 51 classically puts it. The whole of the further discussion moves along this tack. For both Taylor and Wesley alike, the authority of the Bible is beyond question. But whereas Taylor continually tries to evade its statements by rationalistic watering-down, Wesley insists on complete acceptance of them, even if at first they alienate and run counter to our natural inclinations. Consequently his book becomes a running commentary on Taylor's would-be Biblical proof-texts. As matters progress, the central emphasis in the ensuing discussion is detailed elucidation, though matters of logical principle are also raised. Thus, for instance, the principle is asserted that man's bias to sin does not annul the guilt attaching to sin;[48] and cogent objections are brought against the confusion of human weakness with impurity in the sight of God.[49] In expanding on the statement of Job 15[14]: 'What is man, that he should be clean? And he that is born of a woman, that he should be righteous?', a statement which Taylor had used as such a confusion, Wesley unfolds in this connexion the principle that this text simply cannot be taken on its own, but must be understood on the one hand against the background of all the dialogues in the Book of Job and on the other hand in the light of the whole of the Old Testament. In reply to the special pleading of human weakness in mitigation, he immediately rejoins: Was Adam made defective and imperfect? He even continues—and theologically this is a moot point—that every man is now born in the same excellent original state. It is only against the background of such a highly emphatic and richly developed creational theology that John Wesley's doctrine of original sin really gains its cutting edge and reaches its peak.[50] This is of the utmost importance. It corresponds to the whole trend of his theological thought, as this was to be particularly and repeatedly observed in his favourite formula of the correlation between holiness and happiness. This is why he opposes Taylor's argument, the final outcome of which is to make God the Author of sin. God, for Wesley, is the *primo mobile*, the Author, of all life in its manifold forms; but not of sin. Between these two lines of thought there is a great gulf fixed. Just as Taylor identified sin with man's common weakness, so he also contested the idea that the Fall of Adam and Eve destroyed communion with God. In both cases Taylor relativized what really happened. Over against this, Wesley vigorously maintained that the sinful pair disrupted their communion with God of their own free will. They fled from Him and hid themselves from

His presence, which made them sore afraid. Thus he adhered firmly to the literal sense of the Biblical narrative in all its rigour. He took it to its extreme logical conclusion. Communion with God signified for Wesley substantially more than it did for Taylor: it meant not only the possibility of hearing Him as the Lord who is provoked to anger and the Judge who punishes, but also, on the authority of the Paradise narrative, the possibility of having intimate and uninhibited communion with Him. The first men had undoubtedly lost this capacity, but not only they; today, too, it is by no means the norm. Just as in his evangelistic work Wesley acted on the assumption that England was not a Christian country, so the whole bent of his theological thought founded on the principle that mankind is for the most part made up of people without God, atheists in the strict sense.[51]

For Taylor the next and perhaps the greatest stumbling-block in the doctrine of original sin consisted in imputing Adam and Eve's guilt to the whole of their progeny for all time. To accept this imputation meant accusing God of injustice. How could He make innocent people suffer for misdeeds which are not their own? Taylor rightly inferred that if even man recognizes the injustice in this, how much more so God Himself. Wesley answers, with the Bible: God's thoughts are not our thoughts, and His ways are not our ways. To his mind Taylor overlooked the radical difference between God and man. In answer to the allegation of injustice in God's dealings, he rejoined first of all, and in an almost aggressive manner, that it is possible to sharpen the issue even more by further observations. Is it not unjust that God permits millions to be born into a world which bears on every hand the stigmata of His displeasure? Is it not horrifying that He forces human souls to enter into bodies which are conceived and born in sin? Now Wesley comes in with a loud 'But': namely, that God has provided a Saviour for all men. He redeems the whole situation, and by so doing has completely resolved the tension between justice and mercy.[52]

Wesley sees the paradox as being resolved not by logic but by action. Grace is not a principle, but a deed. Moreover, the fact of the matter is that not only punishment, as Taylor thought, but sin itself, was transmitted from Adam to his progeny. Here Wesley underscores the Pauline text: 'The wages of sin is death' (Romans 16[23]). In other words, death is not a mere fate which breaks in upon man unexpectedly and undeservedly. In seeking to sum everything up, he then makes his own, via Hervey, the picture of man which a leading and late Puritan preacher of the preceding century had sketched under the catch-phrase 'Living Temple'. Man is a deserted temple, which bears on its façade the inscription: 'Here God once dwelt'. The edifice allows this to be surmised from the size and beauty of its layout, the clarity of its lines and the rhythm of its proportions; and yet the lamps are extinct, the altar overturned. Disorder reigns, darkness and stench fill the place. The hushed beauty of holiness has given way to the noise and bustle of vulgarity. The pillars have been shivered, and in their attempts at restoration people have put the separate pieces in the wrong place. Nothing really and convincingly coheres with anything else. Before the eyes of the beholder lies a field of ruins.[53]

The book could have ended on this note. But Wesley felt constrained to probe sundry questions and objections which Taylor had raised—palpably with a view to undermining the traditional doctrine of original sin. He had said, e.g., that if original sin is man's common inheritance, does it not follow that present-day humanity is living under worse conditions than Adam prior to the Fall? He had further objected that if all men are saddled with a corrupt nature and can hardly change it, why does every generation try to improve the world? Is this not sheer folly? In answer to the first question Wesley retorted: At no point whatever does the Bible compare the faculties of Adam's progeny with those of the first man, and this with good reason. The disparity between the state of innocence and that of guilt is so vast as to preclude any and every comparison. A new situation has set in. Thus here again he preferred practical to rational asseverations and in this respect anticipated Kierkegaard's criticism of Hegel on this matter. The same data governed the thinking of both the evangelist of the eighteenth and the thinker of the nineteenth century: namely, the infinite qualitative difference between God and man; the leap from sin to righteousness, a leap which can never be a transition. Granted this, it is possible, of course, on first thoughts to regard the latter state of humanity as worst than the first. This must be the case. For the seriousness of sin consists in the fact that it is not possible to put the clock back. On the other hand, however, by sending Jesus God has created a new state of affairs and opened up a new and living way. Anyone who puts his trust in the Saviour obtains not only forgiveness of sins but the power to lead a new life, power to effect a potent improvement. These are blessings which previously did not exist. Herein the tribes of Adam boast more blessings than their father lost, but only insofar as they take the offer seriously, i.e. insofar as they become Christian. Meantime, four-fifths are still Muslims or pagans; and so everything depends on their conversion.[54] The missionary idea again gains expression.

Since Taylor, according to his own lights a radical thinker, never made things easy for himself, he could not evade an exhaustive treatment of the main New Testament passage on original sin, i.e. Romans 7. He concluded from the parenthesis in the first verse of this celebrated chapter ('I speak to them that know the Law') that Paul is addressing himself to the Jews, the People of the Law. Wesley now puts the record straight. In the mind of the apostle, the Law can equally well be the law written in the heart which the heathen also know; for the point at issue here is not the origin of the Law and its particular contents, but its power to convict. Therefore the statement applies to all men, Jews and heathen alike. Thus Wesley secured in principle the universal validity of the Pauline statement about the Law against an historicizing relativization and constriction. In the same way, he demolished Taylor's rationalistic alternative: Either man sins intentionally, in which case he is guilty in the sight of God, or he acts compulsively against his own will, in which case it is improper to speak of sin. Taylor could not conceive that Paul might just mean *both* a deliberate act *and* a compulsive act. Against such superficial one-track-mindedness Wesley urged the Biblical truth that man is a self-contradictory creature, driven to and fro by forces which he does not wish upon himself, but which prove to be stronger than himself. Man's weakness is his inner self-contradictoriness, not simply his succumbing to, and weakening in the face of, temptation. The man of the Bible, who does not have the mastery of himself, was set over against the man of the Enlightenment, who is the master of his fate. Here the profound saying of Jeremiah(17[9]): 'The heart is deceitful above all things, and it is desperately wicked; who can know it?' served evidence for Wesley.[55]

In this section Wesley withstood a final assault by Taylor on the subject of Redemption and Regeneration. Here his central concerns are affected, and here, therefore, the repulse turns out to be particularly crucial. Taylor had put forward the opinion that Jesus Himself does not speak of man's natural depravity; still less does He trace it back to Adam. Consequently, forgiveness of sins could only relate to individual sinful acts on the part of each individual person. Wesley alludes to the saying of Jesus about seeking the lost. Being lost is more than what we bring upon ourselves through our own fault. The whole act of redemption in all its implications—and this for Wesley is the crucial evidence, the 'fundamental truth'—only has meaning if it was preceded by an all-implicating inculpation. Are the apostles wholly silent, as Taylor opines, about original sin? If they are, then it is because the heathens themselves, as Seneca and Horace testify, waxed eloquent on this point. It is only in the present day that people have begun to question man's sinfulness. For antiquity it was an established fact. To Wesley's mind Taylor had precipitately equated regeneration with being created and destined for the kingdom of God, as well as with a commensurable moral performance. Which was understandable enough, because he did not want to admit sin to be a deep, even fatal wound. What he understood by regeneration was a progressive acceptance of morally valuable habits, in his eyes clearly a form of self-education, i.e. a growth in virtue. Here the favourite concept of the Enlightenment—furthering our education till we attain perfection—made its presence felt. Taylor saw in the doctrine of original sin a threat to moral endeavour, and asked: What good, then, does this doctrine do? Wesley's reply was that first it brings about conversion, repentance, self-knowledge; then faith, knowledge of salvation in Christ crucified; and finally, love. And thus we have holiness, but from faith, and not from a moral yearning for perfection.[56]

The vigour with which Wesley upholds the Bible against the spirit of the age is readily discernible. He works both with its literal meaning and with its general tenor. He weaves together the Old and the New Testaments. Sayings of Jesus and statements of the apostles, dogmatics and exegesis, lend support to each other. At the same time he is at pains to do justice to his opponent despite his fundamental disagreement with him. He never dismisses him abruptly or cuttingly, but meets him on his own ground. Indeed, he looks afresh and seriously at every idea on its merits. Nevertheless, for him the truth of the Biblical statements was beyond question from beginning to end, as was their unity. This unqualified Biblicism gave him a more natural affinity to the position of the Reformers than to that of Pietism, in that Scripture was for him the instigator and criterion, not the confirmation of personal experience. This is also why his personal experiences played no part in this tough, minutely detailed controversy with Taylor. For him the first and last word must rest with the Bible. If the way in which he did this is found to be simplistic, as indeed it is, this judgement is equally applicable to his opposite number. Taylor, too, wanted to teach according to the Scriptures and not without their support. But Wesley remorselessly showed up for him those of his presuppositions which he had derived from other sources and put him right on straight Biblical lines.

This zeal for the Bible also compelled him to take his refutation even further and to pursue his opponent into every nook and cranny. Consequently he took up a series of detached points. Taylor had maintained that nowhere in the Bible was a sin which is not our own imputed against us. Wesley proved to him that the opposite is the case, not only on the basis of the Israelite scapegoat, which Taylor had interpreted symbolically, but above all in the light of the suffering of God's servant spoken of in Isaiah 53. Moreover, Taylor had disputed the idea that the suffering which men have to undergo on earth, and death which has become their lot, are punishments, since God in fact brings great good out of both. Here again Wesley contested the superficial one-track-mindedness behind this kind of thinking and emphasized that the divinely intended good end in no way makes null and void the attendant punishment for man. On the contrary, afflictions attest by their frequency the basic condition of life on this earth, as inhabited, governed and fashioned by man. Wesley was at great pains to bring out the fact that the juxtaposition of Adam and Christ as the originators and representatives of two orders of humanity, the old and the new man, is a fundamental reality. For what was being expressed here was not an historical sequence of events and its dénouement, but rather the choice between two possibilities, or better still two realities. In counter-argument to the interpretation that sin is man's free choice, Wesley brings in the observation that man normally succumbs to temptation, and linked with this the question, How come that this is so? Wesley closed with a discussion of Adam's 'original righteousness'. Consistently with his whole approach, Taylor had conceived this in static terms: Adam could not fall. Wesley understood it dynamically: Adam could stand or fall. In this respect he had the Bible itself on his side. His interpretation of original righteousness was richer and deeper, not only by

95

virtue of its element of dynamism, but also by its very essence. For Taylor, righteousness meant correct conduct; for Wesley, it meant the right condition of the heart, which must be regarded as the fountain-head of conduct.[57] Thus he sought to probe deeper and deeper below the surface at every point.

He further demonstrated that he was not putting forward his own pet ideas in all this by reproducing extracts from three refutations of Taylor. An added reason for feeling constrained to do this was that Taylor had manhandled them and in particular had broken in smithereens the architectonically impressive edifice erected in the first of the refutations. The first of these replies originated from the eminent Congregationalist hymn-writer Isaac Watts.[58] the second from the Anglican clergyman Samuel Hebden of Wrentham in Suffolk,[59] the third from Thomas Boston senior.[60] No doubt Wesley brought in this last mainly because of his highly developed theology of creation. At the same time he believed that, having previously bored or confused the reader by the minutiae of his detached discussions,[61] he could in this way offer something creative by way of a change. Such was the modesty with which he deferred to others in his interpretation, thereby at the same time placing on record his sense of making common cause. Every mania for originality was quite foreign to him. This is also why he compiled so many extracts from books which were not his own and why in his 'Christian Library' he created for the first time in history a popular series of Christian classics.[62] Oneness with the Christian witnesses to the truth in every epoch, confession and nation counted more with him than his own opinion or his own renown.

This comprehensive and to some extent sluggish work is singularly characteristic of Wesley the theologian, and in more respects than one. It reveals, first of all, how totally committed he was to the matter in hand. He sacrificed everything to it—readability, directness in pursuing a line of argument, large horizons. He turned aside into detailed discussion in the same way as had happened time and again at key points in the history of the church: for example, with Origen in his dialogue with Celsus on the truth of Christianity; with Tertullian in his controversy with Marcion on the concept of God; with Anselm of Canterbury in his discussion with Gaunilo of Marmoutiers on the same question; with the sharp clash of opinion between Luther and Erasmus of Rotterdam on free will. Then again, Wesley's

3

treatise indicates how to him the Biblical witness was the only court of appeal to which he would listen. The key that unlocked the Biblical evidence had to be found and kept. This applied to the great fundamental declarations about God and man, the righteous and the sinful, creation, redemption and regeneration, sanctification and perfection. But it was equally applicable to a specific proposition, which in point of fact never failed to give coherence to the whole. In the third place, this book evinced Wesley's sense of justice, which he demonstrated in the way he treated his opponent. He never gave vent to rash invective, even though he regarded Taylor's theology as absolutely pernicious. On the contrary, he invariably retraced in detail his lines of thought. But he gave equal proof of his sense of justice in his speech for the defence of his colleagues in the debate, who had been unfairly treated by his opponent. Finally, it is impressive to see how naturally Wesley ranged himself with these his precursors in the cause, by concluding his own book with extracts from their writings, thus rounding the whole work off on a positive note.

At first glance his second major doctrinal work, his *Plain Account of Christian Perfection*, from the year 1766,[63] gives an entirely different impression. Here Wesley adopted a style which is completely different from that of the preceding work, in that he proceeded autobiographically and historically.

He attested the truth rather than argued a case, with the result that everything has a simpler and clearer look about it. There is no trace of the close attention to detail which encumbered his debate with Taylor on original sin. Certainly the same underlying factors were involved, because here, too, Wesley indicated that he had a sense of being called, even constrained. In the one case he did what he did because of a basic affront against Christian truth, in the second instance because of his personal experiences of faith and life. In neither case had he acted on his own initiative. The stages of his spiritual pilgrimage were defined by books which had an impact on him. Every one of them pointed in the same direction. If a man wants to serve God, then he must resolve to be serious and utterly dedicated. The first work belonged to the year 1725—Jeremy Taylor's exposé on the *Rule and Exercise of Holy Living and Dying*. This was a summons to purity of intention. Next, in 1726, came Thomas à Kempis' *Imitatio Christi*. From this he learned that it would profit him nothing if he were to sacrifice his life for God; what mattered was to offer Him his heart. A year or two afterwards he hit upon William Law's books, *Serious Call* and *Christian Perfection*. Here it became clear to him that in God's eyes half-heartedness had no place, and he determined to place all he had and was completely at God's disposal—his soul, his body, and his possessions. In 1729 things came to a head with his reading of the Bible, which he now no longer merely read, but studied thoroughly. The Bible became for him the only standard of truth and the only model for genuine piety. The harvest is gathered in the first of his published sermons, from the year 1733, which had as its subject the circumcision of the heart. Even at that time he saw this circumcision as consisting in love, which he perceived to be the first and great Christian commandment. With this realization, as he now asserted retrospectively, he had arrived in principle at Christian perfection, and he also termed it such. In the year 1738 a long conversation which he had had in Herrnhut with the Swede Arvid Gradin assumed great significance for him. Wesley asked him for a definition of full assurance of faith, and Gradin wrote down for him in Latin the following words: 'Repose in the blood of Christ; a firm confidence in God, and persuasion of his favour; the highest tranquillity, serenity, and peace of mind, with a deliverance from every fleshly desire, and a cessation of all, even inward sins.'[64] It is worth noting that it was precisely this interview and the instruction he received that he spoke of, and not his own conversion. Obviously he did not find his conversion to be a complete and final state, because temptations still harassed him, temptations which from the outset he experienced not only as a spiritual torment but as a practical problem which he had sought to overcome. It is also striking, however, that in contrast to the direct account in his carefully kept diary he did not stress the sermons of and conversations with Christian David, which had brought to a conclusion his search to understand justifying faith. Obviously this question was now no longer a live issue. The fact is that justification meant for him only the gateway to the Christian life. He for his part, however, strove might and main to discover its wholeness, its goal—this regardless of the fact that Gradin's description was sketched exclusively from man's side in terms of his spiritual experience. At the same time, however, it becomes clear from this emphasis that he had superseded the legalistic stage in his understanding of Christianity. Christian perfection no longer meant fulfilling a commandment, albeit the first and great commandment, but living in the saving presence of God. At this point it becomes clear yet again how much he owed to his encounter with the Moravians and how his heritage from Mysticism still continued to influence him.

This autobiographical introduction is followed by a word-for-word reproduction of his early pamphlet on *The Character of a Methodist*.[65] which culminated in love of God, a love which springs up in his heart freely and naturally, being the life-principle of the perfect Christian. It was significant in this connexion that he was predisposed to quote his brother's and also his own hymns.[66] Christian lyrics, which poured forth from the Methodist movement in such plentiful supply, revealed in a unique way the originality, the spontaneity of its heart-stirring message: Love, joy in salvation, earnest desire for sanctification based on the new birth. On the other hand, contentions arose. Wesley emphasized that the perfection which was experienced and commended by the Methodists was no justification whatever for a silent self-sufficiency on the part of the pious man in enjoying the presence of God, as had been the case with the Quietism of France in the eighteenth century and as Molther in turn had slavishly repeated; and did not, therefore, result in dispensing with worship, prayer and sacrament, nor by the same token with loving service of our neighbour. Neither did it lead to having an arrogant self-admiration, as if one had attained to freedom from errors or temptations.[67] Under no circumstances did it lift a man out of the human situation. Much as John Wesley, in line with the Anglican tradition, laid stress on holiness as a characteristic quality of the Christian and derived the right to do so from the New Testament, he firmly rejected the traditional ideal of holiness held by the Greek and Roman church, which was built on the foundation of miraculous experiences and superhuman phenomena. The life of the perfect Christian was not a proof of the existence of God, but a sacrifice continually offered up to Him, as he so aptly said, linking up with the eminent Archbishop James Ussher (1581–1656), a classical author on spirituality.[68]

By virtue of its importance, Wesley continues, Christian perfection was bound to grow and become a fundamental plank in the platform of the Methodist movement generally. His own experiences, his own evolution, his own vicissitudes, questions and answers, were no more than a sign of things to come. Wesley always saw his destiny and that of the Methodist movement as running in parallel with each other.

Precisely in exercising the leadership in it, he knew himself to be a member of it and its instrument. This is why even at the First Conference of Preachers on 25th June 1744, Christian perfection was the subject of conversation. This was taken up again more fully at the second Conference on 1st August 1745. Wesley reported on this matter in the question and answer form of a catechism, by posing questions to each of which in turn a Biblical answer had been given. Matters again took a similar course at the Conference of 1759. In the ensuing period, especially from the time of the astonishing growth of the Methodist movement in London in the year 1762, Christian perfection assumed an increasing importance, particularly when enthusiasts suddenly came on the scene predicting the end of the world in the very near future; for they combined with this the assertion that Christian perfection was not attainable in this life and in the present dispensation.[69] By way of counter-evidence Wesley cited personal testimonies by members of the movement who lived and died in the assurance of attaining Christian perfection and of being inwardly happy in it. Thus Jane Cooper confessed immediately before her death that nothing could separate her from the love of God which was given to her in Jesus Christ. In 1763 the importance of this subject led Wesley to write a new treatise on it, in which, in addition to what has been previously set forth, he warned Christians against lodging superficial claims. Christian perfection meant, says Wesley in language most strongly reminiscent of the Romanic mysticism of France, complete resignation to God's will, self-sacrifice, naked following of the naked Jesus to the crib at Bethlehem, to the judgement hall, to His scourging before Pilate, to His cross on Golgotha. Humility and patience were the surest proofs of growth in love. Each supported the other. Part and parcel of this was the unrepining acceptance of failure in the attempt to win men for God and that everything—both our own endeavours and the other person whom we have not reached[70]—was left in God's hands. In the year 1764, too, Wesley took up the pen on the subject of perfection and expressly presented it as a climactic of justification. He left the question of sinlessness open, to the extent that its purport is salvation from sin. On the other hand, now as always, perfection was in essence pure and genuine love. At the same time he urged his preachers to expound this message of perfection unremittingly and to develop it closely. In his concluding words he asked impressively: Who can love enough?[71]

The perfection of the Christian and of the Church was from the very outset a favourite subject of German Pietism. In his *Pia Desideria*, a manifesto in which he struck a highly optimistic note, Spener had voiced the absolute certainty that God had promised better things for His Church, and, in the confidence of the Reformers that God keeps His promise, had concluded from this that just such an improvement was also attainable. Despite all the persecutions and accusations of fanaticism, the leader of Pietism had held fast to this expectation.[72] In the preface to the work of his pupil Balthasar Köpke (*Discourse on the Temple of Solomon*), he had given a detailed, learned exposition of the New Testament word τέλειος.[73] Joachim Just Breithaupt, the first professor of theology at the Pietist University of Halle, had in the dogmatic sphere complemented this exegetical Biblical study by a Latin dissertation on perfection,[74] and August Hermann Francke had given practical advice relative to Christian perfection.[75] Important as all this was and much as it altered the situation, it was of a different ilk. It bore the marks of a piece of studied theologizing and was directed in a polemical way against Lutheran Orthodoxy, which in the opinion of the Pietists had sold the Biblical truth short at this point. It thereby smacked of being contrived. In Wesley, however, we hear the voice of the early Church and an originality which stems from a balanced consideration of the subject on its own merits. By giving this discussion of his central theme an historical foundation, he evinced the fact that this subject had been the fundamental principle governing his own personal development and the inner history of the Methodist revival. In this way he achieved a convincing unity of life and doctrine. Against such an appeal to facts which attested an increasing inner conformity to the New Testament both in his own life and in the life of his followers, no objections could be raised. The disinterested, even the antagonistic had to see, acknowledge and respect this congruity as a practical reality. Here we already have direct appeal to and positive demand for a silent awe in the face of the facts of Christian faith which characterizes the modern age. This was completely in line with Pietism, which regarded the theoretical apologetics of Orthodoxy as a spent force with no future and in its place enlisted examples of real-life Christianity.[76]

The massive literary enterprise, Wesley's selective compilation of 'A Christian Library', given over entirely to the history of Christianity, pointed in the same direction.[77] Since he was completely void of every mania for originality or any need to have the pre-eminence—so void that he unfairly slighted pretensions of this kind on the part of others, as in the case of Samuel Johnson's controversial pamphlet to the North American colonies to the effect that taxation imposed by the mother country is not tyranny—he appropriated to himself from every part of the Christian tradition what he considered to be good, adapting it to the purposes of the Methodist movement by abridgement, revision and clarification. The idea as such follows the same lines as Zinzendorf's London hymnbook, which reproduced hymns from every age and place so as to give it a truly ecumenical character. The original design for this work certainly arose in Wesley's mind very early on, possibly in Georgia.[77a] In any event it was there that he produced the first of his own extracts from Christian writings of the past. Now, however, he thought of 80 to 100 books on fine paper. He intended, therefore, to publish something special, something grandiose.[78] He exchanged ideas on the list of books to be included with Philip Doddridge (1702–51), the highly distinguished Congregationalist theologian who through his commentary on the whole of the Bible, which has also been translated into German, had won himself a secure place in eighteenth-century England. He was principal of the Dissenting Academy in Northampton, which he himself had founded in 1729—originally in Market Harborough—and which he made into the best theological seminary of its time for non-Anglican theological students. It is worth noting that the Bishop of London, Thomas Sherlock (1678–1761), who in 1748 had succeeded to Edmund Gibson, an opponent of the Methodists, and whose outlook was quite different, sent him a letter in which he emphasized their mutual commitment to the Gospel of Christ crucified and their mutual antagonism to the fashionable natural theology with its idle speculations.[79] From earliest days John Wesley had entered into close association with this gifted, earnest contemporary. On 22nd March 1739, he wrote to him his first and apparently non-extant letter.[80] At the height of his controversy with the Moravians in London at the end of July 1740, Doddridge, who also knew the Moravians well and to some degree held them in esteem, was present at a conversation of Wesley's with Molther.[81] Doubtless, therefore, he was conversant with the points in dispute. On 9th September 1745, Wesley paid him a personal visit in Northampton, when he was just about to expound the Bible to a class of students, and was invited to take over the lecture.[82] Doddridge had queried Wesley's proposals regarding the books to the extent that he wanted to exclude those which were emphatically Anglican. Nevertheless, he allowed himself to be persuaded and thanked him for the amiable and soundly argued way in which he had convincingly removed his reservations and had demonstrated the common spiritual ground between Anglicans and Dissenters.[83] Among the leading figures of Nonconformity he was John Wesley's only friend. The fact that Wesley had chosen him of all people underlined the comprehensive nature of the project and the breadth of his sympathies. Wesley could not have enlisted the help of a strict, exclusivist Anglican. Doddridge, who clearly fulfilled in the eighteenth century the same kind of eirenic rôle between the various denominations as Baxter had in the seventeenth, seemed the right man for the job.

Wesley began the Preface, written on 25th March 1749, by asserting that there was available in the English language an abundance, indeed a superabundance of devotional literature, particularly from the previous century, the golden age of Anglicanism and Puritanism alike. On this score he was indubitably right. The plethora of writings of this kind really is astonishing and has not its equal in any other country, neither in the wealth of individual originality nor in the consistency or near-consistency in the basic stance. Wesley's concern, however, was not to exhibit national peculiarities, still less national achievements; for he immediately went on to say that in addition to these works there was a large supply of translated books. Truth to tell, the abundance made confusion worse confounded; it was impossible for anyone to read everything, even if he lived to be eighty. But the nature of the writings themselves also makes for practical difficulties. Many are written in the style of controversial literature and are for this reason unpalatable. Conversely, others take it upon themselves to be obscure, whereas surely Christian faith is the plainest, clearest thing in the world. Consequently there is wheat mixed with chaff, gold with baser metals. He (Wesley) has made a bold attempt to extract the genuine gold that is of lasting value. In doing so, he has especially aimed at precluding any inconsistencies between the various items. Thus the whole work, which appeared in fifty volumes between 1749 and 1755, may be taken as an expression of his personal theological convictions.[84]

What, then, did he in fact select and thereby assess to be fundamental for a Christian? Even the very first volume shows a notable
catholicity, but also a clear line. It includes the early Christian
writings of the Apostolic Fathers (Clement of Rome, Polycarp of
Smyrna and the Epistles of Ignatius of Antioch), separate discourses
of the monastic Father, Macarius, and in apt conjunction John
Arndt's *True Christianity*, the classical devotional book of German
Pietism. In the next four volumes there follow numerous accounts of
martyrs from a major work of the English Reformation, John Foxe's
*Acts and Monuments* (1564), among these accounts being the histories of Hus and Jerome of Prague; but the biography of Martin
Luther, who was not in fact a martyr, also had a place here, and in
Wesley's mind no doubt a place of honour. This proves that he considered the German Reformer, to whose doctrine of the Law he took
vigorous exception, to be one of the key figures in the entire history of
the church. Here one observes yet again the predominance of narrative literature. For Wesley, the personal life of the Christian was of
overriding significance. He knew from his own experience about the
high educational value of biographies, about the edifying power of
example. At the same time due stress is laid on the circumstances of
the martyrs. Genuine Christianity was authenticated under persecution. This basic principle, to which he himself had subscribed in his
youth even to the point of over-emphasis, was one which he wanted
to impress on the members of his movement. This is what lay behind
the detailed, well-nigh exhaustive account which he gave of the late
medieval and modern persecutions of Protestants, from the fate of
the Albigensians, the Waldensians, the adherents of Wyclif and Hus,
down to the Huguenots, the Beggars, the Irish Protestants and the
Protestants in the remote areas of Piedmont, the Valteline and Lithu-
ania. Then the Puritan devotional literature of the seventeenth century was given extensive coverage. By including the authors Joseph
Alleine, Isaac Ambrose, Samuel Annesley (his maternal grandfather),
Richard Baxter, Robert Bolton, John Brown, John Bunyan, Edmund
Calamy, Stephen Charnock, Nicholas Culverwell, William Dell,
Thomas Goodwin, John Howe, Richard Lucas, Thomas Manton,
John Owen, John Preston, Richard Sibbs, John Smith and John
Worthington, he made a thoroughly representative selection from the
welter of literature, not least in his choice of subjects. Thus Ambrose
was pressed into service as a sponsor on the cardinal doctrine of re-

generation, Preston on the unity of faith and love, Goodwin and Owen on temptations, Bolton on the temptations to despair, Bunyan with his *Holy War* on the struggle between God and the Devil for man's soul, Baxter on the expectation of everlasting rest with God.

Comparatively speaking, the Anglicans were somewhat less fully represented and had less distinct subjects. Clearly Wesley's major concern here was for churchmanship. Outstanding eirenic figures were in evidence: the highly esteemed and widely read William Beveridge; the Cambridge Platonists Ralph Cudworth and Henry More; Bishop Joseph Hall of Exeter; Henry Hammond, who had inspired and recommended one of the most consequential and seminal books in the English Christianity of his time, i.e. *The Whole Duty of Man* (1659), and who with this had bridged the gulf between Anglicanism and Puritanism; this very book; then the naturalized Englishman of German birth Anthony Horneck, who in 1678 had started the Religious Societies in London, and Simon Patrick, the co-founder of the Society for Promoting Christian Knowledge. Thomas Ken, the great hymnographer among bishops, was represented by his *Exposition on the Church Catechism*; Robert Leighton, the mystically disposed Archbishop of Glasgow, by several books; Jeremy Taylor, one of the great classical authors who had strongly influenced Wesley himself and a theologian who inclined toward the centre; then William Cave with his classical delineation of *Primitive Christianity*; but next to this the friend of the Puritans John Reynolds, Dean of Lincoln, and John Tillotson, later Archbishop of Canterbury, a man of universal sympathies of whom the strict Anglicans said that through him Canterbury had turned into an Amsterdam in which every religious tendency made rendezvous.[85] In addition, Wesley incorporated writings of Nicholas Sanderson, Robert South, Seth Ward and Edward Young. Avowed Anglo-Catholics like Lancelot Andrewes, John Bramhall, William Laud and John Pearson, were omitted, but also, astonishingly, Lewis Bayly's *Practice of Piety*, which would really have been in Wesley's line, in that it, too, embodied the Puritan spirit within Anglicanism. This omission must surely be attributed to a basic flaw in Bayly's general stance. Bayly had no concept of creation; for him man was to an inordinate degree the bearer and the living proof of earthly misery.[86] This was at variance with John Wesley's conviction. We recall that his concept of original sin gained its cutting-edge precisely against the background of a vigorous doctrine of creation. It was secured against every form of naturalistic pessimism, to which Bayly remained exposed.

Among the biographies, which took up a large amount of space, there appeared the Reformation figures Philip Melanchthon, John Calvin, his pupil Peter Martyr, who between 1547 and 1553 had in fact taught at Oxford, but not Martin Bucer (1491–1551) who had spent the last years of his life in Cambridge and had made a significant contribution to the English Reformation and not least to the cherished English idea of the Christian State.[87] This brings out into the open the fact that John Wesley's selection was not entirely unfortuitous. From among his precursors, John Wyclif was, as we would expect, represented, and in addition his Czech followers John Hus and Jerome of Prague, who have already been mentioned among the martyrs. From the post-Reformation period, Huguenot France was thrown into relief by a place being given to the theologian and statesman Philippe du Plessis-Mornay, the adviser of Henry IV, the co-draftsman of the Edict of Nantes and a literary apologist for Christianity in his widely read book *On the Truth of the Christian Religion* (1581).[88] The 'Christian Library' then offered a biography of the early Puritan William Whitaker, who had engaged in debate with the Counter-Reformation figure Cardinal Robert Bellarmine, and brought to life a succession of figures from the Presbyterian Church of Scotland: to wit, Hugh Kennedy, Patrick Simpson, Andrew Steward, Robert Bruce, Robert Blair, John Weish and Thomas Cawton, but not the militant leader John Knox or the constitutional lawyer and polemicist George Buchanan. Understandably enough, Oliver Cromwell, too, was missing. The theologians Richard Hooker, John Donne, George Herbert and James Ussher, the laymen Sir Philip Sidney, Sir John Hale and Sir Henry Wotton, were put forward as distinguished Anglicans.

Mysticism was represented by the Scotsman Henry Scougal, whose book *The Life of God in the Soul of Man* had pointed the way for Wesley himself and for George Whitefield in their youth. From among non-English works, as is to be expected from Wesley's own life-story, witnesses from the Romanic mysticism of Spain and France gained admission. There were spiritual letters of John of Avila, Brother Lawrence, the *Spiritual Guide* of Miguel de Molinos, and pastorals of Fénelon. Then, noteworthily, the *Pensées* of Blaise Pascal are reproduced in Volume 23. Wesley was probably already familiar with them from his childhood days. He used turns of phrase from them in his early correspondence with Mary Pendarves and commended them along with Thomas à Kempis' *Imitation of Christ* and the works of Fénelon as models of inward Christianity forged on the anvil of personal experience. This is also why they had already been included in the reading-syllabus prescribed for his lay preachers. He felt keenly that the disparity between them and Voltaire, who as is well known had furnished them with annotations, was so vast that he could only make sense of the arch-fiend of the Enlightenment's association with them in terms of satirical design.[89]

Taken in general, the 'Christian Library' was a cross-section through early and modern Christianity with very definite emphases. The emphasis fell unmistakably on the seventeenth century, whose fecundity had patently made a deep impression on Wesley. Important aspects of the Christian tradition were left out. *The Epistle to Diognetus*, Tertullian and Augustine, were omitted from early Christianity, as was the Byzantine world, and the whole of the Middle Ages, with which he must have felt a natural affinity in such figures as Anselm of Canterbury, Bernard of Clairvaux, Francis of Assisi, and his numerous travelling preachers, and which he must have welcomed as providing historical precedents for his movement. Even the Reformation period was poorly represented, but the Reformed line was sustained to 'within a hair's breadth of Calvinism', with the result that he was suspected of Calvinism. The inclusion of Romanic mysticism, with its voluntaristic character, modified and balanced this emphasis. The significance of this selection in point of principle can hardly be exaggerated.[89a] This was the first time in the history of the church that anything of its kind had been attempted and put out. Both the so-called church canon of Scholasticism and Lutheran Orthodoxy,[90] and equally the Lutheran symbolic books from the Reformer's *Catechisms* down to the *Formula of Concord*, exhibited an endeavour to establish a legally binding norm in matters of dogma. Here, however, the interest lay in personal fortification, encouragement in and nourishment of one's faith. For Wesley, as is crystal clear, what was involved was the harmony of the polyphonic choir of witnesses. The books were to further the merging together of different styles of spirituality. The unity of the Church at its most inward point, i.e. personal faith—this was the unspoken design. Looked at from a literary point of view, his 'Christian Library' became the harbinger of the 'Everyman's Library' in the nineteenth and twentieth centuries, designed for general education. In addition, the 'Library' led to a wider literary enterprise. In the year 1782 John Wesley and his young associate Thomas Coke published a series of short devotional treatises partly written by men of the Methodist movement and partly taken from older writings on the model of the 'Christian Library', which were expressly not to be sold, but given away. With this began the tract mission, which has been such an important factor in Anglo-Saxon Christianity and which from 1833 on supplied the outward vestment for the renewal of Anglo-Catholicism under John Henry Newman. Nevertheless, it would be wrong to say that the selection entirely reflected Wesley's theological standpoint and literary preference. It lacks, for example, an author whom he held in exceptionally high regard: namely, the Cambridge Platonist John Norris, whose books he himself not only read time and again, but particularly commended in his pastoral correspondence.[91]

In direct continuation of this purpose is Wesley's biography of his friend John William Fletcher.[92] The latter, whom he had chosen to be his successor, was closer to him than any other person. Wesley narrated his life-story concisely, concentrating on its essential features, and yet painting in at various points affectionate personal touches. Fletcher, a French Swiss by birth, came from Nyon on Lake Geneva, where his father lived as an Army officer. In his early childhood he had undergone seering personal experiences of faith and had twice been saved from drowning. He then studied at the University of Geneva, but contrary to his parents' wishes did not become a pastor in the Reformed Church, but like his father pursued a career as an officer. At first he wanted to join the Portuguese navy and travel to Brazil. For reasons outside his control this came to nothing. Then, with the help of an uncle, he set out for the Netherlands, and from there came to England. The rude reception he had at the hands of the customs officers on his arrival upset him greatly; they confiscated his letters of recommendation, which mattered so much to him, with the remark that all letters must be sent by post. Not knowing the language, he and his friends availed themselves of the help of an unknown French-speaking Jew, who helped them out of their financial difficulty. A French minister, to whom he had been recommended, procured a post for him as a private tutor at Tern-Hall in Shropshire, where he taught his mother-tongue and familiarized himself with the

English language. During a visit which he made to London with his employer, a longish stay was made at St. Alban's. At this time a woman talked to him pressingly about Jesus and salvation, but at the same time spoke in such a naïvely convincing manner that he was touched by what she said. Back at home the mistress of the house said mockingly that this simply must have been a Methodist woman, and that the day might yet dawn when he himself would go over to them. Many a true word was spoken in jest! Fletcher made enquiries and did in fact join a class in London. On 12th January 1755, he was converted. On the previous day he had gone to the Lord's Supper inwardly unmoved. Wesley recounted in Fletcher's own words—and this typifies his scrupulous regard for facts—what he had inwardly experienced on the day of his conversion. With the later decisive experiences, too, he chose this method of confining himself to the original witnesses. In its basic composition the conversion resembled John Wesley's own. Like the latter it consisted in assurance of salvation, understood as assurance of justification in the forgiveness of sins, Fletcher having been previously afraid that he had forfeited himself to the Devil. But it had its own distinctive features to the extent that even prior to the consoling assurance of his being accepted by God, he resolved that he would testify to God in hell as a monument to His justice if he were not permitted to celebrate His mercy in heaven[93]—an idea most strongly reminiscent of the young Luther,[94] which found a fainter echo in Romanic mysticism with its disinterested love of God. The fundamental principle of unconditional surrender to God's will governed Fletcher's thoughts and feelings more strongly than in Wesley's case. On the other hand, the dependence of the new convert on the older man was so great that the latter's *Journal*, with its summons not to rely on our own feelings but to hasten with every sin to Jesus Christ, afforded him decisive help.[95] For him as for Wesley, faith, peace with God and victory over sin constituted an indivisible unity. To these love of God and neighbour were soon added.

John Wesley narrated the further course of John Fletcher's life after the conversion simply as an unfolding of that conversion. The biography turned into the life of a Methodist hagiographer. Structurally, this came to light in the fact that the biographer consciously broke with the binding rule of placing the portrait of his hero's character at the end. He justified this step by the fact that Fletcher's death, as described by his wife, revealed such a closeness to God that nothing more could be added to it.[96] His pastoral concern for the parish of Madeley near Bristol, where he had become the Anglican vicar; his refusal to accept a preferment offered to him for political reasons as a reward for his royalist pamphlet to the North American colonies; his work in the Countess of Huntingdon's college for Methodist preachers in Trevecca (South Wales), which he relinquished because he disagreed with the harsh doctrine of predestination to which he was required to subscribe; his unflagging labours as an itinerant preacher, which he continued even in spite of tubercular coughing of blood until he was absolutely forbidden to do so by doctors; his attitude towards his health and this world's goods, both of which he set little store by for the sake of the heavenly treasure and yet did not condemn out of hand; his love of solitude, his physical over-exertion whenever he preached: all this built up a picture of a perfect Christian of the immediate present. His marriage painted the same picture. This is reflected in the very fact that the wedding—not only at church but subsequently at home—was solemnized with singing of hymns and prayers. More importantly, however, the shared life of the married couple increasingly bore the stamp of a Pietist fellowship for the mutual observation of the soul, spiritual nurture and readiness to serve Christ. Outstanding as a specific piece of service was his work in connexion with a Sunday School, in which the children of the parish were led to God. But as with the Marquis Jean-Baptiste de Renty, his ruling passion was for the uninterrupted presence of God in his heart. This is also why he felt himself to be at home in God's house.[97] The very fact that at this point the prosaic, critical Wesley could be so eloquent confirms his passion for Christian perfection.

These examples of his theological output are only samples which may serve to demonstrate his basic concerns and his treatment of them. In addition, Wesley turned his attention to a whole series of other subjects. Thus he defended the divinity of Jesus against the Socinians and Deists,[98] and the Biblical miracles against Congers Middleton.[99] Time and again he contested the doctrine of predestination, seeing in it both an affront against God's boundless love and a dangerous undermining of man's sense of moral responsibility. He saw in it the vanguard of Antinomianism and diagnosed it as a cancerous growth which had long been eating into Christianity. He also discussed its positive reverse side—the doctrine of the irrevocable perseverance of the elect in divine grace—and modified it along Biblical lines by issuing a warning against a false sense of security.[100] He kept precisely this controversy on the requisite level of debate and, significantly enough, opened it with an appropriate verse from John Milton's Prologue to *Paradise Lost*.[101] Equally, he did not evade the attendant controversial questions which in part are only loosely connected with this subject.[102] He took mysticism very seriously as a rival to faith and treated it in various ways. He held that Romanic mysticism in high esteem which laid stress on the will and which extolled disinterested love of God as the crowning glory of a Christian character, and repeatedly recommended its biographical monuments, such as Gaston Jean-Baptiste de Renty, Brother Lawrence and Armelle Nicolas.[103] With equal vigour he discountenanced the German mysticism which he found in Jakob Böhme [Behmen] as mediated to him by William Law, on the grounds (a) that it obscured the truth of justification and faith by superfluous cosmological speculations, (b) that it distorted the doctrine of creation and our understanding of sin by its androgynous fantasies in clear contradiction to the Bible, and (c) that with all this it revolved round a false centre. He did not burke a second difficult controversy on these very questions with his erstwhile patron William Law, who was now seventy years old. Even in the year 1782, at the age of seventy-nine, he wrote a concise, cautionary summary of Jakob Böhme, in which he vehemently censured his slipshod way of drawing conclusions from analogies and association of ideas.[104] He vindicated the divine inspiration of the Scriptures.[105] Above all, drawing on Philip Doddridge, John Guyse and Johann Albrecht Bengel, he published concise, pertinent *Notes on the New Testament*.[106] He arranged Johann Lorenz Mosheim's church history for his Societies.[107] Borrowing from Johann Franz Buddeus, he also wrote a natural theology to display the wonders of God even to the non-Christian.[108] On more than one occasion he turned his attention to Roman Catholicism, particularly as his evangelistic work in Ireland repeatedly thrust him up against it in a practical way. He drafted and answered a *Roman Catechism* based on the doctrinal decisions of the Council of Trent, the writings of Bellarmine, the Index of prohibited books, various Papal Bulls and decrees of the Lateran Councils, in order to demonstrate fully the disparity between the Roman Catholic system and the Scriptures. In this connexion he greatly extolled the wider latitude allowed in the Church of England, but at the same time insisted on this his mother church remaining loyal to the Bible, and repudiated the principle of tradition. Finally, he summoned individual Catholics to a Biblical Christianity and fervently hoped that from this would issue a true overcoming of confessional differences. At the same time, however, he protested against every disposition towards inter-denominational persecution, thus throwing into high relief this very tendency on the part of Roman Catholics.[109]

His writings exclude no area of theology, until it comes to the Old Testament.[110] He shared this one-sidedness with the dominant strain in German Pietism. In this matter he did not follow in his father's footsteps. Wesley's writings were essentially occasional, and with a man as fully preoccupied as he was and with his life-style this is not to be wondered at; for he hardly ever sat quietly at his study desk. He read and wrote as he rode round the country, a thing which is hardly conceivable to modern man. Only when he was forced through illness to rest for a while did he lead a half-way normal life. The spirit in which he wrote is certainly the same throughout: absolute commitment to the New Testament. Whatever he wrote about, the purpose behind putting pen to paper was to make primitive Christianity into a contemporary reality.

One group of his writings still remains outstanding: namely, the ethical ones, in which he declared himself clearly and concisely on contemporary society. He had both feet firmly on the ground, and observed very accurately what was going on around him—and not just what directly confronted him within his Societies as he faced the problems of pastoral care. We have already come to know his condemnation of war in his book on original sin. He also did not take slavery for granted, as his contemporaries did. Rather, giving a thorough survey of its development, he attacked it root and branch.[111] In reading the literature on the subject, his heart had bled for individual African countries and their inhabitants. The perhaps somewhat idyllic picture of Guinea painted by Allanson, and Brues' picture of Senegal, published between 1749 and 1753, had particularly affected him. From the time when the Portuguese first sold African natives to the American Spaniards in 1508, this evil, to which early medieval Christendom had put an end throughout its borders, once again reared its ugly head in Christendom. Men, especially Africans, were plundered in large numbers from their native country, where they were living in peace and contentment. Small boys and girls, whom parents had anxiously protected from wild animals, especially birds, were pitilessly snatched away. Anyone who resisted was slaughtered. Nowadays, admittedly, things are done in a rather more 'civilized' way. But what can possibly be said in answer to the fact that those who have been singled out, irrespective of whether they are men or women, are led before the English surgeons for examination as to their work-fitness; that they are branded with their owner's number with red-hot irons; that they are then made over to the highest bidder, before whom they must again stand, stark naked, for examination of their flesh? On the plantations they are given wretched food (potatoes and roots) and paltry blankets for the cold nights. They have to slave away the whole day long. Of course, they are supposed to be able to endure the heat well which gives the Europeans so much trouble. In this connexion he (Wesley himself) has seen, when he was living in torrid Georgia, how well a man from Western Europe can work there. At that time he and his household and the Germans had felled trees alongside the slaves, and enjoyed much better health than the indolent colonial masters, who could only complain perpetually about their aches and pains. What attitude, then, is taken towards their mental capacity? It is claimed that they are stupid, slovenly, cunning, work-shy, it being entirely overlooked that it is precisely slavery which breeds such qualities. They are beaten and flogged if people are not satisfied with them; a price is put on their head if they escape. Wesley asks the people who talk in this kind of way whether they have made even one single serious attempt to relate in a human way to the slaves. He once knew a slave-owner who had put this to the test, and the experiment was a huge success. The Africans revered him as a father and obeyed him for love's sake. Having enumerated all the known facts and demonstrated how all this is an affront against justice and humanity, Wesley adopts an extremely grave tone and reminds his contemporaries of their Lord and Maker. God rules over them and will judge them for all these monstrous crimes. It is their bounden duty to restore to every man his freedom. Every individual has a right to it; no man is born to slavery. They cannot afford to delay any longer. The price paid for ostensible necessity—economic advantage—is that of losing their own soul. Finally, Wesley invokes God Himself to hear the cries of the oppressed and the outcast and to set the captives free.

This voice cried out in the year 1714. Yet another generation was to pass before the slave trade was prohibited in the British colonies, and two generations before slavery was finally abolished. For Wesley as a theological writer it was noteworthy that here he deployed the concept of creation as his decisive argument. With this concept he was able to develop directly humanitarian, legal and ethical themes and in this way forge a link with the general spirit of his age.

Conversely, Wesley could take strong exception to the fact that the century which was obsessed with freedom had unjustifiable fears for the personal freedom of the individual in contemporary Britain. In this connexion he pointed to the totalitarian systems in France and Turkey, and asserted that in contrast to them the United Kingdom was 'governed according to law' (the Rechtsstaat idea).[112]

In his pamphlet, *Thoughts concerning the Origin of Power* (1772), he sought to invalidate the modern principle of the sovereignty of the people by exhibiting the inconsistencies with which this principle was being put into effect on the contemporary scene: above all, denial of female suffrage and restriction of the vote to a definite social status. However, it was neither his wish nor his intention to undermine this principle and to plead for a monarchical or aristocratic constitution. Rather, he wanted to persuade people to acknowledge that God is the Author and Bearer of all legitimate power. By making man its starting point, the Enlightenment left this fundamental truth out of consideration, thereby misread the true situation, and was therefore to be opposed on principle.[113]

At this same time he expressed his views on the current high cost of living and food shortage. He unerringly traced back their outward forms and causes. In doing so, he finally arrived at the workshyness of the landed gentry, who further financed their life of luxury by ruthless rent increases. Wesley cited appalling examples of starving men which he had seen with his own two eyes. As with slavery, so here the misery cut him to the quick. He also made a series of proposals for relieving the situation. Thus in order to lower the price of corn he recommended a luxury tax on horses, which as coach-teams only served the convenience of their owners. He gathered everything up into a call to repentance addressed to the God-forsaking nation, and asked whether by such phenomena God might not be choosing to punish the failure to serve Him.[114] Since he regarded the War of Independence engaged upon by the North American Colonies as an unjust and ungrateful action against the lawful king, he held up to his fellow-countrymen the blessings that accompany the impartial administration of justice as contrasting with the confusions of war in that place.[115]

With these writings he addressed himself to the generality of the people. But besides these he wrote special short treatises relating to specific life-situations: calls to repentance addressed to drunkards, Sabbath-breakers, swearers, prostitutes and loose women, smugglers, condemned criminals, but also to a thoughtless elector, soldiers and nominal Christians. Every one of them culminated in a summons to take God seriously.[116] It was his firm conviction that the outstanding characteristic of the English people of his day was godlessness.[117]

It is surely impossible to pass a more severe sentence than that. This is also why he traced out inexorably all its outward forms. Thus he cast his beady eye on the dress and costly apparel at which people gazed wide-eyed, and admonished the members of his Societies not to conform to such modish ways. They could be neatly and plainly dressed like the Quakers, without having to copy their idiosyncrasies. He conceded only one exception: namely, women who lived with an unreasonable husband, and daughters who were decked out by parents of the same character. Here obedience takes priority. For the Christian only those items of apparel are permitted which he can take with him into eternity.[118] He gave advice to those who live alone and to married couples. Although, consistently with the Bible, he held back from commending celibacy outright, he saw its value in securing us against the strong temptation to love a creature more than the Creator.[119] He believed himself duty bound to warn against deluding ourselves into thinking that we could lay hold of true happiness simply by having a loved one, by having the permanent mutual society which would then follow automatically.[120] In this way the ascetic streak in Wesley's morality makes its presence felt. No wonder he took it upon himself to vindicate the character of Montanus, the rigorist of the Ancient Church, and let him be seen as a true Christian.[121] The concept of creation, which so profoundly coloured Wesley's dogmatics, was not extended into his ethics. In his mind God always came first, and this meant that everything, even the good and precious things of life, the things which have been bestowed by God Himself, had to be offered back for His sake.

This idea of letting God be God was further asserted in an extreme case. Wesley also voiced his opinion on the Lisbon earthquake, which, as is common knowledge, shook to the core the optimism of the Enlightenment.[122] He directed his attack against the purely natural explanation, which dismissed what had happened far too easily. In following this explanation through in detail, he did not do so primarily as a means of making himself credible to the spirit of the age, but rather so as to exhibit to his stupefied readers other far worse ways open to the Almighty of destroying life on earth. With this idea he pursued a line of thought which ran along similar lines to modern discussion about nuclear weapons. The proper response was to let oneself be summoned by what had happened to conversion, to genuine fear of God. God could at any moment bring down the same and worse things upon any town or even upon the whole of humanity. Only the Christian, the genuine convinced Christian, is able to cope with such a disaster, because he knows true happiness.[123] Strictly Biblical as all this was, even to the point of imbalance, Wesley made apt use of quotations from the classics—Homer, Pindar, Sappho, Horace, Virgil—in order to lend occasional support to his interpretation. Despite his over-emphasis, he was not world-denying and narrow-minded. Certainly he devoted all the resources of his literary and historical learning to a single objective: namely, complete and utter loving obedience to God.

In retrospect, the predominant impression left by all this is one of varied themes and unitive interpretation, but also, first and foremost, certainty of judgement. There is never the slightest suggestion of vacillation, still less evasion. This man, with his clear decisive point of view, was a born leader for ordinary people. They could depend on him, and his advice was good enough for the majority. An immediate result of this paternalism was the legalistic strain which runs through all his ethics, but which is not its underlying theme. This latter lay unmistakably with his sense of God's God-head. God first and last: this was his platform. This was true of his exposition and vindication of Christian truths, his narration of the lives of individual Christians, his accounts from the history of the Christian Church. This is also why the short pamphlet on the Lisbon earthquake culminated in an appeal to love God above all else.[124] On this note Wesley's programme as a theological author is complete.

The result of examining the formal literary character of Wesley's theological output is that one perceives a similarity to Martin

Luther,[125] a fact which attests the profound and direct affinity between these two theologians. With both the German Reformer and the founder of Methodism, the oustanding characteristic of every writing is its conversational style. Wesley needed the other party—whether it was someone who wished for instruction, advice and encouragement from him, or an opponent who provoked him by affronting Christian truth, or the Societies which called for guidance from him, support through him or advocacy by him. Like Luther he was not bound by the prevailing literary device, which in his period was the epistolary style. In this respect he was fundamentally different from his friend and opponent James Hervey, who fully embraced the literary fashion, and this to great effect. Like Luther, Wesley made almost exclusive use of traditional and readily available forms of religious literature—sermons, treatises, controversial writings, open letters, collections of prayers, catechisms—and used them in as unsophisticated a way as possible. The statement that 'Luther thought almost always as an expositor'[126] is equally applicable to him. The same is true of another statement: 'Luther does not write in dialogue; he lives in dialogue.'[127] As is so often the case in the history of the church, the spectator, observing such affinity, is faced with the impressive fact that the inner logic of the subject evokes commensurate forms of expression.

# EIGHT

# John Wesley as Pastor

CONCERN for souls had been the *raison d'être*, the sphere of activity and the rule of life of the student circle at Oxford. With the Methodist movement proper it seemed at first that things were going to take a different course. The feature of the movement which at that stage caught the public eye[1] as the predominant one was preaching—both in its form and in its content. The subjects of regeneration, justification and sanctification startled the people of the time just as much as the massive congregations, the field-preaching and the high incidence of nervous fits which caused people to shake their heads. In reality, however, pastoral care remained a key factor. Both together gave the movement its distinctive character. Pastoral care lent support to the preaching, for having made necessary the linking together of the converts, it entailed the setting up and internal organization of the Societies. The solid structure which was erected was for purposes of pastoral care and secured its permanence.

What kind of rôle, then, did John Wesley himself play in this regard? Without any doubt his very nature, endowed as it was with educational aptitudes and ideally suited for the formation of character, made him singularly well equipped for this rôle. Even the still only semi-serious correspondence with Mary Pendarves between 1727 and 1731 had made this abundantly plain. By this time, however, he had also had to win his spurs as a pastor in no uncertain fashion not only in his day-to-day relationships with his undergraduates but also in that agonizing correspondence with the father of one of them, who blamed him for the untimely death of his son. Only a few pastoral interviews and letters have come down to posterity from the first years of the movement's turbulent advance. Without any shadow of doubt there was hardly any time left for counselling in depth and still less for making any record of it. Dramatic confessions of sin and indeed manic-ecstatic outbursts forced their way to the forefront of his attention; less clamant and more profound spiritual needs were overshadowed. Nevertheless, both occasional references in John Wesley's *Journal* and the rules of the Methodist Societies show that people were very much preoccupied with the state of their souls and were encouraged to be so. People examined themselves and others; they laid bare the state of their own soul to others and could even claim the right to peer into the hearts of their brethren. In November, 1738, at Oxford, Wesley himself held a conversation of this very kind with Charles Delamotte, his 'old companion in affliction', as he calls him. During this conversation the young man told his mentor, with whom of course he was more intimately acquainted than almost anyone else as a result of their daily association with each other in distant Georgia, certain uncomfortable home-truths to his face without mincing words. Every word smacked of Moravian influence, and this could have given Wesley a golden opportunity for dismissing the strictures. In these very months he certainly began to become critical of the *Unitas Fratrum*, as his (unposted) letter of September 1738 proves. Delamotte admittedly recognized, first of all, that the one to whom he was speaking had made distinct progress since the Savannah days. He had come to realize that his basic attitude at that time was mistaken. Nevertheless, he had not left it entirely behind him. Traces of it were still discernible; the same mentality still conditioned his life. For his humility, far from being the natural simplicity of Jesus Christ, was assumed and affected. He only imagined himself to be no longer building on his own works. In reality he was still clinging on to them. He had not conquered sin—and was not self-reliance the basic sin?—but had only held it down temporarily. In any real crisis —for example, at the onset of death—his supposed peace of heart would prove to be an illusion. All his fears would then return.

John Wesley took careful note of everything and went away troubled. Was his critic right? He did not know what to do, other than look for an answer in the Bible; and this he found when he hit upon Galatians 6[16]: 'As many as walk according to this rule, peace be on them, and mercy, and upon the Israel of God.' That evening he prayed that God would fulfil His promises, and understood Jesus' words to Mary on the occasion of the marriage at Cana: 'My hour is not yet come' (John 2[4]) to mean that he had to bide his time.

Both the incident as such and Wesley's response to it are significant in several respects. He paid close attention to the reproach levelled against him by the other person and rejected out of hand every excuse which might take the sting out of the rebuke. He took the strictures seriously, particularly if they related to the heart of the Christian life—justifying faith. But if the cap fitted, he did not allow himself to accept purely human comfort, whether it was his own self-communing or the consolation of a friend. On the contrary, he resorted for help to the highest authority of all, the New Testament, albeit in a somewhat mechanical way dictated by his doctrine of Biblical inspiration. For him, only God Himself was capable of resolving heart-searching questions. We hear no word of rebuke to the younger man, no hint of having lost trust, no suspicion of a prior judgement fed into his mind by others, no attempt to vindicate or justify himself. The hard facts, the essential question which they posed, the Biblical answer—these three elements totally determined the basic structure of his exercise of pastoral care.[2]

The fact that shortly afterwards, in December 1738, John Wesley wrote from Oxford to several members of the Methodist Societies in London, requesting them to communicate to him their spiritual experiences, again demonstrated the overriding importance he attached to pastoral care. On the basis of these testimonies he wanted to form, for his own benefit, a picture of the spiritual condition of the movement at that time. At the same time there was a critical factor inherent in this request, in that it implied that not every personal experience could claim the same validity. The experience was to be measured against the New Testament as the classical, primitive Christian model, and must if necessary be rejected. He incorporated into his *Journal* two of the replies which he received, and these merit special notice as the earliest testimonies to spiritual experience from within Methodism. The first correspondent set down an eloquent confession of his new birth, which he had experienced some eighteen years before this and therefore long before Wesley himself. He described the event of conversion as the work of a moment and defined it as consisting of the forgiveness of sins, of a profoundly personal assurance as to this fact. This had also been the case with Wesley himself on 24th May 1738, and Wesley insisted on reproducing the letter unaltered and on adhering to its Biblical phraseology with such scrupulous exactness that he even felt words like 'assurance' and 'certainty' to be inadmissible amplification.[3] This is the self-same characteristic that compelled him, when writing his biography of John William Fletcher, to narrate the latter's conversion in the very words of the convert himself.[4] There was no difference whatever between the experience of the correspondent and what later happened to Wesley so far as the suddenness of the event and the fact that forgiveness of sins was its content were concerned. The way in which the account went on, too, was in entire accord with John Wesley's experience, even though its distinctive certainty of tone was a feature in which they differed. The correspondent had immediately afterwards been endowed with a strange power which he compared with a 'mighty rushing wind', in other words, which he experienced as a glorious verve of spirit. This enabled him to conquer all the sins by which he had previously been laid low. It was conversion that had brought about this great transformation. From that moment onwards Christ and Christ alone indwelt his heart. He could only reiterate the words of Paul: 'I live; yet not I, but Christ liveth in me.' (Galatians 2[20]).[5]

This, then, is what the early Methodists experienced. The second correspondent (man or woman?)[6] expressed himself in similar terms, the only difference being that he used the formulae of justification with greater precision, clearly under the formative influence of John Wesley's sermons, for he honoured him as his father in Christ. He described his temptations graphically, and just as graphically a vision in his garden which manifested to him the Crucified with the open wound in His side. In this vision he had been given the assurance that a single drop of blood from this wound could wash him clean, even if the sins of the whole world cleaved to him. Finally, he brought his account to its climax in a fervent, almost fanatical protestation of love for Jesus, which drew on the Song of Solomon. Here the distinctively Methodist combination of joy in salvation with earnest pursuit of sanctification was placed on record for the first time.[7]

John Wesley did not adopt a position on these testimonies: consistently with his whole approach, he respected them as scientific evidence. The fact that he incorporated them into his *Journal* might well indicate that he allowed them a degree of normative authority. But this is not necessarily the case. Certainly they were not in his view simply poetic exuberances on the part of people who loved Jesus. His own testimony at this same time had a quite different ring about it, being one of ruthless self-condemnation. He was suffering under the tension between the old and the new Adam, between earthly and heavenly desires, but he stated this tension with his usual sobriety, without indulging in self-pity. All he said was that his dearest wish was that Jesus Christ might be formed in his heart.[8] He judged that although he had indeed for many years had the outward form of godliness, kept God's commandments, given his goods to the poor, denied himself, suffered hardships, taken up his cross, nevertheless he was not a Christian, because he lacked the fruits of the Spirit— love, joy and peace. Nine months previously, shortly after his conversion he had stirred up a hornet's nest in the Hutton household and had brought down upon himself the suspicion of being an insane fanatic[9] when he said this, looking back on his previous life. Even now, therefore, he still thought just as little of his own standing as a Christian. It went as deep as that! Was it deliberately, and for the sake of contrast, that he put this disparaging account of his own spiritual condition immediately after the exuberant testimonies to the possession of salvation which emanated from his adherents?[10]

All this is not in itself pastoral care, but only one of its prerequisites, i.e. the study of souls. And yet it is an essential prerequisite. One gains the impression that this study of the human heart led to John Wesley's caution as a pastor. For him, it was primarily a matter of reading the situation accurately, taking due note of the features unique to each spiritual case. The paroxysms which occurred in his meetings did not commend themselves to John Wesley one bit, and doubtless he would gladly have thrown overboard this top-hamper from his evangelistic work. But these things happened. One way or another, God found ways of revealing Himself.[11]

Pastoral care, in the strict sense, first fell to his lot on 21st January 1739, when at an evening meeting a well-dressed, middle-aged woman suddenly cried out as in the agonies of death. She was calmed down. At John Wesley's invitation she visited him the next day and told him that three years previously she had been tormented by strong convictions of sin and that nothing had been able to comfort her. At that time she turned for help to the incumbent of her parish, but he had no idea what to make of her, obviously regarded her as mentally disturbed, and recommended immediate medical treatment. The physician came, bled her, and gave her several other then fashionable treatments, which naturally enough were unable to heal her wounded spirit. Then yesterday evening a sudden change had taken place. Wesley's proclamation of the central saving truths had touched the sore point. It had awakened in her a faint hope that the One who atones for every sinner could espouse her cause and heal her soul, which had transgressed against Him.[12] Here again Wesley's caution dominates the scene, which is readily understandable in psychological and psycho-analytical terms. The tension which was still present in her soul and had been aggravated by the spurious medical treatment was triggered off again by the irritant term 'sin' to the point of abreaction, and was released. There was nothing left for Wesley to do. He could take what had happened to be a direct result of the preached Word.

Wesley adopted an even more reserved attitude towards a young French Camisard woman, who prophesied the imminent coming of Jesus Christ. He did not see the Spirit of God at work here at all, but rather regarded the whole affair as either hysteria or gratuitous self-indulgence. However, he refused to get involved and went away unmoved.[13]

In the case of a Mrs Compton at Oxford, who appeared on the scene as a rabid opponent of the Methodist movement, matters took the following course. He argued with her, but suddenly broke off the argument because it only raised her hackles, and invited her to join him in prayer. Surprisingly, she knelt down with him. Then she took a fit, and while she was in convulsions she cried out: 'Now I know I am forgiven for Christ's sake.' With this, her resistance broke down.[14] Here again he had no responsibility beyond recognizing what had happened.

These unexpected but indisputable occurrences were in turn used by Wesley as the evidential raw material for his pastoral advice. He did this particularly in the case of his elder brother Samuel, to whom he had been so closely attached as a child. Ever since his conversion they had been estranged. Samuel regarded the whole Methodist movement as nonsensical and extremist. He foresaw a sectarian development based on self-delusion and vanity. John referred him to the facts. The paroxysms were traumas which were resolved by the preaching of the Gospel and by prayer. The proper thing to do, therefore, was not to focus on the fits, but rather on the fact that they were cured. But he also drew attention to the more significant facts: namely, that people had turned from their evil ways and taken up a new and good life; indeed, that people who had been pronounced neurotic and melancholic and been given up as hopeless, became healthy, hard-working and happy. He eschewed any high-powered attempt to convert his brother. Nonetheless, he had confidence in the potency of the facts. This sober, purely factual propaganda was another instance of his caution. Here, again, he put his trust in the God who attested Himself by facts, rather than in his own pastoral adroitness.[15]

The hostility which the Methodists encountered must certainly have necessitated many a pastoral conversation between Wesley and individual members of his movement who needed strengthening. But he hardly mentions this. For him, the all-important thing is the outcome—that like Paul they learned to count all things but dung and dross.[16] Consequently he educated them very clearly and concisely in the early Christian attitude. The general impression that one might gain, perhaps, about his style is that he exercised pastoral care by issuing short sharp orders. He did not enter overmuch into people's troubles, but was convinced that depression originated in lack of faith[17] and was therefore to be combated by preaching and overcome by faith.

In the early years of the movement he encountered in and around Bristol cases which he did not resolve overnight. At Kingswood he was called on 23rd October 1739 to Sally Jones, a girl of nineteen or twenty, who was suffering from strenuous imaginary struggles with the Devil. It took two or three people to hold her down in bed. She imagined herself to be completely in the power of the Evil One. A week ago, she said, it would still have been possible to save her, but now it was all over with her. Then she warned those standing round with the words: 'Break, break, poor stony hearts! Will you not break? What can be done more for stony hearts? I am damned, that you may be saved.' She then turned her eyes to the ceiling, where she caught sight of the Devil. 'There he is; aye, there he is,' she cried. 'Come, good devil, come. Take me away, take me away. You said you would dash my brains out; come, do it quickly. I am yours.' Everyone was terror-struck, but they overcame their terror by prayer, during which the girl fell asleep. They continued in prayer until 11 o'clock at night. Then the tormented girl woke up and seemed to be cured. All those present then sang hymns of praise in gratitude for the deliverance, and the girl joined in as well.[18] The convulsions recurred for several days and became more and more violent; the cursing and the ridiculing of Wesley, faith, Jesus, became worse. The Devil seemed to have won the day. True, during prayer the girl quietened down, but nobody had any idea how she would be the next day. A decisive victory could not be claimed. Here again Wesley did nothing special, but confined himself to prayer, from which in early Christian fashion he expected everything.

Only two days later a similar thing happened in neighbouring Bristol, so that one is tempted to suspect an epidemic which must be traced back to John Wesley's own personality or the style of his meetings. Nevertheless, the usual evidence for conjectures of this kind is lacking. His preaching was absolutely normal. One thing we may venture to say: the fact that so many people were together for hours on end, mainly in the evenings and well into the night, and were preponderantly female in composition, put too great a strain on people's nerves, all the more so because these meetings centred on the fundamental choice between eternal salvation and eternal damnation. This made for outbreaks of hysteria. Here John Wesley's respect for facts went a little too far. When, on 11th August 1740, he left forty or fifty people, who wanted to spend the whole night praying for salvation, to do as they desired while he went to bed, and was woken up by them in the night to a deafening noise of groans and shrieks, he had no right to be surprised. As he prayed, the cacophony increased at first, but later sudsided.[19]

In Bristol, too, there was a woman who had fits. She gnashed her teeth and shrieked vociferously. When the name of Jesus was spoken, three or four people were scarcely able to restrain her. Those present prayed, but it seemed to them that only a momentary lull set in. At the request of the family Wesley reluctantly paid her a further visit in the evening, having beforehand turned in dejection to his New Testament and opened it at the parable of the pounds. Here the word about the unfaithful servant who buried his pound for fear of his hard master had struck right home. As he was going into the house, he heard the possessed woman screaming. When he entered the room, she burst out in a horrible laughter, which was soon intermingled with blasphemy. One of those present asked the evil spirit: 'How didst thou dare to enter into a Christian?' and received the reply: 'She is not a Christian. She is mine.' Cursing followed. When Charles Wesley appeared on the scene, she cried out: 'Preacher! Field-preacher! I don't love field-preaching.' She continued to spit curses for the space of two hours. They stayed with her until midnight and visited her next day even before noon. As they prayed, she became tranquil, and they began to hope that she was cured.[20] But they could not be sure. Wesley knew well from his own previous experience that there were such things as compulsive neuroses, e.g. irresistible, prolonged, maniacal laughter. This had been his experience in Oxford as he and his brother Charles strolled across the Meadows singing psalms together, and suddenly Charles was unable to contain himself any longer, but rather infected John as well. The same thing was now cropping up in his meetings, sometimes attended by streams of blasphemy against God and Jesus and at other times by screaming terror of the Judgement.[21]

John Wesley allowed all these extraordinary phenomena to take their free course, without taking any measures other than resorting to prayer. He made no attempt at exorcism. It was always others from among his associates who directed questions or issued commands to the evil spirits. He himself deduced from the phenomena the truth that the state of the Christian on earth is the lot of a warrior who is engaged in a continual fight against Satan. In principle he was glad that in these phenomena this challenge was now becoming unmistakably clear, in that these things extended far beyond individual experience and confronted everyone in common.[22] This common challenge made for the spiritual cohesion of his Societies. Such an analysis brings out an underlying factor in his conception of pastoral care: namely, that spiritual anguish and salvation in the individual were of no value in isolation. They had their proper locus within the Christian fellowship. They must serve to edify the fellowship and in turn be the common responsibility of the fellowship. Pastoral care was not an individual responsibility. This exactly corresponds to the purpose behind the formation of the Bands. Thereby the circle was fully drawn. The basic psychological fact which Wesley faced was invariably fear. But this was not the only thing to claim his attention and set him problems.

In these months he was also deeply involved with yet other people and in another way. In Bristol he visited daily a soldier who had been sentenced to death as a deserter and spoke with him about eternal salvation. However, he terminated his visits once the unfortunate man had come to faith and was able to stand on his own two feet.[23] A young man who had become one of Wesley's adherents but had then gone back to his former bad company, had committed a highway robbery and was now in Bristol prison. Wesley found time for him too, and witnessed a true repentance and a fresh start.[24] These were the months in which, as a result of Spangenberg's and Molther's Mystic-Quietist propaganda, he became increasingly estranged from the Moravians. There once came to him a woman with whom previously he had often discussed to his own profit questions of faith. But now she talked to him in fanciful phrases which were obviously inspired by mystical notions. He could only register his disapproval and confided to his *Journal* the following regretful but at the same time unequivocal declaration: 'My soul is sick of this sublime divinity. Let me think and speak as a little child! Let my religion be plain, artless, simple! Meekness, temperance, patience, faith, and love, be these my highest gifts; and let the highest words wherein I teach them be those I learn from the book of God!'[25] Once again his enduring Biblicism thundered forth. A similar thing happened to him nine months later with a certain Betty Bush, who wanted to pass on to him personally her private revelations and speculative ideas. He strongly admonished her and his companions to settle for the Bible and practical Christianity.[26] Thus he ruled egotism and high-mindedness out of court.

He exercised pastoral care in a quite different way when dealing with a shameless assailant. On one occasion his opponents had arranged for a woman who was well known for her irreligion and impudence to interrupt him during a public meeting. The instant she began to do this, he turned directly towards her and spoke in personal terms about the love which God had for her soul. Then he prayed with the congregation that God would confirm his word. This really touched her; she blushed with shame, and the evening passed by without disturbance.[27] Seemingly she remained in the meeting until the end.

During this period he went to people's death-beds on several occasions. To his surprise he found in impoverished, pain-racked people a robust joy and an expectation of deliverance. Everything of this world had been eliminated, and their one and only heart's desire was for full communion with God.[28] During hospital visits he was occasionally asked by patients in adjacent beds to pray with them or to conduct a service of worship. During these visits he came to realize the general importance and the special nature of ministering to people in hospital. He complained bitterly at not having the time which needs to be spent on this and envisaged a great harvest which

127

could be reaped here.[29] A moving case was the death at Bath of John Woolley, a boy of thirteen, whom he himself buried on 21st February 1742. This problem child had been causing his parents anxiety for some considerable time, having been expelled from school because of his misbehaviour and then wandered about all over the place for days and nights on end. One day he came into the Methodist 'New Room' in Bristol and heard John Wesley preaching about disobedience to one's parents. He took these words to heart and returned home a changed child. He was now devout and prayed regularly, not only for himself, his parents, his brothers and sisters, but also for John and Charles Wesley. He once said to a farmer that he should desist from speaking contemptuously about religion because, according to the apostle, 'Without holiness shall no man see the Lord' (Hebrews 12[14]). He was very attentive to the welfare of his younger brothers and sisters and brought his parents great joy by his modest, obedient behaviour. Shortly before he died, he was troubled about the fact that his father, who looked after his own family so well, clearly had no faith in God, and longed that a change might yet come about. Doubtless John Wesley had visited him several times while he lay on his sick-bed. Whilst he was there, the boy had made request that Wesley would bury him.[30] Thus John Wesley's pastoral care extended to concern for children. Here again the complementary relationship between preaching and pastoral care was confirmed.

Wesley's respect for the facts as the first principle behind his pastoral care could easily make him seem callous. His sister Martha Hall, who since 1735 had been married to the totally unreliable clergyman, Westley Hall, a vain unstable philanderer, lost nine of the ten children by their marriage soon after they were born. It sounds almost heartless that her brother could write to her: 'Dear Sister,—I believe the death of your children is a great instance of the goodness of God towards you. You have often mentioned to me how much of your time they took up! Now that time is restored to you, and you have nothing to do but to serve our Lord without carefulness and without distraction until you are sanctified in body, soul and spirit.'[31] Here the relationships of creaturely existence have been completely obscured by the relationships opened up by redemption. This rigorism was entirely in keeping with his basic make-up. He was capable of writing a lengthy letter to a friend with the express purpose of dissuading him from drinking tea. Brushing aside the objection that this was surely no more than sheer pettifogging and that it is permissible to gratify such a minor indulgence, he countered that we must start precisely with little things in order to meet the weightier claims of self-denial. For him, a general issue is decided by the particular. It is in the particular that it becomes clear whether we are convinced, resolute, cheerful servants of God.[32] Equally, he expressed to his brother Charles his utter astonishment at the fact that he spent his money entirely on himself and his wife, and called this robbery.[33]

In a letter written late in life to his erstwhile pupil, the lawyer Richard Morgan in Dublin, the younger brother of his prematurely deceased friend William Morgan, he exhibited an isolated instance of something that probably only he was capable of—a combination of ruthless severity with a residual sympathy, or if you will, an amalgam of tactlessness and tact. Unlike his elder brother, Richard had at first resisted every attempt on the part of the Wesley brothers to influence his frivolous ways as an undergraduate, so that even his father, critical as he was of the Wesleys, was forced to give them his backing.[34] But then James Hervey succeeded in actually winning him over to them.[35] When they were about to set out for Georgia, he had bidden them farewell in Gravesend and had expressed a desire to join them later. Evidently a true-blooded, blithe, quickly enthused Irishman, he had later changed his mind and had returned to his native land, where the Court of Exchequer appointed him as his father's assistant. After his father died, he took over his position. He had obviously not joined the Methodist movement, but retained a certain goodwill towards it, so that on 15th July, 1769, Wesley paid him a visit.[36] In the year 1775 he suffered the tragedy of losing his only daughter Sophia, who was presumably in her adolescence. Shortly before she died, during her fatal illness, Wesley wrote to him a downright cruel letter, which he prefaced with the words: 'I am now going to give you one of the greatest and yet most thankless instances of friendship. Prudence (so called) would restrain me from it but love is stronger than prudence.' Then followed an open admission of how deeply Sophia Morgan had disappointed him by her peevish, demanding, selfish behaviour. He could not imagine that the discipline exercised by her parents had ever made even the slightest impression on her. He pitied the man who would one day have her as his wife and predicted that she would only be a torment to him. For the space

I

of fifty years, travelling in Europe and America, he had never met such a good-for-nothing creature. In view of this, added Wesley, the sooner God took her the better for her and her father alike. Not satisfied with this, he accused her father of having ruined her by bringing her up wrongly. He then went on to exhort him at long last to take the Christian life seriously. How often he had bidden fair to do this! What, then, was holding him back? Perhaps it was the desire to scrape some money together? Wesley could hear him object: 'What, would you have me idle?' and countered: 'Am *I* idle? But I labour for eternity, for treasure in heaven, for satisfying riches. Go thou and do likewise!' He concluded his dunning in a curt and at the same time conciliatory manner with the priggish words:'If you receive this in love, you may profit thereby. If you show it to your wife and daughter, you will not hurt me, but you will thereby renounce all future intercourse with me.'[37]

On the other hand, when it came to fostering fraternal relations as between Christians, he could be surprisingly amiable. Thus on 18th July 1749, in Dublin, he asked an unnamed Roman Catholic not to condemn Protestants over-hastily, and made a general plea for him to sow love in place of malice and bitterness. In order to win his confidence, he set down a detailed confession of faith, which drew principally on statements from the New Testament and made love of God and love of neighbour its focal point, but also placed justification in a key position. His climactic theme was common sonship with God: his pastoral endeavours were directed to this end.[38] Here we are already confronted by the distinctly modern outlook, in which relations between the various Christian denominations were determined not so much by doctrinal issues as by spiritual emulation.

The severity and the gentleness are one and indivisible. This is also how John Wesley himself felt, and why he warned the preacher Joseph Cownley against offering his hearers the love of God in Jesus Christ over-hastily. The Law must prepare the way for the Gospel.[39] At this point he sharply contrasted his method of teaching with that of the Moravians: it was legitimate to preach the Law with the utmost stringency, so that it searched the inmost recesses of the heart with inquisitorial power. Initially the Gospel must remain in the wings; at this stage it may only shine forth in all its splendour momentarily and must remain in the background as a remote reality. But even when faith has been attained, the Law should resume its rôle, but in a new character. Now it speaks as a distinct and concrete possibility of doing good, no longer as an imperious command or as a condemnatory judgement, but as an offer of freedom.[40] Here Wesley puts forward an original concept of the Law. The Law spells out God's will and thereby speaks to particular situations. Here obedience is not understood as static but as dynamic, as determined by development. Herein lay the quintessence of both Wesley's pastoral care and his preaching. The Law and the Gospel were related to each other in the closest possible way. On this he could not give an inch. In this respect he was closely akin to Pietism and far removed from the Luther of the Reformation, and he was unable to reiterate the strong asseverations which Paul makes against the Law—'the letter that killeth' of 2 Corinthians 3, or even Romans 8. On the contrary, he wanted a 'legal spirit', and said as much precisely in his pastoral correspondence.[41]

It was with such considerations as these in mind that he drew the attention of Ebenezer Blackwell, one of his trusted friends, to the enemies in his own soul. He identified these as firstly an all too blithe cheerfulness, which, though admittedly highly desirable as a basic human quality, could degenerate into a lack of seriousness; secondly, and conversely, as a false diffidence, a mistaken attempt at the true virtue of humility. The motivating force behind both was self-will, which must be overcome if God is to accomplish His will.[42] Thus here again unconditional surrender to God was the goal. With keen insight he recognized lukewarmness to be man's chief danger. Blackwell for his part criticized Wesley in return. He warned him against courting popularity, against lust for power and—like Charles Delamotte before him—against an affected humility.[43]

Wesley meted out the same kind of reproof as he had to Blackwell when he dissuaded the young Cambridge undergraduate Samuel Furly from getting mixed up with harmless but superficial gossips and recommended solitude to him.[44] He held up before him the principle that one should only do things which either are conducive to holiness or could be useful to others, such as, say, learning foreign languages or gaining academic degrees.[45] In his correspondence with him Wesley was exceptionally forceful. When it came to advising in matters of the heart, he urged him, in the very words of the Sermon on the Mount, to cut off his right hand and throw it away, to stop writing to the girl he loved and not to discuss her with anybody.[46] He

impressed on him the simple truth that he would only be freed from
fears when he took leave of his desires. To achieve complete freedom
for God—this was the Christian's aim in life.[47] For, as Wesley wrote
to a potential opponent around the same time, he must love God with
all his heart and serve Him with all his strength.[48] The fact that at this
same time he recommended with exceptional emphasis a book by the
Cambridge Platonist John Norris on the relationship between
Christian living and scholarly learning,[49] shows that his emphasis on
the one thing needful was not to the neglect of the duties of everyday
work.

Understandably enough, the doctrine of Christian perfection gave
rise to several misunderstandings. It is characteristic of John Wesley's
pastoral tact that here he warns against extremism and insisted on
avoiding sweeping generalizations. He advised others to commend
rather than command this highest stage of the Christian life, to lead
men rather than drive them to this state, although he in no way
detracted from the fundamental importance of this high calling.[50]
One of the people who were sorely troubled by this very thing was
Elizabeth Hardy, a woman who could only think in the extreme
categories of Either/Or. She felt herself to be the chief of sinners and
deemed herself fit to belong nowhere but in hell. She found nothing
but wickedness in her heart. In her own eyes she was a person who
had no knowledge of God whatever and felt no love of any kind towards Him. Wesley set her mind at rest at various levels. First of all,
he told her of his own similar self-condemnation in earlier years.
Then he pointed her to the one Advocate and Saviour Jesus Christ,
who is able to supply every spiritual need.[51] The emphasis lay on the
second. Furthermore, he ventured, albeit reluctantly, to give a clari-
ficatory exposition of Christian perfection. Indeed, he could do no
other, because a Methodist lay preacher had deeply alarmed her by
asserting that a believer lives under the curse of God and in a state of
damnation unless and until he has attained perfection. Wesley made
clear what he meant by perfection—a perfect love of God, a love
which came from the heart, so that one constantly rejoiced in God,
prayed to Him and gave thanks to Him. Admittedly he was fully
persuaded that every believer could attain this state. But this did not
mean that until he did he was accursed of God. God Himself, he
urged, leads man to perfection and awakens this love, which He
brings to its final consummation. Faith is the first decisive step; and

one may confidently leave the rest to God. Of course, God only admits that which is pure into His eternal world. This is why for Wesley it was certain that God ultimately made man 'ripe for glory', even the man who died before he had attained to undivided love for Him.[52] These were simple, clear and strong words, which could surely banish spiritual doubts. But this did not happen overnight with Elizabeth Hardy. Three and a half years later he had to spell out for her the very same thing again. In doing so, he pointed to the contrast between the soul which has been completely surrendered to God and the weak, fragile body in which it lived and with which it had to come to terms.[53] Although this linked up with the Pauline image of treasure in earthen vessels (2 Corinthians 4[7]), it was a dangerously Platonizing way of looking at things. This way of thinking was brought easily to Wesley's mind by the Anglican tradition, which had been given its characteristic stamp by the close interplay between Christianity and Platonism ever since the Renaissance. He did not teach complete cleansing from evil impulses, i.e. sinless perfection, still less that perfection could not be lost.[54] He comforted Dorothy Furly along similar lines, telling her that nervous disorders could assuredly exist alongside it;[55] and in writing to a certain Miss March he expressly took up the Pauline dictum about treasure in earthen vessels.[56]

This way of handling problems at once analytical and moral, explaining them objectively and easing their tensions by personal address, showed him practising what he preached: 'lead, don't drive.'

From the year 1756 onwards the pastoral correspondence with women who assisted in the work of the Methodist movement claimed more of his attention. The first woman to whom this applied was Dorothy Furly, the sister of the young student of divinity Samuel Furly, whom John Wesley had already been closely advising for some time about his rule of life and his selection of reading. Reading through the exceptionally extensive and intensive correspondence which Wesley carried on with this brother and sister and which was frequently resumed within two to three days, we gain the impression that he looked upon them as his special protégés and felt them to be specially promising examples of Christian living. He would like to help them become truly exemplary or at least to observe precisely how the Word bore fruit in them. In his first letter he exhorted

Dorothy to be faithful in little things, particularly in conversation. God, he said, gives us speech for praising Him with, and therefore it should minister to His glory and serve to mediate His grace to men. We may never think Him afar off; on the contrary, He, the righteous and holy One, is intimately near. She has only to be ready to receive Him.[57] Clearly he feared for her more than for anyone else that she might want to conform to the world, to frivolous conversation, to light-minded company. Therefore he warned her against mixing with rich Methodists of high social standing and admonished her to look out the humble and the poor. He lauded the fact that she had tasted the delights of the simplicity of the Gospel, but he was no longer so sure about this. She was not to deviate one iota from the plain and unadorned character of the Christian message. We are to be Christians 'altogether'. His heart's desire for her was that she might really experience God's love. However, this experience had no connexion with the attitude of waiting Stillness advocated by the Mystics, with William Law at their head, but rather was evinced by involvement. Wesley, a man of decision and a man of action, would have been able substantially to adopt Fichte's dictum: 'Doing, only doing shows your worth.' We do not lose, he says, our sense of God's love by fulfilling our daily duties, but rather by neglecting them. To his mind it was erroneous to see in the hustle and bustle of everyday life the major hindrance to living life in God's presence. On the contrary, we commit sin by giving way to such evil impulses as pride and anger, by setting out without praying and by giving way to spiritual sloth. Therefore we should be wary of our trials and tribulations and be on our guard less self-contemplation and self-pity dominate our mind.[58] Dorothy Furly vacillated. Moreover, she also tended to be depressed and unsure of herself. John Wesley encouraged her, for she had reason to praise God for what He had done, and she could thoroughly rely on Him to fulfil His promise to the very last letter. No human unworthiness could thwart the free love of God. In order to speak to her spiritual condition, he passed on to her the observation of one of the Fathers, which echoed the practical wisdom of the late classical age or the human insight of the Desert Fathers, to the effect that it is easier not to desire praise than not to be pleased with it. Why? Because the sense of honour is as natural to man as the sense of touch. Only when earthly things are passed away will that which is conformable with the Spirit of God entirely determine our

nature. Therefore—this is the purport of this down-to-earth encouragement—we cannot expect any final perfection in this life and
we must not despair because it is lacking. She thought that she had
enemies. Wesley rejoined that it was enough that she had one Friend,
who was mightier than them all. She should let Him, and Him alone,
reign in her heart.[59] What mattered was to believe the Bible, to believe that, as the First Letter of John lays down, perfect love casts out
fear. To be sure, a keen guard against offending God was good;
nevertheless, this had nothing in common with fear. Anyone who
lacked this fear was a mystical Antinomian.[60] John Wesley saw the
young woman as being in this hidden danger, and probably he was as
adamant as he was here because the bitter controversy with Moravian
Quietism was coming to life again. Would he have to witness this a
second time in the next generation? He always had a suspicion that
Dorothy Furly was not telling him everything,[61] and this, too, must
have reminded him of his exchange of brickbats with the Moravians.
He did not want to lose to them again people whom he had won for
Christianity. For this would mean losing them to the Antinomian
heresy. It is only against this background that we can make any sense
of the hypersensitive mood, the phrenetic, almost neurotic manner in
Wesley's letters to her, which at first sight seem at times to border on
suppressed eroticism. His greatest desire was that, now she had ventured upon a true Christian life and was experiencing in her heart the
first signs and tokens of God's Spirit, the second great change would
take place in her. But this change was only effected in those who fought.
Anyone who expected it from a merely human 'stillness' was following a will-o'-the-wisp.[62] The temptations which tormented Dorothy
Furly may have extended even to doubts as to the existence of God,
as in August Hermann Francke's conversion, of which it has been
rightly said that it was Descartes transposed into the realm of
religion.[63] Just like him she had turned to prayer as the crucial means
of grace.[64] If God, Wesley judged, made her walk along thorny
paths, then He did so in order to break her pride and self-will.[65] In
his opinion she still wanted to have a say in things, even in appro-
priating salvation, and she was not content simply to be a mere
recipient of the great gift. At a minimum she wanted to move God by
her behaviour into doing something for her, into endowing her with
more power, into conferring on her a deeper and an abiding assurance of salvation. She had not yet understood that God's grace is

unmerited and free.[66] Her anxiety about her health, which was never far below the surface, seemed to Wesley exaggerated: his constant aim was to redirect her attention to matters pertaining to salvation.[67] At times Dorothy Furly appeared to him to be obstinate, because her basic questions, above all her difficulties with regard to God's free grace, to which the only appropriate response on man's side was faith, constantly recurred.[68] She was obviously prone to idle gossip, against which he had warned her earlier, and on the other hand to abject depression over questions pertaining to salvation. This is why he admonished her to pay careful attention to the prosaic duties of everyday life and particularly to monetary matters.[69] Moreover, she should always hold herself in readiness for an even greater change which God probably had in store for her. In doing so, she should keep herself completely open to either possibility—a sudden transformation or a gradual transition.[70] When she got engaged to the lay preacher Joseph Downes, Wesley gave his approval. He thought she could not find a better partner, becuse he was resolved to be completely devoted to God.[71] In the ensuing period his correspondence with her diminished markedly. The degree of spiritual maturity with which Wesley credited her was demonstrated by the fact that he answered in the affirmative her query as to whether or not she could take part in a Methodist Men's Class.[72]

In the case of her brother, with whom he kept up an even more copious correspondence, he was at times less happy. The high hopes which he had raised at the beginning of their acquaintance had given way to definite disappointments. John Wesley had urged him to lead a secluded life in Cambridge and to choose out his own spiritual director.[73] He had also, however, warned against undue haste and had stressed that Jesus' requirement of the rich young ruler that he sell everything did not apply to him at that time and did not apply indiscriminately to every Christian today.[74] But quite apart from this Samuel Furly had been infatuated by a girl and simultaneously, in a remarkable combination of circumstances, by an inordinate desire for learning. To Wesley both these things seemed dubious, though he gives no details. Clearly he judged the girl of his choice to be a frivolous person and envisaged a spiritual backsliding on the part of his protégé. Wesley therefore invited him to come and stay with him in the event of his not feeling equal to his temptations.[75] After he had given the girl up some time later, his father in God urged him not to squander his freedom again. On the basis of the time-honoured principle *principiis obsta* (look before you leap!), he had to be on his guard right from the start.[76] The young man brought his pastor further heartache by his proposal, which obviously had been suggested to him by somebody else, to seek Anglican orders without any connexion with the Methodist movement—in other words, to break with him.[77] Wesley was happy to accept the detailed account which he then received about his having ended his relationship with the girl: God Himself, he judged, had here convicted 'a poor Pharisee'. Whom he meant by this does not become clear. Either it was Samuel Furly, who had mistakenly believed himself to be in the right, or it was the girl who had only feigned piety: or else—John Wesley himself, who had acted wrongly, whether by his advice or by giving too little advice. All this remains an open question. Furly was not to fear the unpleasant consequences which the break might have for him; God would undertake in this matter, especially as he had acted in the right way when, at the time of parting, he had presented the girl whom he had given up with a devotional tract to take with her as she went her way. But Wesley for his part now reproached himself for having been afraid of giving offence, as a result of which the blame was partly his. In this letter, which is not entirely understandable in its details, the corporate guilt, in which John Wesley included himself along with both the young people, is worthy of note. He of all people, a man who generally lorded it over the members of his congregations and was more ready with orders than words of consolation, here behaved wholly as one needing correction.[78]

This incident was followed by a long spell of mutual understanding. Wesley expected much of Samuel Furly and confided to him many things which brought him joy or concern in the Methodist movement. Suddenly things again became exasperating. On 30th July 1762, Wesley wrote to him: 'You love disputes, and I hate them. You have much time, and I have much work.' The subject at issue was the doctrine of perfection—but the chief thing about it was the whole tone of the proceeding. This was exacerbated by the fact that Furly had not replied to him and had offered as his reason for this the fact that Wesley would brook no argument.[79] Underlying this was the unpleasant feeling that the pupil was accusing his master of being dictatorial. Wesley yielded to him in the debatable propositions, but did so clearly and distinctly against his better judgement and merely for the sake of peace.[80] Then he exhorted him afresh to use simple phraseology; obviously he feared he would lose his way in pedantic obscurity.[81] He read him a penny lecture on good style and quoted Alexander Pope in order to bring home to him its main characteristics. A good style must be clear, pure, pertinent, forceful and withal be astonishingly easy, thoroughly natural and free of all artifice. In saying this, he did not neglect to remark that he himself did not pay any special attention at all to his style but set down the words as they occurred to him. Only when he was preparing something for the press did he work according to the principles derived from Pope's paradigmatic poem. He concluded this weighty letter with the words: 'Use all the sense, learning, and fire you have; forgetting yourself, and remembering only these are the souls for whom Christ died; heirs of an happy or miserable eternity.'[82]

Obviously Samuel Furly replied to this with some reluctance. It is characteristic of John Wesley's meticulous pastoral concern, which is better termed true love, that three months later he reverted to this subject and said to him that he placed no special store by an exchange of letters on such peripheral questions as style. If Furly was unable to agree with his views, then so be it. However, Wesley retracted nothing in principle. In general terms he again advocated simplicity as an absolutely correct standard, and in particular declared himself in favour of short sentences, because they really arrest a man, shake him out of his slumber, cut him to the quick. He gave by way of classical example a free rendering of the declaration of His task which Jesus makes in John's Gospel: 'The work is great, the day is short; and long is the night wherein no man can work' (John $9^4$.)[83] Wesley closed the correspondence by giving thanks for the fact that precisely as Methodists they could agree to differ.[84] In this way he showed in practice the freedom of conscience which he himself had claimed elsewhere[85] and laid his axe to the root of the dictatorial tendencies to which he was undoubtedly exposed.

This correspondence, which mirrored the oscillation between hope and fear, which one day breathed joy and the next disappointment, which jumped from large affairs to small, which combined personal experiences with abstract arguments, which announced clear purposes and concealed a general mood of tension, comes over to the reader with immediacy and realism. It shows that a forceful personality like John Wesley, who could make demands to the point of unreasonable severity, at heart remained human and did not push unscrupulously for things he cared about.

He kept up a regular correspondence on matters of faith with the already mentioned Miss March for almost eighteen years. This correspondence opened with the subject of self-knowledge. Like Elizabeth Hardy, she felt herself to be a great sinner. She reproached herself with pride, wilfulness, and a morose disposition. Wesley set her mind at rest without making light of her harsh self-judgement, by laying down the significant principle that one could condemn oneself with ruthless honesty and yet know peace and joy in the Holy Ghost. Self-indictment and assurance of salvation are reconcilable. To be sure, he did not go as far as the psychologically inevitable equation which the young Luther had once experienced: confession of sin and praise of God are in the last analysis one and the same thing, neither being possible without the other.[86] But his own insight pointed in the same direction. When Miss March thought that she had devoted too much time to reading and too little to prayer, Wesley sought to dispel her misgivings and to commend Christian freedom as a great boon.[87] He took the same line when she asked him about the proper attitude to adopt in doctrinal disputes. Second to none though he was in insisting on clarity in dogma and in seeing in doctrine the crucial front on which the Church triumphed or succumbed, he could here suggest moderation. Even if others developed mistaken interpretations in her hearing, she should bite off any inclination to argue with them and say: 'I believe otherwise, but I think and let think.' This was true, of course, on the assumption that contention did more harm than good.[88] As for taking our own sins and failings seriously, he approved of the humility which was implicit in it. For of all the virtues humility was to him the absolutely cardinal virtue in the Christian ethical tradition, or, as he put it in this passage, 'a preparation for every fruit of the Holy Spirit'. Recognition of sins had the effect of keeping a man earnest and responsible. Revolted by his experiences with the Moravians, for the rest of his life he saw in levity one of the greatest dangers of the Christian life. Despite going into detail here, he nonetheless held hard by his basic subject—complete devotion to the will of God. Anyone who in faith entrusted himself to God, anyone who followed His leading and responded to it with undivided love for Him, could see Him at work in all things—in general providence as well as in personal experience. It was faith which opened one's eyes to the activity of God, not natural knowledge, by which in this context he set little store by contrast with the dominant view of the Enlightenment.[89]

In one of her letters Miss March had asked about the stages of development in the Christian life. Wesley said by way of reply that God could act instantly or gradually; with Him, in whose sight a thousand years are but as a day, periods of time have no significance. He also contested the idea that God uses suffering in order to draw men closer to Himself. He could equally well make joy serve His purpose.[90] Thus Wesley fought might and main for the freedom of God, and against any systematic rigidity. Time and again the question of sin came up. In this connexion Wesley enjoined that a person's being convicted of sin does not mean that such a person is damned. It is worthy of the utmost consideration that on this point he repeatedly warned against excessive severity and pointed to the fact that the status of a child of God was not lost because of human failings. If and when the Christian needed yet more faith than he had when he first believed, he could rest assured that God would give it to him and that His gift would be new every morning.[91] Here in this situation is a living echo of Paul's great words at the beginning of Romans 8: 'There is therefore now no condemnation to them which are in Christ Jesus.' Growth in the Christian way of life became the principal subject. As Wesley perceived with increased misgivings, Miss March sought a self-made form of humility. She went rooting after her own defects; she made odious comparisons between herself and other women to her own detriment; she had an impatient desire to establish that she was making spiritual progress. Wesley replied to all this by admonishing her to be grateful for the abundant blessings which she had received, and to be unfeignedly humble. Faith, complete trust in God's work and God's decree—this was the only counsel he felt able to offer her.[92] True humility, he amplified, echoing Fénelon, meant essentially that she should stop looking at herself.[93] On another occasion he commended to her the dictum of a Father of the Church: Blessed is the man who manages to persevere 'in dry duty'. Continual preoccupation with our own holiness not only meant perpetual self-torment, but led to fanaticism. We have to come to terms with the fact that there are various degrees and various kinds of communion with God.[94] Holiness, he said, is simplicity, faith and love all in one, so that the one supports the other;[95] and it was important to him that in 1 Corinthians 13[7] it was said of love that it endures all things.[96] In any case, *sub specie aeternitatis* things tended to merge, just as for all the difference in circumstances the innermost feelings of a Christian, in life and death alike, could remain constant.[97] This, then, was true wisdom, which had nothing to fear from comparison with fashionable, secular knowledge.[98]

John Wesley had to spell all this out to a woman whom for a time he thought to be a paragon of Christian virtue and whom he regarded as a model of perfection.[99] Thus he was frankly grateful and congratulated her when her character was impeached,[100] and lapses cut her down to human proportions.[101] She became his classic example for teaching that the perfection of the Christian, whatever heights it may attain, was not free from the laws of mutability and was exposed to spiritual uncertainty.[102]

In the later period a new subject of discussion emerged—friendship. Wesley strongly advocated the view that friendship of a reliable and long-lasting kind was only possible as between Christians. For him, friendship merged into one with the love which Paul delineated in 1 Corinthians 13, and it was this Biblical passage which Wesley quoted in his letters to Miss March more than for most other people.[103] When God renewed our friendship with people from whom we had been estranged, this was cause to thank Him with our whole heart. Love for a friend, understood against this background, did not make us blind to the faults of the person we loved. In this context John Wesley made the general observation that now he was seventy-one he no longer, as in his youth, admired the perfect Christian whom Clement of Alexandria had described as an unfeeling Stoic. For him, apathy was not the virtue, the goal, it had formerly been.[104] He openly admitted that one learns to see things differently in old age, and reckoned that wisdom came with the years. He felt that this was only natural, and this is precisely why he was careful not to elevate it to an inviolable principle. After all, God was free to think otherwise and to bestow greater wisdom on young people than on their elders.[105] Part of what he had in mind here was doubtless the hope of now finding in his friend, whom he so admired, genuinely human sympathy, rather than the unworldly aura of a saint.[106] By the same token, he directly admonished her to seek out the humble and the poor in order to do good to them.[107] Equally, he held up to her the example of his own life and that of Francke's disciple Anton Wilhelm Böhme, in order to show her how in the midst of a very busy life one could serve God in His needy children.[108]

As a result of keeping up an extensive and protracted correspondence with an astonishingly large number of women who were often considerably younger than himself, John Wesley not only incurred the jealousy of his wife,[109] but also brought down on himself the mordant sarcasm of his opponents.[110] There were fourteen altogether; the longest correspondence lasted thirty-two years, the shortest four, most of them between fifteen and twenty years.[111] Almost all the women involved had important tasks to fulfil in the Methodist movement as Class Leaders. Correspondence with their leader was one of the duties of their office and naturally widened out from there, because these female correspondents also came to him with their own spiritual needs. These needs in turn stemmed from the fact that these women took to themselves the purpose of the movement—to propagate the authentic Christian life of the early Church within the present age. All this is readily understandable. On the other hand, it is striking that the correspondence did not begin until 1757, some two decades after the evangelistic work had begun. Obviously up to then a great deal was still largely possible for Wesley by personal fiat, and organizational matters took up so much energy that the personal care of souls had to take second place.

His first correspondents were two widows, Sarah Crosby and Sarah Ryan. Wesley was fifty-four at the time. A second fact worth noting is that the real golden summer of this correspondence was the years 1763 to 1769. This reflected, in the first place, the expansion of the movement. Many new people were added to it, and Wesley saw it as incumbent on him to maintain the basically person-to-person character which is one of the essential features of pastoral care. The great strength of Methodism lay in the fact that Wesley never treated people as mere numbers. The leader made time to keep in really close touch with every colleague—male and female alike. How he managed to do this in the midst of his indefatigable labours remains as much of a mystery as his inexhaustible capacity for work in every other sphere. Secondly, although he was still fit and alert, he was now an ageing man, who sought contact with younger people for his own and for the work's sake.[112]

What, then, was the substance of these letters? Wesley kept in touch longest—for fully thirty-two years—with the first of his female

JOHN WESLEY AS PASTOR

correspondents, Sarah Crosby, though not always at the same depth. She was obviously an unbalanced person. On the one hand, she had mystical leanings, and on the other hand tended towards self-flagellating introversion.[113] It was not unknown for her to take too much upon herself and to be ambitious for power, the result being that the classes were infected by a party spirit and their very existence endangered, so that at a critical moment John Wesley deliberately promoted her friend Mary Bosanquet, later wife of his closest colleague John William Fletcher, over her head in leadership of a meeting.[114] Even in the first letters between Sarah Crosby and himself the subject under discussion was perfect love of God, the classical main subject. He wanted this to be the vital principle of her life. In saying this, he made the exaggerated confession that he himself was only just beginning to aspire to God, and very feebly at that.[115] When she had borne testimony to her spiritual experiences in a class meeting, she subsequently reproached herself, for she had seemed to assume the rôle of a preacher, whereas in fact Methodism in accordance with Anglican usage did not allow women to preach. John Wesley allayed her qualms of conscience and judged that she had done no more than her plain duty.[116]

Four years later she bewailed having to record backsliding in her relationship with God. Wesley countered this by saying that he had never held out to her the certainty of freedom from sinfulness or of always remaining on the same high spiritual plane. At the same time he warned her against denying what she had received from God.[117] Christian perfection lodged its claim ever anew, and was at this very moment doing so with such a penetrating challenge that it was also assailing Wesley's own relationship with God. Mrs Crosby accused Wesley of having lost authority with many members and lay preachers because he did not live sufficiently closely with God. She also found him—him of all people!—too lenient towards breaches of discipline in the movement. Here he thundered forth: This is by no means the case. On the contrary, God Himself, he was convinced, was strengthening his position among his people by what she deemed to be mistaken indulgence. Nobody had the right to pass judgement on whether his communion with God was in good case, especially as all that people knew about it was what he chose to tell them. At the end of this pungent letter he hastened to stress that he welcomed plain speaking and regarded it as grossly mistaken to assume that he disliked or even stifled this sort of thing. On the contrary, the truth of the matter was this: 'I love you the more, the more free you are.'[118] However, it was only too clear that these words gave vent to the annoyance of an offended party. Moreover, he had given himself away right at the very outset by admitting that he had hesitated as to whether or not he should reply to her at all, and whether if he did he should exercise discretion or practise complete candour. He strongly upheld his personal liberty and allowed nobody to know everything that was in his heart. Much as he assumed the rôle of the servant of the servants of God, his authority remained that of the Commander-in-Chief.

This contretemps seems to have had a cooling-down effect, because nine months later he bemoaned the fact that Sarah Crosby had written to him so infrequently and expressed the hope that she thought of him more often than she wrote to him. By this he meant that at the very time when he was in such a difficult place as Ireland and was continually coming up against opposition, he specially needed to talk things over with her and to have the support of her prayers. Indeed—and now he resumed the rôle of Commander-in-Chief—if she, perchance, gave credence to innuendoes against him, then she would notice by her loss of power in prayer that she was in the wrong. He strongly exhorted her to insist on the goal of Christian perfection set for everybody, and yet he feared that perfection had been forgotten.[119] Later he urgently entreated her to pray as much as possible both in private and in the meetings, but absolutely forbade her to preach, even if it were only in the form under discussion of her briefly introducing a Biblical text. She could of course link short exhortations with her prayers, but without a text and always with frequent pauses, so that there should not be the slightest suggestion of a coherent form of preaching.[120]

This admonition makes clear that the adoption of female preaching was imminent, and maybe those self-recriminations on the part of Sarah Crosby had been meant as a discreet enquiry.[121] She was fond of introspection and its prerequisite, doubt. She must have loved it, for Wesley expressly warned her against it and recommended her to place herself in God's keeping in child-like, trustful love.[122] On this basis he was able nine months later in one and the same breath to congratulate her on her illness and her recovery from it and to admonish her to use to the full the time which still remained to her, be it long or short,[123] but also to give quite specific advice: for example, to put paid to a cause of offence by means of an explanatory letter, and if this did not entirely succeed, to endure the remaining consequences as a cross ordained by God.[124] In the ensuing period he hardly ever wrote to her at any great length, but merely gave her summary accounts of the progress of the evangelistic work, to which he added instructions regarding her part in it, without the letters sounding unfriendly.[125] On the contrary: it looks as though it was only with her that he shared such a personal matter as his wife having left his house in Bristol again while he was on an evangelistic tour in Wales, and having vowed never again to set foot in that house or in the Foundery in London. His comment on this was that he would have to resign himself to the will of God.[126] Such was the extent to which he could take Sarah Crosby into his confidence. This was underlined by the fact that he immediately burned her letters once he had noted down for his own purposes the most important things in them, clearly so as to spare himself having to give his wife unnecessary explanations.[127] Then, as at the beginning, Christian perfection again became the subject of discussion between them, but from a different angle. Instead of John Wesley having to remove her uncertainties, he now faced her with searching questions for purposes of self-examination. He wanted to know whether she felt a tendency to pride or anger, whether vain desires disturbed her peace of mind, whether she hankered after entertainment, comfort, popularity, more possessions, whether she detected in her heart self-will, stubbornness, sloth or unbelief. Of himself he confessed to her that he bared his soul with the utmost reluctance, because he had been forced to conclude that in doing so he bored others. Accordingly, he had changed his policy and curbed his innate candour; he therefore placed all the greater value on frank discussion with her.[128]

Taken collectively, all this adds up to an earnest, lively discussion about the spiritual foundations and the external life-forms of the Methodist movement. Personal matters took second place to objective questions and tasks, but without them being completely suppressed. It was only to be expected that sharp works were spoken, that reproaches were made, that misunderstandings arose, that a temporary estrangement took place, that the letters alternated between being weighty and banal. One thing, however, remained constant throughout the thirty years—the basic subject of Christian

K

perfection. Neither did anything change in this respect, that John Wesley was the leader, the commander, the patriarch, who always knew best and issued the orders, even though he strove honestly and constantly for fraternal solidarity. He would no more allow people to interfere with the way he treated the members of his movement, particularly his lay preachers and class leaders, than with his personal relationship with God; and his reluctance to bare his soul to others, which he explained as being a matter of expediency, in fact corresponded to his patriarchal rôle, which he did not wish to compromise by exposing his inner self.

The particularly close friendship with Ann Bolton began in the year 1768 when she, still almost a child in Wesley's eyes, refused to marry a man who was not a Christian believer. John Wesley encouraged her to take this step and held up to her the lofty aim of offering God an undivided, celibate service. He described this aim with his favourite expressions: she was to become holy in body and spirit, a flaming sacrifice of love. So that she might prepare herself for this and not live to rue uselessly the day when she missed a glorious opportunity of this life, he invited her to come to London and join in the Methodist fellowship there.[129] After a searching interview he judged that she was called to great things, but that at the time she had only attained the faith of a servant, not yet that of a child.[130] The austere old man became quite tender towards her and, to put it candidly, pulled out all the stops in order to bring home to her both personal knowledge of God's salvation and a holy life on earth.[131] He spoke in quite another key than he had to Sarah Crosby. This fatherly combination of enticement and encouragement, backed up with repeated assurances of love and of a bond reaching beyond the grave, with insistent requests for letters and face to face encounters, and with an avowal that he would sooner forget himself than forget her, is surprisingly sentimental; but it becomes to some degree understandable when we remember that Ann Bolton was probably tuberculous and that John Wesley did not expect her to live long. Indeed he asked that in this eventuality she would let him have her seal as a keepsake.[132] He also gave her detailed medical advice, particularly about outdoor exercise—after all, he had himself written a *Primitive Physick*, a sort of little handbook of homœopathic medicine which drew on the ideas of a then famous physician, George Cheyne.[133] As to the main burden of his letters to her, this

146

consisted in exhortation to entrust herself completely to God, to let the blood of Jesus avail for her soul, in other words, to believe in the reconciliation which Jesus had accomplished and to appropriate the righteousness which God has made available. Granted, she had faith, but it was still too weak; for she lacked the joy of the children of God in the Holy Spirit.[134] All this is reminiscent of his conversations with Peter Böhler in Oxford and London prior to his conversion in 1738, and he obviously saw his young friend, who could almost have been his granddaughter, as being in the same position. She was to come to salvation in the same way as he had. His impression was that what she needed was faith and yet more faith, utter and complete reliance on the truth of God's promise. Just as Peter Böhler had once ridden him of his 'philosophizing', so he now warned her against rationalizing God's saving work in her life, because by so doing she would overestimate her own part in it and underrate God's grace.[135] When yet further temptations arose in her heart, the resemblance was complete; and John Wesley deemed these temptations to be 'a good sign'.[136] There was then a temporary lull in the rapid exchange of letters. But when the correspondence was resumed, he asked her whether she stood fast in the glorious liberty of the children of God.[137] He wanted to know about the onslaughts she had to withstand because he was convinced that the Devil would give her no respite, and warned her not to desire suffering. Jesus, he said, only asked her, as He asked Peter, whether she loved Him more than she loved all others, and wanted to entrust His lambs to her charge. With these words from John's Gospel Wesley appointed her to her office within the Methodist classes.[138] When the temptations recurred, he pointed her to the love of God which was assuredly in her heart. This counsel was put to her with the express purpose of redressing the balance, and everything depended on her remaining steadfast in this love. It also meant that she must not wallow in suffering, but rather cling to God with child-like simplicity.[139] She was to become perfect, an incandescent 'flame of holy love' for God.[140]

Wesley made this hope his life's aim, and in doing so gave supreme expression to the affection in which even into extreme old age he held this young woman because of her unique combination of seriousness and sweetness. The result was that he complained almost like a suitor about unanswered letters, about inconstancy in her affections,[141] about all too infrequent chances to meet,[142] about failure to share things with him,[143] and admitted to a 'friendly jealousy'[144] with which he had watched over her. Thus for a while he saw everything about her through rose-tinted spectacles, indeed in glowing colours. She was, in the flowery phrases of the early Christians, his pride and joy,[145] a city set on a hill,[146] the 'nursing mother of the Society',[147] but also the 'perfect pattern of true womanhood' and 'a mother in Israel'[148] and the 'sister of his choice'[149] with whom he hoped to be united in the divine love through all eternity.[150] This is why even in this life he intended her to lead a life similar to his own. She, the class leader of Witney in Oxfordshire, was not to be pinned down to any one place, but should be at home everywhere, though without having the same measure of responsibility as he. In saying this, he was not unmindful of her health, which would benefit from the change of air as a result of frequent journeys.[151] On another occasion he exclaimed: 'How unspeakably near are you to me!'[152] and also saw in her afflictions a means of consolidating her attachment to him, because sympathy and love had been forging an indissoluble bond.[153] In one and the same breath he could ask her whether she had forgotten him and express the strong hope that in future their exchange of ideas would turn out to be more frank and open, because for some time he had felt himself more closely united to her than ever before.[154] He therefore asked her to correct him in his literary style, because he often had to write in haste. He considered this to be a true service of friendship, which he would regard as further proof of their need for each other. In saying this, he emphasized that these corrections would have to aim at the literary style of the Bible, because this was generally speaking the best and both in the Old and New Testaments there was never a word out of place.[155] He wanted to encourage a friendship between her as an older friend and his thirteen-year-old niece, Sarah, the daughter of his brother Charles, so as to extricate her from her circle of super-ficial young companions.[156] A year previously he had personally warned Ann Bolton against spending too much time socializing, be-cause this militated against being serious in the service of God. In his opinion an hour from time to time was enough.[157]

Although in some respects the position which he conferred on her calls to mind the relationship between Count Zinzendorf and the young Moravian church elder, Anna Nitschmann, who became his second wife, in other respects it differs from it. The Count made the young woman the leader of the female bands and thereby stirred up a hornet's nest; Wesley had nothing of this sort in mind, though he did want to groom her as a model of Christian womanhood. This is why he was over-anxious about her spiritual life,[158] praising her on the one hand but also invariably asking her whether she had made spiritual progress and whether she made it her constant aim to gain a share in God's holiness.[159] At the very outset and at the very end of the correspondence he issued to her the vigorous, almost draconian summons: 'Woman, remember the faith!'[160] Although he proffered her comfort in her afflictions, he did not simply hold out to her the eternal joys as a future reward, but stressed that those who suffer would receive the fairest crown.[161] Nor was he satisfied with the pious remark that in God's purpose suffering is a shorter way of making His people holy than obedience to His commands.[162] Aside from such general observations, he also saw her suffering as yet another way of enhancing the deep spiritual fellowship which existed between them; because she was 'a daughter of affliction', he loved her even more.[163] He exhorted her to embrace suffering and cited the experiences of other devout people who had found inward peace in the midst of their afflictions.[164]

Nevertheless, it would have been at variance with his sober realism if he had persisted in his uncritical idealization of this woman. Sooner or later he was bound to discover her foibles and dangers. About the turn of the year 1773-4 she was given another opportunity to marry. Wesley advised her against the man in question. He did so advisedly, remarking that she needed a husband who was a convinced Christian and not someone who merely pretended to be one in order to please her. Moreover, her husband must excel her, so that she could turn to him for support. In his judgement neither of these conditions was met. It is noteworthy that he made this an occasion for examining his own feelings towards her and exonerated himself on the grounds that his spiritual affection for her was self-justifying, picking up a phrase from Edward Young's *Night-Thoughts*[165] about fever's heat and transient excitement.

The fact that she fretted over this lost opportunity of marriage was in his view ingratitude for God's guidance;[166] the fact that she sought to renew the friendship was disobedience. When she used her native wit and rued having too readily distrusted it, he rejoined that we need the guidance of the Holy Spirit for such a major decision as marriage.[167] He was absolutely convinced in his own mind that he had given her the right advice, and in order to strengthen his argument told her how his sister Kezia had got over having been jilted by Westley Hall.[168] Even so, after Wesley died Ann Bolton did get married.

For a while she felt drawn to Mysticism. Wesley issued an urgent warning. The Mystics, even Mme de Guyon, who as a member of the Romanic branch of Mysticism would have been entitled, on the basis of the principles he enunciated elsewhere, to more charitable comment or even to praise, were for him dangerous gourmets who lured believers from their Biblical simplicity and purity. People who followed their advice became solely preoccupied with themselves, forgot their neighbour and despised the everyday duties imposed by love. He vigorously reminded her of the Sermon on the Mount and the Hymn to Love (1 Corinthians 13).[169] In particular, the dark night of the soul which they so extolled as the pre-condition for divine grace being made manifest, was a great temptation for people who suffer to immerse themselves in their pain instead of doing good.[170] He found all this corroborated by her behaviour; she seemed to be making the most of her illness. At this point he felt he had to intervene. At the very end of their correspondence, four months before his death, his pastoral tone became shrill, almost threatening. She had given up involvement in pastoral care and was living only for herself. He could no longer tolerate this. He earnestly entreated her to remember her erstwhile leading rôle and demanded that she resume it immediately: 'The day after you receive this go and meet a class or band. Sick or well, go! If you cannot speak a word, go; and God will go with you. You sink under the sin of omission! My friend, my sister, go! Go, whether you can or not. Break through! Take up your cross. I say again, do the first works; and God will restore your first love! and you will be a comfort not a grief to me.'[171]

This was the irreparable end to a correspondence stretching over twenty-three years, which was followed by only one other letter, a brief Thank you for a present.[172] Nowhere else had Wesley spoken in such deeply heart-felt terms. Had he been mistaken in his estimate of this woman, and especially in his evaluation of their relationship? We are driven to ask this by the fact that the severity which marks this closing chapter, but which detracts nothing from his love for her, reads very much like a well-earned punishment for the indulgence and undue ardour of the early and middle chapters. Had he been an ardent admirer struck with calf-love, who had exposed himself to ridicule? Throughout the whole of this correspondence one sees signs of his human, his all too human foibles. Occasionally he must have seemed over-demanding, and one can understand why the young woman fought shy of him. A great deal in her behaviour looks suspiciously like a wholesome rebuff, and a rebuff of the very attitude of which he suspected her. On the other hand, there were solid grounds for his enthusiasm. It seemed that here he had been given someone who not only came up to his *beau idéal*—perfect love of God —and embodied it with the kind of consummate ease which only a woman could attain, but also someone who enhanced this impression by her conduct in the face of sickness and suffering. The fact that he could follow closely the course of her development from her youth up to, say, her fortieth year, helped to satisfy his Pietist desire for visible attestations of God as well as his efforts to form character. Perhaps this correspondence shows more clearly than any other the limitations in John Wesley's make-up and in his dealings with his associates. He, too, could succumb to *idées fixes* and be mistakenly enthusiastic. But ultimately his basic demand—perfect love of God— remained the criterion to which he subjected even himself and to which he sacrificed an idol.

The correspondence with Lady Darcy Maxwell, *née* Brisbane, in Edinburgh, who had lost her husband after being married for two years and six months later had lost her only child, a son, and who was herself in feeble health, was bound from the very outset to have suffering as its enduring theme. Wesley saw in this a mark of distinction: God had brought her low in order to turn her mind to Him exclusively. But he immediately asked, in what can only be called an inquisitorial manner, whether her depression really struck bed-rock, by which he meant, whether her depression had led her to sorrow over sin and over her own sinfulness. For only then was she in accord with the Scriptures. Only if and when she could echo in her heart Paul's confession to being the chief of sinners would God come to her aid and make a complete Christian of her, a purpose over which He had taken unusual pains precisely in her case. He apologizes for jumping in with both feet in this way and asked her to reprove him if he caused her offence.[173] In his second letter, which followed within a matter of three weeks, he resumed the subject and toned down his demand considerably. If sorrow over her sin was not sufficiently profound, he now wrote, she ought not to despair, for Jesus

151

Himself had borne our griefs long ago, and for her sake too. He found
words of a directness worthy of the Apostles or of the Reformers:
'You are nothing; but Christ is all and He is yours.' God's offer had
even greater force than His demand. The possibility of becoming a
Christian in the full sense, of preserving not only the form but also
the power of faith, as he said in an allusion to Timothy 3[5], surmounted the danger of becoming lukewarm or of being unrespon-
sive.[174] In the next letter he struck a classically Pietist note. Faith, in
the traditional conventional sense, is of no use; indeed, it is not faith at
all. 'Faith, living, conquering, loving faith, is undoubtedly the thing
you want' . . . God's 'precious promises' are not 'afar off . . . Do not
put them off a day, an hour.' And he concluded this exhortation with
the confession, indeed the prayer of the father of the epileptic boy
who said to Jesus: 'Lord, I believe; help my unbelief' (Mark 9[24]).[175]
Shortly afterwards she had joined Methodism, and Wesley was
delighted to hear this, but immediately asked her not to let the 'half-
Methodists', who sought to hold Christ in one hand and the world in
the other, be a stumbling-block to her. The words of the risen Lord
to Peter applied to her: 'What is that to thee? Follow thou me'
(John 21[22]). She was to become a true Christian, like the Marquis de
Renty and the Mexican recluse Gregory Lopez; and he was convinced that she gave him reason for entertaining the highest hopes.
One thing he particularly urged upon her: She was to be wary in her
choice of company and only mix with serious people, but in so doing
not to look down on people of a different sort.[176] This was also the
main feature of his next letters: Christianity is no half-hearted affair.
But the doctrine of justification was now brought into even sharper
focus: Anyone who fondly imagines that he can achieve his aim by
virtue of his own achievements, by works of the Law, will come to
grief. It is wrong to suppose that we have to offer something to God,
that we need to make ourselves worthy of the Lord. No; Jesus Christ
has accomplished everything; it is only for us to receive. We have
moved from a letter to a sermon, which culminated in a summons to
take all this to heart.[177]

This key note was sustained in the further correspondence, especially when Lady Maxwell, who lived in Edinburgh, fell in with
avowed Calvinists who preached double predestination and rejected
Christian perfection. A friend of hers, Lady Glenorchy, had hired a
disused Roman Catholic church, which she had placed at the dis-

posal of the Methodist preachers for one evening per week. One day late in the year 1770 she refused it to them because they did not preach predestination, which, as everybody knew, John Wesley regarded as a dangerous heresy. One of his people, an Irishman from Dublin by the name of Richard De Courcy, had gone over to the Calvinists. Even then Wesley still put a kindly construction on things and regarded this action as simply a case of temporary aberration. Evidently the young man, who had but recently arrived, had immense success in his preaching, and this success gave rise to fulsome praise. His like had never been heard before in Edinburgh. Whitefield could not hold a candle to him! An angel of a man! This deeply grieved Lady Maxwell, who in July 1770 had opened a Methodist school, and John Wesley even feared that she too, if only out of loyalty to her friend, might allow herself to be led astray and to be won over to De Courcy, and he pressed her to report to him with as complete a candour as before. He took this opportunity to reiterate his principle that it had never been his wish to preach on controversial Christian issues, at any rate not in a contentious spirit.[178] He exhorted her more than ever to remain loyal to the fundamental doctrines of justification and perfect love of God.[179] He prayed that she would have the kind of hunger and thirst for righteousness commended by Jesus in the Beatitudes.[180] Much as this was in the foreground of the discussion, however, he tackled her own particular preoccupations and feelings. Evidently she was haunted by thoughts of her departed dear ones. Wesley showed understanding for this and told her that his mother had often felt his father's presence beside her so intensely that they seemed to be walking arm in arm and that this had been a great help to her in times of decision. He confessed that in his dreams he himself had had animated conversations with people who had died in faith.[181] Later she felt the presence in her heart of the blessed Trinity, of each of the three divine Persons in particular, after the pattern of the Romanic mystics so dear to Wesley's heart, the Marquis de Renty and Brother Lawrence. Wesley's comment on this was that formerly he had supposed that this was the experience of all those Christians who had attained perfect love for God, but that now as a man of eighty-four he realized that it was granted only to a few chosen people. She could count herself fortunate to be among them. Even so, he did not neglect to warn her against forsaking the humble path of the simple Christian.[182]

This correspondence was characterized by the fact that in it doctrinal questions played a dominant part. Admittedly suffering, illness, spiritual experiences and the progress of the Methodist movement also came up for discussion time and again, and yet all this yielded pride of place to the Gospel truth pertaining to salvation. Here we have a classic example of the objective character of Wesley's pastoral care.

This objectivity was also true of his dealings with his closest associates, where the bonds of love, trust and friendship had already been established. Chief among them was his brother Charles, who became his closest associate right from the very start and remained such for over fifty years, until his death on 29th March 1788. It was he who had gathered together the student circle in Oxford. It was he who had gone with him to Georgia. And it was he to whom John had confided his spritual difficulties. Then with Peter Böhler's help they had almost simultaneously come to know the truth of justifying faith and assurance of salvation. Together they had taken up the evangelistic work. It was only natural that John exchanged ideas with him on all questions posed by the work itself and that in doing so he generally bested his less self-assured junior in the argument. Charles was by no means convinced about everything that John did. He showed a tacit disdain for John's enthusiasm for the German Moravians.[183] Again, he saw the dangers in the employment of lay preachers, which could lead to complete separation from the Church of England. But he had no bright ideas and so preferred to adopt a mediating position and to try to slow things down rather than stir up trouble.[184] Equally, he had grave misgivings about field-preaching. John gave him a brief but by no means dismissive answer, in which he made everything hinge on the decision of the early Christians to obey God rather than men. The first claim on a preacher was preaching the Word of God, the second thing was church order; in the event of a head-on clash between the two, therefore, the latter had to give way. Even in the face of a bishop who forbade him to fulfil his ordination vows, this was the way he must go. John Wesley deduced that God approved of the extraordinary way in which His Word gained a public hearing through the Methodists from the results which it achieved, i.e. the creation of a fellowship of faith, and not, say, the strange, neurotic side-effects.[185]

In 1741, during the controversy with the Moravians, Charles (contrary to his earlier position) was for a while well disposed towards them, and could therefore exclaim: 'No English man or woman is like the Moravians.' John did not remonstrate with him, but spelled out his disagreements with them under seven heads, and concluded his letter with the prayer: 'Lord, if it be Thy Gospel which I preach, arise and maintain Thine own cause!' The disagreements, as he understood them, were sufficiently serious and radical to point clearly to the need for a separation. The basic outlook of the Moravians seemed to him to be mystical rather than Biblical, to be elaborated at every point by strange views, and to be obscure instead of plain and simple. This obscurity carried over into their behaviour, which was secretive, not to say deceitful. They slighted the command of Jesus to take up one's cross daily and to deny oneself. Indeed, they were thoroughly conformed to this world, and this was made abundantly clear by their luxurious appearance, their wearing of gold and finery. They extended Christian freedom far beyond the precepts of the Bible, so that on the basis of their rules a Christian could make things very convenient for himself. They set no value whatever on good works; at best these were to be found within their own fellowship. With them the spiritual relationship with God—and with this he reverted to his initial reproach that their outlook was basically mystical— completely swallowed up the outward and visible relationship to God.[186] In other words, they were at best Christians for themselves and among themselves, but betrayed the Lord's world-wide commission. This ran counter to his basic understanding of Christianity as being completely apostolic. This uncompromising tone of voice won his brother back.

Doctrinal questions and matters of principle maintained their dominant rôle right through their correspondence, which stretched over decades. In this regard the matters under discussion were justification and its relation to sanctification, with its final consummation in perfection;[187] secondly, the aptness of the term merit;[188] and finally, loyalty to the Church of England.[189] On the first catena of questions John Wesley submitted to his brother in the form of propositions a series of definitions and clarifications, and asked him to state his attitude to them, be it assentient, dissentient, corrective or supplementary.[190] Much as he gave him the right to hold his own opinions, he was equally emphatic in wanting a common platform, because he considered this to be necessary for the work's sake.[191]

Significantly enough, however, he allowed a greater measure of liberty on the question of whether or not one remained loyal to the Church of England. To be sure, he hoped that here, too, it would be possible for them to be of one mind; but if not, then at least Charles, the more rigid churchman, should not hinder him.[192] Even with him he remained the commander-in-chief, who in the final analysis bore the sole responsibility for everything; but he refrained from forcing him to toe his line.

Charles was indispensable to him. He often bewailed the fact that they were working separately from each other, longed for more frequent news of him and criticized him for being independent, this having to his mind already gone on far too long,[193] but always kept him well posted as to the progress of the movement and the anxieties which it caused him. The fact that Charles had taken a house in London so far away from him, the older man, had been a grave error.[194] Undoubtedly he often reprimanded him and at times all too severely, e.g. when he reproached him for the fact that despite having an adequate salary he accepted money from the Methodist societies without any sense of having compromised his honour.[195] He also found him too lenient: in particular, he did not oppose predestination strongly enough.[196] He took exception to the fact that he could even think of demanding that the older man set a limit on his authority.[197] To his mind loyalty to the Church of England went too far in the younger man, even though his attitude was basically the same. He called Charles' attitude bigotry as to church order.[198] On the other hand, he opened up to him his inmost heart. In his letters to him one comes across moving testimonies about himself, from his admission of the trials he had had to face in Georgia[199] and the unvarnished account of their mother's death[200] to the confession of his most recent failure before God and of the only thing that helped him overcome this—the command to preach the Word and to care for souls, a command which sustained him and the whole Methodist movement with the force of the calling of an Old Testament prophet.[201] He passionately summoned his brother to the work in a way that he did with nobody else.[202] He charged him with joint responsibility for giving flesh and blood to the two fundamental doctrines of the movement, justification and perfection, as well as loyalty to the established Church.[203] In his discussion with him he passed in review his own destiny and that of the Methodist movement. He divulged to him his pining for the days of the student circle in Oxford.[204] He admitted to him that they both held obstinately to their opinion.[205] He confided to him that at seventy-eight he felt just the same as at twenty-eight.[206] And when the younger man was already staring death in the face, he bade him remember that Christians not only believed in the God to whom nature was subject but in the God who was greater than His own creation and raised the dead to life.[207] Nor did he neglect little kindnesses. He praised him to Lady Maxwell as the better letter-writer,[208] and on one occasion he thanked Charles himself for having justifiably reproved him.[209]

Even more than in his letters to his brother, doctrinal matters played a predominant part in his correspondence with the man whom he had chosen as his successor, John William Fletcher (Jean-Guillaume de la Fléchère, 1729–85). Since coming to England at twenty-four years of age and becoming a private tutor, this erstwhile officer from Nyon on Lake Geneva[210] had joined the Methodists as a result of sermons he had heard in London and had followed the recommendation of his personal adviser, John Wesley, to take Holy Orders in the Church of England. Ordained on 6th March 1757, by the Bishop of London, he hurried almost at the double from the place of his ordination to the church where John Wesley had just been preaching in order to place himself at his disposal. From that time on a close friendship had been forged, and his cure at Madeley in Shropshire, where he worked from 1760, became a base for the Methodist movement as well as the place of retreat for its leader. Late in life, at fifty-two, on 12th November 1781, Fletcher married Mary Bosanquet, one of the women who had found their way into Methodism in those halcyon days. As governess of a home for orphan children she had very soon attracted Wesley's attention. At the time of the couple's wedding he stated that there was nobody to whom he would have more readily given her than to his friend Fletcher.[211]

The first subject to be raised with him was as usual Christian perfection, but in discussing it with him the subject was given a more sharply polemical edge than elsewhere: in opposing the false notions of Antinomians and Predestinarians, he was to become the key spokesman. When the controversy with George Whitefield and his patroness Lady Huntingdon and their circle as to God's eternal election and its immutability reached its peak in the years 1768 to 1773, John Wesley put him to use, and this with good reason. The fact that in 1768 he had accepted after some hesitation the position of first 'Superintendent' of the new college for preachers at Trevecca in Wales founded by the Countess, but resigned in 1771 on the grounds of conscientious disagreement,[212] made him peculiarly suited for this task. Moreover, he was without peer in his theological lucidity. He was later to refute the Arian Richard Price[213] and above all the Deist Dr Joseph Priestley, the theologian and analytical chemist whom Wesley considered to be one of the most dangerous enemies of Christianity.[214] He charged him with all this, although he was not entirely satisfied with his literary style and argumentative method. These were too mild for his taste, but he thought it possible that they would not be without effect on others.[215] The letter in which he summoned him to become his successor is a classical example of his objectivity precisely in personal matters.[216] He began by reviewing the phenomenal strides which the Methodist movement had made in forty years. In the course of this review he looked at each and every sphere of activity and named not only the Three Kingdoms (England, Scotland and Ireland) but also New York, Pennsylvania, Virginia, Maryland and Carolina. Impressive as this looks, the wise of this world rightly say: When John Wesley passes from the scene, it will all be over! In this way he indirectly but unmistakably establishes his rôle as leader. Indeed, he assumed it as the indisputable point of departure for what follows. According to the well-known verse from the *Iliad*, 'the rule of many is not good'; and in his moments of realism he too could not shut his eyes to this fact. The preachers were not united—and this was the very thing that he so urgently wanted.[217] Who could unite them and at the same time be set in authority over every member? Only a man who had faith and love and whose sole intent was to further God's Kingdom. He must be a man of discrimination and decision, of human understanding, familiar with Methodist doctrine and discipline, and able to express himself. He needed diligence and drive, tenacity and fixity of purpose. This required sound health—obviously he had no idea of Fletcher's proneness to consumption. In addition to the aforementioned qualities he needed to have the confidence and loyalty of the members; he must be a winsome personality. As Methodism encountered a great deal of opposition, learned and considered as well as crude and violent, its leader needed erudition as well as resolution. He had to be able to hoist them with their own petard and to expose their presuppositions. Was there any one at all who commanded so many gifts all at once? 'Thou art the man!', exclaimed Wesley to his younger friend in his imperious way. But he also anticipated his objections. 'I'm not equal to the task', he hears him saying; 'I have neither grace nor gifts for such an imployment'. 'You say true', Wesley rejoined. 'But do you not know Him who is able to give them? perhaps not at once, but rather day by day; as each is, so shall be your strength.' He further anticipates Fletcher saying: 'But this implies a thousand crosses, such as I feel I am not able to bear.' 'You are not able to bear them now', says Wesley, 'and they are not now come. Whenever they do come, will He not send them in due number, weight and measure? And will they not all be for your profit, that you may be a partaker of His holiness? Without conferring therefore, with flesh and blood, come and strengthen the hands, comfort the heart and share the labour of your affectionate friend and brother.' The command at the end was integral to the matter in hand: the fact that the choice fell precisely on him had an objective basis. The task and the situation dictate matters; personal qualities were secondary to them; and Fletcher's scruples were quashed with the most powerful objective argument of all—the support of God Himself. In this matter John Wesley by no means assumed the rôle of an absolute monarch who would brook no argument. He had, one can safely reckon, weighed everything carefully and showed understanding for the recipient of his letter. In singling him out and grooming him to succeed him, he protected him from becoming arrogant by telling him that God would make good his deficiencies, and in a way abased him again by immediately summoning him to come and be with him while he (Wesley) was still alive, so as to make him thoroughly acquainted with the work and to present him to the Societies in his future rôle.[218] This is how John Wesley exercised pastoral care over his associates.

In both cases—with Charles Wesley and Fletcher alike—there was no spiritual scrutiny, no inquiry as to their inward condition; difficulties, temptations, mystical impulses have no place here. Indeed, flights of fancy were entirely absent from this correspondence, which was task-orientated, objective, manly—though without it being void of human touches. But these human traits consisted essentially in the fact that the task was discussed, doctrinal views were weighed against each other, and responsibility was shared, ready as John Wesley was, when it came to the crunch, to take the whole thing on his own shoulders. Even humour was not completely suppressed. Thus on 6th March 1763, he wrote to Charles that of his two chief helpers the time one was love-sick, the other 'physick-sick', and neither was really supporting him.[219]

But what was he like, then, as a pastor to the one person who should have been closer to him than anyone else—his wife? Mary Wesley,[220] *née* Goldhawk, was the widow of a Huguenot merchant in London, Antoine Vazeille (Anthony Vazeille), and was herself probably of Huguenot descent. Mother of two sons, Noah and Anthony, and two daughters, she inherited a considerable fortune, investment of which Wesley secured on behalf of her children. It is hard to offer reasons for his choosing this particular woman, whom he married on 18th February 1751. Two and a half years previously, at the same time as his brother Charles, he had already thought of marriage. At that time the woman of his choice, a thirty-three-year-old widow, Grace Murray, *née* Norman, in Newcastle-upon-Tyne, whose husband had been lost at sea, had been snatched away while his back was turned, by one of his closest associates, John Bennet.[221] Possibly she herself had encouraged this to happen. John Wesley had come to know and esteem her as a result of the service she gave to the movement. She was the matron of the Methodist Orphan-House in Newcastle, and together with other associates had taken part in several of his evangelistic tours. In August 1748, a definite verbal contract had been made between them; in our terms, they had become espoused. Undoubtedly he was bitterly disappointed by the breach between them and by her hasty decision to marry someone else.[222] Who was to blame for this is not easy to decide. According to the rules of the Methodist Societies, which on this specific point followed closely those of Herrnhut, the brethren had to be consulted prior to any marriage. But the outcome of this consultation was not binding. It would appear that Charles Wesley, who as his brother by nature and grace deemed it his prerogative to be the first to be consulted, had felt he had been slighted. Clearly he intervened with the highest of motives, i.e. in order to avoid scandal being brought on John's good name and that of the movement. It was possibly he who introduced Grace Murray and John Bennet to each other; at any rate it was he who finally brought them together. There ensued several heart-rending scenes, which took place in George Whitefield's rooms in Leeds. There John Wesley was in deep distress. For a while he was unable to utter a single word. Then, when he was told that the newly-wed John Bennet had arrived, he refused to see him. Whitefield, however, then succeeded in showing him in. They embraced each other without saying a word and with tears running down their cheeks. Then John Wesley spoke with his brother Charles, who seems to have recognized his false position in this matter and to have regretted having interfered.[223] Amazingly, the estrangement between the two brothers was only short-lived.[224] John also had no wish to see his betrothed again. However, she then came into the room and fell at his feet. Subsequently he met her on only two occasions.[225] It was magnanimous of him to forgive both Grace Murray and John Bennet, and to see himself as partly to blame, though not without speaking to them plainly about the way they had behaved.[226] This experience hurt him deeply, and it may be that at forty-eight he settled for getting married to a forty-one-year-old woman, whom he had hardly got to know, without there being any of the joyful abandonment of love's young dream. The fact that despite his basic ascetic outlook he originally held out high hopes for the ultimate union between a man and a woman and valued matrimony as a unique life-partnership was clearly expressed by him to a friend to whom he unburdened his heart after his betrothal had been shattered.[227]

It was in fact a man of the same age as himself, Ebenezer Blackwell, a commercial banker in London, from 1739 onwards a generous patron of the Methodists, who first drew Wesley's attention to the widow Mary Vazeille, who was one of his acquaintances. No local history of London Methodism can fail to take him into account. He helped not only financially but also by his advice on every conceivable matter, and was one of Wesley's most frequent correspondents. He readily made his country house at Lewisham in Kent available to Wesley, and it was there that the latter wrote most of his apologetic articles for the press.

Shortly before his marriage Wesley had had occasion to re-visit his alma mater, Lincoln College, Oxford, because his personal vote was necessary at an election. Received in an exceptionally friendly and respectful way, he felt strongly drawn to go back there on a permanent basis. He certainly felt at home in these cloistered surroundings and would have been glad to spare himself the many petty annoyances with which the movement plagued him daily. He could have started all over again with a fresh band of pupils, left the movement to its own devices and let it merge with the Church of England. The alternative to this temptation was total involvement in the world with all its pressures, including marriage. It would seem that the course of his life up to then had struck him as having fallen between two stools. If he were to remain celibate, then his place was the cloistered life of the university; if he were to serve the movement, he must marry. The clear-cut legal and financial rule that he was only permitted to hold the position of Fellow as a bachelor, underlined this straight choice.[228] He hurried back to London and there injured himself so seriously on slippery ice on London Bridge that he had to stay in bed for a few days. Through Ebenezer Blackwell's good offices he spent these days in the nearby residence of Mary Vazeille. As with so many other decisions, therefore, his decision to commit himself to indissoluble union was taken on a sick-bed.

This incident is highly illuminating. According to the rules of the Methodist Society, John Wesley should now have informed his closest colleagues, of whom his brother Charles was one. This he did not do. This omission was probably deliberate on his part, because the repercussions of his annoyance over his betrothal to Grace Murray having been broken up had still not died away, and perhaps also because as leader he arrogated to himself a special position. He simply informed Charles that he would be getting married, and withheld his prospective wife's name. Charles learned her name from Vincent Perronet, in whom John had confided, and was in high dudgeon. He refused to go to the church with Perronet or his brother —the original source is ambiguous here—and together with his wife went into silent mourning for several days, being incapable of preaching, eating or sleeping. At the Foundery, the headquarters of the movement, he listened on the day before the wedding to the address in which John justified his decision. Those present were so taken aback that they 'hid their faces'. The secretive and arbitrary way in which the leader of the movement had acted annoyed them all. There was a distinct feeling: We cannot stand for this, but nobody dared to voice his dissent. It was presumably the incumbent Charles Manning, a close acquaintance of Mary Vazeille's, who on 18th February 1751 conducted a quiet wedding ceremony in Hayes. How different things had been with Charles, whose marriage had been solemnized by John on 8th April 1749, at Garth in Wales![229]

The following Sunday witnessed a distressing scene. Ebenezer Blackwell, Charles Wesley confided to his diary, forced Charles to go and see the newly-wed couple, dragging him along to his sister-in-law in his own inimitable officious manner. Charles greeted his brother affably, his new relative formally, and took his leave as soon as propriety allowed. Then, some three weeks later, a reconciliation took place which was sincerely meant but which fell short of its object.[230] Charles Wesley refused, it would seem, to attend the Methodist Conference which was held shortly after in Bristol and was the first to discuss separation from the mother Church. This refusal put John out greatly, because this was the very time when he needed him so desperately—obviously in the discussion as to separation.[231]

Thus John Wesley's marriage got away to an unhappy start. This reaction was not exactly calculated to inspire his wife, who was not a committed member of the Methodist societies, with confidence in her husband and his life's mission or in the large circle of new company. Later she assisted in the Methodist Book-Room at the Foundery.[232]

Legally, the first consequence of his marriage was that he lost his position and salary as a Fellow of Lincoln College: he sent in his formal resignation on 1st June.[233] From this time on he was financially straitened, whereas previously he had always been in a position to support his brothers and sisters and many others. This was another marked change in terms of proving himself in the world and its tribulations.

One thing had already been clearly understood between the married couple. He would not give up a single item of his previous activities: he must not preach one sermon fewer, write one letter fewer, compose one tract fewer, make one journey fewer.[234] A life marked by self-sacrifice lay before Mary Vazeille, and even though she did not realize all the implications of this, she must have had more than an inkling of what lay ahead of her—all the more so because, being an older man, Wesley was less likely to change his ways. The very first letter that he sent to her, on 27th March 1751, from Tetsworth, some forty-two miles from London, followed assurances of love and gratitude to God for having brought the two of them together for mutual support, with a whole series of tasks relating to the service she was giving the Methodist movement. He concluded with a pressing summons for her not to let any daily business come between God and her soul and to devote at least one hour a day to reading the Bible, to prayer and meditation.[235] Only three days later he wrote again. His first lines were profuse with avowals of his love for her, and special gratitude was due to God for having given him this helpmeet to travel the road of life with him. Then he told her that the wives of several preachers, who apparently knew her slightly, had strongly approved of his choice. This should encourage her to win over the women who had previously been antagonistic towards her and who obviously lived in London. She was to make repeated attempts to this end.[236] A year later he was able to pass on fresh eulogies of her and news of the favourable impression she had made when in Newcastle-upon-Tyne, where his débâcle with Grace Murray had probably predisposed the Methodists in favour of accepting his wife, and where her unaffected manner had particularly commended itself. At the same time, however, he blamed himself for not having spoken seriously and emphatically enough with her, seeing that they were surely meant to be guardian angels to each other, and he did not hesitate to apply directly to them both the full rigour of the lofty words of the Epistle to the Ephesians about marriage as an analogy for the union between Christ and His Church. He understood these words to mean not a sacramental, but a pastoral and moral bond, a responsibility before God for the person closest to us.[237] It would be wrong, therefore, to say that he was unmindful of his pastoral commitment to her. On the other hand, he was not over-solicitous in this regard; his letters were extremely matter-of-fact, and there are several among them where there is not even a single mention of spiritual things.[238] Obviously mistrust on the part of individual Methodists made life hard for her. He exhorted her not to become bitter and biting, but rather to possess her soul in quiet and patient love. If her own strength was insufficient for these things, she must take to herself the rule of Thomas à Kempis: 'Do what is in thee and God will supply what is lacking.'[239] Then he again acknowledged the gracious way in which she was willing to leave a female visitor alone with him undisturbed until she had said what she wanted to say. However, he laboured this point for a suspiciously long time, and stressed in an unmistakably pointed manner that this was the only way to win and secure a person's affection; that, as Paul lays down (1 Corinthians 10[29]), everyone must be left to his own conscience, and that nothing was to be gained by violent methods; finally, that a wife is not to use a rod on her husband, a rod being for a fool's back.[240] This was in October

1758. In the January of this year there had already been a row between the married couple when, while searching his pockets, she had come across a letter to Sarah Ryan, a simple trustworthy member of the Methodist Societies, but on reading it had realized that it was of a purely pastoral nature.[241] Something of the same sort must have happened at the end of this same year. In any event he complained bitterly to her on 23rd December that she was trying to choose his company for him. He could not allow this to happen, and asserted his independence, which he regarded as his inalienable right before God and men, but at the same time remarked that this point had been a continual bone of contention between them for seven years—in other words, since the beginning of their marriage.[242] On 20th January 1758, she had already left him for the first time, vowing that she would never see him again, but her temper had calmed down on the evening of the same day. Later she twice broke into his bureau, took out all his papers and showed his letters to some twenty people in order to humiliate him. The reason behind this was jealousy of Sarah Crosby and Sarah Ryan, the matron of Kingswood School. Shortly afterwards, when the married couple met one another in Colchester, Mary Wesley gave vent to taunts and jibes in front of others and to reproaches as soon as they were alone. Even though prior to this she had written him two affectionate letters, which in the light of events he could only suspect as being hypocritical, daggers had been drawn, and they were not to be sheathed. Ebenezer Blackwell's attempt to reconcile them proved abortive. Wesley found him too biased in favour of his wife, and Blackwell had to defend himself against the outraged husband. He remonstrated with his wife, saying that if she imagined he was unable to defend himself because she had taken his papers away from him, she was deluding herself, because his word was good enough for anyone who knew him. He concluded by voicing a sour wish that God would give her the one blessing which she now needed—strength to repent unfeignedly and profoundly.[243]

From now on these discordant notes never died away. On 23rd October 1759 he listed ten points which he disliked about her, and gave her ten pieces of advice on how things could be put right and she herself could become content again. He disapproved, firstly, of the fact that she showed his letters and papers to other people without his consent; that she did not allow him to be master in his own house but continually watched over him like a prisoner; that he could not call anything his own in his own house, and even when he was away on tours had to list out to her every place he visited and every person he met; that she browbeat the servants in the house and set them about the ears in such a manner that they no longer felt at ease, a thing which had not been the case prior to her moving in; finally, that when she was in a rage she forgot her good breeding and talked Billingsgate. It cut him to the quick that she talked about him behind his back and made his faults her standing topic of conversation; that she fabricated lies about him, for example, that he had beaten her and had driven to Kingswood with Sarah Ryan; that from the very outset of their marriage he had insisted that she only sit down with his permission. It grieved him that she immediately became caustic and rude to anyone who dared to defend his good name, for instance his brother Charles and others; indeed, that in doing so she did not hesitate to use lewd words which were neither consistent with the Bible nor with common decency.

What she should do followed automatically from these reproaches. She should not touch any more the letters she had stolen from him, even if she did not intend to hand them back to their rightful owner. She should leave him free to arrange his life for himself, so that anyone could come and see him. He must not be required to give an account of every move he made and every conversation he held. She must promise not to take his papers or any other belongings of his without his consent. She should treat all the servants with courtesy and consideration, not speak ill of him behind his back or accuse him falsely, and in general keep to the truth and avoid all acrimony. He gave her this advice in the fear of God and out of loving concern for her soul.[244] These words were rough, but honestly meant. A month later he made a further attempt to win her over, this time by kindness, by asking what after all had she gained by taking away his papers. Did this give her satisfaction? Did not the doubt sometimes cross her mind as to whether she was doing the right thing? Was what she was doing even prudent? Would not people start saying of her: First she steals from her husband, then she exposes him to criticism in public? But even if she did find satisfaction in all this, had she considered what she stood to lose? Willy-nilly she was forfeiting his esteem; she was dealing his love a severe blow, and killing his trust in her. More than that: she was making it impossible for them to pray together; for how could he pray to God with someone who was daily plotting to do him injury? Finally, he entreated her to quench the fire raging in her heart and to see him, her husband, in a true light.[245]

All this was to no avail. He therefore curtly claimed obedience from her as a wife by invoking the divine ordinance,[246] but a little later made further overtures for a peaceable attitude on her part. In doing so, he emphasized her good points—her indefatigable industry, her thriftiness and unpretentiousness, her neatness, her patience, her skill and tenderness in looking after the sick—virtues which she seemed to forget in her relations with him. He exhorted her not to keep bringing up the past, but to work towards a happy future which could still be theirs and to make the eventide of life beautiful for them both. He wanted to walk towards eternity hand in hand with her.[247] Nine months later he sent her a pastoral letter. God had bestowed on her countless temporal blessings. Might He not have spiritual ones in store for her as well? He had sent her afflictions. Might they not have some divine message in them? Might they not help her master her faults, her impetuous, harsh, blustering disposition? Might they not bring her to a true love of God in which she would be able to endure and overcome every adversity?[248]

In the summer of 1768, when she lay ill in London, he had hurried to her side post-haste from Bristol, where he was holding the Conference with his preachers, and spent an hour with her—he could not spare any more time. In his ensuing letter he gratefully acknowledged how fifteen years previously she had spared herself no pains in nursing him back to health. But the letter culminated in a pastoral exhortation. He said to her that she must not become impatient if she did not immediately recover her health, especially as the time of year was not favourable. But above all there was a divine purpose behind her illness. She should become entirely devoted to God, be sanctified for Him; and His favour was better than strength, health or life itself.[249]

She left Wesley himself or his house on several occasions for longer or shorter periods of time, more often than not without telling him. This first happened in April 1755, when Charles Wesley mediated between the married couple to heal their estrangement; but, although according to the notes in his Diary Charles acknowledged the truth of his brother's views, according to John's account he maintained complete silence towards him, so that it was absolutely impossible to make any progress. Here, too, jealousy must have been the main factor, for she had voiced her suspicion that the two brothers had only brought her to Bristol during John's stay in Leeds in order to keep her out of his hair.[250] Why she went away on 23rd January 1771 he could not imagine; she betook herself to her married daughter in Newcastle-upon-Tyne, intending 'never to return'. At the time he was incensed, and wrote into his *Journal*: 'I have not left her, I have not sent her away; I will not recall her.'[251] In the event she did come back to him; but in September 1774 she had gone off again while he was on an evangelistic tour in Wales, and this time, too, he apparently made no efforts to get her back home.[252]

Prior to this, a stern letter had been sent to her from York on 15th July 1774. In this letter he on the one hand held her to strict account by enumerating to her from memory, whose unretentiveness for evil deeds he provocatively emphasized, all the things by which she had wounded him and indeed wounded him deeply. Part of this hurt was the fact that she never replied to the numerous letters he wrote when he was away, and yet for all that asserted to other people that although he never wrote to her, he was meantime no doubt corresponding regularly with Sarah Ryan; that she had said to a lay preacher with whom she was on friendly terms that her husband's parting words had been: 'I hope to see your wicked face no more.' The cardinal sin of jealousy brought forth evil fruit. Not satisfied with putting names to several women with whom she suspected her husband of having had an affair, Mary Wesley even went so far as to believe him capable of having relations with prostitutes, and this is how she justified taking charge of his money. Having had more than his fill of major and minor rows, he was forced to the conclusion that she was as implacable as ever, regardless of whether he answered her back or kept his own counsel—something which he could only partly excuse by her hasty temper. On the other hand he exhorted her to let bygones be bygones and make a fresh start, not to meddle in his affairs, not to hanker after wearing the trousers, not to contend for power, money and admiration—things which she obviously envied him. She should be content in her secondary and supportive rôle and no longer withstand God's manifold attempts to break her stubborn will and to curb her violent temper, instead of (as had been the case up to now) only becoming more and more intolerable. Then her husband, who was ready to forgive all, would again love her as Jesus

Christ loved His Church. Reasonable as this offer sounded, however, at no point did the letter consider the possibility that he for his part might have been in the wrong. Only in the opening words did it contain a hint along these lines, when he mentioned that his wife had originally laid the blame for the quarrels at both their doors, only to put the blame entirely on him.[253] It was precisely this detailed letter in which, more than in any other, pastoral tones were drowned by a disputatious attitude. Wesley should have shown greater understanding for the fact that he was not easy to live with; he should have put himself in his wife's shoes instead of dressing her down. But above all he erected an insuperable barrier between them by the fact that he harped on his sense of mission, and that although at first he only alluded to this aspect of the matter, the longer he stressed it the more emphatic he became. By slandering him, she disrupted God's work in the world and prevented people from being saved. This was what was at stake in her undermining his authority, whereas her insignificant life was of no consequence in this respect.[254]

There is no disputing the fact that it was no longer possible for things to work out between the two of them. Two years before, on 10th July 1772, he had informed his brother Charles of the amazing change which had taken place in her; he suddenly found her all sweetness and light; she did not find fault with anybody; she was thoroughly pleased with life.[255] Now things looked hopeless. The proposal of a reconciliation which he put to her on 1st September 1777, brought into sharp focus the last-mentioned reproach, i.e. the placing in jeopardy of many people's salvation. This damage could not be repaired simply by an act of pardon on his part. It was impossible for him to accept his wife back again without further ado. This would look like a corroboration of her accusations; but then again, she herself was hardly in a position to offer any way of making amends. So he reduced his claims to a minimum: namely, that she retract all the things she had said against him, above all the assertion that he had been living in adultery for the past twenty years.[256] The whole affair leaves a nasty taste, but also has a numbing effect. He was again playing high and mighty, and she had to receive grace and favour from him. The basis for a partnership before God and for God no longer existed. This letter was an ultimatum, at best a treaty, but not really a peace treaty, only an armistice. This was not adequate for a renewed mutual commitment which bore even the remotest resemblance to the summons of the Epistle to the Ephesians to reflect the union between Jesus Christ and the Church. His piercingly cold letter of final parting, written on 2nd October 1778, in which he laid upon her the sole responsibility for every evangelistic failure, for the whole current increase in the forces hostile to God and Christ, and expressly emphasized that even if she lived to be a thousand years old she could not undo the mischief which she had caused, ended the affair once and for all.[257]

Thus from a given moment in time John Wesley failed as a pastor in the most intimate of all relationships. If we compare his letters to the women of the Methodist movement with those to his wife, we are immediately struck by the fact that spiritual and Biblical matters take second place to personal and mundane affairs and to establishing who was in the right and who was in the wrong. One cannot but ask whether he made any serious efforts at leading her to the same heights as the others, whether he shared with her the things that mattered to him most. None of her letters is extant, and we learn about what they discussed only through him. The impression given by this is an indistinct picture of an unsophisticated woman who spiritually and mentally is not particularly well advanced, a woman of simple needs who did not find the support she had hoped for in the man whom she wanted to have entirely to herself, a woman at the mercy of her own temperament who saw her vocation in life as one of nursing and looking after the family, an example of Gertrude von Le Fort's 'timeless woman'.[258] She was certainly not the ideal partner for John Wesley, not even in his middle age; and one can only marvel that he made such a stupid choice. Nevertheless, once having irrevocably committed himself to her, and that with the whole force of Ephesians $5^{32}$, he was duty bound to knit her into the Methodist Society and to share his life's purpose with her, even if she did not measure up to his and others' expectations. There were enough straightforward, uncomplicated people in the movement with whom she was on an equal footing and to whom she could turn. It probably came hard to her to be left behind, and in this respect her jealousy was justified, but not the incredibly base means by which she gratified her vindictiveness. Her husband asked too much of her; she was to live as ascetically as he himself did, lay every consideration for herself on the altar of service to the Methodist movement. In requiring this, he overlooked the fact that whereas for him the Methodist movement meant fulfilment, for her it meant self-denial. Admittedly it was more congenial from his point of view to exchange ideas about matters of faith and life, about Christian perfection, about the validity and the limitations of Mysticism, with people like Miss March, Lady Maxwell, Dorothy Furly, Mary Bishop, a highly cultured teacher, or even with the young women Ann Bolton, Ann Roe, Philothea Briggs, Elizabeth Ritchie and all the rest, and to enjoy a deepening fellowship of heart and mind with them. But he should have informed his relationship with his wife with his essential concerns in a quite different way and nipped their estrangement in the bud by showing even greater love and concern, by striking even more deeply into the Bible, instead of resorting to vigorous assertions as to the rights and wrongs of the affair. He did try to do this, but gave up trying too easily. All things considered, he exercised too little patience.

In the closing years all relations between them ceased to exist. When she died in London on 8th October 1781, and was buried on 12th October, he only learned of this after the event.[259] To this day it is astonishing that his authority was not adversely affected by the long tragic drama and its dénouement. This could have given a golden opportunity for a serious and spirited opposition party within his movement which also rebelled against his stance as the leader, to call his whole position in question.

Pastoral care inevitably includes pastoral care for one's own soul; it demands, to put it in secular terms, self-criticism. Was John Wesley sufficiently able to look at himself dispassionately? Although at times of crisis in his life he looked to his own failings as well, these failings never consisted in his having taken the wrong course, but always and solely in his not having pursued his course to its logical conclusion. Thus he had let his love for Grace Murray and John Bennet get the better of him and had failed to reckon with the possibility that they were deceiving him.[260] He had not talked seriously enough with his wife;[261] he had also been too ready to take her back without the necessary safeguards.[262] Radical self-questioning, therefore, did not arise in these relationships. It was much the same in his dealings with the members of his movement. Here, too, he was prone to blame himself for not being severe enough, rather than for being too gentle.[263]

However, there is one impressive instance of an extremely severe self-indictment. Significantly enough, this is a confession made to his brother Charles.[264] At sixty-three John Wesley here passed on himself the judgement: 'I do not love God. I never did.' Therefore he also had no true faith in the Christian sense of the word. He judged himself to be an honest heathen, a God-fearing proselyte such as adhered to the Synagogue.[265] These were words spoken of himself by a man for whom Christian perfection was the sum and substance of life, the aim and object of education, a subject for preaching which could never be impressed on people enough and an inexhaustible topic of pastoral conversation, as well as a problem of theological definition which is posed ever abew and can never be definitively solved—a man who would not allow anything to come between him and his God and who thereby gave people the impression of being self-contented and at one with his eternal Lord. He was therefore taken all the more completely aback by the fact that God was making him such an effective instrument of His purposes and had brought him to a position where he could 'neither get forward nor backward'. He had no irrefutable evidence of the invisible world, nor any for the fact that he was a child of God—all this was no more than a bare postulate, an inference drawn from reason. And yet he dare not preach any other Gospel. His major themes—faith, love, justification, perfection—had to remain his message. Nevertheless, he whose very faith in God was failing gave evidence to an increase, rather than a decrease, in his zeal for God's cause. He was under compulsion to invite all the world to the mighty Lord whom he did not know. But it was not fear which lay behind this compulsion; he had no terrors of falling into hell, but, if of anything at all, then of 'falling into nothing'. This was a thoroughly modern feeling which seized his soul. The traditional concepts had lost their potency, and Nihilism was beginning to make itself felt in the form of a horror of complete emptiness and absurdity. But in the very throes of such feelings and misgivings he confessed that he was being 'borne along'.[266] In the abyss he became all the more assured of God; in the midst of his own failure he entrusted everything to His keeping. If these words are taken seriously—and it is unwarrantable to tone them down—then they throw clear light on his severity and his self-assurance, which looked like self-righteousness. He trusted God not only with a child-like faith in providence, but with all the tenacity of a mature man who was clear in his own mind as to what he was doing and what he was risking, but who in his decisions and actions knew himself to be only a tool in the firm grasp of Him who had laid His hand upon him.

What the two brothers did together for people in their movement— he as the head, Charles as the heart[267]—was expressly termed by Wesley the care of souls, *cura animarum* in the strictly personal, all-embracing, profound and precise sense of the tradition in Christendom associated with Gregory the Great. It went far beyond preaching, the primary form of evangelism, and gathered to itself all the gravity of being accountable before God for men.[268] It had not first fallen to their lot in and with the Methodist movement or even been chosen by them. Truth was that already their ordination as Anglican priests could only be understood as establishing pastoral care to be their sole business, the sum and substance of their lives. Pastoral care later proved to be the fountain-head of Methodism, the spring of its whole action. These were the underlying principles in concise, simple and clear terms: Doctrine is of prior importance, because it articulates the truth, the whole truth, and nothing but the truth. This is also why he and his colleagues had the ineluctable duty constantly to improve their formulations of this truth. On the human side respect for reality was tantamount to the first commandment; it necessitated, first and foremost, a dispassionate stance—a summons to which, in view of the staggering results of his activity, he had repeatedly to subject himself. Unpleasant and suspicious facts like the nervous fits and symptoms of hysteria could not be pushed aside, but had to be brought under God's dominion, for He was able to reveal Himself as He willed. Part of a sense of sobriety was a basic recognition of the fact that God's 'drawings from above' take different forms and that individual souls had to be guided in different ways.[269] Fellowship was the bringing together of unlike minds. This explains why biographies of devout men came to have greater importance for him than all other kinds of devotional writings and why the word 'experience' was one of his favourite terms.[270] None of these biographies was recommended by him more frequently or more emphatically than that of Gaston Jean-Baptiste, the Marquis de Renty, because here he saw a living embodiment of everything that he looked for: the abiding presence of God in the heart; perfect love of God; obedience as a self-authenticating principle of living; an utter detachment in our attitude to possessions ('let me have all things, let me have nothing');

utter and complete readiness to help one's fellow-man.[271] He faithfully strove to give pastoral care the individual stamp intrinsic to it. Fixed though his principles were, he made no attempt to force his people on to a Procrustean bed.[272] He himself was aware of the fact that in exercising pastoral care he did not always have at his command the requisite sensitivity to people, and excused this lack in himself on the grounds of the imperious nature of his task—God's claims on men's hearts.[273] The goal of Christian perfection was never lost sight of; in the end it came to the same thing as recovery of the primitive Christian outlook, the plain Scriptural way, entire love for God.

# NINE

# John Wesley as Educationalist

PASTORAL CARE is closely related to education. Anyone who not only wants to advise men as occasion affords but also to guide them continually, to instil their lives with purpose and meaning and to lead them to some high goal, will endeavour to win them very early in life, if possible in childhood. In Germany, as one would expect, it was Pietism which realized that education was its great task. It did so at a time when secularization of the Baroque period was on the horizon and was being exhibited with particular clarity in the education of the aristocracy according to the French model of the chevalier. Whereas Luther[1] had directed the attention of the corporations of the cities to their duty of founding and accepting responsibility for schools in an era when the Christian basis for every kind of education was taken for granted and the secular school was still not even emerging as a possibility, in Pietism the Church again assumed responsibility for every aspect of education and culture, albeit in a different way from what pertained in the Middle Ages. August Hermann Francke's Orphan-school in Halle, which had been partly shaped on the model created by Duke Ernest the Pious in Gotha, gave classical expression to this aspiration. There for all to see, it came to have world-wide influence.

In Britain the independent bodies in the Church of England known as the Religious Societies were yet again, as in many other things, the precedent for and the precursor of what Methodism attempted. The most important of them, the 'Society for Promoting Christian Knowledge', had in fact set itself two main tasks. It disseminated improving books and founded schools for the children of the poor. For in the England of the time education was as much a matter of ability to pay as of ability. Samuel Wesley the elder, an enthusiastic friend of the Religious Societies, who notwithstanding every opposition and his own misgivings had founded such a religious society in his parish at Epworth in 1702, set his sights on a charity school from the outset.[2] In fact he probably managed to build it. His oldest son Samuel was a schoolmaster in Tiverton, and the student circle centred round John and Charles in Oxford had itself started a charity school.

The Society for Promoting Christian Knowledge had been formed in 1698—three years after August Hermann Francke's important educational work had begun in Halle. Very early on Francke had sought and made contact with the Society, the result being a brisk correspondence between Halle and London in which *inter alia* the important educational question of which classical authors should be read in class was discussed.[3]

The new Methodist foundation in Kingswood near Bristol became an integral part of this lineage. But once again it was not John Wesley who took the initiative. It was Charles who had gathered together the student circle in Oxford. It was Whitefield who had first preached in the open air before large crowds. And the idea of founding a school for the children of the poorest people in the mining village likewise originated with the latter. This idea was realized by him at least to the extent that, on the afternoon of Monday 22nd April 1739, he conducted a stone-laying ceremony at which, in the presence of several colliers, he knelt in prayer and asked God to grant that the gates of hell would not prevail against the good designs of the Methodists. He was already on his way to North America; the previous day he had preached his farewell sermons to large gatherings at two places near Bristol, Hanham Green and Rose Green, and on the Monday morning many had come to thank him personally and to bid him farewell.[4] Just as in general John Wesley entered into Whitefield's labours in Bristol, so he also took over this particular task.

The site for the school proved to be ill-chosen. And so on 15th May 1739, under John Wesley's supervision, a better site was selected; and on the following Monday, 21st May, at 7 o'clock in the morning, the foundation-stone was laid, this time by John Wesley.[5] It was significant that the decision in favour of having a school was taken at such an early stage and that it was implemented precisely in Kingswood. Wesley himself gave an account of this development.[6] In the winter of 1738–39 various people had scoffingly remarked à propos of George Whitefield's stirring sermons, that if he wanted to convert the heathen, why did he not go to the colliers of Kingswood? He had taken this comment to heart, his evangelistic work had been effective, and Kingswood had become a respectable village. What could be more natural than a desire that their children, too, might be brought up to be the same? Understandably enough, the place which had once been a byword for brutality had no wish to relapse into its former ways. So the leaders of the Methodist movement and the local community shared one and the same desire. The simple building which was completed about a year later consisted of a large schoolroom and four small rooms at either end, of which two were intended for the two teachers and two perhaps for impoverished, homeless children. The strong impact which the Orphan-school in Halle had made on John Wesley in 1738 probably contributed to this plan. Whitefield supported the new foundation by making collections for it.

Naturally enough, the morning was to be given over to teaching the children. But over and above this Wesley had given thought to adult education. He hoped for pupils of every age-group, even for a few of venerable years, who were to be taught in the side-rooms either in the early morning before they went to work or late in the evenings after work.

The first to become teachers were Robert Ramsey and Gwillam Snowde, two young men who unfortunately let Wesley down badly. They had come to him seeking help, i.e. asking for work, and he had (in our view inexplicably) immediately appointed them to the new school. There they admittedly fulfilled their duties, but embezzled money collected for the school building and together committed highway robbery. Ramsey was sentenced to death, but as an act of clemency Snowde's sentence was reduced to deportation.[7] At a future date the school gained one male and one female teacher.[8]

The establishment opened in debt. John Wesley had only a quarter of the building costs when he began the work, and even when the building was complete he did not have the money to hand. But not only that: the school also gave rise to a quarrel between him and Whitefield, who claimed a right to it. However, Wesley made it crystal clear to him that his only contribution was the collections he had made, and declared his willingness to refund them to him. Whitefield complained that children at a Methodist charity school in Bristol had received clothing, whereas those in Kingswood had not. Wesley pointed out for the record that the clothing, which had not as yet been paid for, had been provided without his approval. Behind

M

the quarrel over the school lay the more important dispute over sound doctrine. Whitefield championed the harsh doctrine of predestination and had denounced Wesley as a false teacher. The long letter which he had sent to him from Georgia, deliberately written at Christmas, on 24th December 1740, had been printed without authorization and distributed at the Foundery in London in order to alienate people's affections from John Wesley.[9]

After this difficulty had been surmounted, the school prospered. Wesley gave a favourable report on a visit made by him on 15th March 1744.[10] However, his long-term plans were much more far-reaching: he wanted to have a more advanced school suitable for the education of his lay preachers. The impressions he gained from Germany, from Halle, Jena and Herrnhut, confirmed him in this view, especially as in Herrnhut Latin, Greek, Hebrew, French and English were taught. In the year 1744 he had discussed several educational programmes with the corset manufacturer Richard Viney, a Moravian Brother who had been excommunicated by Spangenberg and who believed himself to be particularly gifted for teaching children. He thought in terms of a three-tier system, which was to include a boarding school for children of gentle folk, presumably in London, an orphan school after the pattern of Halle, and a school for apprentices, an industrial or commercial school for ordinary young people. He had considered making Viney the inspector of this project—whether for the whole of it or only for a part is not entirely clear.[11] On the other hand, there were fundamental differences of opinion between the two men. Viney criticized Wesley because he, to use his own phrase, wanted to admit only 'justified children', that is to say children who had already gone through the basic experience of the sinner who has been justified by Jesus Christ. He thought this to be exclusivist and unrealistic.[12]

All this shows that Wesley was continually exercised by the responsibilities of education and devised ways of transposing thought into action. Two years after his discussions with Viney, on 7th April 1746, he laid the foundation-stone for the second school in Kingswood, the 'New House',[13] quite close to the charity school. Although this was not given special mention by him, it was undoubtedly a deliberate step. Just as in the Methodist Societies high and low, rich and poor, rubbed shoulders with one another, and just as a person of exceedingly low intellect, perhaps even mentally retarded, was assured of full respect,[14] so the children also had to grow accustomed to the fact that there were differences of class and culture without being filled with envy and jealousy or contempt. It may also be that the proximity of alms-houses to Charterhouse School in London, which he had seen for himself as a boy, was still in his mind's eye. Nonetheless, the new foundation was to educate an élite. On 24th June 1748, construction was so far advanced that it was possible to open the new school with its spacious grounds. He took as the basis for his sermon the words of Proverbs 22[6]: 'Train up a child in the way he should go, and even when he is old he will not depart from it.'[15] From the outset he had laid down firm, general rules which he insisted on having rigidly observed. These rules were derived from the German school which had made the strongest impression on him in the Summer of 1738. This was not, as might be supposed, the Orphan-school in Halle, but the now forgotten foundation of a Pietist group in Jena, which had been begun there about 1700, perhaps even earlier, by Johann Ernst Stolte.[16] This man, who after proceeding M.A. had begun his career at Jena University in 1695, must have been a dynamic personality of relentless diligence. In addition to his lectures, he made his home, where he opened his lunch table to students, into a focal point of Christian life. A Bible class was held there every day, and on Sundays a prayer meeting; and over a period of weeks he prepared the students to take their Communion by discussing Luther's *Smaller Catechism* with them. This acknowledged spiritual father of the students also gained the confidence of individual citizens of the town, with whom Erhard Johann Brumhard, the pastor of Little Jena, had established contacts, and the opening of a Christian school seems to have originated with them, the school then being naturally accepted as part of this group's area of responsibility. The growth of the Pietist movement incurred the displeasure of the University authorities; as with Francke in 1689 at Leipzig, Stolte's licence to teach was withdrawn. But unlike Francke he was a mature man. He was given a pastoral charge in the parish of St James Weimar, where he subsequently fell into further difficulties. His student circle in Jena survived: there was a constant supply of other dons who looked after it; and above all Johann Franz Buddeus (1667–1729), a Professor of Theology who had come from Halle, gave it his protection, albeit with his characteristic caution. This is the student body in which the young August Gottlieb Spangenberg

179

found his spiritual home in 1722.[17] It also provided the model for the work among children which, from the time when a Prince of Sachsen-Weimar-Eisenach gave it his patronage, increased to three schools, one in each of the three suburbs, with some three hundred pupils and thirty teachers. This was the state of affairs which John Wesley encountered in August 1738 and from which he derived his impressions.[18] The decisive feature of these schools was the family-like common life of the members under God. This point was the main thing that John Wesley took over in creating his school at Kingswood.

In his mind this idea became the key idea.[19] And so he went beyond the Jena model and in line with the best traditions of the British Public Schools created an entirely residential school for fifty pupils in eight classes. He required the parents to agree to the boys—it was only a question of boys—having no holidays. The whole of their life was spent in the school. Following the example of Jena, they were admitted between the ages of six and twelve; only up to that age, he believed, was it possible for him to eradicate bad habits.[20] He expressly debarred pampered sons.[21] Since every part of life was to be given to God, he also refused to allow any time for play. Here he was quick to pass on the harsh judgement: 'He that plays when he is a child, will play when he is a man', which, he said, was a quotation from a relevant German proverb.[22] Fear of God, holiness and wisdom were the cardinal principles of education. Everything had to be subordinated to them; everything must serve them. For first and foremost he wanted to train soldiers for Jesus Christ, men who could fight and sacrifice, men of the calibre of the early Church; and he rejoiced in the knowledge that he was not alone in this aim.[23] This is also how he justified the rigorous discipline. In this connexion he did not conceal his surprise at the fact that right from the start he had more pupils than he was able to take in.[24] Because every moment was meant to be given to God, something useful must be happening all the time. In fine weather the boys had to work in the garden, on rainy days in the house; and—again in line with the Jena model—a teacher always had to be present as a supervisor. He fully realized that he thereby asked a great deal of the teacher, but he wished to avoid the uncomfortable feeling of a police force by the very fact that the master was a 'father in Christ' who exercised due authority, and rightly stressed that prevention is better than cure.[25] Also in the service of the family-like community life was the rule, likewise derived from Jena, to the effect that a teacher only taught for a few hours: in Jena, where there was a large supply of teachers, probably from among the students, the teaching duties were restricted to one hour per day.[26] In this way the human aspect of the teacher's rôle was rated higher than his technical task. However important it was to communicate and appropriate knowledge—and this was the primary function of the school—this was not the be-all and end-all of things. The first and foremost thing was the common life.

The daily regimen took the following form. The pupils rose at 4 a.m., summer and winter alike; they went to bed at 8 o'clock in the evening. Which meant that eight hours were allowed for sleeping. The first hour of the morning, from 4 to 5 a.m., was spent in private reading and singing, probably done in free association. The older boys were already to engage in self-examination, to meditate and pray. At first a form of prayer was available to them; later, however, they were to pray in their own words. From 5 to 6 a.m. they worked in the garden or went for a walk or even did music practice. Then came breakfast, which consisted of milk porridge or thin gruel. School began at 7 a.m., and in the lessons languages were taught until 9 o'clock, then writing, arithmetic and other subjects from 9 to 11 a.m. From 11 to 12 o'clock physical activities in the form of manual work or outdoor exercise were again on the time-table. At 12 o'clock the simple mid-day meal was taken. The menu had on it cold roast beef for Sunday, for Monday minced meat and apple dumplings, for Tuesday boiled mutton, for Wednesday vegetables and dumplings, for Thursday boiled mutton (again) or boiled beef, for Friday vegetables and dumplings (again), for Saturday bacon and fresh vegetables. The strange thing is that, in a country surrounded by sea, fish is nowhere on the menu. Only water was permitted as a drink, and nothing whatever could be drunk between meals. On Fridays anyone who so wished could fast until 3 o'clock, and Wesley expressly recommended this, on the grounds that, far from being injurious to health, it was good for it. From 1 to 4 o'clock languages were again taught, then the other subjects until 5 o'clock, when the hour of private prayer began. This was followed by another short period of physical exercise. Supper was at 6.30, when bread and butter, milk and cheese were provided. Shortly before 7 o'clock evening worship took place, and at 8 p.m. everybody went to bed, the youngest first. Each boy had his own bed, a thing which at that time was not a matter of course. Every bed had a mattress, but it was not a feather-bed. John Wesley also had an eye for detail, rather like Ignatius of Loyola had had as father to his Jesuits. Sundays were different from weekdays in that at 7 o'clock the boys learned hymns and poems, at 9 o'clock and 2 o'clock attended public worship, and at 4 o'clock were given private instruction. It was a Spartan, ascetic regimen that awaited the young people, and Wesley allowed nothing to be deducted from it.[27] In the instruction[28] what stands out is the great importance attached to languages. Latin, Greek, Hebrew and French were all on the curriculum, but a great deal of care and attention was also given to the mother tongue, doubtless because the pupils left much to be desired in this regard. Instruction in the Christian faith was of overriding importance. Even in the second form the pupils read the English translation of Claude Fleury's delineation of primitive Christianity, which Wesley himself had got to know so well as a youth, and in the third form this was taken a step further by means of William Cave's representation of the early Christians. From a doctrinal point of view, these books firmly established the standpoint of Anglican churchmanship from the very outset. In the fourth form the distinctively Puritan note of John Bunyan's *Pilgrim's Progress* was added, which meant in turn a new element of personal religion to counterbalance that of corporate religion. Anglicanism meant Christian life in the enduring forms of the common life, available to everyone as a binding tradition. Puritanism meant personal communion with God, working out one's own salvation. Even in the first stage of education the institutional and the personal aspects of the life of faith lent support to each other. Wesley wove the two strands together skilfully and effortlessly here as in his 'Christian Library'. At the same time the pupils read Thomas à Kempis's *Imitation of Christ (Imitatio Christi)* in the Ciceronian dress with which Sebastian Castellio had clothed it. They also translated the *Imatatio* into English and Fleury's depiction of the early Christians into Latin. The line of study begun with Bunyan's *Pilgrim's Progress* was continued in the fifth form by a close study of the biography of Thomas Haliburton (1674–1712), a Presbyterian minister who died early in life, who at the time of his premature death was a Professor at St Andrew's and had had to contend with grievous doubts about God. This biography, of which John Wesley was very fond, was translated into Latin in the next form. As is to be expected, the next stage of reading was in the biography which he considered to be the normative model of Christian living, that of Marquis Gaston Jean-Baptiste de Renty. This latter work was part of the sixth form course, in which a comparatively large amount of time was devoted to classics, with Caesar, Terence, Velleius Paterculus and Kennet's *Roman Antiquities*. Translation of selected Colloquies of Erasmus was also used to further the acquisition of Latin.

William Law's *Christian Perfection* was prescribed for the last year but one. Thus although Wesley had twice roundly parted company with its author, who had been the guide and counsellor so greatly admired by him in his youth, he still held this book in esteem. Bengel's introduction to Biblical chronology was read; from English poetry John Milton was on the syllabus and from classical literature Cicero's *The Offices* and Virgil's *Aeneid*; and included here, too, was the *Greek Antiquities* of John Potter, who was Bishop of Oxford in Wesley's younger days and later became Archbishop of Canterbury. In the final year William Law's *Serious Call to a Holy and Devout Life* was to be read, and then, by way of conclusion to the historical studies, Lewis's *Hebrew Antiquities*. From classical literature the prescribed books were Cicero's *Tusculan Questions*, selected passages from Ovid, Virgil, Horace, Juvenal, Persius and Martial, and in addition six books of Homer's *Iliad*. The reading of Biblical books in the original took the following form. The Epistles of St John were not to be studied until the seventh year; in the eighth year the Gospels and Genesis were read. No mention is made of the Pauline Epistles, much though they meant to John Wesley. This remains all the more enigmatic because he saw in justifying faith the essence of Christian truth.

Apart from mathematics, importance was attached to geography and to a limited degree to physics as well, in which John Wesley was particularly fascinated by electrical phenomena.[29] But broadly speaking the teachers gave the pupils instruction in Christian theology and classical antiquity, instruction which, as is only to be expected, conformed to the educational standards generally accepted in Britain at the time, particularly by taking over the medieval heritage in the liberal arts—logic, rhetoric and music.[30]

Wesley asked a great deal of the teachers and admitted that it had become difficult for him to find suitable ones, even though he had been in the favourable position of being in touch with the whole of England.[31] For, much as he expected great things of the pupils academically, his first and last concern was for genuine Christians. What mattered to him was combating the worldly bias built into the education and culture of the Enlightenment and replacing it by a Christian education which was at least its equal.[32] In point of fact, however, he was convinced that he offered something even better, and passed disparaging judgements, describing the situation in vivid, racy style, on the waste in time at Oxford and Cambridge, where lazy young men got their degrees on the cheap, because the examinations were so off-hand that nobody who had not known them at first hand would credit it.[33] If someone were to praise the professors of the two universities, his reply was that they were indeed learned, but that they had no real rapport with the undergraduates and kept on churning out the same old stuff with their noses stuck into their lecture notes while a mere handful paid any attention. But someone may ask: What about the tutors, who are surely supposed to have a direct responsibility for the undergraduates? Of their number only very few were worth their salt; the great majority had no mastery whatever of Latin, Greek, philosophy and mathematics, and were therefore quite incapable of fulfilling their task, even if they wanted to. Such abuses, he went on, were to have no place at Kingswood School. Wesley had sufficient confidence in the school to believe that youngsters who for three years had taken a regular and industrious part in the classes could hold their own with any undergraduate.[34] In the prescribed books, too, he reckoned that he set a higher standard than those of the generality of higher education, in that only morally unexceptionable authors with high principles were included. Like the Society for Promoting Christian Knowledge, he adhered firmly to the principle that formal qualities like stylistic elegance had to take second place.[35]

Wesley thought highly of Milton's *Treatise on Education* and took up one particular requirement made by him: namely, that the boys receive the whole of their education at the same place. This idea of not changing schools had imprinted itself on his mind as being a necessity.[36] Further, he had given thought to the proper site for a successful school. He decided, first of all, against a foundation in the midst of a large town. In such circumstances the many distractions prevented the children from accumulating knowledge; mixing with boys of the same age who had been brought up in an entirely different way was totally subversive of genuine Christian character. Secondly, he dismissed the idea that every type of child be admitted indiscriminately. What would be the inevitable result if the children came from homes with no Christian commitment? He referred to the experience of his eldest brother who, at Westminster School in London, had seen at first hand a father remove his son from boarding in his House because he (Samuel Wesley) had taught him the Catechism.[37] Nevertheless, proximity to a town made sound sense, and with his foundation his aim had been to reap the advantages and preclude the disadvantages. Kingswood was in just the right position, tucked away and yet within easy reach of Bristol, a buzzing commercial metropolis with a cosmopolitan atmosphere.

The educational and communal advantage of such an overtly Christian attitude on the part of teachers and pupils alike was seen by Wesley to consist in the fact that here unlike elsewhere knowledge was not pursued largely with a view to a career in church or state, but so to speak for its own sake. Knowledge was one of God's good gifts, and Christian knowledge sets us on the way that leads to eternal life. This was the only thing that mattered, and measured against this standard all values are seen in their proper perspective.[38] Wesley concluded his description of Kingswood School by placing the strongest possible emphasis on his own rôle and authority, citing the same Pauline text as he had invoked in 1739 in his dispute with Joseph Butler, Bishop of Bristol: 'For necessity is laid upon me; for woe is unto me if I preach not the gospel '(1 Corinthians 9[16]). He also quoted the apocryphal utterance of Luther at the end of the Diet of Worms, which he left untranslated in the German even in the midst of his English text: '*Hier stehe ich : Gott hilffe mich*,'[39] In conclusion, he alluded to time's wingéd chariot—he was sixty-five at this time— and stressed that he could no longer afford to lose any time.[40]

At few points in his endeavours did the radical, resolute, rigorous and remorseless bent in his make-up, his utter willingness to spend and to be spent in and for the service of God, his imperious authoritarianism, his riding rough-shod over others, come out into the open more blatantly than here in the field of education. At the same time, however, this ruthlessness of his here stands out in its full extent and stature because it meant renunciation on his own part; his human traits were completely suppressed for the sake of the cause, the task, the goal. But it was clear that in this sphere circumstances were bound to alter cases. The comparison which the venerable founder drew in 1781 and 1783 between what he had intended and what had become of his intentions proved in the event to be quite unfavourable from his point of view. The school had become unrecognizable: the rules were being flaunted, and instead of their rebellious spirits being trained with stern discipline for Jesus Christ, the boys were playing and rollicking about the place.[41] But he was not the sort of man to concede defeat. Far from it: that same year he reiterated his basic principles, and did so in this instance by disagreeing sharply with the chief authority of the time on education, Rousseau's *Émile*.[42] But now there is no longer any trace of a harsh, dictatorial 'Thou shalt not', a drill-major's bark, no harping on unquestioning obedience. Instead, John Wesley held up the lofty aim of a genuine Christian life in all its magnificence and potential. He described this life as a constant indwelling of holy tempers, as a genuine love of God and neighbour, as humility, gentleness, patience and contentedness, in fine, as the image of God, as the heart, the soul, the mind which was in Jesus Himself.[43] Could any demand be too exacting, any sacrifice too great, any price too high for such a life?[44]

# TEN

# John Wesley: Take Him for All in All

JOHN WESLEY'S career and his extremely arduous endeavours from the time of his conversion up to his death cover a time-span of virtually fifty-three years, more than half a century. Throughout this period he had a single, steady aim. The way in which he set about his task, the principles which he followed, the objectives which he set himself and also largely achieved, the methods by which he worked and the rôles which he assumed, the people with whom he dealt (not only his associates and the members of his societies, but also the opponents with whom over the years he had to do): all this remained amazingly consistent. Only in physical extent did his way of life change; in essence it had received its distinctive stamp in and with his conversion and its implications. Every supervenient factor served to enrich and deepen, to confirm and strengthen, but not to modify this life-style. Right through his life it was restoration of the primitive Christian stance in the present age that coloured his thinking. He had come to recognize with increasing clarity that its focal point was justification and regeneration, a conjunction in faith of earnest penitence with joy in salvation; and he saw its goal as being perfect love of God, Jesus Christ and our neighbour. Convinced as he was that both true Christianity and the success of his movement depended on it, he inculcated these principles with unflagging zeal. From the time when as a man of thirty-two he had resolved to seek out the true understanding of the Christian message on the mission field, taken as the authentic context of its origin, he held fast by his missionary obligation, critically to examine his own country, which for him was his primary field of responsibility. Equally, he refused to allow anything to shake his loyalty to the Church in which he had been born and nurtured and which by ordaining him had conferred on him his office and his evangelistic life's work.

This made his life self-contained to the point of stereotyped sameness—as is aptly reflected in his utterly unpretentious ways in matters of dress, food, sleep and relaxation. There was never at any point the slightest danger that external pressures—friends, colleagues or opponents, unforeseen events and special problems—might force him to alter his course. The expansion of his movement, the public stir which it caused, the powers of resistance which it developed in the face of ridicule, contempt, hostility and ostracism, did not puff him up with inordinate pride. Nor did misunderstanding and misrepresentation make him bitter in heart.

The diversity of his activities did not, therefore, threaten to tear him apart. In expending his energies in these different spheres, he did not dissipate them. At bottom the voice of the preacher, the theological writer, the biblical expositor, the pastor, the letter-writer, the educator, the organizer and the general commander was always pitched in the same key. Whether he read or wrote, whether he thought or spoke, whether he worked out his strategy or marshalled his troops for battle, whether he wooed people or laid down the law, he always remained the same. He identified himself completely with his movement; he lived through and shaped its history as if it were his own, and in so doing exemplified the modern objectification which ruthlessly demands the involvement of the individual as an impersonal obligation and completely eliminates human individuality. This is why for him the challenge to evangelize was never out of his mind for a single moment. This challenge was just as immediately real to him when he was preaching in a church or a preaching-house or in the open air as when he was riding through the countryside, observing its special features, and unexpectedly gained a travelling companion, or when he put up at some modest hostelry. In vain does one search for evidence in his life of relaxation and recreation. Like Otto Dibelius in our own time, his motto could have been: 'A Christian is always on duty.'[1] For him, as for Tertullian, the Christian life was discipline, obedience, rigorous training and self-denial. The fact that he could not infrequently be alarmingly and hurtfully brusque in manner and—how un-English of him!—would rather part company than compromise, stemmed from this implicit obedience to his Lord. In the *militia Christi*, of which he himself was a living embodiment and which he set over his school at Kingswood as the aim of education, there was no furlough. This would have belied the very nature of Christ's army.

The same was true of his theological thinking and opinions. For

him, matters of doctrine were of prime importance: he was remorseless in refuting false teaching. It was on this rock that his relations
with the Moravians foundered, relations which had passed through
every phase possible as between those who make common cause and
share a common faith—from glowing admiration and cordial agreement to profound mistrust and hostility for which he was prepared
to give reasons. Throughout all this the carrying note was disappointed love and abiding gratitude. Things had never sunk to
mere indifference. But the doctrinal question was also the determin-
ing factor in John Wesley's opposition to the prevailing theology of
the Enlightenment, an opposition to which he gave full vent in his
major controversy with John Taylor of Norwich over original sin
and in his denunciation of the Deistic scepticism of Conyers Middleton about the miracles of the Bible. His attitude to Roman Catholicism, too, was in the final analysis determined by doctrinal considerations, even though he neither made any secret of his admittedly
qualified admiration for Ignatius of Loyola as a warrior of Jesus
Christ nor had the slightest compunction in recommending Gaston
Jean-Baptiste de Renty and Gregory Lopez as models of Christian
piety. He conceived of and longed for Christian unity as an agreement in the truth of God's holy Word.[2] For him, theology was never
purely a matter of theory,[3] but meant searching out Christian truth
and translating it into life. To his mind, its implications in and for
practical personal piety productive of Christian fellowship were not a
result or an application of it, but of its very essence. Theology was
faith, and faith was by definition theology. His theological sermons
and his pastoral correspondence proved this just as clearly as the
catholicity of his 'Christian Library', which selected from all that was
available on the basis of the guiding principle of taking truth to ourselves and deriving support from it for our Christian life. It was no
coincidence that he gave biographies pride of place. Their efficacy
and importance ranked second only to the maxims and narratives of
the Bible; and conversely, the latter could have no finer corroboration
than personal experiences of those who had taken them seriously.

Both Wesley's colossal work-rate and his keen interest in multi-
farious subjects, including physics, medicine and foreign languages
(living and dead), only become explicable when we see that their
hidden source lay precisely in his single-mindedness. As is often the
case with men of small stature, this singleness of mind was matched

by its physical prerequisites—a tough constitution which defied repeated breakdowns in health and a spartan disregard for personal needs. His sinewy, upright figure, his firm gait, his piercing eyes and his aquiline nose gave the immediate impression of meeting a man utterly self-possessed. He had a commanding presence.[4] His labours had one end in view; whatever he did was aimed at the one target. All this exhibits a singularly modern style of deliberateness and purposiveness; there is in him no trace of a carefree abandonment to life, a happy-go-lucky or even improvident use of time, a dreaming or idling away of life which leads on the grand scale to absorption in the cosmos or in the historical process, and on the small scale to creative brain-waves. In having such a deliberateness, which was not, however, taken to the point of the crippling self-flagellation inherent in the dissection of one's own ego or one's own destiny, Wesley was a child of his times and a debtor to the Puritan tradition of the custody of oneself.

To be self-contained means in turn to be profoundly lonely. Wesley had many friends, but not one who was really and truly close to him. The circumstances of both his betrothals speak volumes here: he let nobody in on the secret, indeed he blatantly ignored the precepts of his own movement by turning his back on the advice and opinions of others. He hardly ever availed himself of the pastoral opportunities provided by the Bands, although he originally intended to do so. Instead, by confiding his thoughts and feelings to his *Journal*, and by having this published at intervals shortly after he had written it up, he made his thoughts known to the general public in vindication of decisions already taken. Although he was not averse to complaining that he was so much on his own,[5] in his heart of hearts this was just the way he wanted it, and undoubtedly his movement would have vacillated in its course, especially in its relations with the mother Church, if it had been led by a collective leadership. For his closest colleague, who had specifically hitched his wagon to John's star, his brother Charles, had wavered time and again, particularly with regard to the Moravians and concerning the system of lay preachers. On the other hand, despite his misgivings as to the rightness of the course upon which John entered, he had never gone so far as even attempting to part company with him. This makes it abundantly plain who supported whom and who depended upon whom.

Seen in the perspective of church history, the striking thing about

John Wesley and his movement is the disparity between the background situation and the end if view. To be precise: the eighteenth century, within which the whole of his long life fell, was the age of reason, as Thomas Paine (1737–1809), the Anglo-American political writer, has aptly called it.[6] This age saw itself destined to push through wide-sweeping social reforms, a radical transformation in every aspect and every department of life based on the principles of reason. In the case of Christianity this meant setting natural religion above God's revelation in Jesus Christ. Most of those who pursued this aim did so not with the intention of replacing Christianity but of supplying its deficiencies. They were convinced that their programme would liberate the basic Christian principles from the suspicion of being gratuitous assertions and ensure their general credibility. John Wesley could not go along with enterprises of this kind. Here he could only voice an emphatic No. To his mind, the pristine Christianity of the apostles supplied man's every need. All his zeal was devoted to this. He was utterly convinced that primitive Christianity could be restored in his own day and age, as in every generation. At the same time, however, he was thoroughly modern both in his diagnosis of, and his remedy for, the situation. He realized that the era in which Christianity had held institutional dominion and the way in which this dominance had been reflected in privileges for the Church, had run out. England and Europe generally could no longer be regarded as Christian countries; their inhabitants were no better placed than the heathen whom he had known in North America. And so, with a dynamism unprecedented in church history, he sought to free Christianity from the shackles of custom and tradition, without jettisoning them completely. Like the early Church, he was a revolutionary in his fundamental purpose and the methods he used. At the same time, however, he was conservative in his churchmanship, respecting as he did the tradition which he inherited. His endeavours were aimed at fostering the personal life of faith as that for which institutional custom was the humble foundation, at a 'free church' which would be the apotheosis and *raison d'être* of the national Church as by law established. And yet 'the Church' was not, strictly speaking, the object of his interest. It would be nearer the truth to say that everything he did, everything he planned, everything he put forward, everything he took under his direction, gave expression to an endeavour to approximate more closely to the true aim and goal of the Church, i.e. each individual's life with God. For him, the pro-visional nature of the Church, its taking second place to Christian perfection in finding personal fulfilment in and through the restora-tion of the divine image, was beyond dispute, though without him thereby setting up a dichotome between the two. Wesley never en-gaged in polemics against people or institutions, but only against doctrines—a fact which was particularly high-lighted by his rejection of the doctrine of predestination. For him, what was at stake was the purity of the Gospel and its being appropriated by men. This con-cern for truth did not prevent him from showing respect for the Church as an institution at every opportunity, from loving its liturgy, from reviving its rule on fasting or from readily acknowledging the markedly Patristic features in its own self-understanding. All this, however, was not an end in itself, but a means to an end. Restoration of the primitive Christian stance in its totality was always his guiding principle; never for a single moment did he diverge from this. This concern for repristination was also what had basically attracted him to German Pietism: he saw in the Moravians the early Christian com-munity exemplified, just as he saw in Gaston Jean-Baptiste de Renty a living embodiment of an individual Christian worthy of the early Church. One might be tempted to call this attitude to early Chris-itanity conservative, especially as it was directed against the rational-istic Deism of the Age of the Enlightenment so effectively and com-prehensively championed by William Whiston (1667–1752) in his Unitarian masterpiece, *Primitive Christianity revived* (published in 5 Volumes, 1711–12), as a result of which Whiston had broken with the Religious Societies,[7] particularly because they were based on a pre-critical faith in the infallibility of the Bible which carried with it an indiscriminate treatment of the Old and New Testaments as the literal word of God. In a deeper sense, however, this attitude of Wesley's was revolutionary. For in Wesley's view Scriptural Chris-tianity was an indictment of, and dynamite to, the present age. He took the criterion of canonicity so seriously that for him every sub-sequent epoch stood in principle at the bar of the early Church. At the same time, for him as for the German Pietists, the early Christian period guaranteed by its very historicity that it could be realized in the present age.

This interplay of modernity and adherence to the old, or more correctly the original ways, can be fascinatingly observed in yet another connexion. Wesley was never triflingly employed, and was all too easily fascinated by the attempt to calculate work done, or, taking this principle to extremes, by the sheer volume of work done. Time and motion, the dominant forces in our modern way of life, were also highly determinative for him. His daily routine, which involved sixteen to eighteen hours' work per day between 4 a.m. and 10 p.m.; the vast numbers in his congregations, which went into thousands or at least hundreds; his preaching three to four times in one day; his rides and journeys from one preaching engagement to another, during which he read or wrote; his able, efficient and even in the external sense successful organizing ability—all this gives the feel of a business man of drive and ambition, almost of the organization man. The horse which carried him from one place to another is the precursor of the motor-car. The time spent in the solitude of his study and little oratory was the exception that proves the rule. It is impossible to point convincingly to any historical precedent for the way in which he ordered his day and his work. The Reformers Luther, Zwingli, Calvin, Melanchthon and Bucer were doubtless just as tirelessly occupied as he was. But they did not travel anything like as much as Wesley, who was nearly always on the move. Calvin steered Protestantism from Geneva by writing letters and books—just as Luther had done from Wittenberg. Similarly, wide influence was exercised by the Pietist figures, Philip Jakob Spener and August Hermann Francke, but they too based themselves primarily at home. They propagated their ideas by letters of counsel and made their own places of work into Christian centres. Count Zinzendorf, to be sure, travelled very frequently indeed. But his journeyings bore quite another stamp; they were tours of reconnaissance with a view to founding communities, rather than a modern itinerant preaching ministry. In Britain itself no parallel whatever can be drawn, because the Church of England attached the utmost importance to continuing the medieval parish system. Finally, the social aspect of Wesley's evangelistic efforts was modern. Although he owed the first inspiration to his younger friend George Whitefield, his own concern too was for the neglected strata of society, and he expressed this concern without the class-conscious overtones of aristocratic benevolence, but rather with the direct, convincing spontaneity of Christian love, which goes out to men in their situation of need. Another modern aspect of his movement was its rapid growth from small beginnings which resulted in the members having a direct say in many decisions: for instance, in the purchase of a plot of ground, the erection of a preaching-house or a school (as at Kingswood), the raising of a collection for the poor, but also and especially in the admission or exclusion of individuals or groups and in doctrinal controversy. All this was democracy in action, and ran counter to the authoritarian character and hierarchical structure inherited by the Church of England from the Middle Ages, a difference of ethos which, though never deliberately put into words, was nevertheless part of the very air it breathed. But all this was done in fulfilment of the age-long task of bringing men to God by conversion and faith, by forgiveness of sins and re-dedication to the will of Jesus. The outward forms were novel, but the message was the historic Gospel, and had a claim to be accepted. If it was not, then the fault did not lie with the message, but with the age. What was taken in hand here by Wesley for the first time in church history, i.e. an attempt to bring the Christian Gospel to men who were estranged from it, and to do this by using the most up-to-date methods possible, methods which only latched on to traditional structures as springboards for action, was to happen again and again in time to come. To this extent Methodism was a pioneer design for the history of the modern church. Another essential aspect of the same matter was the conscious use of tracts as a means of propaganda.[8] John Wesley was aware that the exhortation of people to regular Bible reading would fall on deaf ears unless and until the prior necessity of evoking an interest in it on the part of eighteenth-century man was met. Hence his books; hence his 'Christian Library'; hence his periodical the *Arminian Magazine*, which he published from 1778 on; hence his emphasis on biography and letters; hence, lastly, the pastoral conversation in small groups and the organization built up around them. Wesley gave real leadership; and the ready response to this lead proves that for all its rigour it met the spiritual needs of those who were led.

The obverse side of Wesley's being self-contained, i.e. his Pietist preoccupation with saving souls, was inevitably a narrow, limited outlook on life and the world. The things which in other quarters met the needs of the eighteenth century—the delight in nature, which was then just beginning to come into bloom; the enthusiasm for independent thinking, which took the form of a *philosophia ab oro*; the early stages of the psychological novel as an independent literary form in Samuel Richardson and Henry Fielding; the transformation of Puritanism into a rationalist and pre-Romantic outlook in Daniel Defoe; the portraiture in the grand manner, taking the whole landscape as its backdrop, in Sir Joshua Reynolds, and the landscape painting of Thomas Gainsborough—all this made scarcely any impression on Wesley, although he did sit for Reynolds and for George Romney.[9] On the other hand, Edward Young's *Night-Thoughts* did make an impression on him, and he went to untold lengths to include them in his lay preachers' select library by slightly modifying and elucidating them. He accorded Thomas Gray, whom he justly esteemed for his greatness as a poet, no more than lukewarm admiration, his reason being that Gray had forfeited every friendship because of his touchiness and hurtful arrogance.[10] On 17th August 1758 he heard Handel's 'Messiah' sung in Bristol Cathedral and commented that several choruses surpassed his expectations. But it was significant that he also immediately went on to draw a comparison with the attentiveness of this congregation during a sermon, a comparison which proved unfavourable to the latter.[11] He was widely read in the classics, a cultural standard taken for granted at the time. He was so familiar with Shakespeare and Milton that he was able to quote them with facility.[12] But was he really seized by what they had to say about reality and man? This is a very moot point. The fact that he detested Bernard Mandeville's *The Fable of the Bees*, which founded English utilitarian ethics by cold-blooded commendation of private vices as public virtues, and that he saw in this book a cynical intensification of Machiavelli's Prince, [13] was a foregone conclusion. He certainly did not live in cloud cuckoo land. Rousseau's anthropology, which placed more than a generation of poets and educators under its spell and spurred men to great endeavours, met with his strong disapproval. However, he paid no further attention to the French Revolution.

Thus for all his detailed criticism and for all his assiduous, discriminate reading, Wesley lacked an all-encompassing, balanced, circumspect stance towards his own age. In this respect he was unable to become a trail-blazer and leader. He was aware of this limitation in himself, but regarded it not as a strait-jacket but rather as a divinely imposed responsibility. It was significant that he insisted on defending the ascetic, rigorist Montanists as genuine, scriptural Christians.[14] Thus he could only oppose the advancing secularization in every sector of life, which, one must admit, on British soil proceeded more slowly than on the Continent and without the aggressive tone that it adopted there; he could not overcome it by means of any profound theological concept of creation worked out on a grand scale. Yet who, at the time, could have recognized here a challenge to Christianity, or risen to meet it? The only alternatives conceived of in the England of the day were (on the one hand) the facile accommodation to secularism exemplified by the rationalistic, Supranaturalist apologetics which accepted natural religion without reserve, and (on the other hand) the radical repudiation of secularism which Wesley adopted. There was not a single theologian who was really and truly more than a match for the spirit of the age.

Within its limits, however, Wesley's impact on his own people must be described as powerful and significant. Through him and in him they realized the full gravity of Christianity and were saved from mere conformity. His narrow-minded attitude to the world contrasted sharply with an open-mindedness towards fellow-Christians and different denominations. He was a loyal Anglican who kept to the liturgy of the Book of Common Prayer. But he felt free to introduce the observance of the Covenant Service, which was a development of the original Scots Presbyterian idea. He felt equally free to enter upon the closest collaboration with the Congregationalist leader Philip Doddridge, a collaboration which bore fruit in his 'Christian Library' and his Biblical exegesis. Although he did not enjoy or foster any special friendships with Baptists and Quakers, it was not his deliberate intention to stand aloof from them.[15] Quite the reverse: he seized every opportunity that came his way to discuss matters with them, and in these discussions general agreement constantly alternated with disagreement over particular points. His physician, Dr Fothergill, who saved his life in November 1753, was a Quaker.[16] This is Wesley as we see him through modern eyes.

But how was he regarded within in his own ranks—by those who were closest to him, but over whom he exercised the strictest authority? When he died on 2nd March 1791, several of his most loyal colleagues were gathered round his sick-bed and testified that he who had been to them a 'beloved pastor, father and friend' was now to receive his starry crown.[17]

The repercussions of his life's work which are to be heard in the various funeral orations and obituary addresses give us some indication of what he meant to his own people. The man who succeeded him as leader of the movement was the erstwhile lawyer and Anglican clergyman, Dr Thomas Coke (1747–1815), who in 1776 had experienced a conversion centred on assurance of salvation through faith in the forgiveness of sins under the Methodist lay preacher Thomas Maxfield. Prior to this he had had repeated doubts as to whether he was worthy of the priestly office, especially as in his early manhood he had been a leading and highly popular member of the local corporation of his native Brecon in South Wales after completing his studies at Oxford. These misgivings were now overcome, and he requested an interview with John Wesley. A year later, in August 1777, he identified himself fully with the Methodist movement and won the confidence of its leader so swiftly that in 1784 the latter appointed him along with Francis Asbury as 'Superintendents' or 'Bishops' for North America. The circumstances leading up to this were singular and significant. After the triumph of the cause of independence in North America, which he deeply deplored, John Wesley had become convinced that in future there would no longer be any place there for the Church of England. Which is what in fact happened when a new independent body emerged with the name of the Protestant Episcopal Church. This meant in turn, of course, that the Methodist Societies, formerly of Anglican allegiance, had to relinquish their dependence on the mother-country. Now more than ever before, they had to be really autonomous. Because in 1780 John Wesley had received no reply from the competent authority—Dr Lowth, Bishop of London—to his request that he (Lowth) ordain at least one Methodist preacher to assist the pastoral work in the New World, he now felt doubly compelled to take matters into his own hands. Now that independence had been achieved in North America, a further approach to an Anglican prelate was nonsensical and could only make confusion worse confounded. So he appointed Thomas Coke and Francis Asbury. He had thought the matter over carefully. The procedure followed by the Church of Alexandria in the fourth and fifth centuries, according to which when a bishop died the presbyters chose the next Bishop from their own ranks so as to avoid becoming dependent on some external power, served as his model. He deduced the constitutional basis for this procedure from the parity between bishops and presbyters in the ancient Church which Lord Peter King had proved to his satisfaction. He had chosen Coke (along with Asbury) not least because if need arose he would be able to defend property rights in his professional capacity as a lawyer.[18] In other ways, too, Coke was a man after Wesley's own heart. Like Wesley himself and like his original designated successor, John William Fletcher, he had Anglican orders. Above all, he had realized, perhaps more fully than any other colleague, the thoroughly apostolic stamp of the Methodist movement, and had put this awareness into practice both in his evangelistic work in England and in going overseas as a missionary to the heathen in the West Indies. True enough, he had only adhered to John Wesley at a late stage, but this made him all the more able to weigh and assess Wesley at a developed stage in his work and thought.

The funeral oration on Wesley which he delivered at Baltimore and Philadelphia on 1st and 8th May 1791, was based on 2 Kings 2[11-12], and compared the deceased with Elijah. The only possible result of such an approach was an idealized picture, but one not without quite realistic traits. It began at the very heart of things—with his communion with God, the like of which was hard to find.[19] It then moved on to the abundant evidence of God's providence in his life. In this context he instanced the way in which time and again Wesley had been preserved from physical harm when he was thrown off his horse. Stress was then laid on the central part which self-sacrifice and self-denial played in his life, and particularly on his abandonment of the ease and comfort of Oxford, which was so congenial to his great liking for ancient literature and places. Instead of Oxford he had chosen the privations of Georgia. A sharper contrast than this it is impossible to imagine—life in the raw in place of culture of the highest order! Then, when he returned home again, he did not resume the academic life, which had such an appeal for him, but devoted himself to serving the poor and uneducated by the proclamation of the Gospel of salvation. Nor did Coke omit to mention such an apparently unimportant detail as the fact that his diet in Georgia had been as meagre as possible and had consisted solely of vegetables, milk and water. What governed him was an insatiable desire to do good.[20] Finally on this head, Coke openly admitted that he had never known anyone who had sacrificed his own comfort and pleasure, personal advantage and friendship, for the sake of Christ's Church as freely and willingly as Wesley had.[21] There then followed a eulogy of his courage. Wesley proved this by his vigorous protests against the besetting sins of England and North America. In the case of England it was the widespread superficiality, dissipation and worldliness, the very antithesis of the godliness of yore, against which he directed his attacks; in the case of North America, as Coke said with an obvious dig at the contemporary situation with its atmosphere of intoxication with victory and liberty, it was slavery and the oppression of the coloured people.[22] Then Coke mentioned his wholeheartedness, his exacting way of life. Apart from never being in one place for two minutes as a result of his incessant travels, he referred in this connexion to the profusion of his writings and the constant necessity for him to switch from one activity to another. He had no hesitation in setting him alongside the greatest men in church history, including Origen, Athanasius or even Paul. The whole of this evaluation of his life's work may be summed up by the one word: unsparing. Wesley paid regard neither to himself nor to others nor to the enemy whom he confronted, i.e. the world. 'Wesley *contra mundum*': in this pithy phrase from the ancient Church, originally coined with reference to Athanasius, Coke found the key to the meaning of the deceased Wesley's life.[23]

On 26th July 1791 another leading associate, the Anglican clergyman Joseph Benson (1748–1822),[24] who had taught classics at Kingswood School and had been appointed to be the principal of the college for the Calvinist Methodist preachers at Trevecca in Wales, but who because of the anti-Calvinist position which he shared with Wesley had incurred the wrath of Selina, Countess of Huntingdon, had returned to Kingswood, preached his funeral oration at a critical juncture, i.e. at the first Conference after Wesley's death, held in Manchester. It was Benson who had summoned Wesley, along with John William Fletcher, to reform the Church of England. Now he based his final tribute on the Biblical text: 'Remember them which have the rule over you, who have spoken unto you the word of God: whose faith follow, considering the end of their conversation (Hebrews 13[7]).

In the first part of his appreciation, which is biographical, he quoted several paragraphs from Wesley's *Journal*, thereby committing himself to Wesley's self-critique. What was particularly striking was that he included in these quotations Wesley's harsh self-judgement of 8th January 1738, in which he accused himself of unbelief, pride, irrecollection and frivolity. Then he spotlighted the part which

Peter Böhler had played in helping him find true faith and concluded with the triumphant outcome in his conversion. From then on Wesley was strong in faith and mighty in prayer, with the result that he took in his stride superhuman efforts, dangers, persecutions and difficulties. He set his course and ran full steam ahead with absolute trust in God, with enviable assurance and rare courage, with exemplary patience and genuine friendliness. His life was one continuous good work; his own catch-phrase, 'doing good', which he had taken over from the Religious Societies, fitted him to a tee. His humility and self-possession; his abstemiousness, which led him to make do with neat, simple clothing and only one square meal a day; his amiable sociability; his prolific and extensive reading, which never left him at a loss for a topic of conversation—all this made him a veritable paragon of Christian virtues and human qualities.

Nevertheless, these were only the external features of his character and activity. His real self only came out in his preaching. Here Benson emphasized his simplicity and clarity, which went straight to the matter in hand and dispensed with every unnecessary word, so that when he spoke, the Word of God, as Hebrews 4$^{12}$ puts it, was living and active and sharper than a two-edged sword. The same was correspondingly true of his written work: in his clear, manly style he reminded Benson of a celebrated author of the time, Joseph Addison.

But Wesley was even greater as a bishop and pastor than he was as a preacher. Or to put it another way: his preaching and writing find their fulfilment in episcope. In Benson's opinion, nobody had since the Apostolic Age exercised as much immediate pastoral responsibility for so many people as Wesley had. What is more, he took the apostles as models for his own work. The vast numbers of people who turned to him for help and cleaved to him as their guide and counsellor, made assistance indispensable. The class system, the pastoral care, created the need for the lay preachers; and the need was met.

The content of his sermons became the real distinguishing mark of the Methodists in an age which looked to quite different ideas and experiences for fulfilment: justification through faith, regeneration, entire santification—these were the truths which he pressed home with all the force at his command. But he did not simply require these things or mouth them as mere slogans. No; they were to become real in his own personal experience, lest he be guilty of hypocrisy. The experience did not in itself prove the truth, the latter being derived from the Biblical promise, but it secured against a counterfeit or a meaningless, nominal Christianity.

Benson roughly calculated that on average Wesley had preached 1,000 to 1,200 sermons a year, had travelled 3,000 to 4,000 miles a year, and that he had been in personal communication, by word or letter, with 10,000 to 12,000 people a year. In addition to this, he had been an avid reader and written books of his own. All this had only been made possible because he used to the full every available moment of his time. In this way his long life had, as it were, been made even longer. Here the typically modern, organized approach to life which he put into practice was recognized and appreciated by one of his most devoted colleagues as a rudimentary element in every aspect of his work. This indicates the degree to which he was felt to be a Christian of modern times.

The phenomenal success with which he met was a God-given increase. For him, as for Paul, his congregations were his credentials. They can do no other than remain true to his teaching, transpose it into their own lives, pass it on to others, take care not to bury in the ground the talent entrusted to them.[25]

Benson did not hit upon the kind of striking formula which Coke had with the motto, 'Wesley *contra mundum*'. Broadly speaking, his representation of Wesley does not come across with the force which results from concentrating on some central point. In addition to the above, he had also enlarged upon Wesley's culture. In harmony with the spirit of the age, he had drawn special attention to his keen interest in mathematics, praised his historical bent, which made him able to draw a sharp distinction between the probable and the certain, and, finally, had extolled his capacity for logical thinking and his knowledge of the modern languages French and German. Even so, Wesley's real concerns in his basic understanding of Christian truth had been clearly identified: justification through faith, regeneration, radical transformation and sanctification in love. Full justice had been seen to be done to the part played by his conversion in the whole course of his spiritual development. Again, it is significant that from among Wesley's writings he had specified his *Notes on the New Testament*, a commentary which drew on Bengel's *Gnomon*, his *Sermons*, his *Earnest Appeal to Men of Reason and Religion*, and his refutation of John Taylor's book against the doctrine of original sin.[26]

This was yet another indication that he had clearly recognized his rightful claims as a theologian.

A simpler memorial to the deceased Wesley than those of Coke and Benson was given by the lay preacher Richard Rodda, in a sermon preached at Oldham Street Methodist chapel, Manchester, on 13th March 1791. The text was Hebrews 11[4]: 'Through faith he being dead yet speaketh.' In the biographical part he gave Wesley's conversion special emphasis by quoting Wesley verbatim. He made particular mention of how indebted Wesley had been to Christian David on the occasion of his visit to the Moravians at Herrnhut, but also did not omit to assert that he was unable to approve of several things about them. He then deftly sketched his evangelistic work, emphasizing the class system and the use of lay agency, the organization into circuits, and the annual Conferences of the preachers, to which Rodda ascribed the utmost importance for the corporate endeavours of the movement. At these Conferences the scrupulosity and integrity which marked his discipline of the servants of the Word had particularly impressed him. He was convinced that no comparable eruption had taken place in the history of Christianity since the Apostolic Age.

Admittedly the earthen vessels which God used for this purpose were quite inadequate for the work itself, but he adjudged of Wesley that he was singularly gifted for it, and specifically as a preacher. He was the very acme of the Christian orator, being as he was earnest, decisive, above party and totally dedicated to the cause. He never wasted words, but went straight as a die to the heart of the matter and pricked the consciences of his hearers. He knew what was in man and the devious paths which sin takes. Thus he could set forth with equal trenchancy both man's total depravity and his utter inability to save himself. He could persuade people that only the blood of Jesus Christ had the power and efficacy to do this.[27] Justification and sanctification alike took place by grace alone; only firm reliance on God's promises guaranteed that we attain salvation. The righteousness which God bestows on us as an unmerited and free gift by forgiving our sin was the quintessence of his message—though he roundly rejected the Antinomian error that men are given licence to sin.[28] Indeed, he attached the utmost importance to both his preachers and the members of the Methodist movement yearning for Christian perfection and setting their hearts on being filled with all the fullness of

God. He answered with a resounding No his closing rhetorical question as to whether the flock was left without a shepherd now that the shepherd had died, and replied that God would provide and indeed had already done so insofar as a large number of itinerant and local preachers were ready to continue the work in the spirit of its founder.[29] Here the movement and its origin—Wesley's conversion and his message of salvation—were set right at the centre of the picture. It was clearly recognized that both his conversion and his message were essentially the same in meaning—justification of the sinner by God's free grace, which had been realized once and for all in and with the death of Jesus Christ and which was appropriated by us in faith. For this Rodda quoted a favourite verse from John Wesley himself.[30] He had reproduced in simple language the decisive thing about his leader. The special merit of this panegyric to Wesley lay in the fact that Wesley was not understood as the master and fashioner of the movement, but as its servant and instrument.

Another lay preacher, Samuel Bradburn, began his characterization of Wesley with the concept of the 'great man'. His definition, unlike Schleiermacher's at a later date, was not in terms of his impact on history—namely, that he founded not so much a school as an era[31]—but in terms of his spiritual orientation. For a great man to arise, he says, outstanding gifts must be stretched to the full in an exceptional way. It is then that extraordinary results follow.[32] Wesley was endowed with a wide range of abilities, which were brought together to great effect. In thinking, he was clear and penetrating; in language, he was decisive, articulate and eloquent; and his memory was excellent. He would therefore have made a first-class lawyer. He never preached without preparation, and never got carried away on a wave of emotion. Doubtless he did himself a disservice by preaching the Word three or four times a day; if he had preached twice, his preaching would have been more effective. The opinion once passed on him in Edinburgh that 'it was not a masterly sermon but only a master could give it', hit the nail right on the head.[33] His style was simple, clear and concise, never circumstantial, boring or laborious. Earnestness was the hall-mark of everything he said.[34] This made Bradburn all the more surprised to find that apart from when he was preaching he was an amiable, cheerful companion who enjoyed a good joke. Indeed, he had heard him say even in the pulpit that 'sour godliness is the devil's religion'.[35] His punctilious courtesy would have made him an ideal courtier; and yet he could converse with equal ease with simple peasants and trades-people. His friendly disposition was particularly noticeable when he was talking to young people. In connexion with such conversations he frequently voiced the thought: 'I reverence a young man, because he may be useful when I am in the dust.' He loved children and liked having them around him, being mindful of Jesus' words that we should take them as an example. He was by disposition deeply sensitive to little things.[36]

He was a guileless, honest kind of man, who would trust completely those with whom he was dealing, at times to his own hurt; for he was not seldom exploited by hangers-on. Equally, he had a keen sense of justice, but an even stronger inclination to love. Sensible of the proprieties though he was, and not slow to realize when he was being put upon, he could forgive and forget.[37]

Hard to believe as it may sound, he was extremely reluctant to reprove people. Least of all would he remonstrate with a servant, though he was of the social standing to do so. To be sure, he could be bitingly sarcastic; nevertheless, he seldom was so and then only half-heartedly. At bottom he had a sensitive spirit. Bradburn had seen him weep and his lips quiver when he was speaking about the sufferings of Jesus and the torments of hell. He gave all he had to the poor. The amount he gave away in the Connexional year 1780–81, which as his secretary Bradburn knew exactly, totalled the phenomenal sum of £1,400. He himself was hauled with his master from door to door in London, the two of them freezing in the bitter cold winter weather, while they begged money, coal and clothes for the poor. Thus no effort, no self-sacrifice had been too much for this over-worked man.[38]

He wanted nothing for himself in life; what he received in money, chiefly for the devotional tracts sold by his preachers, was the common property of all the preachers. He looked after them like a father, particularly by means of legacies and gifts which were entrusted to him. Thus he lived by the Pauline maxim: 'As poor, and yet making many rich' (2 Corinthians 6[10]). The way in which he distributed money or goods to the poor, far from humiliating the recipients, was always thoroughly unaffected and courteous.[39]

He brought God into the minor events and problems of everyday life. Similarly, he had no hesitation in praying about them. Thus for him there was nothing in life outside the sphere of God's influence.[40]

Deserving of mention was his neatness, orderliness and punctuality. Everything he undertook was done advisedly, not precipitately, haphazardly or in the heat of the moment. Because he used every moment to the full and, as he advised his preachers, was never unemployed, he was never in undue haste. Again, his writing, which he normally did while standing at his desk, went slowly. This is why his works were consistent and clear. It is truly astonishing how he wrote so many pages while keeping to such a steady pace.[41]

He never spoke of himself. His modesty precluded him from doing so, although he had a great deal to offer others out of his vast experience. He had a deep-seated, acute sense of his own sinfulness, and his one desire was that God Himself might kindle a flame of sacred love on the mean altar of his heart.[42]

A saint: this is how Bradburn summed up his portrait of Wesley,[43] which he hoped had done him justice. In fact he had offered more than the others, because he had depicted him primarily as a man. In so doing, he had preserved for posterity traits which otherwise would have been lost.

The most original and the most fertile obituary address was given by the lay preacher and physician, Dr John Whitehead, who attended him during his last days and also became his first biographer. This was the official funeral sermon at his burial service, held in London on 9th March 1791. It gains a unique position by virtue of the fact that as far as possible Whitehead related to Wesley the categories of thought which typified the Enlightenment, and thus sought to explain him to his contemporaries. In choosing for his text 2 Samuel 3[38]: 'Know ye not that there is a prince and a great man fallen this day in Israel?', his aim was to give full play to the senses of the Hebrew root שַׂר (šar), which moved between the connotation of a leader and that of a man of outstanding moral character. He stressed first of all his extensive learning, which, in addition to his knowledge of ancient and modern languages and their respective literature, included above all such a thorough familiarity with the New Testament that generally speaking the wording of the original Greek text came more naturally to mind than that of the English Version.[44] Such was the harvest reaped by his daily reading in the original text! Whitehead hastened to mention particularly, and to commend to an age with a predominately scientific outlook, a unique work of Wesley's— his theological *Compendium of Natural Philosophy* derived from

Johann Franz Buddeus.[45] Although he was not conversant with the various branches of higher mathematics, he nevertheless mastered Newton's *Principia mathematica* and his theory of light and colours. Whitehead saw his penchant for logic as a proof of a search for truth and a love of truth which would never rest content until it had succeeded in getting to the very root of things.[46]

These intellectual assets, says Whitehead, again entirely in the spirit of the Enlightenment, were matched by moral qualities. From early youth Wesley was punctilious in the performance of his duties; he was a conscientious man, who submitted himself even to uncomfortable truths, related them to his own life and resolutely translated them into action. But he was also a man dedicated to God, who learned from the Bible that all his own deeds were unable to put him in a right relationship with God. Thus by bitter experience he won through to the conviction that he could only be justified by the grace of God and that he had to accept this in faith, or rather that he was permitted to accept this in faith. This new-found conviction alienated his former friends. It must have seemed incomprehensible to them that a man like him, a paragon of virtue and the very epitome of conscientiousness, should suddenly deem himself to be a sinner, and so they simply took him to be mad. But this opinion of himself was far from being fanaticism; it had been compellingly borne in upon him by the nature of God, by ruthless self-examination and by the asseverations of the Bible. Is it at all conceivable, asks Whitehead, that a man like him, a thinker who formed his judgements rationally and carefully, a thinker who went to the root of matters, a thinker who was totally committed to the truth, should turn out to be an 'enthusiast'? The fact of the matter is, as he himself relates, that when he heard the startling experiences of counsellors and pastors of his acquaintance who had known justifying faith for themselves, he took out his New Testament and insisted on what had been said to him being endorsed by it.[47]

Hence it was reason, highly critical reflection, sustained independent thinking, that was his criterion, whatever he heard or thought, desired or undertook. In coming to close grips with the Bible, he exercised his reason to discover its true meaning. Indeed, Whitehead goes so far as to make the daring statement that he did not accept any doctrine—not even from the Bible—which was not for him agreeable to reason.[48] However, everything ultimately depended on what was meant by reason. Wesley meant eternal reason, the primal reason which was expressed in the nature of things. This is how he formulated matters, in harmony with the Platonic tradition of Anglican theology. A religion is rational if and when it is consonant with the nature of God and the nature of man. This he certainly claimed to be true of Christianity as evinced by the Bible. The Gospel disclosed God's perfection in every way. It revealed the love of God, in that He gave the world a Redeemer. It made known the wisdom of God in the whole plan of salvation. It proved the justice of God in the death of the Redeemer. It set forth the omnipotence of God in transforming a man into a child of God, a transformation which brought in its train holiness and happiness at the very point where previously there had been nothing but sin and despair. Finally, God's perfection was made manifest in effecting life eternal where previously eternal death had reigned supreme. Therefore, in Whitehead's opinion, the Gospel thoroughly corresponded to the rational concepts held by all men of the harmony and unity existing between the divine attributes. No one was more given to showing the harmony of these attributes than John Wesley himself. Did not this prove the magnitude of his whole outlook and what a great person he was altogether?[49]

Conversely, the Gospel corresponded to the nature of man. For man is a blind, misguided, ignorant creature. Only the Gospel as a system of moral truths enlightens him and puts him on right lines. Question is, however, Is man also capable of complying with these instructions? Does he not time and again lack the strength to do so? Does he not constantly fail in the line of duty? Does not his conscience convince him that he is doing wrong? Therefore, says Whitehead, skillfully pursuing his line of argument within the terms of reference prescribed by the Enlightenment, the Gospel must be more than a system of moral truths, which is how it initially presents itself. Man is, in the words of the Bible, dead in trespasses and sins. The Gospel comes to him as a promise; the Spirit of God accompanies the Word of promise and the other means of grace; He effects repentance in the sinner and enables him to appropriate the offered pardon. For grace is in essence forgiveness, a personal offer and a personal gift. Was this not the message that was repeated over and over again by this great servant of the Gospel now gone to his rest?[50]

Nevertheless, the Gospel does not stop short at forgiveness. It goes on to entire sanctification of our hearts and our whole manner of life.

Dead to the world and alive to God: such is the motto of the Christian. This means loving the Lord our God with all our heart and our neighbour as ourselves. To this end God has promised in the Gospel continual support through His Spirit. Could we desire more than this message of salvation reveals?[51]

Since this message is a long-term and carefully considered plan, everything depended on communicating the divine plan in its proper sequence. This, too, was done by John Wesley in an exemplary manner. He began with the first step that leads to Christianity, i.e. with repentance, and thus pointed the way to a genuine personal experience of devotion. By making this observation, Whitehead had in mind the Enlightenment's passion for methodical clarity and certainty, a passion which corresponded to its enthusiasm for education. However, this was not for him the main point. His real emphasis fell on Wesley's having followed the example of Jesus and the apostles. And so he unobtrusively recommended to those who took the Enlightenment for granted the very figures which the Deists had tried to discredit in the eyes of their own age. The suggestion that progress in the Christian life was comparable with the process of learning and maturation in every skill, whether practical or academic, met half-way the Enlightenment's bent for method, its enthusiasm for education and instruction.[52]

Repentance brought in its train faith, which seized upon justification, and justifying faith was followed by sanctification. Here, too, Wesley had minted the right concepts by making clear distinctions; and in taking the idea of growth to the point of Christian perfection, he had never left people in any doubt as to what he meant: namely, such a degree of love for God and neighbour, but also for justice, truth, holiness and purity, that no impulse displeasing to God any longer took root in our hearts. In view of such an exacting challenge, Whitehead asks: Is it not 'irrational', i.e. inconsistent with reality, to proclaim the omnipotence of the God who makes sinners new men? Must we not be grateful to Wesley for having restored to us true and sublime views of God, His plan of salvation, His power, His help, His Spirit, and for having thus afforded men the whole counsel of God?[53]

Let those, many as they may be, who have a mind to disapprove of the singling out of faith in the *ordo salutis* and in the Christian attitude as a whole, take note of the fact that strictly speaking all human behaviour, all our dealings with one another, are based on a kind of faith, on trust. Whenever something is purchased, it is taken on trust that the commodity in question is genuine and that the purchaser is paying for it with legal tender; in every projected transaction, it is assumed that the one who makes the plans will keep his health and that the circumstances are predictable. Just as every relationship to our neighbour is animated by faith, so faith in Jesus Christ unites the believer with the total vitality of His being, with the divine life itself. He is thereby transformed, and transformed into the new reality of such life. This is offered to all. Which is why Wesley embraced Arminianism, the universality of God's saving grace, in despite of the advocates of predestination, and not without good reason.[54]

With all this Wesley proved Christian experience to be a reality which claimed and secured for itself no less a validity than the external reality which is perceived by the senses. By drawing this analogy with empirical knowledge, Whitehead yet again fastened on to the principles of the Enlightenment.[55]

He now turned his attention to Wesley's colossal work-rate. The indefatigable application of this man must have called forth a sympathetic response in the apostles of the Enlightenment, who had chosen as their totems the society-forming insects—ants and bees. Whitehead stressed that the lack of understanding and the hostility which Wesley encountered, far from diminishing his zeal, in fact increased it. In this context he like others took up Wesley's favourite formula, that 'doing good' was the quintessence of his life. To this end his methodical way of life and work was subservient: he squeezed the last drop from every moment, and from his own energies too. He had no compunction in setting aside the matter in hand, once the moment had come for him to move on to some other task.[56]

Whitehead described his activity as consisting essentially in mission, although he himself did not use this catchword. His concern was to proclaim the message of salvation among those who sat in darkness and in the shadow of death. It was just such people whom he helped to have an experimental Christianity, Christianity as their own personal experience, so that the great words of 1 Peter were unquestionably true of them: 'In time past ye were not a people, but are now the people of God' (1 Peter 2[10]).[57] In passing this judgement, Whitehead had divined the essential thing about Wesley—restoration of the early Christian stance by means of evangelism.

But Wesley was also a solicitous, compassionate father to his own

O

people, even though he often came across as being very severe, an impression which was certainly the case in his treatment of himself. He knew his Societies, and had at heart the interests of every single member.[58]

Such unremitting labours in the service of men for God's sake brought forth a living harvest. Myriads of people were won to a life of decency, industry and respectability as a result of their becoming Methodists. Sometimes their way of life was so radically transformed that they were no longer recognizable. They became better workers in their daily job, better spouses and parents, better citizens and subjects. Society is highly indebted to Wesley, and inane accusations of political subversion stand self-condemned. If every British subject had been converted to Methodism, there would be no public unrest, no disaffection or conflicts; instead, peace and order would prevail throughout the realm.[59]

The Church of God grew daily as a result of his exertions. The example of his life demonstrates, Whitehead concludes, how meaningful and how happy life becomes when a man sees his purpose in life as doing good and is entirely committed to God, and God alone. Summing up John Wesley as he had been in his maturity with this apt phrase, he took his leave of the venerable father whose labours had been so blessed and owned of God.[60]

The strongly apologetic tone of this final tribute may leave an unfavourable impression on later readers, particularly because a burial service is not the occasion for addressing the wider public. Even so, in a deeper sense he struck the right note. Whitehead touched the very nerve-centre of Wesley's life's work; he put his finger on the underlying purpose and distinctive nature of his public ministry. What Whitehead offered was a theological interpretation of Wesley's message, which he clearly characterized as instruction in the Faith and a summons to the imitation of Christ. Everything else in the deceased leader's life had been subordinated to this end, and in Whitehead's representation clearly emerged as being of secondary importance. And thus, for all its brevity, what he offered was a theological biography. Like all the other obituarists, he too had recognized that Wesley's vital concerns were justification, regeneration and Christian perfection and had recognized that what made these purposes the governing factors of Wesley's life was their New Testament, evangelistic character. Moreover, he had succeeded in making the content of Wesley's message intelligible to the basically anti-pathetic, and at best unsympathetic outlook of the Enlightenment, without in any way detracting from its Biblical thrust. In this respect his funeral address put forward something unique; at all events, anything comparable would be hard to come by. At the same time he had entered into the mind and spirit of the deceased, who had not spoken in timeless propositions, but rather to his own age and times. The motto applied to Wesley by Coke—'Wesley *contra mundum*' (Wesley against the world)—had been closely substantiated on the basis of his proclamation of the Gospel.

In addition to these strictly theological funeral orations, in which abstract ideas played a greater or lesser, but always a dominant part, there appeared short modest poems, anonymous and ephemeral, which found their way into the hands of the common people. In one such elegy on the death of Wesley the content of his preaching was reproduced with the greatest possible brevity and in simple, everyday language: namely, that all men are lost in sin and that their salvation comes solely through Jesus, the Saviour whom God has sent. This résumé, somewhat mawkish in style, was calculated to pluck at the heart-strings and had no lack of sighs and exclamations. Stress was laid on Wesley's ceaseless activity, his arduous journeyings up and down the country, his wise allocation of time, his countless converts, but mention was also made of the exemplary simplicity of his preaching, and the unaffected way in which he moved among the people. This was followed by yet another expression of approval for his being no respecter of persons but a plain man for plain men. This poem, which is utterly lacking in logical progression, which reproduces impressions and is consequently full of repetition, and which does not follow any immediately discernible pattern, ended with a proleptic vision of the eternal glory which was already his but which still lay in the future for his followers. Until their journey ended, they were to remain loyal to the teachings which he had given them.[61]

Another poem depicts two shepherds who were mourning his death while tending their flocks. By his preaching he had opened up the very gate of heaven to them and unlocked the true meaning of life. From that day on the Psalms of David and the hymns of John and Charles Wesley had been their spiritual nourishment. They used to the full the ample opportunity they had while guarding their flocks to discuss the stories of the Bible. They felt themselves to be in close affinity with the patriarchs, who had been shepherds too, and similarly close to the shepherds of Bethlehem, to whom the birth of Jesus had been announced. It was not this, however, that counted with them, but the message conveyed by these narratives, the message of the sin into which the first men and all subsequent generations had fallen, the message of eternal damnation as the great danger to which men are exposed. It was their constant endeavour to impress this message upon one another. They acquainted themselves with the prophets, who had predicted the coming of Jesus, and finally called to mind the Good Shepherd who brought home His sheep. Although they lived out their lives within a set routine and within an extremely modest setting, they were content with their lot and thanked God both for their livelihood and for their wholesome, peaceful way of life. Every evening they joined together in praising His loving kindness and told their children and grandchildren about Him. This idyllic scene, conceived and painted on the 'classical' lines favoured in eighteenth-century nature-poetry, finds its acme in terms of human relationships when the shepherds, as young men, are shown as falling in love with the same girl and yet rather than vie with each other, they agree to do the noble thing by each other by both giving her up. Into this bucolic Elysium the news of Wesley's death bursts like a bomb-shell. They would have been more easily able to come to terms with a personal loss, such as the disappearance of a cow or a sheep. Wesley's death meant grief for 'thousands and tens of thousands', a grief through which only God's help could bring them. The shepherds had sustained the loss of their most faithful friend and brother, a man who, endowed with the most excellent gifts of the Spirit, had seen it as his true life's vocation to espouse their cause. In this hour of mourning they thought not merely of his eminent qualities and his Christian virtues, nor yet of his self-denial and modesty, which turned a great theologian into a humble Christian, but also of the thousands who like themselves mourned his death. This multitude were those to whom he had opened up new vistas in life by his message of sin and forgiveness. The sole aim and object of all his endeavour had been to further God's Lordship on earth; and for this reason things had been made possible which could only be regarded as miraculous.[62]

Thus both these poems, which were not of a very high standard and which were limited by the taste of the times and the sentimentality of the lower orders, also presented in their evaluation of Wesley the same picture as the theologically orientated obituaries: namely, that his impact stemmed from his preaching, which was sensed to be the essence of his life's work. His own people had understood him correctly. He was, and intended to be, an ambassador of the crucial truths of the Apostolic Faith which had called the Church to life, an ambassador of the forgiveness of sins and the new obedience which culminated in entire sanctification, complete dedication to God. One feels a liberation of soul when one sees how, in the light of this basic fact, cultural differences and theological capabilities ceased to be of any importance, and how the profound solidarity of all Christians became the unconscious genetic principle of the Methodist movement. At the same time the unanimity of these characterizations of Wesley bears witness to the consistency of his whole make-up, which impressed itself on all who came into contact with him. The modern and the contemporary judgement are at one.

Whereas Wesley ceased to keep his detailed *Journal* four months before his death, he maintained his short-hand diary up to the penultimate week of his life. He preached for the last time the week before he died. This sermon was delivered in a private house outside London, in Leatherhead. His text was Isaiah 55[6]: 'Seek ye the Lord while he may be found, call ye upon him while he is near.' On the preceding evening he preached his last sermon at the City Road chapel in London, where he also lived. This sermon had as its text Galatians 5[5]: 'For we through the Spirit wait for the hope of righteousness by faith.' Yet again, therefore, it centred on the heart of his message and bore final testimony to what he had taught for well-nigh fifty-three years.[63]

Thus everything is neatly rounded off. For all his constant communion with God, a communion which he so admired in the Marquis de Renty and which he so ardently desired for himself, Wesley confessed that he was an unprofitable servant,[64] a sinner who lived by grace alone. His last days were shot through and through with this awareness; he kept on repeating and singing to himself hymns which had this as their purport.[65] This was what he had confessed to his brother Charles twenty-five years before,[66] and he meant what he said. If the distinctive thing about the leading figures in church history is the fact that in them their human destiny, their personal piety and the theological expression of their inmost being are all of a piece, that inner consistency is reached between life and doctrine, between word and deed, this is certainly the case with Wesley.

This awareness of being a sinner and of being in need of divine grace, by which our sins are forgiven, resolved in turn the profound dichotome which ran through John Wesley's life: he taught, even required perfection in love, and yet was to a large extent such a severe and, when need be, such a ruthless man. He rejected Antinomianism, which in the case of the Moravians he had recognized as the great peril of Christian liberty, and yet fell himself into a legalism which found expression in his fundamentally ascetic outlook and rigorism, even though at heart he was a preacher of grace and a champion of freedom. It was entirely consistent with this that his marriage represented no more than an abortive interlude, a kind of mishap in his life, and that he frequently advised his female correspondents against getting married, on the grounds that looking after a husband and children militated against devotion to God.[67] And yet in the final analysis this austerity was not the decisive thing. What he really wanted was to let the final word in the life of a Christian rest with the Spirit of God and His spontaneous working.[68] His important equation of total devotion to God with human fulfilment and his formula that holiness is happiness, a formula which had seized and activated him from his youth up—all this was equally true of him in his old age. John Whitehead rightly stressed this in his funeral address.[69] For Wesley, God is the Creator who brings all things to perfection, who restores His image in man and gives him the very mind which was in Christ Jesus.[70] Thus the restoration of primitive Christianity reached its acme in the life of the individual and achieved its goal in the realization of the presence of the eternal world in life here and now.[71]

It cannot be gainsaid that Wesley was a man of an *idée fixe*. The predominant impression left by his personality will always be its ascetic and rigorist character. He shared this characteristic with those eminent and normative representatives of Christianity in modern times who sharply recognized and vindicated the essence of the Biblical message in the face of the spirit of the age: men such as Johann Georg Hamann, Johann Christoph Blumhardt, Sören Kierkegaard, and, to mention lesser figures, Claus Harms, August Tholuck and Wilhelm Löhe. The great polymaths, the more fertile minds—men like Isaac Newton, Gottfried Wilhelm Leibniz, Johann Gottfried

Herder, Georg Friedrich Hegel, and also, to some extent in a different category, Friedrich Schleiermacher and Richard Rothe—were advocates of, and witnesses to, the harmony between Christianity and the universe. This harmonization was also congenial to the dominant theology of Wesley's age. But figures of this sort failed to do justice to the basic datum of a sense of exile which marks the situation of the Christian on earth.[72] The public philosophy dominated by simplistic, this-worldly assumptions provoked with imperative force this sense of exile with a vigour worthy of apostolic days. One may perhaps elevate this acute sense of being aliens to the status of a law of modern church history and thereby justify the one-sidedness of these great figures. Just as in refusing to compromise John Wesley gave eloquent expression to the direct confrontation of the church with the world, so with equal eloquence he pointed to its resolution with his favourite formula equating holiness with happiness.

# Notes

## Chapter 6: John Wesley as Preacher

1. 'Let me be *homo unius libri.*' *Sermons on Several Occasions,* I (1944) [3rd imp., 1948], Preface, p. vi.
2. *Journal,* II. 274–6, 13th September 1739, esp. 275–6: '(Fourthly): They speak of sanctification (or holiness) as if it were an outward thing—as if it consisted chiefly, if not wholly, in those two points: (1) the doing no harm; (2) the doing good (as it is called); that is, the using the means of grace, and helping our neighbour. I believe it to be an inward thing, namely, the life of God in the soul of man; a participation of the divine nature; the mind that was in Christ; or, the renewal of our heart after the image of Him that created us. Lastly. They speak of the new birth as an outward thing—as if it were no more than baptism; or, at most, a change from outward wickedness to outward goodness, from a vicious to (what is called) a virtuous Life. I believe it to be an inward thing; a change from inward wickedness to inward goodness; an entire change of our inmost nature from the image of the devil (wherein we are born) to the image of God; a change from the love of the creature to the love of the Creator; from earthly and sensual to heavenly and holy affections, —in a word a change from the tempers of the spirits of darkness to those of the angels of God in heaven.'
3. *Journal,* II. 335–6, 6th February 1740.
3a. [Translator's note: This principle was not in fact medieval, but comes from the Treaty of Westphalen, 1638.]
4. On this point, cf. my study of Christian Hoburg (1607–1675), chief spokesman of the 'spiritualizing' mysticism, critical of the Church, which substantially paved the way for Pietism: *Die spiritualistische Kritik Christian Hoburgs an der lutherischen Abendmahlslehre und ihre orthodoxe Abwehr* ('The "spiritualizing" attack by Christian Hoburg on the Lutheran doctrine of the Eucharist, and its Orthodox refutation'), in *Bekenntnis zur Kirche: Festschrift für Ernst Sommerlath zum 70. Geburtstag* (1959), pp. 126–38. On Pietism, see esp. pp. 133–4. For Zinzendorf's position on this issue, see also Vol. II, Part 1, of this present work, p. 48.
5. On this point, cf. also *Letters,* II. 46, Newcastle-upon-Tyne, 28th September 1745, to 'John Smith', in which Wesley, discussing

accusations against himself and the Methodists, picks out the doctrinal issue as the decisive point of controversy. See Vol. II, Part 1, of this present work, p. 201.

6. In altering freely the text of Romans $8^1$ to highlight faith, Wesley clearly deduces his right to do so from the logical sequence worked out in his discussion of faith, in which he developed the theme of the indwelling of Jesus, in whom the Christians believed, in their hearts (based on Galatians $2^{20}$).

7. On this point, cf. the terminology, almost word-for-word the same, of August Hermann Francke, *Nicodemus oder Tractätlein von der Menschenfurcht*, 3rd edn, Halle, 1707, p. 158: 'Happy is the man who, in the midst of all manner of onslaught and struggle, even when the enemy boasts that he has defeated him, stands fast and fights on (Joshua $4^{10}$); he will go on from faith to faith in might, and finally overcome all things and inherit all things with Christ.' [See Vol. I, p. 271, n.3]. Cf. also the earlier use of this language in Christian Hoburg's 'Elias Praetorius', '*Spiegel der Misbräuche beym Predigt-Ampt in heutigen Christenthumb, und wie selbige gründlich und heilsam zu reformiren*' (1644), p. 152: '*Die wahre Kinder Gottes aber gehen täglich von Krafft zu Krafft / von Macht zu Macht / aus einer Klarheyt in die Andere*': '*The true children of God, however, go on from strength to strength, from power to power, from one glory to another*' (*italics original*).

8. 'These, while they trust in the blood of Christ alone, use all the ordinances which He has appointed, do all the goods works which He had before prepared that they should walk therein and enjoy and manifest all holy and heavenly tempers, even the same mind that was in Christ Jesus.' J. Wesley, *Sermons on Several Occasions* (1944), [3rd imp., 1948], pp. 6–7. Further examples: in the same collection, p. 520 (Sermon XXXI: *The New Birth*): . . . 'gospel holiness is no less than the image of God stamped upon the heart; it is no other than the whole mind which was in Christ Jesus; it consists of all heavenly affections and tempers mingled together in one';
*Letters*, I. 89, 17th June 1731, to Ann Granville: 'that is to be happy, to be renewed in the image in which we were created, to have that mind in us which was also in Christ Jesus';
*Letters*, I. 117, 28th February 1732, to his mother.

9. Op. cit. *(Sermons)*, p. 8: 'But this, it is said, is an uncomfortable doctrine.' This accusation is very significant in the eighteenth-century context. The great concern of this century was to ease human life in every respect—hence its thorough-going hostility to asceticism. Cf. the concept of religion cited in note 8.

10. Franz Volkmar Reinhard: 'Wie sehr unsere Kirche Ursache habe, es nie zu vergessen, dass sie ihr Dasein vornehmlich der Erneuerung des Lehrsatzes von der freien Gnade in Christo schuldig'—'Our Church has indeed good reason never to forget that it owes its very existence above all to the renewal of the doctrine of free grace in Christ'—*Sämtliche Predigten,* Vol. 17 (1818—vol. 2 of the 1800 series), pp. 232–53.
11. *Sermons on Several Occasions* (1944), [3rd imp., 1948], pp. 11–19.
12. Matthew Mead(e) (1630–1699) 'Εν ὀλίγῳ Χριστιανός *The Almost Christian Discovered or the False Professor Tryed and Cast.* Being the Substance of Seven Sermons. First Preached at Sepulchers London 1661 And now at the Importunity of Friends made Publick London 1662 (35th edn, 1825). I have used the copy in the Bodleian Library, Oxford (2nd edn, 1663). The book takes its stand completely with the Puritan tradition of self-examination (esp. pp. 152 ff.). Translated into German under the title *Der falsche Bekenner,* it was drawn on particularly by Gottfried Arnold. (See *Die Abwege oder Irrungen und Versuchungen gutwilliger und frommer Menschen aus Beystimmung des gottseeligen Alterthums angemerket,* 1708, 2nd edn—with *Theologia experimentalis,* 1714, section 64).
13. John Wesley's *Sermons on Several Occasions* (1944), [3rd imp., 1948], pp. 12–13. 'He not only avoids all actual adultery, fornication and uncleanness but every word or look that either directly or indirectly tends thereto! nay and all idle words, abstaining both from detraction, backbiting, talebearing, evil speaking, and from "all foolish talking and jesting"—εὐτραπελία, a kind of virtue in the heathen moralist's account—briefly, from all conversation, that is not "good to the use of edifying" and that, consequently, "grieves the Holy Spirit of God, whereby we are sealed to the day of redemption".' It is noteworthy that John Wesley expressly weaves the commendation of εὐτραπελία into his argument.
14. Op. cit., p. 19.
15. Op. cit., pp. 32–49, Sermon IV: *Scriptural Christianity* (Sermon III: 'Awake, thou that sleepest . . ., on Ephesians 5¹⁴, is from Charles' pen).
16. Op. cit., p. 33: 'It was, to give them (what none can deny to be essential) . . . labour of love (1 Thessalonians 1³).' It is noteworthy that Wesley renders πίστις, not as *faith,* as Luther did in German *(Glauben),* but as *fidelity.* He sees clearly that here, according to the general sense of the passage, a virtue in the proper sense must be the true connotation.
17. Cf. Vol. I, p. 98 and note 8 there. [E.T.]

NOTES

18. See particularly *Sermons on Several Occasions* (1944), [3rd imp., 1948], p. 39: 'For the more Christianity spread, the more hurt was done, in the account of those who received it not.'

19. Op. cit., p. 41: 'But shall we not see greater things than these? Yea, greater than have been yet from the beginning of the world. Can Satan cause the truth of God to fail, or His promises to be of none effect?'

20. Op. cit., p. 41: Isaiah $2^{2 \text{ and } 4}$, $11^{10-12}$, $11^{6-9}$.

21. Op. cit., p. 43: 'And, first, I should ask, Where does this Christianity now exist? Where, I pray, do the Christians live? Which is the country the inhabitants whereof are all thus filled with the Holy Ghost? . . . Why then, let us confess we have never yet seen a Christian country upon earth.'

22. Sermon I: *Salvation by Faith*, preached at St. Mary's, Oxford, before the University, June 18, 1738.
Sermon II: *The Almost Christian*, preached at St. Mary's, Oxford, before the University, July 25, 1741.
Sermon IV: *Scriptural Christianity*, preached at St. Mary's, Oxford, before the University, August 24, 1744.

23. Op. cit., pp. 514–26, Sermon XXXIX: *The New Birth*, on John $3^7$.

24. Op. cit., p. 516: 'Yea, so little did he retain even of the knowledge of Him who filleth heaven and earth, that he endeavoured to "hide himself from the Lord God among the trees of the garden" (Genesis $3^8$); so had he lost both the knowledge and the love of God without which the image of God could not subsist. Of this, therefore, he was deprived at the same time, and became unholy as well as unhappy.'
There appears here John Wesley's favourite formula, the collocation of holiness and happiness, the association of the earnest pursuit of sanctification with joy in salvation, expressed here in its negative aspect. Further examples of this formula: in this same sermon, p. 521: 'For it is not possible, in the nature of things, that a man should be happy who is not holy';
*Letters*, I. 92–3, 19th July 1731, to Mrs Pendarves;
*Letters*, I. 114, 17th November 1731, to his brother Samuel;
*Letters*, I. 128, Oxford, 18th October 1732, to Richard Morgan.

25. Op. cit., pp. 519–20: 'From hence it manifestly appears, what is the nature of the new birth. It is that great change which God works in the soul when He brings it into life; when He raises it from the death of sin to the life of righteousness. It is the change wrought in the whole soul by the almighty spirit of God when it is "created anew in Jesus Christ"; when it is "renewed after the image of God in righteousness and true holiness"; when the love of the world is changed

into the love of God; pride into humility; passion into meekness; hatred, envy, malice into a sincere, tender, disinterested love for all mankind. In a word, it is that change whereby the earthly sensual, devilish mind is turned into the "mind which was in Christ Jesus". This is the nature of the new birth: "so is every one that is born of the Spirit".'

26. On this revival of the early Christian idea of sacrifice in Romans 12[1], cf. the parallel lines of thought in Wilhelm Löhe, *Vorschlag zur Vereinigung lutherischer Christen für apostolisches Leben*, in *Werke* (ed. Klaus Ganzert), Vol. V, 1 (1954), pp. 248ff., especially pp. 248-9: 'One of the ideas which from the first age of the Church lived on in its various parts, but was then gravely misused and was therefore discarded at the time of the Reformation, is the idea of sacrifice. It is from the Father through His only-begotten Son Jesus Christ that we derive everything that we are or possess—and all this must be brought back to Him in the Holy Spirit, so that all things may be of Him, through Him and unto Him. It is because of this 'bringing-back', or sacrifice, that Christians, on whom this responsibility lies, are called a βασίλειον ἱεράτευμα, a royal priesthood (1 Peter 2[9]). In this offering up and 'bringing back' of all things to the Lord is a heavenly joy which God grants to His Christians.

'There are many duties which fall on the Christian, which he perhaps carries out to the best of his ability, but which for him become difficult and oppressive, whereas they could become easy and delightful for him if he were profoundly convinced that their fulfilment were an act of worship, not only in theory but in very truth. The bare, chilly sense of obligation brings neither pleasure nor courage—quite unlike the thought that by doing my duty I am offering to God an acceptable sacrifice. Thus, for example, the better kind of Christian neophyte struggles for continence, yet cannot attain to the spiritual virginity for which he longs. The merely negative command is no source of strength. However, if this beginner in Christianity grasps, as a living reality, the thought that by his continence he is showing his Lord love and worship, that his is an offering to his heavenly Father acceptable in Christ Jesus,—then, what to the natural man is hard or impossible becomes a labour of joy.

'The man who has no regard for the idea of sacrifice or despises it will also be unable to find much or any reference to it in the New Testament; but an attentive and well-disposed man will find traces of it everywhere, and with the passage of time the whole of the N.T. writings, particularly the apostolic letters, will display themselves to him as being full of this idea, even where it does not appear expressly in the text. The entire Christian life, understood in its noblest terms, is sacrifice. Seen from the vantage-point of this idea, all the exhortations of the apostles and the whole process of living by them are bathed in the light of a holy, heavenly fulfilment. The Church returns to its Lord, bringing with it and offering to Him all that it has or is.'

27. Cf. Vol. I, pp. 53–58.

28. Op. cit., *(Sermons on Several Occasions)*, p. 523: '. . . it is sure all of riper years who are baptized are not at the same time born again. "The tree is known by its fruits". And hereby it appears too plain to be denied, that divers of those who were children of the devil before they were baptized continue the same after baptism; "for the works of their father they do": they continue servants of sin, without any pretence either to inward or outward holiness.'

29. William Law, *Grounds and Reasons of Christian Regeneration* (1739).

30. *The Marks of the New Birth* (Sermon XIV), op. cit., pp. 162–74.

31. Cf. supra, p. 15.

32. Sermon XV: *The Great Privilege of those that are Born of God,* op. cit., pp. 174–84: 'For, from the moment we are born of God, we live in quite another manner that we did before; we are, as it were, in another world' (p. 175).

33. 'A change in the whole manner of our existence': op. cit., p. 175. This early appearance of the existentialist concept along Kierkegaardian lines is particularly remarkable.

34. Op. cit., pp. 183–4: 'From what has been said, we may learn, secondly, what the life of God in the soul of a believer is; wherein it properly consists; and what is immediately and necessarily implied therein. It immediately and necessarily implies the continual inspiration of God's Holy Spirit; God's breathing into the soul, and the soul's breathing back what it first receives from God; a continual action of God upon the soul, and a reaction of the soul upon God; an unceasing presence of God, the loving, pardoning God manifested to the heart, and perceived by faith; and an unceasing return of love, praise and prayer, offering up all the thoughts of our hearts, all the words of our tongues, all the works of our hands, all our body, soul, and spirit, to be a holy sacrifice, acceptable unto God in Christ Jesus.'

35. Sermon VIII: *The First-fruits of the Spirit*, op. cit., pp. 85–96.

36. Op. cit., pp. 89–90. 'They are not condemned, thirdly, for inward sin even though it now remain. That the corruption of nature does still remain, even in those who are the children of God by faith; that they have in them the seeds of pride and vanity, of anger, lust, and evil desire, yea, sin of every kind; is too plain to be denied, being matter

of daily experience. And on this account it is, that St. Paul, speaking
to those whom he had just before witnessed to be "in Christ Jesus"
(1 Corinthians 1[2, 9]) to have been "called of God into the fellowship"
(or participation) "of His Son Jesus Christ"; yet declares, "Brethren,
I could not speak unto you as unto spiritual, but as unto carnal, even
as unto babes in Christ" (1 Corinthians 3[1]); "babes in Christ"; so
we see they were "in Christ"; they were believers in a low degree.
And yet how much of sin remained in them! of that "carnal mind,
which is not subject to the law of God"!

'And yet, for all this, they are not condemned. Although they feel
the flesh, the evil nature in them; although they are more sensible,
day by day, that their "heart is deceitful and desperately wicked" yet,
so long as they do not yield thereto; so long as they give no place to
the devil; so long as they maintain a continual war with all sin, with
pride, anger, desire, so that the flesh has no dominion over them, but
they still "walk after the Spirit"; "there is no condemnation to them
which are in Christ Jesus". God is well pleased with their sincere
though imperfect obedience; and they "have confidence towards
God", knowing they are His, "by the Spirit which He hath given"
them (1 John 3[24]).' It is important to notice this point, or we risk
branding Wesley as a thoughtless or fanatical perfectionist.

37. Sermon IX: *The Spirit of Bondage and of Adoption*, op. cit.,
pp. 96–110.
38. Sermon X: *The Witness of the Spirit*, op. cit., pp. 111–23.
39. Cf. Vol. II, Pt. 1, of this work, pp. 32–6, esp. p. 35.
40. Schleiermacher's idea of 'feeling' is a concept of immediate self-
awareness: See *Glaubenslehre (Der christliche Glaube nach den
Grundsätzen der evangelischen Kirche in Zusammenhange dargestellt)*,
Vol. I (1821), [2nd edn, 1830], § 3 (Hendel ed., reprint of the 2nd
Berlin edn, no date), pp. 5–12. [E. T., H. R. Mackintosh and J. S.
Stewart as *The Christian Faith*, 1928].
41. Cf. my paper '*Biblizismus und natürliche Theologie in der Gewissens-
lehre des englischen Puritanismus*', in the *Archiv für Reformations-
geschichte*, vol. 42 (1951), pp. 198–219; Vol. 43 (1952), pp. 70–87.
[Translator's note: see also R. C. Monk, *John Wesley: His Puritan
Heritage* (London, 1966), pp. 157–67.]
42. Sermon XI: *The Witness of our own Spirit*, op. cit., pp. 123–33.
43. Sermon XV: *The Great Privilege of those that are Born of God*, op. cit.,
pp. 174–84.
44. For the opposite view, cf. the rejection of justification as a 'fiction' in
favour of the new birth as a 'fact', usual in 'spiritualizing' mysticism.
This is classically formulated by Christian Hoburg, as in Ch. 12

('How present-day Preachers fail to understand the spiritual union with Christ; and also the imputation of the death and merits of Christ') of Elias Praetorius, *Spiegel der Misbräuche beym Predigt-Ampt im heutigen Christenthumb* (1644), pp. 174–6: 'What manner of immensely precious and splendid mystery this is, is known only to God's faithful children, who cleave to their Head and Saviour with firm faith, and are united and bound to Him in their very soul; for He lives, works and reigns in them like a King on his throne, in his Temple; He gives them food and drink; He, the heavenly Vine, fills His tendrils with sap, power, life and blessing. This doctrine is as vitally necessary in true Christianity as it is extremely comforting; but their openly published books and sermons testify how miserably the present-day preachers treat this doctrine on all hands. No small evidence on this point is afforded by their interpretation of Imputation: namely, that it is sufficient for salvation that one should externally appropriate Christ with His life, passion and merit—thus, forsooth, one can come to salvation. The other matter, however, that of union with Christ the Head with His members, and of His indwelling, that is a mere figure of speech, whether used of the essence of the matter or used emotively—and they cannot even bear to hear this word "essence". And so they show that they have in their hearts nothing of the essence of Christ—only knowledge or histories or "letters" (sc. both letters as literary productions and "the letter" that "killeth"). Believing Christians, however, who cleave to Christ their Head and are united with Him, have nothing in their hearts but the pure essence, Spirit, life, sap and power of Christ; hence they experience nothing less than life, essence, sap and power. In Christ, that is to say, is genuine essence (ἀλήθεια *verum, solidum, non imaginativum imputativum quid*), and in Him are all things new.

'Now because they are unwilling to allow of such a thing, they betray that they have not yet tasted Christ inwardly in their hearts with His righteous new nature, life, Spirit and power, nor yet have they the essence of the New Man dwelling in them through faith, the substance of things hoped for; indeed, that they have not yet savoured the heavenly gifts, the gracious Word of God, nay, the powers of the world to come. In their minds they can, to be sure, admit that this be acknowledged as union, but they do not want it to be regarded as the essence of the matter. Surely, therefore, it is not unreasonable to ask whether, when Christ dwells in us with His Spirit, His nature too is at the same time in us, or whether Christ's Spirit is separable from His nature, whether Christ's Spirit is anything less than divine in essence and power?'

In Spener, for all his extended discussions on this subject, no clear distinction is drawn between purely imputative justification and substantial regeneration.

45. Cf. supra, note 35.

46. Sermon XVI, Upon our Lord's Sermon on the Mount, Discourse I, on Matthew $5^{1-4}$, op. cit., pp. 185–200.

47. Op. cit., p. 189: 'He now addresses us with His still small voice, "Blessed", or happy, "are the poor in spirit". Happy are the mourners; the meek; those that hunger after righteousness; the merciful; the pure in heart: Happy in the end, and in the way; happy in this life, and in life everlasting! As if He had said, "Who is he that lusteth to live, and would fain see good days? Behold, I show you the thing which your soul longeth for! See the way you have so long sought in vain; the way of pleasantness; the path to calm, joyous peace, to heaven below, and heaven above!" '

Similarly, p. 190: ' "Blessed" saith He (or *happy*—so the word should be rendered, both in this and the following verses), "are the poor in spirit". He does not say, they that are poor as to outward circumstances, it being not impossible that some of these may be as far from happiness as a monarch upon his throne; but "the poor in spirit"—they who, whatever their outward circumstances are, have that disposition of heart which is the first step to all real, substantial happiness, either in this world, or that which is to come.'

48. Op. cit., p. 194: 'One cannot but observe here, that Christianity begins just where heathen morality ends, poverty of spirit, conviction of sin, the renouncing ourselves, the not having our own righteousness (the very first point in the religion of Jesus Christ), leaving all pagan religion behind. This was ever hid from the wise men of this world; insomuch that the whole Roman language even with all the improvements of the Augustan age, does not afford so much as a name for humility (the word from whence we borrow this, as is well known, bearing in Latin a quite different meaning): no, nor was one found in all the copious language of Greece, till it was made by the great Apostle.' On this point, cf. Albrecht Dihle, *Antike Höflichkeit und christliche Demut*, in the *Estratto dagli studi italiani di Filologia Classica*, N.S., Vol. XXVI (1952), pp. 169–90, esp. pp. 180ff.

49. Sermon XVII, Upon our Lord's Sermon on the Mount, Discourse II, op. cit., pp. 201–17.

50. Sermon XXVIII, Upon our Lord's Sermon on the Mount, Discourse III, op. cit., p. 220: 'The pure in heart see all things full of God.'

51. Op. cit., p. 223: 'But the great lesson which our blessed Lord inculcates here, and which he illustrates by this example, is, that God is in

all things, and that we are to see the Creator in the glass of every creature; that we should use and look upon nothing as separate from God, which indeed is a kind of practical Atheism.'

52. Sermon XIX, Upon our Lord's Sermon on the Mount, Discourse IV, op. cit., pp. 235–51.

53. Ibid., p. 237: 'First I shall endeavour to show that Christianity is essentially a social religion; and that to turn it into a solitary religion, is indeed to destroy it.'

54. Sermon XX, Upon our Lord's Sermon on the Mount, Discourse V, op. cit., pp. 251–69.

55. The most important passages read as follows (ibid., p. 255, paras. 2 and 3):

'2. From all this we may learn, that there is no contrariety at all between the law and the gospel; that there is no need for the law to pass away, in order to the establishing the gospel. Indeed neither of them supersedes the other, but they agree perfectly well together. Yea the very same words, considered in different respects, are part both of the law and of the gospel; if they are considered as commandments, they are parts of the law; if as promises, of the gospel. Thus, "Thou shalt love the Lord thy God with all thy heart", when considered as a commandment, is a branch of the law; when regarded as a promise, is an essential part of the gospel—the gospel being no other than the commands of the law, proposed by way of promise. Accordingly, poverty of spirit, purity of heart and whatever else is enjoined in the holy law of God, are no other, when viewed in a gospel light, than so many great and precious promises.

'3. There is therefore, the closest connexion that can be conceived between the law and the gospel. On the one hand, the law continually makes way for, and points us to the gospel; on the other, the gospel continually leads us to a more exact fulfilling of the law. The law, for instance, requires us to love God, to love our neighbour, to be meek, humble, or holy; we feel that we are not sufficient for these things; yea, that "with man this is impossible". But we see a promise of God, to give us that love, and to make us humble, meek and holy: we lay hold of this gospel, of these glad tidings: it is done unto us according to our faith; and "the righteousness of the law is fulfilled in us", through faith which is in Christ Jesus.

'We may yet farther observe, that every command in holy writ is only a covered promise. For by that solemn declaration. "This is the covenant I will make after those days, saith the Lord. I will put My laws in your minds, and write them in your hearts", God has engaged to give whatsoever He commands. Does He command us then to "pray without ceasing", to "rejoice evermore", to be "holy as He is holy"? It is enough: He will work in us this very thing: it shall be unto us according to His word.'

56. Ibid., p. 260: 'We must cry aloud to every penitent sinner, "Believe in the Lord Jesus Christ, and thou shalt be saved". But, at the same time, we must take care to let all men know, we esteem no faith but that which worketh by love; and that we are not saved by faith, unless so far as we are delivered from the power as well as the guilt of sin. And when we say, "Believe, and thou shalt be saved" we do not mean "Believe and thou shalt step from sin to heaven, without any holiness coming between; faith supplying the place of holiness"; but "Believe, and thou shalt be holy; believe in the Lord Jesus, and thou shalt have peace and power together: thou shalt have power from Him in whom thou believest, to trample sin under thy feet; power to love the Lord thy God with all thy heart, and to serve Him with all thy strength; thou shalt have power by patient continuance in well-doing, to seek for glory, and honour and immortality"; thou shalt both do and teach all the commandments of God, from the least even to the greatest: thou shalt teach them by thy life as well as the words, and so "be called great in the kingdom of heaven".'

57. Ibid., p. 267.

58. Sermon XXI, Upon our Lord's Sermon on the Mount, Discourse VI, op. cit., pp. 269–86.

59. Sermon XXII, Upon our Lord's Sermon on the Mount, Discourse VII, op. cit., pp. 287–304.

60. Ibid., p. 301: 'Lastly: Had you been with the brethren in Antioch, at the time when they fasted and prayed, before the sending forth of Barnabas and Saul, can you possibly imagine that your temperance or abstinence would have been a sufficient cause for not joining therein? Without doubt, if you had not, you would soon have been cut off from the Christian community. You would have deservedly been cast out from among them, as bringing confusion into the church of God.'

61. Sermon XXIII, Upon our Lord's Sermon on the Mount, Discourse VIII, op. cit., pp. 305–22.

62. Sermon XXIV, Upon our Lord's Sermon on the Mount, Discourse IX, op. cit., pp. 323–38.

63. Sermon XXV, Upon our Lord's Sermon on the Mount, Discourse X, op. cit., pp. 339–50.

64. Ibid., p. 343: 'The thinking of another in a manner that is contrary to love, is that judging which is here condemned.'

65. Sermon XXVI, Upon our Lord's Sermon on the Mount, Discourse XI, op. cit., pp. 351–9.
66. Sermon XXVII, Upon our Lord's Sermon on the Mount, Discourse XII, op. cit., pp. 360–70.
67. Sermon XXVIII, Upon our Lord's Sermon on the Mount, Discourse XIII, op. cit., pp. 370–80.
68. Sermon XXXV, *Christian Perfection*, op. cit., pp. 457–76.
69. In this context John Wesley also cites Romans 6[7] in his support. On p. 463 the original text is given: ὁ γὰρ ἀποθανὼν ϛεϛικαίωται ἀπὸ τῆς ἁμαρτίας. Luther's translation is literal: 'Wer gestorben ist, der ist gerechtfertigt von der Sunde' ('Whoever has died is justified from sin'). The rendering in the Authorized Version of 1611 (King James' Bible): 'For he that is dead is freed from sin', lends considerable support to Wesley's argument.
70. Ibid., p. 466: 'It is of great importance to observe, and that more carefully than is commonly done, the wide difference there is between the Jewish and the Christian dispensation.'
71. Sermon XXX, *The Law established through Faith*, Discourse I, op. cit., pp. 395–406.
72. Dietrich Bonhoeffer, *Gesammelte Schriften*, ed. Eberhard Bethge, Vol. III (1960), pp. 322–4 (Lecture: *Vergegenwärtigung neutestamentlicher Texte*, 1935), and *Nachfolge* (3rd edn, 1950), pp. 1–12. E. T., R. H. Fuller as *The Cost of Discipleship*, London, S.C.M., 1959, 6th imp., 1971, pp. 35–47.
73. Thomas Müntzer, *Von dem getichten Glauben*, Quire A, Leaf 4, *recto*: 'One must not creep in at the back door through another basis of faith, but have the whole Christ, not the half Christ; whoever refuses to have the bitter Christ will drown himself in honey.' Cf. *Hochverursachte Schutzrede wider das geistlose, sanftlebende Fleisch zu Wittenberg* (1524), ed. Ludwig Enders (*Flugschriften aus der Reformationszeit*, Vol. X: *Aus dem Kampf der Schwärmer gegen Luther*, in the series *Neudrücke deutscher Literaturwerke des 16. und 17. Jahrhunderts*, No. 118), 1893, pp. 21–2. See also Carl Hinrichs, ed., *Thomas Müntzer, Politische Schriften* (*Hallische Monographien*, No. 17), 1950, pp. 75–6: 'It is as plain as a pikestaff that the latter-day scribes and doctors of the law behave no differently than the Pharisees of yore: they preen themselves on their knowledge of Holy Writ; they reel off their vast tomes; and the more they prate on, the more nonsense they produce. "Believe, believe", they say; and yet they close the path to faith itself. . . . Things are no different, we find, in the present day. For when the godless are apprehended by the law, they say as glib as you like: "Ah! It has been abolished". But when it is properly

explained to them how it is written in the heart (2 Corinthians 3) and how we are commanded to pay respect to the things that lead to the fountain of life (Psalm 36), then the godless man overwhelms the righteous man and makes play with Paul with such a doltish understanding that even the children think they are watching Punch and Judy.'

74. Sermon XXI, *The Law established through Faith*, Discourse II, op. cit., pp. 407–15.

75. Ibid., p. 411: 'What St Paul observes concerning the superior glory of the gospel, above that of the law, may, with great propriety, be spoken of the superior glory of love, above that of faith.'

76. *Works* [3rd edn, 1829], VI, pp. 54–65.

77. Ibid., p. 65.

78 Sermon LXI, *The Mystery of Iniquity*, *Works*, [3rd edn, 1829], VI, pp. 253–67. The text is 2 Thessalonians 2⁷.

79. Ibid., p. 257: Acts 6¹.

80. Ibid., p. 258: Acts 15²⁸⁻²⁹.

81. Ibid., pp. 258–65.

82. Ibid., p. 264: 'When Tomo Chachi, the Indian Chief, keenly replied to those who spoke to him of being a Christian, "Why, *these* are Christians at Sanannah! These are Christians at Frederica!"—the proper answer was "No, they are not; they are no more Christians than you and Sinauky". "But are not these Christians in Canterbury, in London, in Westminster?" No; no more than they are angels. None are Christians, but they that have the mind which was in Christ, and walk as he walked. "Why, if these only are Christians", said an eminent wit, "I never saw a Christian yet". I believe it; You never did; and, perhaps, you never will; for you will never find them in the grand or the gay world. The few Christians that there are upon the earth, are only to be found where *you* never look for them. Never, therefore, urge this objection more: Never object to Christianity the lives or tempers of Heathens. Though they are called Christians the name does not imply the thing: They are as far from this as hell from heaven!'

83. *Sermons on Several Occasions*, pp. 576–88 On this point, cf. Ernst Sommer, *John Wesley und die soziale Frage*, 1930, (Beiträge zur Geschichte des Methodismus), [2nd edn, n.d.], esp. pp. 20–1 and p. 34, note 60.

84. Cf. Vol. II, Part 1 of this present work, p. 180, and supra p. 39. [Translator's note: *The Whole Duty of Man* is usually accredited to Richard Allestree (1619–81). For a more detailed discussion of the question of its authorship and an assessment of its influence on

J. Wesley, see G. Thompson Brake, 'The Whole Duty of Man', LQHR, 182 (October, 1958), pp. 293–7.]

85. Sermon LXXIX, on *Dissipation*, based on 1 Corinthians 7[35]: 'This I speak—that you may attend upon the Lord without distraction.' *Works* [3rd edn, 1829], VI. 444–52.

86. Ibid., pp. 444–5. 'Almost in every part of our nation, more especially in the large and populus towns, we hear a general complaint among sensible persons, of the still increasing dissipation. It is observed to diffuse itself more and more, in the court, the city and the country. From the continual mention which is made of this, and the continual declamations against it, one would naturally imagine that a word so commonly used was perfectly understood. Yet it may be doubted whether it be or no. Nay we may very safely affirm, that few of those who frequently use the term understand what it means. One reason of this, is, that, although the thing has been long among us, especially since the time of King Charles the Second (one of the most dissipated mortals that ever breathed), yet the word is not of long standing. It was hardly heard of fifty years ago; and not much before the present reign. So lately has it been imported: and yet it is so in every one's mouth, that it is already worn threadbare; being one of the cant words of the day.'

## Chapter 7: John Wesley as Theological Writer

1. *Works* [3rd edn., 1830], VIII, pp. 340–7. He was first prompted to write this work around 1731 by the description of the perfect Gnostic in Clement of Alexandria, which he greatly admired. But when, ten years later, he started on the first draft of his own book, his concern was to give it a more strictly Biblical form. In doing so, he emphasized that neither he himself nor his people had attained the lofty goal which had been set before them. See *Letters*, V.43, London, 5th March 1767, to the Editor of *Lloyds' Evening Post*. Leslie F. Church has rightly given this tract the key position in his book, *The Early Methodist People*, 1948, 2nd edn, 1949, p. 11.

2. Ephesians 4[5–6].

3. Cf. vol. II, part I of this work, p. 180. He stated how reluctantly he acted in this way in his letter to Elizabeth Hardy of 5th April 1758 (*Letters*, IV, 10, Dublin): 'It is with great reluctance that I at length begin to write: first because I abhor disputing and never enter upon it but when I am, as it were, dragged into it by the hair of the head.'

4. *Plain Account of Christian Perfection*, 1765.
5. *Works* [3rd edn, 1830], VIII. 3–42.
6. 'Doing good', ibid., p. 9. Cf. Vol. I of this work, p. 98, p. 101; Vol. II, Part I, p. 131.
7. Ibid., p. 11: 'scriptural Christianity'. This deliberately and pointedly chosen expression is clearly distinguished from the catchphrase 'primitive Christianity', which served as the platform on the one hand for the Patristic stance adopted by orthodox Anglican theology and on the other hand for the counter-view put forward in the Arian —Deistic manifesto of William Whiston (*Primitive Christianity Revived*, 5 vols., 1711–12). In this way John Wesley gave expression to the fact that in contradistinction to the humanist outlook of the prevailing Anglican theology, 'Primitive Christianity' meant for him biblical Christianity. On Arianism and Deism, cf. esp. Roland N. Stromberg, *Religious Liberalism in Eighteenth-Century England*, OUP, 1954, passim, esp. pp. 34–87.
8. It merits notice that Wesley speaks in the following terms about the New Testament: 'It is undeniably proved by the original charter of Christianity' (ibid., p. 11). He thereby confers on the N.T. both a binding importance in its own right and an importance in the historical sense of providing documentary evidence. In other words, he takes into account the Enlightenment's desire for historical authenticity.
9. 1 Corinthians 14[20]. Wesley's full text is as follows (ibid., pp. 12–3): 'And the strongest reasoner whom we have observed (excepting only Jesus of Nazareth) was that Paul of Tarsus; the same who has left that plain direction for all Christians "in malice" or wickedness "be ye children"; but "in understanding" or reason "be ye men".' In this connexion it is worthy of note that John Wesley follows without qualification the rendering of the King James' Bible and makes no play with the original Greek word τέλειοι, which is so crucial here, clearly because he wanted to remind his readers of what was familiar to them. The objective meaning of 'reason' and 'natural', as connoting a reflection of the true order of things or their constitutive principle, which is here basic to Wesley's argument, is Greek, and in particular Platonic. This thought-pattern had been given a permanent place in Anglican theological thinking through Richard Hooker: see *Of the Laws of Ecclesiastical Polity*, Book I, ch. viii, Everyman's Library Edition, Vol. 201 (1907), 1958 imp., pp. 174–84. This notion reappears in typical form in Susanna Wesley's *Conference with her Daughter* (ed. G. Stringer Rowe, 1898, *Publications of W.H.S.*, 3), *passim*, esp. pp. 6, 29–31, 35–7. We may assume that this advice to her daughter, which reads largely like a paraphrase of Hooker, was

also part of John Wesley's unconscious heritage. The equation of beauty with goodness, too, traces back to Hooker, and indeed Hooker expressly describes this equation as a Greek presentiment of the true state of affairs on the basis of the word-combination καλοκἀγαθία. Inherent to this equation is that of holiness with happiness and the favourite Anglican formula 'the beauty of holiness' (Psalms 29², 96⁹; 110³). Cf. Richard Hooker, ibid,. p. 175.

10. Cf. the same line of thought in the young Luther, above all in his *Lectures on the Epistle to the Romans* and in his *Ninety-Five Theses* on Indulgences *(accusatio sui)*. From among the copious literature, see esp. Ernst Wolf, *Staupitz und Luther*, 1927, pp. 223–61.

11. *A Farther Appeal to Men of Reason and Religion, Works* [3rd edn, 1830], VIII, 46–247.

12. The passages are Luke 6⁴³; Mark 1¹⁵; Matthew 3⁸, 6¹⁴⁻¹⁵; Luke 3⁴,⁹; Matthew 7⁷, 25²⁹ (p. 147).

13. Ibid., p. 48: 'The first sowing of this seed I cannot conceive to be other than instantaneous; whether I consider experience, or the word of God, or the very nature of the thing;—however, I contend not for a circumstance, but the substance: If you can attain it another way, do.'

14. Ibid., pp. 49–50. The works in question are: *The Notions of the Methodists fully disproved*, Newcastle, 1743; *The Notions of the Methodists farther disproved*. No place or year.

15. *Letters*, II, 116–28, Bristol, 10th February 1748, to Thomas Whitehead (?).

16. Robert Barclay, *An Apology for the True Christian Divinity as the same is held for and preached by the people, in scorn, called Quakers* (1676).

17. *Letters*, II, 117 (see above, note 15): 'If by these words—"The Scriptures are not the principal ground of truth and knowledge, nor the adequate primary rule of faith and manners"—be only meant that "the Spirit is our first and principal leader", here is no difference between Quakerism and Christianity. But there is great impropriety of expression. For though the Spirit is our principal leader, yet He is not our rule at all; the Scriptures are the rule whereby He leads us into all truth. Therefore, only talk good English; call the Spirit our "guide", which signifies an intelligent being, and the Scripture our "rule", which signifies something used by an intelligent being, and all is plain and clear.'

18. *Letters*, II, 125: 'In what Robert Barclay teaches concerning the Scriptures, Justification, Baptism, and the Lord's Supper lies the main difference between Quakerism and Christianity.'

19. *Letters*, II, 127–8: 'Friend, you have an honest heart, but a weak head; you have a zeal, but not according to knowledge. You was zealous once for the love of God and man, for holiness of heart and holiness of life: you are now zealous for particular forms of speaking, for a set of phrases and opinions. Once your zeal was against ungodliness and unrighteousness, against evil tempers and evil words: now it is against forms of prayer, against singing psalms or hymns, against appointing times of praying or preaching; against saying "you" to a single person, uncovering your head, or having too many buttons upon your coat. Oh what a fall is here! What poor trifles are these, that now well nigh engross your thoughts! Come back, come back to the weightier matters of the Law, to spiritual, rational, scriptural religion. No longer waste your time and strength in beating the air, in vain controversies and strife of words; but bend your whole soul to the growing in grace and in the knowledge of our Lord Jesus Christ, to the continually advancing in that holiness without which you cannot see the Lord.'

20. On this, besides the letter to John Taylor of 3rd July 1759, mentioned in note 23, see also *Journal*, V, 47, 16th March 1764: 'I have long desired that there might be an open, avowed union between all those who preach those fundamental truths. Original Sin and Justification by Faith, producing inward and outward holiness; but all my endeavours have been hitherto ineffectual. God's time is not fully come.' This is what gives Wesley's preaching its ecumenical dimension. He conceived the unity of Christendom as a doctrinal unity.

21. On the progress of Unitarianism in England, see the first-rate accounts given by H. John McLachlan, *Socianism in 17th-Century England*, 1951, and Stromberg (see note 7). From 1733 John Taylor (1694–1761) was in Norwich and from 1759 theological tutor at the Warrington Academy. He caused a great stir with his Unitarian book: *The Scripture Doctrine of Original Sin*, 1740 [2nd edn, 1741; 3rd edn, 1746; 4th edn, 1767]. John Wesley wrote in 1757, and Taylor replied in the 1767 4th edition.

22. *Letters*, IV, 48, London, 9th December 1758, to Augustus Montague Toplady in Dublin. Similarly, *Journal*, IV, 199, London, 25th March 1757; IV. 200, London, 1st April 1757.

23. *Letters*, IV, 67–8, Hartlepool, 3rd July 1759, to Dr Taylor.

24. *Journal*, III, 374, 28th August 1748, in Shackerley (Lancashire): 'We came to Shackerley, six miles farther, before five in the evening. Abundance of people were gathered before six, many of whom were disciples of Dr Taylor, laughing at Original Sin, and, consequently, at the whole frame of scriptural Christianity. Oh what a providence is it which has brought us here also, among these silver-tongued

Antichrists! Surely a few, at least, will recover out of the snare, and know Jesus Christ as their wisdom and righteousness!'

Similarly, *Journal*, III, 520, 10th April 1751, (likewise in Shackerley); *Journal*, V, 308, 6th April 1769, in Belfast.

25. *Letters*, IV, 67–8 (see above, note 23): 'Either I or you mistake the whole of Christianity from the beginning to the end! Either my scheme or yours is as contrary to the scriptural as the Koran is. Is it mine or yours? Yours has gone through all England and made numerous converts. I attack it from end to end. Let all England judge whether it can be defended or not!'

*Journal*, IV, 39–40, 2nd August 1752, Drumcree (Ireland): 'Mr. Booker, the minister of D(elvin), met me here—the last man I should have expected. But it cannot last. The same person cannot long admire both, John Wesley and John Taylor.'

26. Acknowledgement of Taylor's merits and abilities in formal matters is given in *Works* [3rd edn, 1830], IX, p. 192 (Preface) and p. 431: 'What I have often acknowledged, I now repeat. Were it not on a point of so deep importance, I would no more enter the lists with Dr Taylor, than I would lift my hand against a giant. I acknowledge your abilities of every kind; your natural and acquired endowments; your strong understanding; your lively and fruitful imagination; your plain and easy, yet nervous, style. I make no doubt of your having studied the original Scriptures for many years. And I believe you have moral endowments which are infinitely more valuable and more amiable than all these. For (if I am not greatly deceived) you bear "good-will to all men". And may not I add, you fear God?

'O what might not you do with these abilities! What would be too great for you to attempt and effect! Of what service might you be, not only to your own countrymen, but to all that bear the Christian name! How might you advance the cause of true, primitive, scriptural Christianity; of solid, rational virtue; of the deep, holy, happy, spiritual religion which is brought to light by the gospel! How capable are you of recommending, not barely morality (the duty of man to man), but piety, the duty of man to God, even the "worshipping him in spirit and in truth!" How well qualified are you to explain, enforce, defend, even "the deep things of God"; the nature of the kingdom of God "within us"; yea, the interiora regni Dei! (I speak on supposition of your having the "unction of the Holy One", added to your other qualifications). And are you, whom God has so highly favoured, among those who serve the opposite cause?'

27. Cf. esp. Romans 1²¹ff. *Works* [3rd edn, 1830], IX, pp. 202ff.: 'How well was Rome represented in the prophetical vision by that beast

"dreadful and terrible", which had "great iron teeth, and devoured and brake in pieces, and stamped under his feet" all other kingdoms!'

28. The book in question is the widely used book of Edward Brerewood (Bryerwood) (1565(?)–1613), Professor of Astronomy at Gresham College, London, and at Oxford, and Fellow of Mary Hall. See note 29.

29. Ibid., p. 210: 'Are they eminent for justice, for mercy, or truth? As to mercy, they know not what it means, being continually cutting each other's throats, from generation to generation, and *selling for slaves as many of those who fall into their hands* as on that consideration only they do not murder' (italics original). As is well known, the protest against the slave trade, on which the whole wealth of seaport towns like Bristol and Liverpool was based, only began after John Wesley's death, and the fact has always been deplored that he himself did not initiate it and provide it with the strongest possible Christian motivation, but rather was not ashamed to accept help from the wealth of these particular towns. In this passage he seems to pioneer a condemnation of the slave trade.

Edward Brerewood, *Enquiries touching the Diversities of Language and Religions through the chief parts of the world,* London, 1614, [2nd edn, 1622; 3rd edn, 1635; 4th edn, 1647]; French edn, 1640. On this, see Richard Simon under the pseudonym Sieur de Moni, *Histoire critique de la créance et des coûtumes des nations du Levant,* Frankfort (= Amsterdam), 1684.

30. On the subject of the noble savage before Rousseau, which admittedly the young Wesley did not take into consideration, because it was not till later that he joined the discussion, see Frank J. Klingberg, who in *Anglican Humanitarianism in Colonial New York,* 1940 (Church Historical Society of Philadelphia Publications, no. 11), pp. 49–86, traces the idea back to Las Casas.

31. On Admiral Lord Anson, see Sir John Barrow, *The Life of Lord Anson* (1839). George Lord Anson (1697–1762), Admiral, served 1723–35 on the coast of South Carolina, 1737–9 on the coast of West Africa, 1739–41 in the West Indies, 1741–4 in Chinese and Philippine waters, 1745–6 in London, then in command of the Channel fleet against France. From 1748 he was virtually First Lord of the Admiralty, between 1751 and 1756 officially as well and again from 1757–62. [In 1761 he was made Admiral of the Fleet.] His principal work, which John Wesley makes use of here, is *Voyage round the World* (1748), published by Richard Walter, M.A., chaplain of His Majesty's Ship *Centurion* in that expedition.

32. What Wesley probably has in mind is the translation by George Sale

(1697(?)-1736), 1734, which Voltaire particularly commended. A German translation was published by Thomas Arnold Lemgo in 1746.

33. This observation, which was developed by Theodore Trede (*Das Heidentum in der römischen Kirche, Bilder aus dem religiösen und sittlichen Leben Süditaliens*, 4 Vols., 1889–91) into a comprehensive, copiously documented work, is of long standing. It seems that it was first made by François de Croy, who went over from Roman Catholicism to Calvinism and became a Reformed pastor in Uzès near Montpellier (see *Fortgesetzte Sammlung von Alten und Neuen Theologischen Sachen*, 1742, pp. 408–9). His book, *Les trois conformités, sçavoir l'harmonie et convenance de l'église romaine avec le paganisme, judaisme et les anciennes hérésies*, 1605, was Englished under the title: *Harmony of the Romish Church with Gentilism, Judaism and Ancient Heresies*, 1626. Did Wesley know it? He nowhere mentioned it. An abridged edition by Johann Jakob Grasser appeared in German under the title: *Heydnisches Pabsttum, das ist, Gründlicher Bericht, was für Gebräuche und Ceremonien die römische Kirche habe aus dem Heydenthum genommen*, Basel, 1607.

34. *Works* [3rd edn, 1830], IX, p. 222: 'If then, all nations Pagan, Mahometan, and Christian, do in fact, make this their last resort, what farther proof do we need of the utter degeneracy of all nations from the plainest principles of reason and virtue? of the absolute want both of common sense and commun humanity, which runs through the whole race of mankind?'

35. On this, see Karl Holl, *Die Bedeutung der grossen Kriege für das religiöse und kirchliche Leben innerhalb des deutschen Protestantismus. Gesammelte Aufsätze zur Kirchengeschichte*, Vol. III: *Der Westen*. 1928, pp. 352–5. See also Wilhelm Lütgert, *Die Religion des deutschen Idealismus und ihr Ende*, Vol. I [2nd edn, 1923], pp. 177–9.

36. On this, see esp. the impressive chapter on 'The Ladder of Preferment' in Norman Sykes, *Church and State in 18th-Century England*, 1934, pp. 147–88.

37. *Works* [3rd edn, 1830], IX, pp. 231–4. The introductory sentences read: 'I ask, then, First, Are you thoroughly pleased with yourself? Say you, Who is not? Nay, I say, Who is? Do you observe nothing in yourself which you dislike, which you cannot cordially approve of? Do you never think too well of yourself? Think yourself wiser, better, stronger than you appear to be upon the proof? Is not this pride? And do you approve of pride? Was you never angry without a cause, or farther than that cause required? Are you not apt to be so? Do you approve of this? Do not you frequently resolve against it, and do not

you break those resolutions again and again? Can you help breaking them? If so, why do you not? Are you not prone to "unreasonable desires", either of pleasure, praise, or money? Do not you catch yourself desiring things not worth a desire, and other things more than they deserve? Are all your desires proportioned to the real intrinsic value of things? Do you not know and feel the contrary? Are not you continually liable to "foolish and hurtful desires"? And do not you frequently relapse into them, knowing them to be such; knowing that they have before "pierced you through with many sorrows"? Have you not often resolved against these desires, and as often broke your resolutions? Can you help breaking them? Do so; help it, if you can; and if not, own your helplessness.

'Are you throughly pleased with your own life? *Nihilne vides quod nolis?* "Do you observe nothing there which you dislike?" I presume you are not too severe a judge here; nevertheless, I ask, Are you quite satisfied, from day to day, with all you say or do? Do you say nothing which you afterwards wish you had not said? do nothing which you wish you had not done? Do you never speak anything contrary to truth or love? Is that right? Let your own conscience determine. Do you never do anything contrary to justice or mercy? Is that well done? You know it is not. Why, then, do you not amend? Moves, sed nil promoves. You resolve, and resolve, and do just as you did before.'

38. Ibid., pp. 234–5.
39. Ibid., p. 235: 'Universal misery is at once a consequence and a proof of this universal corruption. Men are unhappy (how very few are the exceptions!), because they are unholy.'
40. Ibid., p. 236: 'I have not touched upon envy, malice, revenge, covetousness, and other gross vices. Concerning these it is universally agreed, by all thinking men, Christian or Heathen, that a man can no more be happy while they lodge in his bosom, than if a vulture was gnawing his liver. It is supposed, indeed, that a very small part of mankind, only the vilest of men, are liable to these. I know not that; but certainly this is not the case with regard to pride, anger, self-will, foolish desires. Those who are not accounted bad men are by no means free from these. And this alone (were they liable to no other pain) would prevent the generality of men, rich or poor, learned or unlearned, from ever knowing what happiness means.'
41. Ibid., pp. 237–8. James 4[1ff].
42. Luther, Schmalkaldic Articles, 1537, III, 1, On sins. See *Die Bekenntnis-Schriften der Evangelisch-Lutherischen Kirche*, Edn of the Deutsch-Evangelischer Kirchenausschuss [2nd edn, 1952], 434, 8.

43. In Wilhelm Hopf, *August Vilmar. Ein Lebens-und Zeitbild,* Vol. 1, 1912, p. 71 (following Vilmar's autobiography). The theological teacher in question was the supranaturalist rationalist, Albert Jakob Arnoldi, in Marburg.

    Sören Kierkegaard, *Der Begriff Angst,* translated into German by Emanuel Hirsch, 1952, pp. 13, 17. [E. T., *The Concept of Dread,* W. Lowrie, Princeton University Press, 2nd edn., 1957.]

44. Philip Jakob Spener, *Pia Desideria,* 1675, ed. Kurt Aland, 1940, [2nd edn, 1955], $11^{14}$–$43^{22}$, esp. $28^{19}$–$33^{10}$.

45. *Works* [3rd edn, 1830], IX, p. 255.

46. David Jennings (1691–1762) was from 1744 a Congregationalist theological tutor in London, having previously been minister of a church. He set special importance by Biblical and dogmatic orthodoxy. In 1749, on the recommendation of Philip Doddridge, he was made D.D. *honoris causa* at St Andrews University in Scotland. His principal works are:

    1. *The Beauty and Benefit of Early Piety,* 1730;
    2. *A Vindication of the Scripture Doctrine of Original Sin,* 1740 against Taylor).
    3. *The Scripture Testimony . . . an Appeal to Reason . . . for the Truth of the Holy Scriptures,* 1755.

47. *Works* [3rd edn, 1830], IX, pp. 274ff.

48. Ibid., p. 274.

49. Ibid., p. 281: 'Infirmities! What then, do innocent infirmities make a man unclean before God? Do labour, pain, bodily weaknesses or mortality, make us "filthy and abominable"? '

50. Ibid., p. 279, cf. esp. pp. 280–1. 'You conclude the head thus: "Man, in his present weak and fleshly state, cannot be clean before God!" Certainly as clean as the moon and stars at least; if he be as he was first created. He was "made but a little lower than the angels"; consequently, he was then far higher and more pure than these, or the sun itself, or any other part of the material creation. You go on: "Why cannot a man be clean before God?" because he is conceived and born in sin? No such thing. But because, if the purest creatures are not pure in comparison of God, much less a being subject to so many infirmities as a mortal man!' . . . (for the continuation, see previous note).

51. Ibid., p. 281.

52. Ibid., pp. 284–5.

53. Ibid., pp. 286ff.

54. Ibid., pp. 288ff.

55. Ibid., pp. 296ff. The Authorized Version of 1611 (King James'

Bible), which Wesley follows, is much more pointed than Luther's translation: 'Es ist das Herz ein trotzig und verzagt Ding, werkann es ergründen?'

56. Ibid., pp. 302–14. Cf. also his statement of fundamental principle in *Letters*, VI, 297–8, London, 7th February 1778, to Mary Bishop: 'Indeed, nothing in the Christian system is of greater consequence than the doctrine of Atonement. It is properly the distinguishing point between Deism and Christianity. "The scriptural scheme of morality", said Lord Huntingdon, "is what every one must admire; but the doctrine of Atonement I cannot comprehend." Here, then, we divide. Give up the Atonement, and the Deists are agreed with us.'

57. *Works* [3rd edn, 1830], IX, pp. 314–53.

58. Isaac Watts (1674–1748), *The Ruin and Recovery of Mankind*, 1741. John Taylor replied to this in his book, *Remarks on Original Sin*, 1742, and included this reply in the third edition of his work on *Original Sin*, Belfast, 1746.

59. Samuel Hebden wrote three times in quick succession against John Taylor:

a. *Man's Original Righteousness;* and God's covenant with Adam, as a publick person; asserted and plainly proved . . . with an appendix, relating to a book lately published by . . . John Taylor . . . against the Doctrine of Original Sin, 1740.

b. *Baptismal Regeneration disproved.* The Scripture account of the nature of Regeneration explained . . . with remarks on some passages in a late book against Original Sin, 1741.

c. *The Doctrine of Original Sin,* as laid down in the Assembly's Catechism explained and vindicated, 1741.

The following remarks of Doddridge in A Postscript to the 2nd edition of his *Sermons on Regeneration* is also indicative of the repercussions caused by Taylor's writings. 'Now as no Book can fall more directly under this [sc. Taylor's] censure [sc. of having "taken away the very Ground of the Christian Life" by maintaining the doctrines of Original Sin and New Birth], than this of mine . . . I thought it not improper in this Postscript, briefly to acquaint my Reader with the Principles, on which I continue to think the View in which I have put the Matter to be Rational and Scriptural, and do still in my Conscience judge it far preferable to what the Advocates of Baptismal Regeneration on the one Hand, or Mr Taylor [in *A Key to the Apostolick Writings,* a preface to his Paraphrase and Notes on Romans] on the other, would introduce. It seems to me, that the Points in Dispute with *him* are much more important than our Debates with them, as a much greater number of Scriptures are concerned, and the whole

Tenor of our Ministerial Addresses would be much more sensibly affected.' (Philip Doddridge, *Practical Discourses on Regeneration, in Ten Sermons*, London, 2nd edn, 1745. Postscript, pp. xvii–xix). [Translator's note: Being unable to obtain a copy of this work in English, Dr Schmidt quotes from E. F. Rambach's not completely accurate German translation of Doddridge. I have here quoted more fully and used the copy of the 2nd edn of Doddridge's sermons in Dr Williams' Library, London.]

Further books against Taylor were: S. Niles, *A Vindication of the Scripture Doctrine of Original Sin from Mr. Taylor's free and candid examination of it*, London 1740; idem., *The true Scripture Doctrine of Original Sin stated. . . . In the way of Remarks on The Scripture Doctrine of Original Sin. By John Taylor*, 1757; and Jonathan Edwards the elder (1703–58), *The great Christian Doctrine of Original Sin defended containing a reply to the Objections of Jeremy Taylor in his book intitled 'The Scripture of Original Sin'*, 1758 [1760², 1766³, 1768⁴, 1789⁵, 1798⁶].

60. Thomas Boston senior (1677–1732), a distinguished Presbyterian minister in Scotland, wrote the popular book, *Human Nature in its Fourfold State . . . in several discourses by a minister of the Gospel in the Church of Scotland*, 1720 [20th edn, 1771; 22nd edn, 1784], to which Wesley alluded in discussing this point. It is also to be observed that he did not hesitate to make the maximum use even of Calvinist authors, even though he regarded predestination as a pernicious heresy. An edition of Thomas Boston's complete works has also been published: *The Whole Works of Thomas Boston*, 12 Vols., Aberdeen, 1848–52. On Boston, see Andrew Thomson, *Thomas Boston of Ettrick, his life and Times*, 1895.

61. *Works* [3rd edn, 1830], IX, p. 353. The extracts are spread over pp. 353–464, vol. cit.

62. See Ferdinand Sigg, *John Wesley und die 'Christliche Bibliothek'. Einblicke in die verlegerische Tätigkeit des Methodismus im 18. Jahrhundert*, in the *Schweizer Evangelist* (Special number for 250th Birthday of the Founder of Methodism), 1953, pp. 381–5. See above, pp. 101–8.

63. *A Plain Account of Christian Perfection as believed and taught by the Rev. Mr. John Wesley, from the Year 1725 to the Year 1765*. Bristol. Printed by William Pine, 1766.

64. *Works* [5th edn, 1861], XI, p. 369: '*Requies in sanguine Christi.*' One has no difficulty in recognizing in this description a reflection of the 'Stillness' advocated by Molther.

65. Cf. supra, pp. 67–9.

66. *Works* [5th edn, 1861], XI, pp. 369, 370, 382, 385–7, 392–3, 403, 433, 443.
67. Ibid., p. 383.
68. Ibid., p. 384. Wesley is probably quoting from a sermon of James Ussher (1581–1656). Ussher, Archbishop of Armagh from 1625 and thereby Primate of all Ireland, held a unique position in the early history of the Anglican Church insofar as he pursued and advocated an eirenical policy which was well disposed towards the Calvinists in contradistinction to William Laud, with whom, however, he was on friendly terms. He had no altar in his church, rejected theological positions which Calvinists might not be able to accept and was an advocate of synodical episcopacy.
69. Ibid., p. 408.
70. Ibid., pp. 436–7.
71. Ibid., pp. 441–5.
72. Spener, *Pia Desideria* (1675), ed. Kurt Aland, 1940 [3rd edn, 1964], 43,[31]; 45,[18].
73. Balthasar Köpke, *Dialogus de templo Salomonis ...* 1695.
74. Joachim Just Breithaupt, *De perfectione partium*, 1704. On the other side of the question, see Valentine E. Löscher, *Unschuldige Nachrichten*, 1704, p. 43.
75. August Hermann Francke, *Von der Christen Vollkommenheit* (before 1690), reproduced in Gustav Kramer, *August Hermann Francke*, Vol. I, 1880, pp. 273–5.
76. See August Hermann Francke's manifesto in his preface to *D. Hieronymi Welleri Marter-Buch*, 1700, Quire A, Sheet 3, *verso*: 'The whole of the sacred writings are given to us by the deliberate counsel of God as a sort of model alphabet for clear testimony to the truth that we may be taught more forcibly through example than in any other way, indeed that even the Son of God Himself has taught us for the most part through the example of His holy and pitiful life, whereby He has left us an example that we should follow in His footsteps (1 Peter 2[21]).'
77. On this, cf. Ferdinand Sigg (see above, note 62).
77a. [Translator's note: on this point, see R. C. Monk, *John Wesley: His Puritan Heritage*. London, 1966, p. 33, note 5.]
78. Cf., e.g., *Letters*, II, 151–2, Newcastle-upon-Tyne, 14th August 1748, to Ebenezer Blackwell: 'I have had some thoughts of printing, on a finer paper and with a larger letter, not only all that we have published already, but, it may be, all that is most valuable in the English tongue, in threescore or fourscore volumes, in order to provide a complete library for those that fear God. I should print only an

hundred copies of each. Brother Downes would give himself up to the
work; so that, whenever I can procure a printing-press, types, and
some quantity of paper, I can begin immediately. I am inclined to
think several would be glad to forward such a design; and if so, the
sooner the better, because my life is far spent, and I know not how
soon the night cometh wherein no man can work.' The citing of such
a central Biblical text as John $9^4$ shows the great importance Wesley
attached to this very project. See also *Letters* II, 152–3, Newcastle-
upon-Tyne, 14th August 1748, to a Friend: 'I have often thought of
mentioning to you and a few others a design I have had for some years
of printing a little library, perhaps of fourscore or one hundred
volumes, to the use of those that fear God. My purpose was to select
whatever I had seen most valuable in the English language, and either
abridge or take the whole tracts, only a little corrected or explained,
as occasion should require. Of these I could print ten or twelve,
more or less, every year, on a fine paper, and large letter, which
should be cast for the purpose. As soon as I am able to purchase a
printing-press and types, I think of entering upon this design. I have
several books now ready, and a printer who desires nothing more than
food and raiment. In three or four weeks I hope to be in London, and,
if God permits, to begin without delay.'

79. On Philip Doddridge (1702–51), see Geoffrey F. Nuttall's definitive
work, *Philip Doddridge, His Contribution to English Religion*, 1951.
The German translation of his biblical commentary, *The Family
Expositor*, (6 vols., 1739–56), by Friedrich Eberhart Rambach, under
the title *Paraphrastische Erklärung der sämtlichen Schriften des Neuen
Testaments* (4 vols., 1755–8), especially at such an early date, shows
the high regard in which he was also held abroad. His *Sermons on
Regeneration*, 1740 (2nd edn, 1745), were also translated by the same
man in 1755. With regard to the correspondence between Sherlock
and Doddridge, see Charles John Abbey and Henry Overton, *The
English Church and its Bishops in the 18th Century*, 1878, II, p. 52.
[Translator's note: On Thomas Sherlock (1678–1761), see Edward
Carpenter, *Thomas Sherlock*, London, S.P.C.K., 1936. Further to
Doddridge's international renown even within his own lifetime, see
J. Orton, *Memoirs of the Life, Character, and Writings of the Late
Rev. Philip Doddridge* (London, 1766; new edn, 1819), p. 105: 'His
sermons on Regeneration, Salvation by Grace, on the Power and
Grace of Christ . . . have been translated into Dutch; . . . the Rise
and Progress of Religion, into Dutch, German, Danish and French.']

80. *Journal*, II, 154 (Diary).

81. *Journal*, II, 371 (Diary), Thursday 24th July 1740.

82. *Journal*, III, 206.

83. 15th March 1746, Doddridge to Wesley; 18th June 1746, Doddridge to Wesley; printed in *Arminian Magazine*, I (1778), p. 419; Doddridge to Wesley, 29th June 1746, reprinted in *Journal*, III, 244–5, 2nd July 1746.

84. John Wesley, 'A Christian Library', I (1749), pp. i–vi. He sharply rejects the accusation of not having been Anglican enough in *Letters*, IV, 121, London, 12th December 1760, to Mr T. H., alias Philodemus, alias Somebody, alias Stephen Church, alias R. W.: 'Nothing can prove that I am no member of the Church, till I am either excommunicated or renounce her communion, and no longer join in her doctrine and in the breaking of bread and in prayer. Nor can anything prove I am no minister of the Church, till I either am deposed from my ministry or voluntarily renounce her, and wholly cease to teach her doctrines, use her offices, and obey her rubrics.

'Upon the same principle that I still preach and endeavour to assist those who desire to live according to the gospel, about twelve years ago I published proposals for printing "A Christian Library: Consisting of Extracts from and Abridgements of the Choicest Pieces of Practical Divinity which have been published in the English Tongue". And I have done what I proposed. Most of the tracts therein contained were written by members of our own Church; but some by writers of other denominations: for I mind not who speaks, but what is spoken.' Ibid. 122: XXX '"Is not your Christian Library an odd collection of mutilated writings of Dissenters of all sorts?" No. In the first ten volumes there is not a line from any Dissenter of any sort; and the greatest part of the other forty is extracted from Archbishop Leighton, Bishops Taylor, Patrick, Ken, Reynolds, Sanderson, and other ornaments of the Church of England.'

85. See the anonymous tract, *The Bishop of London's Doctrine of Justification in his late Pastoral Letters* (London, 1740), which contains by way of appendix a 'Vindication of the Rev. Mr. Whitefield's Assertions, relating to the Errors contained in the Book called The Whole Duty of Man and Archbishop Tillotson's Works.' P. 40: 'It was the general language of the Clergy that Lambeth-House was the Rendez-vous of all Religions, that the Archbishop's Palace was an *Amsterdam*' (italics original). This was a reference to John Tillotson (1630–94), Archbishop of Canterbury from 1691.

86. See my article, *Eigenart und Bedeutung der Eschatologie im englischen Puritanismus*, in *Theologia Viatorum*, IV (1952), pp. 250–3.

87. See Wilhelm Pauck, *Das Reich Gottes auf Erden, Utopia und Wirklichkeit. Eine Untersuchung zu Butzers De regno Christi und zur englischen*

*Staatkirche des 16. Jahrhunderts,* 1928. (In Emanuel Hirsch und Hans Lietzmann, edd., *Arbeiten zur Kirchengeschichte,* Vol. 10). [Translator's note: See also C. Hopf, *Martin Bucer and the English Reformation* (Oxford, 1946), esp. chpt 1; and W. Pauck, *Martin Bucer's Conception of a Christian State,* in: *The Princeton Theol. Review,* Vol. XXVI, 1928, pp. 80–8.]

88. Concerning Du Plessis-Mornay, see Raoul Patry, *Philippe du Plessis-Mornay. Un huguenot homme d'État 1549–1623,* Paris, 1933. Du Plessis-Mornay's apology bears the title, *Traité de la vérité chrétienne* (1583), and may be regarded as a precursor of Hugo Grotius' book under the same title, *De veritate religionis christianae* (1627), which for its part had evolved from a didactic poem for sailors. Grotius had intended to put it into their hands as a missionary and apologetic weapon for their encounter with Muslims and pagans.

89. Cf. *Letters,* I. 76, to Mrs Pendarves, 11th February 1731: 'Who can be a fitter person than one that knows it by experience to tell me the full force of that glorious rule, "Set your affections on things above and not on things of the earth"? Is it equivalent to "Thou shalt love the Lord thy God with all thy heart, soul and strength"? But what is it to love God? Is not to love anything the same as habitually to delight in it? Is not, then, the purpose of both these injunctions this, —that we delight in the Creator more than His creatures; that we take more pleasure in Him than in anything He has made, and rejoice in nothing so much as in serving Him; that, to take Mr Pascal's expression, while the generality of men use God and enjoy the world, we, on the contrary, only use the world, while we enjoy God?' *Letters,* VI. 205, London, 4th February 1776, to Mary Bishop.
*Letters,* VIII. 218, Otley, 29th April 1790, to his nephew Samuel Wesley [1766–1837], an exponent of Bach [but not to be confused with Samuel Sebastian Wesley (1810–76) Jr.] and Charles Wesley's son: 'But I fear you want (what you least of all suspect), the greatest thing of all—religion. I do not mean external religion, but the religion of the heart; the religion which Kempis, Pascal, Fénelon enjoyed: that life of God in the soul of man, the walking with God and having fellowship with the Father and the Son.'
*Journal,* IV. 45, 13th October 1752: 'I read over Pascal's Thoughts. What could possibly induce such a preacher as Voltaire to give such an author as this a good word, unless it was that he once wrote a satire? And so his being a satirist might atone even for his being a christian.' On Pascal's *Pensées* as compulsory reading for the Methodist lay preachers, see Vol. II, Part 1, of this work, p. 110.

89a.[Translator's special note: Without prejudice to Dr Schmidt's thesis about Wesley's selectivity, some specific additional observations on the subject of 'The Christian Library' would seem necessary, in fairness to Wesley and his avowed purpose in publishing the Library, namely, to provide 'Extracts from and Abridgements of the choicest pieces of Practical Divinity which have been published *in the English tongue*' (sub-title, italics mine). Of the authors enumerated as being omitted, we note that: there appears to have existed in Wesley's time no translation of the Epistle to Diognetus or of any suitable work of Tertullian; with minor exceptions, the same applies to Bucer; Cromwell was a statesman rather than a theologian, and besides his letters and speeches wrote nothing of any substance. With regard to the writings of Puritan divines and the inclusion of exemplary Puritan lives in the Library, see above all R. C. Monk, *John Wesley: His Puritan Heritage* (London, 1966), esp. pp. 32–41. For comparative lists of Puritans in the Library, see Monk's appendices (op. cit., pp. 255–64); Duncan Coomer, *The Influence of Puritanism and Dissent on Methodism*, L.Q.H.R., 175 (1950), p. 347; and John Newton, *Methodism and the Puritans* (London, 1964), p. 8.]

90. The concept of canon ecclesiasticus is not widely used. It means two things: the legal decree of the Church as an individual canon and the Church's official list of writings. In the second sense it is apparently distinguished from the canon biblicus. As is well known, Luther wanted to include Melanchthon's *Loci Communes* (1521) in the canon ecclesiasticus as distinct from the canon biblicus: W.A.18,601[6]—the beginning of *De servo Arbitrio*, 1525. This question calls for more thorough research.

91. *Letters*, III, 173, Kingswood, 14th March 1756, to Samuel Furly: 'You are sick of two diseases: that affection for a poor silly worm like yourself, which only absence (through the grace of God) will cure; and that evil disease which Marcus Antoninus complains of—the δίψαν βιβλίων. That you are far gone in the latter plainly appears from your not loving and admiring that masterpiece of reason and religion, the *Reflections on the Conduct of Human Life, with regard to Knowledge and Learning*, every paragraph of which must stand unshaken (with or without the Bible) till we are no longer mortal.' The author of the book which John Wesley here recommended to his young friend was John Norris (1657–1711). [Translator's note: see J. C. English, *John Norris and John Wesley on the "Conduct of the Understanding"*. Proc. WHS, XXXVII (1970), pp. 101–4.] James Hervey (1714–58), John Wesley's erstwhile friend from Oxford days and his later adversary, passed unfavourable judgement on 'The Christian Library' on the grounds that it had been conceived too

hastily and been too little thought out: 'Mr. Wesley has huddled over his performance in a most precipitate, and therefore most imperfect manner. One would think, his aim was, not to select the best and noblest passages, but to reprint those which came first to hand' (Letter to William Cudworth, written in Weston-Fabel near North-ampton [Hervey's parish], 22nd April 1755. Printed in Luke Tyerman, *The Oxford Methodists*, 1873, p. 301.

92. *Works* [5th edn, 1861], X, pp. 273–365.

93. Ibid., p. 283: 'Yet I had a strange thought. "If I do go to hell, I will praise God there. And since I cannot be a monument of his mercy in heaven, I will be a monument of his justice in hell".'

94. W. A. 56, $390^{23}$–$391^{12}$ and $392^1$. '*Iis autem, qui vere Deum diligunt amore filiali et amicitie, qui non est ex natura, sed spiritu sancto solum, sunt pulcherrima ista verba et perfectissimi exempli testmonia. Tales enim libere sese offerunt in omnem voluntatem Dei, etiam ad infernum et mortem eternaliter, si Deus ita vellet tantum, ut sua voluntas plene fiat; adeo nihil querunt, que sua sunt.*

*Verum sancti perfecti, quia abundant charitate, sine tamen magna tristia, faciunt hanc resignationem.*

95. *Works* [5th edn, 1861], XI, p. 284.

96. Ibid., p. 340.

97. Ibid., pp. 349–50.

98. *A Treatise concerning the Godhead of Jesus Christ. Translated from the French*, in: '*A Preservative against unsettled Notions in Religion*', 1758.

99. *Letters*, II, 312–88, London, 4th January 1749.

100. *Serious considerations on Absolute Predestination, Exacted from a late Author*. Bristol, 1741. *A Dialogue between a Predestinarian and his Friend*. London, 1741. *The Scripture Doctrine concerning Predestination, Election and Reprobation. Extracted from a late Author*. London, 1741 (later incorporated in '*A Preservative against unsettled Notions in Religion*', 1758).*Predestination calmly considered*, 1752. *Works* [3rd edn, 1830], X, pp. 204–59. *The Doctrine of Absolute Predestination stated and asserted. By the Reverend Mr. A.T.*, 1770—a tract published in abridged form by John Wesley as a grim warning and almost without any comment on his part. Toplady's book was largely a translation of a treatise by Girolamo Zanchi, *Sermo in Romanos viii, 29–30* (E. T., 1776). Wesley condemned predestination with particular acidity as a deep-seated cancerous growth in the tradition of Christian teaching in his letter of 18th August 1775, to John Fletcher *(Letters*, VI. 174–5, Brecon): 'I have now received all your papers, and here and there made some small corrections. I suppose you have read Dean Tucker's Letters to Dr. Kippis. I read them in my journey from

Gloucester hither, and never before saw so clearly the rise and progress of Predestinarianism. Does not he show beyond all contradiction that it was hatched by Augustine in spite to Pelagius (who very probably held no other heresy than you or I do now); that it spread more and more in the Western Church till the eleventh century; that Peter Lombard then formed it into a complete system; that in the twelfth century Thomas Aquinas bestowed much pains in explaining and confirming it; that in the thirteenth Duns Scotus did the same; that Ignatius Loyola did the same and all the first Jesuits held it, as all the Dominican and Augustine Friars (with the Jansenists) do to this day; that Bellarmine was firm in it, as were the bulk of the Romanists, till the Council of Trent, when, in furious opposition to Luther and Calvin, they disclaimed their ancient tenets.' Here Wesley did not hesitate to range himself with Pelagius against Augustine. Since his essential concern in this connexion was to combat Antinomianism, the question of predestination as dealt with in his literary works has not been given separate treatment here.

101. Milton: 'That to the height of this great argument
     I may assert eternal Providence,
     And justify the ways of God with man.'
                    *Paradise Lost* 1, 1, 22.

102. The tedious and virtually fruitless debate with Roland Hill particularly underlines this. *Some remarks on Mr Hill's 'Review of all the Doctrines taught by Mr. John Wesley'*: Works [3rd edn, 1830], X, pp. 374–414. *Some remarks on Mr Hill's 'Farrago Double-Distilled'*: op. cit., pp. 415–56.

103. He also occasionally warned against the writings of Mme. de la Motte-Guyon. Cf. *Letters*, V. 342, 25th October 1772, to Ann Bolton. For him the 'refined' relationship with God characteristic of Mysticism ran counter to a sober sense of reality: 'You cannot imagine what trouble I have had for many years to prevent our friends from refining upon religion. Therefore I have industriously guarded them from meddling with the Mystic writers, as they are usually called; because these are the most artful refiners of it that ever appeared in the Christian world, and the most bewitching. There is something like enchantment in them. When you get into them, you know not how to get out. Some of the chief of these, though in different ways, are Jacob Behmen and Madam Guyon. My dear friend, come not into their secret; keep in the plain, open Bible way. Aim at nothing higher, nothing deeper, than the religion described at large in our Lord's Sermon on the Mount, and briefly summed up by St. Paul in the 13th chapter (of the first Epistle) to the Corinthians. I long to have you more and

more deeply penetrated by humble, gentle, patient love. Believe me, you can find nothing higher than this till mortality is swallowed up of life. All the high-sounding or mysterious expressions used by that class of writers either mean no more than this or they mean wrong.'

Cf. also *Letters*, VI, 43–4, Bristol, 19th September 1773, to Mary Bishop. Here Wesley quotes a dictum of August Hermann Francke which he may have picked up from oral tradition: 'That wise and good man Professor Francke used to say of them, "They do not describe our Common Christianity, but every one has a religion of his own." It is very true: so that if you study the Mystic writers, you will find as many religions as books; and for this plain reason, each of them makes his own experience the standard of religion.'

104. Letter to William Law from London, 6th January 1756: *Letters*, III, 332–70; cf. also *Journal*, II. 297, 23rd October 1739: 'In riding to Bradford, I read over Mr. Law's book on the New Birth: philosophical, speculative, Precarious, Behmenish, void and vain!'

*Thoughts upon Jacob Behmen* (1780): *Works* [3rd edn, 1830], IX, pp. 509–14; cf. also *Letters*, VI. 298, London, 7th February 1778, to Mary Bishop. Wesley's critical attitude to Friedrich Christoph Oetinger also belongs in this context. Wesley had a copy of the latter's principal work, which was devoted to epistemology *(Inquisitio in Sensum Communem et Rationem, necnon utriusque regulas*, 1753), and wrote on the inside page of the book-cover: 'A Writer so obscure does not deserve the time and pains which are necessary to understand him.' (I saw this in Kingswood School Library, Bath. This copy is inscribed: 'J.W. 1759.').

105. *A clear and concise Demonstration of the Divine Inspiration of the Holy Scriptures,* in *Arminian Magazine*, 1789, p. 211 = *Works* [5th edn, 1861], XI. 484.

106. *Explanatory Notes upon the New Testament*, 759 pp., London, 1755 (11th edn, 1831, not to mention many separate reprints). This work, compiled with painstaking care, in which he included his own comments and interpretations and also corrected the King James' Bible on the basis of the original text, was completed—with the co-operation of his brother Charles—in the astonishing short space of a year and nine months. It deserves a detailed study all to itself. Until a thorough source-analysis has been made, it is impossible to make a proper evaluation of it. [Translator's note: In the body of the original text, by a typological error, the name of Robert Gell has been substituted for that of Dr John Guyse as one of the primary sources of the *Notes* to which Wesley refers in the preface, paras 7–8. Dr Robert Gell (1595–1665) was an Anglican clergyman; Dr John

Guyse (1680–1761) was an Independent minister, who wrote, inter alia, *An Exposition of the New Testament in the form of a paraphrase* (3 vols. 1739–52). Dr Schmidt omits Dr John Heylyn (?1685–1759), who published *An Interpretation of the New Testament . . . containing the Acts of the Apostles and the several Epistles* (London, 1761) and the work upon which Wesley drew, *Theological Lectures at Westminster Abbey. With an Interpretation of the Four Gospels. . . .* (London, 1749). On these sources, see Green's *Bibliography* (1906), pp. 91–2.]

107. *A Concise Ecclesiastical History, from the Birth of Christ to the Beginning of the present Century.* In Four Volumes. 1781.

108. *A Survey of the Wisdom of God in the Creation; or, a Compendium of Natural Philosophy,* Vol. I, Bristol, 1763.

109. *A Roman Catechism,* faithfully drawn out of the allowed Writings of the Church of Rome. With a Reply thereto. 1756 = *Works* [3rd edn, 1830], X, pp. 86–128; *Popery Calmly Considered,* 1779 = *Works* [3rd edn, 1830], X, pp. 140–58; A Letter to a Roman Catholic, *Works* [3rd edn, 1830], X, pp. 80–6. A letter to the Printer of the 'Public Advertiser'. Occasioned by the late Act passed in favour of Popery, 1780: *Letters,* VI. 370–3. To the Editors of the 'Freeman's Journal', 1780; *Letters,* VII. 3–8, 9–16. To the Printer of the 'Public Advertiser'; *Letters,* VI. 371, City Road, London, 12th January 1780: 'With persecution I have nothing to do. I persecute no man for his religious principles. Let there be "as boundless a freedom in religion" as any man can conceive. But this does not touch the point; I will set religion, true or false, utterly out of the question. Suppose the Bible, if you please, to be a fable, and the Koran to be the word of God. I consider not whether the Romish religion be true or false; I build nothing on one or the other supposition. Therefore away with all your commonplace declamation about intolerance and persecution in religion! Suppose every word of Pope Pius' Creed to be true; suppose the Council of Trent to have been infallible; yet I insist upon it that no Government not Roman Catholic ought to tolerate men of the Roman Catholic persuasion. I prove this by a plain argument (let him answer it that can). That no Roman Catholic does or can give security for his allegiance or peaceable behaviour I prove thus: It is a Roman Catholic maxim, established not by private men but by a public council, that "no faith is to be kept with heretics". This has been openly avowed by the Council of Constance; but it was never openly disclaimed.' Here Wesley has in mind the reason offered for breaking faith with Hus.

See also 'A Disavowal of Persecuting Papists', in the *Arminian Magazine,* 1782 = *Works* [3rd edn, 1830] X, pp. 173–5. To this is to be added a pamphlet from the year 1752: *A Short Method of Converting all the Roman Catholics in the Kingdom of Ireland. Humbly proposed to the Bishop and Clergy of the Kingdom*. Dublin, 1752 = *Works*, [3rd edn, 1830], X, pp. 129–33.

110. J. Wesley was himself thoroughly aware of this and on occasion offered reasons for it. See *Letters*, IV. 11, Dublin, 5th April 1758, to Elizabeth Hardy: 'I do by no means exclude the Old Testament from bearing witness to any truths of God. Nothing less. But I say the experience of the Jews is not the standard of Christian experience.' Thus—and this is a genuinely modern approach—it is the experiential criterion which is taken as the norm, and not that of Biblical canonicity. This also corresponds to Pietist thought, which used the historically (i.e. experientially) proven attainability of primitive Christianity in support of its challenge to the life of the modern Church. This argument was first used effectively in Spener's *Pia Desideria* (49, [6]). On the latter, see my article, 'Spener's Pia Desideria', in *Theologia Viatorum*, III (1951), pp. 91ff. This shift in basic approach has profound and far-reaching implications and has become of critical importance for modern Old Testament scholarship among Protestant theologians. Be that as it may, Wesley rectified his omission by his *Explanatory Notes upon the Old Testament* (Vol. I, 1765; Vol. II, 1767), which were excerpted from Matthew Henry's *Exposition of the Old (and New) Testament* (1708–10) and Matthew Poole's *Annotations on the Holy Bible* (2 Vols., 1683–5). In describing his position vis-à-vis the Bible, he sometimes used the immoderate phrase 'bigotry': *Letters*, V. 313, 25th March 1772, to Ann Bolton: 'you and I are bigots to the Bible'. [Translator's note: on the Wesleys and Henry, see A. K. Lloyd, *Charles Wesley's Debt to Matthew Henry*, LQHR, 171 (1946), 330–7.]

111. *Thoughts upon Slavery*, 1774, *Works* [5th edn, 1861], XI, pp. 59–79. Cf. also his vehement letter to Samuel Hoare: *Letters*, VIII. 275–6, Isle of Guernsey, 18th August 1787.

112. *Thoughts upon Liberty*, 1772: vol. cit., pp. 34–46.

113. Vol. cit., pp. 46–53.

114. Vol. cit., pp. 53–9. *Thoughts on the Present Scarcity of Provisions*, 1773.

115. Vol. cit., pp. 129–40. *A Calm Address to the Inhabitants of England*, 1777.

116. Vol. cit., pp. 164–202. In addition, *Thoughts on the Sin of Onan. Chiefly extracted from a late Writer (Dr. Tissot)*, 1767 [2nd edn, 1774; 3rd edn, 1770].

117. *An Estimate of the Manners of the present Times*, 1782. Vol. cit., p. 159:

. . . 'what is the present characteristic of the English nation? It is ungodliness. This is at present the characteristic of the English nation. Ungodliness is our universal, our constant, our peculiar character.'

118. Vol. cit., p. 476.

119. Vol. cit., p. 459. *Thoughts on a Single Life*, 1765.

120. Vol. cit., pp. 464–5. *A Thought upon Marriage*, 1785.

121. Vol. cit., p. 485. *The Real Character of Montanus*. Cf. *Journal*, III. 490, 15th August 1750.

122. See Wilhelm Lütgert, *Die Erschütterung des Optimismus durch das Erdbeben von Lissabon 1755* (1901).

123. *Works* [5th edn, 1861], XI, pp. 1–13 (1755).

124. Ibid., p. 11: 'But how shall we secure the favour of this great God? How? but by worshipping him in spirit and in truth; by uniformly imitating Him we worship, in all his inimitable perfections? without which the most accurate systems of opinions, all external modes of religion, are idle cobwebs of the brain, dull farce and empty show. Now, God is love: Love God then, and you are a true worshipper. Love mankind, and God is your God, your Father; and your Friend. But see that you deceive not your own soul; for this is not a point of small importance. And by this you may know: if you love God, then you are in God; If you love God, then you are happy in God; if you love God, riches, honours, and the pleasures of sense are no more to you than bubbles on the water: You look on dress and equipage, as the tassels of a fool's cap; diversions, as the bells on a fool's coat, and your whole life is a sacrifice to him. And if you love mankind, it is your one design, desire, and endeavour, to spread virtue and happiness all around you; to lessen the present sorrows and increase the joys of every child of man; and, if it be possible, to bring them with you to the rivers of pleasure that are at God's right hand for evermore. But where shall you find one who answers this happy and admirable character? Wherever you find a Christian; for this, and this alone, is real, genuine Christianity. Surely you did not imagine that Christianity was no more than such a system of opinions as is vulgarly called faith; or a strict and regular attendance on any kind of external worship. O no! Were this all that is implied, Christianity were indeed a poor, empty, shallow thing; such as none but half-thinkers could admire; and all who think freely and generously must despise. But this is not the case; the spirit above described, this alone, is Christianity. And, if so, it is no wonder that even a celebrated unbeliever should make that frank declaration, "Well, after all, these Christian dogs are the happiest fellows upon earth!" '

125. On this point, cf. the superb, thoroughly researched characterization by Heinrich Bornkamm, *Luther als Schriftsteller* in *Sitzungsberichte der Heidelberger Akademie der Wissenschaften*, phil.-hist. Klasse, Jahrgang 1965, Vol. I, 1965, esp. pp. 19 and 24ff.

126. Rudolf Hermann, *Die Gestalt Simsons bei Luther* (1952), in *Gesammelte Studien zur Theologie Luthers und der Reformation*, 1960, p. 428.

127. Heinrich Bornkamm, op. cit. (see note 125), p. 31.

## Chapter 8: John Wesley as Pastor

1. Cf. Friedrich Michael Ziegenhagen to Gotthilf August Francke, 15th March 1738.

   Samuel Berein to G. A. Francke, 4th December 1738.

   Also his letter to Francke of 1st June 1739: 'In London a great movement has now been occasioned by the so-called Methodists. The most eminent among them, and the one who has called the greatest stir, is Mr. Whitefield. Both before his departure to Georgia and after his return thence, this man has preached to such vast crowds that in various places the churches and churchyards have been damaged by the immense number of people. But some time ago now the pulpits were forbidden not only to Mr. Whitefield but also to the rest of the Methodists: and yet Mr. Whitefield did not allow his eager desire to preach to be stifled by this, but has since then preached almost daily in the open air on a platform before 20,000 people and sometimes on Sundays before 50,000 people. At these gatherings he has also taken up several collections on behalf of the poor colonists to Georgia, and only last Tuesday collected over £20 for the poor refugees from Salzburg now at Ebenezer. At several places in the city of London and Westminster certain meetings have been established by the Methodists, where they edify one another by praying and studying the word of God. In their preaching they place exceptional stress on the necessity of the new birth, on the repudiation of all human righteousness and on justification by faith. Opposition to them is becoming stronger and stronger: not only are they preached against, but also denounced in writing. Meantime there is said to be a large number of them from every station and walk of life, who receive the word of the cross and of grace, which to the majority in this country is foolishness, as the power and the wisdom of God, and show the proofs of this in their changed behaviour.'

Similarly, Berein to G. A. Francke, 20th July 1739. All this is in manuscript in the archives of Francke's Institution at Halle an der Saale, h I L 5.

2. *Journal*, II, 23rd November 1738. Even in extreme old age Wesley still found fluent words with which to express his axiom of absolute allegiance to the Bible, by sharply contrasting his own approach to that of Count Zinzendorf, words which were both a personal testimony and a pastoral counsel. On 24th February 1786, he wrote to Elizabeth Ritchie as follows (*Letters*, VII, 319): 'Count Zinzendorf observes there are three different ways wherein it pleases God to lead his people: some are guided almost in every instance by apposite texts of Scripture: others see a clear and plain reason for everything they are to do; and yet others are led not so much by Scripture or reason as by particular impressions. I am very rarely led by impressions but generally by reason and by Scripture.'

3. *Letters*, III, 222, Penryn, 19th September 1757, to Samuel Walker in Truro, 'Assurance is a word I do not use because it is not scriptural. But I hold a divine evidence or conviction that Christ loved *me* and gave Himself for *me* is essential to if not the very essence of justifying faith' (italics original).

4. See above, pp. 108–10.

5. *Journal*, II, 108, 7th December 1738.

6. On this, cf. Nehemiah Curnock's detailed discussion in *Journal*, II, 111–2, note 1.

7. *Journal*, II, 109–11.

8. *Journal*, II, 115–6, Saturday, 16th December 1738.

9. *Journal*, I, 479–80, Sunday, 28th May 1738.

10. *Journal*, II, 125–6, Thursday, 4th January 1739.

11. *Journal*, II, 239–40, 7th July 1739: 'I had an opportunity to talk with him of those outward signs which had so often accompanied the inward work of God. I found his objections were chiefly grounded on gross misrepresentations of matter of fact. But the next day he had an opportunity of informing himself better: for no sooner had he begun (in the application of his sermon) to invite all sinners to believe in Christ, than four persons sunk down close to him, almost in the same moment. One of them lay without either sense or motion; a second trembled exceedingly; the third had strong convulsions all over his body, but made no noise, unless by groans; the fourth, equally convulsed, called upon God, with strong cries and tears. From this time, I trust, we shall all suffer God to carry on His own work in the way that pleaseth him.'

In the year 1774 he again expressly defended this attitude of his, and very characteristically did so by using the catchword 'simplicity'. *Letters*, VI, 113, Bristol, 16th September 1774, to Miss March: 'You want more simplicity. I will give you the first instance that occurs of that simplicity which I mean. Some years since, a woman sitting by me fell into strong convulsions, and presently began to speak as in the name of God. Both her look, motions, and tone of voice were peculiarly shocking. Yet I found my mind as ready to receive what she said, as if she had spoken with the look, motion, and accent of Cicero.' He adopted a similar attitude on 21st January 1784. Cf. *Letters*, VII. 207, from near London, to Mrs. Parker: 'But, while one of them was preaching, several persons fell down, cried out, and were violently affected. Have you never read my Journals? or Dr. Edwards' Narrative? or Dr. Gillies' Historical Collections?' The following books are meant: Jonathan Edwards, *A Faithful Narrative of the Conversion of many hundred Souls in Northampton* (1736) and John Gillies' *Historical Collections relating to Remarkable Periods of the Success of the Gospel* (1754)—both being testimonies from similar revival movements, particularly in New England. 'Do not you see, then, that it has pleased the all-wise God, for near these fifty years, wherever He has wrought most powerfully, that these outward signs (whatever natural or not) should attend the inward work? And who can call Him to account for this? Let Him do as seemeth Him good.

'I must therefore still think that neither these nor any other reasons can justify the discarding the messengers of God, and consequently that all who do, or abet this, are maintaining a bad cause.'

12. *Journal*, II, 131–2, Sunday, 21st January 1739.
13. *Journal*, II, 136–7, Sunday, 28th January, 1739.
14. *Journal*, II, 147, Friday, 2nd March 1739.
15. *Letters*, I, 290–1, Bristol, 4th April 1739.
16. *Letters*, I, 334–5, Bristol, 23rd August 1759, to Ebenezer Blackwell.
17. *Journal*, II, 241, 12th July 1739: 'I went to a gentleman (Mr. Cutler) who is much troubled with what they call lowness of spirits. Many such have I been with before; but in several of them it was no bodily distemper. They wanted something, they knew not what, and were therefore heavy, uneasy, and dissatisfied with everything. The plain truth is they wanted God, they wanted Christ, they wanted faith. And God convinced them of their want, in a way their physicians no more understood than themselves. Accordingly nothing availed till the Great Physician came. For, in spite of all natural means, He who made them for Himself would not suffer them to rest till they rested in Him.' This description and analysis can only be called classic in its conciseness, realism, perspicuity and purposiveness. It

brings out in a unique way John Wesley's basic view both on the interrelation between physical and spiritual phenomena and on their relation to faith. Equally, it exemplifies his use of language.

18. *Journal*, II, 298–302, 23rd–29th October 1739.
19. *Journal*, II, 375–6, Monday, 11th August 1740.
20. *Journal*, II, 299–300, 25th and 26th October 1739.
21. *Journal*, II, 346–7, 9th and 21st May 1740.
22. *Journal*, II, 347, Saturday, 17th May 1740: 'I found more and more undeniable proofs that the Christian state is a continual warfare, and that we have need every moment to watch and pray, lest we enter into temptation. Outward trials indeed were now removed, and peace was in all our borders. But so much the more did inward trials abound; and if one member suffered, all the members suffered with it. So strange a sympathy did I never observe before: whatever considerable temptation fell on any one, unaccountably spreading itself to the rest, so that exceeding few were able to escape it.' This judgement is tantamount to a statement of fundamental principle on Wesley's part.
23. *Journal*, II, 338–9, 12th and 29th March 1740.
24. *Journal*, II, 334 and 336, 31st January and 12th February 1740.
25. *Journal*, II, 328, 30th December 1739.
26. *Journal*, II, 381–2, 3rd September 1740.
27. *Journal*, II, 374, 4th August 1740.
28. *Journal*, II, 378–9, Friday, 22nd August 1740; *Journal*, II, 383, 10th September 1740; *Journal*, II, 384, 11th September 1740; *Journal*, II, 456, Friday, 15th May 1741; *Journal*, II, 482–3, Friday, 31st July 1741.
29. *Journal*, II, 503, 7th September 1741: 'Oh what a harvest might there be, if any lover of souls who has time upon his hands would constantly attend these places of distress, and, with tenderness and meekness of wisdom, instruct and exhort those on whom God has laid His hands to know and improve the day of their visitation!'
30. *Journal*, II, 529–32, Sunday, 21st February 1742.
31. *Letters*, II, 12, Newcastle-upon-Tyne, 17th November 1742, to Mrs Hall (Martha Wesley). The fifth line of this letter challenges her to serve the Lord 'without carefulness and without distraction'. In this context 'carefulness' means carking care, a heart weighed down with anxiety. He wrote to her in similar vein on 15th September 1750 from London: *Letters*, III, 199. For full quotation, see below, note 65.
32. *Letters*, II, 158–70, Newington, 10th December 1748, to a Friend.
33. *Letters*, III, 17, London, 4th December 1751, to his brother Charles.
34. Richard Morgan senior to Richard Morgan junior: *Letters*, I, 156–7.

35. *Journal*, VIII, 268: John Gambold on John Wesley and the Holy Club (reprinted from the *Methodist Magazine*, 1798, pp. 117–21, 168–72).

36. *Journal*, V, 329, Saturday, 13th July 1769.

37. *Letters*, VI, 148–9, Waterford, 28th April 1775.

38. *Letters*, III, 7–14, Dublin, 18th July 1749, to a Roman Catholic. Similarly: *Letters*, III, 35–7, Bandon, 22nd May 1750, to Gilbert Boyce (a Baptist preacher); *Letters*, III, 40–1, Birr, 28th June 1750, to the Quaker Joshua Strangman.

39. *Letters*, III, 34, Dublin, 12th April 1750, to Joseph Cownley.

40. *Letters*, III, 79–85, London, 20th December 1751, to Ebenezer Blackwell (?), esp. pp. 80–1. It is worthy of note that John Wesley employed against Count Zinzendorf a similar train of theological argument to that employed against him by the Halle Pietists—but quite independently of them. This shows conclusively that his encounter with the Pietists in Georgia in the persons of the pastors of the Salzburg refugees, and in particular his becoming familiar with Francke's book *Nicodemus* and with Freylingshausen's hymn-book had made a profound impression on him. As evidence of the polemic of Halle, cf. esp. the preface of Johann Adam Steinmetz, 'abbot' of the monastery of Berga, to Johann Jacob Heinold's book *Die nötige Verbindung des Gesetzes und Evangelii, aus unwidersprechlichen Gründen erwiesen, und aus Liebe zur Wahrheit so wol, als aufrichtiger Begierde, einigen und gegenwärtigen Zeiten darwider aufkommenden Lehr-Arten zu steuren, ans Licht gestellet* (Halle, 1748), pp. 3–66. This is probably the most perceptive book on this subject so far as basic principles are concerned. Cf. also Sigmund Jacob Baumgarten, *Theologische Bedenken*, Vol. I (1742) [2nd edn, 1744], pp. 156–62; Vol. III (1744) [2nd edn, 1747], pp. 130–201; Vol. IV (1745) [2nd edn, 1749], pp. 540–9. For John Wesley, Antinomianism remained one of the chief dangers, and he kept coming across it on every hand. See, e.g., in *Journal*, III, 539, 20th September 1751, his judgement on Ralph Erskine's sermons, *Law-Death, Gospel-Life*. Cf. also Vol. II, Pt. 1, of the present work, p. 44 and pp. 55–6.

41. Esp. *Letters*, III, 219–20, York, 11th July 1757, to Dorothy Furly: 'A jealous fear of offending God is good. But what have you to do with any other fear? Let love cast it all out, and at the same time make you tenfold more afraid of doing anything small or great which you cannot offer up as an holy sacrifice acceptable to God through Jesus Christ.

'All who are without this fear (and much more all who call it legal, who revile the precious gift of God, and think it an hindrance to "the growing up in Christ") are Antinomians in the inmost soul. Come not into their secret, my dear Miss Furly; but pray for more and more of that "legal spirit", and you will more and more rejoice.'

42. *Letters*, III, 99–100, Birstall, 28th May 1753; similarly, *Letters*, III, 119, Bristol, 24th September 1754.

43. *Letters*, III, 103, London, 27th June 1753.

44. *Letters*, III, 117–8, Bristol, 30th March 1754.

45. *Letters*, 125, London, 15th February 1755; *Letters*, III, 173–4, Kingswood, 14th March 1756; *Letters*, III, 175, Dublin, Good Friday, 16th April 1756.

46. *Letters*, III, 175: 'If you have either sense or religion enough to keep you close to the College, it is well. If not, I see but one possible way to save you from destruction, temporal and eternal. Quit the College at once. Think of it no more, and come away to me. You can take a little advice from me; from other people none at all. You are on the brink of the pit; fly away, or you perish.'

47. *Letters*, III, 164, London, 21st February 1756, to Samuel Furly; cf. *Letters*, III, 206, London, 20th November 1756, also to Samuel Furly: 'stand fast in the liberty wherewith Christ hath made you free.'

48. *Letters*, III, 157, London, 5th February 1756, to William Dodd; cf. also *Letters*, III, 211–2, London, 11th February 1757, to Samuel Furly.

49. *Letters*, III, 173, Kingswood, 14th March 1756, to Samuel Furly: 'You are sick of two diseases: that affection for a poor silly worm like yourself, which only absence (through the grace of God) will cure; and that evil disease which Marcus Antoninus complains of—the δίψαν βιβλίων. That you are far gone in the latter plainly appears from your not loving and admiring that masterpiece of reason and religion the *Reflections on the Conduct of Human Life, with Regard to Knowledge and Learning*, every paragraph of which must stand unshaken (with or without the Bible) till we are no longer mortal.'

50. *Letters*, III, 212–3, Lewisham, 24th March 1757, to Thomas Olivers (a lay preacher).

51. *Letters*, IV, 20, May 1758.

52. *Letters*, IV, 10–3, Dublin, 5th April 1758.

53. *Letters*, IV, 167–8, London, 28th December 1761.

54. *Letters*, IV, 187, September 1762, to his brother Charles. *Letters*, IV, 212–3, to Mrs Maitland: 'Both in the former and in the Farther Thoughts on Perfection I have said all I have to say on that head. Nevertheless, as you seem to desire it, I will add a few words more.

'As to the word, it is scriptural; therefore neither you nor I can in conscience object against it, unless we would send the Holy Ghost to school and teach Him to speak who made the tongue.

'By that word I mean (as I have said again and again) "so loving

God and our neighbour as to rejoice evermore, pray without ceasing and in everything give thanks". He that experiences this is scripturally perfect. And if you do not yet, you may experience it: you surely will, if you follow hard after it; for the Scripture cannot be broken. What, then, does their arguing prove who object against perfection? Absolute and infallible perfection? I never contended for it. Sinless perfection? Neither do I contend for this, seeing the term is not scriptural. A perfection that perfectly fulfils the whole law, and so needs not the merits of Christ? I acknowledge none such—I do now, and always did, protest against it.

' "But is there not sin in those that are perfect?" I believe not; but, be that as it may, they feel none, no temper but pure love, while they rejoice, pray, and give thanks continually. And whether sin is suspended or extinguished I will not dispute; it is enough that they feel nothing but love. This you allow "we should daily press after"; and this is all I contend for. O May God give you the taste of it today!'

On this, cf. esp. *Letters*, V, 38, London, 27th January 1767, to his brother Charles, and *Letters*, IV, 216, Birmingham, 22nd June 1763, to Henry Venn: ' "But you hold Perfection". True—that is loving God with all our heart, and serving Him with all our strength. I teach nothing more, nothing less than this. And whatever infirmity, defect, ἀνομία, is consistent with this any man may teach, and I shall not contradict him.'

55. *Letters*, IV, 188, St Ives, 15th September 1762.
56. *Letters*, IV, 208, London, 7th April 1763.
57. *Letters*, III, 208, London, 22nd December 1756. Cf. also particularly the beginning of the letter in *Letters*, III, 218, Newcastle-upon-Tyne, 18th June 1757: 'I am the more jealous over you, because I know you are liable to be much influenced by fair words especially when they are spoken by persons of sense and in an agreeable manner. And flesh and blood are powerful advocates for conformity to the world, particularly in little things.'
58. *Letters*, III, 214–5, Birstal, 18th May 1757.
59. *Letters*, III, 217–8, Newcastle-upon-Tyne, 14th June 1757.
60. *Letters*, III, 219–20, York, 11th July 1757. In this Wesley saw the real principal danger. Cf. esp. *Letters*, VI, 113, Bristol, 6th September 1774, to Miss March: 'Bishop Browne thought Arianism and Socinianism were the flood which the dragon is in this age pouring out of his mouth to swallow up the woman. Perhaps it may; especially with Dr. Taylor's emendation. But still the main flood in England seems to be Antinomianism. This has been a greater hindrance to the work of God than any or all others put together.' The Peter Browne men-

tioned here was Bishop of Cork in Ireland. Wesley is probably alluding to his book, *Things Divine and Supernatural Conceived by Analogy with Things Natural and Human* (1733). On this point, see the testimony of his latter years in his Journal: *Journal*, VIII, 105, 13th October 1790: 'In the evening I preached at Norwich; but the house would in no wise contain the congregation. How wonderfully is the tide turned! I am become an honourable man at Norwich. God has at length made our enemies to be at peace with us; and scarce any but Antinomians open their mouths against us.' This underlines yet again the importance which the encounter with the Moravians had for John Wesley.

61. *Letters*, III, 208, London, 22nd December 1756; *Letters*, III, 215, 18th May 1757; *Letters*, III, 218, Newcastle-upon-Tyne, 14th June 1757; *Letters*, III, 220-1, Tremeneare, 6th September 1757.

62. *Letters*, III, 218, Newcastle-upon-Tyne, 18th June 1757: 'Fight on and conquer! Change of place, as you observe, is but a little thing. But God has in some measure changed your heart, wherein you have great reason to rejoice. And, having received the first fruits of the Spirit, righteousness, peace, and joy in the Holy Ghost, patiently and earnestly wait for the great change, whereby every root of bitterness may be torn up.'

63. Cf. Fritz Blanke, 'Das Problem des Pietismus', in *Der Kirchenfreund* (Zürich), vol. 66 (1932), p. 181; idem. (in greater detail), *Francke's Bekehrung*, ibid., vol. 67 (1933), pp. 112-24, 129-33, 145-7, esp. 130-2; vol. 66 (1932), p. 181: 'Francke is Descartes, but translated into the realm of religion and feeling.'

64. *Letters*, III, 230-1, Bristol, 21st October 1757.

65. *Letters*, III, 229, St Austell, Cornwall, 25th September 1757. See the very similar letter in *Letters*, III, 199, London, 15th September 1756, to his sister Martha Hall. The formulation in the latter passage is, we may say, classic in its brevity and directness: 'In what path it is best for us to tread God knows better than man. And we are all well assured He orders all things for our profit, that we may be partakers of His holiness. Probably He withheld you from prosperity to save you from pride; certainly to rescue you from your own will, and from that legion of foolish and hurtfull desires which so naturally attend abundance. Be good and do good to the utmost of your present power, and then happy are you.'

66. *Letters*, IV, 5-6, Lewisham, 9th February 1758.

67. *Letters*, III, 208, London, 22nd December 1756; *Letters*, III, 215, Birstall, 18th May 1757: 'Health you shall have if health be best. And He that gives it will give a blessing with it—an increase of spiritual

as well as of bodily strength, but it is strength to labour not to sit still. And this strength will either increase or decrease in the same proportion with your sense of His love.' Cf. *Letters*, III, 230, Bristol, 21st October 1757; *Letters*, IV, 14, Dublin, 13th April 1758; *Letters*, IV, 50, Colchester, 28th December 1758; *Letters*, IV, 55–6, Norwich, 6th March 1759.

68. *Letters*, IV, 71, London, 19th August 1759; *Letters*, IV, 97, Athlone, 1st June 1760.

69. *Letters*, IV, 245–6, Edinburgh, 28th May 1764.

70. *Letters*, IV, 225, Lewisham, 15th December 1763.

71. *Letters*, IV, 220, London, 16th July 1763.

72. *Letters*, VI, 233, London, October 1776.

73. *Letters*, III, 117–8, Bristol, 30th March 1754; *Letters*, III. 118, Bristol, 21st September 1754; *Letters*, III. 123–4, London, 7th December 1754.

74. *Letters*, III, 128–9, Leeds, 10th May 1755.

75. *Letters*, III, 164, London, 21st February 1756; *Letters*, III, 173–4, Kingswood, 14th March 1756; *Letters*, III, 175, Dublin, 16th April 1756 (see above, note 46).

76. *Letters*, III, 206, London, 20th November 1756; *Letters*, III, 208, London Snowfields, 4th December 1756.

77. *Letters*, III, 229, St. Austell, Cornwall, 25th September 1757, to Dorothy Furly.

78. *Letters*, IV, 7–9, Swindon, 7th March 1758, to Samuel Furly.

79. *Letters*, IV, 185–6, Dublin, 30th July 1762.

80. Cf. particularly John Wesley's reluctant letter from St Ives, 15th September 1762: *Letters*, IV, 189–90.

81. *Letters*, IV, 232, Lewisham, 6th March 1764.

82. *Letters*, IV, 256–8, Liverpool, 15th July 1764. Five Wesley Letters published by Wesley F. Swift, *Proc. W.H.S.*, XXXIII, 1 (1961), p. 13. John Wesley to Peard Dickinsons, London, 15th January 1785: 'My dear Brother, I think the best model that ever was for ye Language of a Christian Preacher is the first Epistle of St. John.'

83. *Letters*, IV, 266–8, Yarmouth, 11th October 1764.

84. *Letters*, V, 21, Yarmouth, 9th July 1766: 'What a blessing it is, that, where we do not think alike, we can *agree to disagree*!' (italics original).

85. *Letters*, III, 74, London, 15th August 1751, to Richard Bailey: 'the privilege of Englishmen—to serve God according to the dictates of their own conscience.' *Journal*, VII, 389, 18th May 1788; *Journal*, VII, 486, 12th April 1789.

86. Cf. Erich Vogelsang, *Der Confessio-Begriff des jungen Luther*, Luther-Jahrbuch, XII (1930), pp. 91–108.

87. *Letters*, IV, 85–6, Wednesbury, 4th March 1760.
88. *Letters*, IV, 90, Liverpool, 29th March 1760.
89. *Letters*, IV, 90–1, Dublin, 16th April 1760. Cf. esp. these sentences: 'It does not require a large share of natural wisdom to see God in all things—in all His works of creation as well as of providence. This is rather a branch of spiritual wisdom, and is given to believers more and more as they advance in purity of heart.'
90. *Letters*, IV, 100–1, Sligo, 27th June 1760.
91. *Letters*, IV, 109, London, 11th November 1760: 'Conviction is not condemnation. You may be convinced, yet not condemned; convinced of useless thoughts or words and yet not condemned for them. You are condemned for nothing if you love God and continue to give Him your whole heart.'
92. *Letters*, IV, 157, Stockton, 17th June 1761; *Letters*, IV, 180–1, Athlone, 13th May 1762; *Letters*, IV, 310, Newcastle-upon-Tyne, 9th August 1765; *Letters*, IV, 310–1, Bristol, 31st August 1765; *Letters*, V, 82, Stroud, 14th March 1768; and VI, 262–4, London, 26th April 1777.
93. *Letters*, V, 192–3, Dawgreen, 6th July 1770.
94. *Letters*, V, 261–2, Cockhill, 25th June 1771.
95. *Letters*, IV, 310–1, 31st August 1765; *Letters*, V, 326, Otley, 1st July 1772; *Letters*, VI, 113, Bristol, 16th September 1774.
96. *Letters*, V, 135, May, 1769.
97. *Letters*, V, 95, 5th July 1768.
98. *Letters*, V, 270–1, Kingswood, 3rd August 1771.
99. *Letters*, IV, 251, Whitehaven, 24th June 1764.
100. *Letters*, V, 95, 5th July 1768. On this, cf. *Letters*, VI. 220, Alnwick, 30th May 1776.
101. *Letters*, IV, 270, Norwich, 13th October 1764.
102. *Letters*, VI, 88–9, Newcastle-upon-Tyne, 3rd June 1774.
103. *Letters*, VI, 92, Sunderland, 17th June 1774: 1 Corinthians 13. Other instances: *Letters*, IV, 124; *Letters*, V, 135, May 1769.
104. *Letters*, VI, 129, Reigate, 30th November 1774, and again p. 133, London, 27th December 1774: 'a Christian is very far from a Stoic,' Also pp. 139–40, 11th February 1775.
105. *Letters*, VI, 132, London, 27th December 1774.
106. *Letters*, VI, 133, London, 27th December 1774: 'I want more of human mingled with the divine. Nay sometimes I want it in Miss March too.'
107. *Letters*, VI, 153–4, Charlemont, 9th June 1775; VI, 206–7, London, 7th February 1776; VI, 208–9, London, 26th February 1776.
108. *Letters*, VI, 292–3, Nr London, 10th December 1777. As to the

admiration accorded to Anton Wilhelm Böhme in Britain, see the testimony of Philip Doddridge.

109. Cf. esp. *Letters*, VI, 98–102, York, 14th July 1774, to his wife, and specifically 99ff.

110. See Vol II, part 1, pp. 160–62.

111. In chronological order: Mrs Sarah Crosby, 14th June 1757–4th June 1789 (32 years); Mrs Sarah Ryan, 8th November 1757–28th June 1766; Mrs Elizabeth Bennis, 23rd August 1763–21st December 1776; Mrs Elizabeth Woodhouse, 23rd April 1764–17th November 1780; Miss Margaret Lewen, June 1764; Lady D'Arcy Mazwell (*née* Brisbane), 20th June 1764–30th September 1788; Miss Margaret (Peggy) Dale, later Mrs Avison, 1st June 1765–17th November 1769; Miss Jane Hilton, later Mrs Barton, 22nd July 1766–11th January 1788; Miss Hanah Ball, 28th January 1768–26th November 1789 (21 years); Miss Ann Bolton, 13th February 1768–12th January 1791 (23 years); Miss Philothea Briggs, later Mrs Thompson, 25th February 1769–30th November 1774; Miss Mary Bishop, 5th November 1769–18th August 1784; Miss Elizabeth Ritchie, 8th May 1774–24th February 1786; Miss Hester Ann Roe, later Mrs Rogers, 3rd May 1776–9th February 1789.

112. He once stated this explicitly; *Letters*, VI, 9, London, 15th January 1773, to Ann Bolton: 'my day is far spent. I am therefore the more desirous to help you forward who are in the morning of life.'

113. This is particularly clear in *Letters*, V, 171, 1st January 1770.

114. *Letters*, V, 174, London, 2nd January 1770, to Mary Bosanquet.

115. *Letters*, III, 217, Newcastle-upon-Tyne, 14th June 1757.

116. *Letters*, IV, 133, London, 14th February 1761.

117. *Letters*, IV, 312–3, Kingswood, 5th October 1765.

118. *Letters*, V, 25–7, St Ives, Cornwall, 12th September 1766.

119. *Letters*, V, 46–7, Sligo, 2nd May 1767.

120. *Letters*, V, 130–1, Chester, 18th March 1769.

121. On this question, see also *Letters*, VI, 290–1, London, 2nd December 1777, to Mrs Crosby: 'For the sake of retrenching her expenses, I thought it quite needful for Miss Bosanquet to go from home. And I was likewise persuaded (as she was herself) that God had something for her to do in Bath and Kingswood; perhaps in Bristol too, although I do not think she will be called to speak *there* in public.

'The difference between us and the Quakers in this respect is manifest. They flatly deny the rule itself, although it stands clear in the Bible. We allow the rule; only we believe it admits of some exceptions. At present I know of those, and no more, in the whole Methodist Connexion.' From among the literature, see above all A. W. Harrison, 'An Early Woman Preacher—Sarah Crosby', *Proc. W.H.S.*, XIV. (1924), pp. 104–9; Theophil Funk, *Die Anfänge der Laien-mitarbeit im Methodismus*, 1941 (Beiträge zur Geschichte des Methodismus, 5), pp. 194ff.; and Leslie F. Church, *More about the Early Methodist People*, 1949, pp. 136ff.

122. *Letters*, V, 171, London, 1st January 1770.

123. *Letters*, V, 205–6, Bedford, 26th October 1770.

124. *Letters*, V, 257–8, Londonderry, 13th June 1771.

125. *Letters*, VI, 87–8, Edinburgh, 3rd June 1774; *Letters*, VI, 191–2, Norwich, 29th November 1775; *Letters*, VI, 114–5, Bristol, 26th September 1774; *Letters*, VI, 290–1, London, 2nd December 1777; *Letters*, VI, 331, Dover, 9th December 1778; *Letters*, VI, 376–7, London, 20th January 1780; *Letters*, VI, 383, Bristol, 3rd March 1780.

126. *Letters*, VI, 115, Bristol, 26th September 1774.

127. *Letters*, VII, 18, Newcastle, 11th May 1780.

128. *Letters*, VII, 19, Edinburgh, 19th May 1780.

129. *Letters*, V, 80–1, London, 13th February 1768; *Letters*, VII, 50, London, 20th February 1781, to Ann Bolton: 'You have known me since you were little more than a child.'

130. *Letters*, V, 86, Liverpool, 7th April 1768; *Letters*, V, 207, 16th November 1770.

131. *Letters*, V, 86, Liverpool, 7th April 1768; *Letters*, V, 88, 9th May 1768; *Letters*, V, 93, Newcastle, 7th June 1768.

132. *Letters*, V, 92, Newcastle-upon-Tyne, 7th June 1768: 'O Nancy, I want sadly to see you: I am afraid you should steal away into paradise. A thought comes into my mind which I will tell you freely. If you go first, I think you must leave me your seal for a token: I need not say to remember you by, for I shall never forget you.' *Letters*, V, 207, London, 16th November 1770: 'To see even the superscription of a letter from *you* always gives me pleasure.' *Letters*, V, 238, Tullamore, 15th April 1771: 'You *did* love *me* a little. Do you still? Do you think of me sometimes?' (italics original.). *Letters*, V, 278, Bristol, 16th September 1771: 'Nancy, Nancy! Why do you forget your friends? Why do you tempt me to be angry? I tell you again you will loose your labour: I can't be angry at *you*.' *Letters*, V, 347, London, 28th November 1772: 'I have some business too, but I know not what business would be able to hinder my writing to *you*.' *Letters*, VI, 83, Whitehaven, 8th May 1774: 'But it would be strange if I were to forget you. I could as soon forget myself.'

133. *Letters*, V, 92, Newcastle-upon-Tyne, 7th June 1768; *Letters*, V, 125, London, 4th February 1769; John Wesley, *Primitive Physick or an*

*Easy and Natural Method of Curing most Diseases,* London, 1747. On this, see the first-rate characterization by Frederick Jeffery, 'John Wesley's Primitive Physick', *Proc. W.H.S.,* XXI. (1937–38), pp. 60–7.

134. Particularly full and clear in *Letters,* V, 197, Bristol, 12th August 1770.

135. Esp. *Letters,* V, 213, Sevenoaks, 15th December 1770: 'reasoning'.

136. *Letters,* V, 215–6, London, 29th December 1770.

137. *Letters,* V, 238, Tullamore, 15th April 1771.

138. *Letters,* V, 240, Bandon, 2nd May 1771.

139. *Letters,* V, 256, Roosky, 8th June 1771; *Letters,* V, 275, Pembroke, 25th August 1771; *Letters,* V, 258, Londonderry, 15th June 1771; *Letters,* V, 325, Otley, 1st July 1772.

140. *Letters,* VI, 174, Gloucester, 15th August 1775: 'I want you to (be) all a flame of holy love!' Similarly, *Letters,* VI, 138, 8th February 1775.

141. *Letters,* V, 197, Bristol, 12th August 1770; *Letters,* VIII, 117, near London, 20th February 1789; and even earlier; *Letters,* VI, 346, Sunderland, 18th May 1779.

142. *Letters,* V, 278, Bristol, 16th September 1771 (see above, note 132); *Letters,* V, 301, London, 29th January 1772; *Letters,* VI, 9, London, 15th January 1773; *Letters,* VI, 97, Leeds, 13th July 1774; *Letters,* VI, 174, Gloucester, 15th August 1775; *Letters,* VI, 345, Sunderland, 18th May 1779; *Letters,* VII, 142, Bath, 15th September 1782.

143. *Letters,* VI, 281, Bristol, 27th September 1777; *Letters,* VI, 345, Sunderland, 18th May 1779; *Letters,* VI, 373, London, 14th January 1780; *Letters,* VII, 142, Bath, 15th September 1782.

144. *Letters,* VI, 190, London, 26th November 1775; *Letters,* VI, 346, Sunderland, 18th May 1779.

145. *Letters,* V, 325, Otley, 1st July 1772: 2 Corinthians 1[14].

146. *Letters,* VI, 70, London, 20th January 1774; Matthew 5.

147. *Letters,* VI, 297, London, 24th January 1778; *Letters,* VIII, 246, High Wycombe, 4th November 1790; cf. also *Letters,* VI, 136, Luton, 11th January 1775, to Francis Wolfe.

148. *Letters,* VI, 144, Worcester, 15th March 1775; *Letters* VIII, 246, High Wycombe, 4th November 1790.

149. *Letters,* VI, 281, Bristol, 27th September 1777.

150. *Letters,* VI, 144, Worcester, 15th March 1775; *Letters,* VI, 279, Bristol, 15th September 1777. He wrote in similar vein to Hester Ann Roe. Cf. *Letters,* VI, 222, Newcastle-upon-Tyne, 2nd June 1776: 'I could almost say it is hard that I should just see you once and no more. But it is a comfort that to die is not to be lost. Our union will be more full and perfect hereafter.'

151. *Letters,* VI, 85, Glasgow, 13th May 1774.
152. *Letters,* V, 309, London, 29th February 1772.
153. *Letters,* VII, 142, Bath, 15th September 1782.
154. *Letters,* VI, 83-4, Whitehaven, 8th May 1774.
155. *Letters,* VI, 14-5, London, 29th January 1773.
156. *Letters,* V, 336, Cardiff, 28th August 1772.
157. *Letters,* V, 275, Pembroke, 25th August 1771.
158. Questions about her spiritual state: *Letters,* V, 240, Bandon, 2nd May 1771; *Letters,* V, 256, Roosky, 8th June 1771; *Letters,* V, 286, Lynn, 7th November 1771; *Letters,* V, 295, London, 28th December 1771; *Letters,* V, 319, Londonderry, 27th May 1772; *Letters,* V, 349, London, 5th December 1772; *Letters,* VI, 191, London, 26th November 1775; *Letters,* VI, 9, London, 15th January 1773; *Letters,* VI, 83, Whitehaven, 8th May 1774; *Letters,* VI, 191, London, 26th November 1775; *Letters,* VII, 83, Bristol, 9th September 1781; *Letters,* VII, 161-2, London, 5th January 1783.
159. 'Partaker of His holiness': *Letters,* VI, 25, Cork, 2nd May 1773; identical phraseology in *Letters,* VIII, 9, Bristol, 18th September 1787; *Letters,* VIII, 157-8, Leeds, 1st August 1789; *Letters,* VIII, 190-1, London, 20th December 1789.
160. *Letters,* V, 256, Roosky, 8th June 1771; *Letters,* VIII, 246, High Wycombe, 4th November 1790. He used the same phraseology in dealing with Miss March: *Letters,* 71, 153, Charlemont, 9th June 1775.
161. *Letters,* VII, 358, Near London, 15th December 1786; *Letters,* VIII, 110, London, 9th January 1789.
162. *Letters,* VIII, 157-8, Leeds, 1st August 1789.
163. 'I love you the more because you are a daughter of affliction': *Letters,* VIII, 84, Brecon, 15th August 1788.
164. *Letters,* VI, 382, London, 26th February 1780; *Letters,* VI, 373-4, London, 14th January 1780.
165. *Letters* VI, 72-3, London, 17th February, 1774. Edward Young (1683-1765), *Night Thoughts,* Book VIII, line 1278. Cf. also *Letters,* VI, 279, Bristol, 15th September 1777: 'My regard for you has been invariable ever since you was with me in London. I then set you down for my inalienable friend, and such I trust you will always be, until the union of our spirits will be complete where our bodies part no more.' [Translator's note: Doubtless following up Telford's suggestion (*Letters,* VI, 73, n. 1) that Wesley's quotation in his letter is 'probably based on Young's *Night Thoughts,* viii', Dr Schmidt gives the reference to Young's *Night Thoughts* (1742) as being to Book VIII, line 1278. I have chased this will-o'-the-wisp with predictable

results! It may be, of course, that Wesley's wording of the 'quotations' is based on his own abridgement, *An Extract from Dr Young's
Night-Thoughts on Life, Death and Immortality* (Bristol, 1770), in
which Wesley sought 'to make that noble work more useful to all,
and more intelligible to ordinary readers' (*Journal*, V, 296–7, December 1768). No copy of this extract was available to me; but in Young's
original composition the nearest equivalent to Wesley's 'quotations'
from 'Virtue's Apology' occurs towards the end of the poem:

'There is, I grant, a triumph of the pulse;
A dance of spirits, a mere froth of joy . . .

Our thoughtless agitation's idle child
That mantles high, that sparkles, and expires,
Leaving the soul more vapid than before . . .

From vice, sense, fancy, no man can be bless'd;
Bliss is too great to lodge within an hour:
When an immortal being aims at bliss,
Duration is essential to the name.'

(See E. Young, *Night Thoughts,* London, 1790, edn, pp. 217–9,
esp. 219.)]
166. *Letters,* VI, 281, Bristol, 27th September 1777.
167. *Letters,* VII, 18, Whitehaven, 8th May 1780.
168. *Letters,* VII, 233, Bristol, 31st August, 1784.
169. *Letters,* V, 342, 25th October 1772, no place; *Letters,* V, 347, London,
28th November 1772; *Letters,* V, 349, London, 5th December 1772;
*Letters,* VI, 115, Bristol, 1st October 1774. Allusion to the Sermon
on the Mount and the Hymn to Love (1 Corinthians 13): *Letters,*
V, 342.
170. *Letters,* VI, 261–2, Near London, 24th April 1777.
171. *Letters,* VIII, 246, High Wycombe, 4th November 1790.
172. *Letters,* VIII, 254, London, 12th January 1791.
173. *Letters,* IV, 250, Newcastle-upon-Tyne, 20th June 1764; similarly
*Letters,* V, 106, Redruth, 9th September 1768: 'It is impossible for
me to give you pain without feeling it myself. And yet the manner
wherein you receive my plain dealing gives me pleasure too. Perhaps
you never had so on complaisant a correspondent before. Yet I think
you hardly ever had one who had a more tender regard for you.' How
highly John Wesley esteemed her is shown by *Journal,* VII, 432,
4th September 1778: 'spending an hour with that excellent woman,
Lady (Maxwell).'

174. *Letters,* IV, 252–3, Manchester, 10th July 1764.
175. *Letters,* IV, 260–2, London, 17th August 1764.
176. *Letters,* IV, 263–4, Bristol, 22nd September 1764.
177. *Letters,* IV, 300–2, Londonderry, 25th May 1765; *Letters,* IV, 308–9, Kilkenny, 5th July 1765; *Letters,* IV, 317, London, 1st December 1765; *Letters,* V, 11, Newcastle-upon-Tyne, 6th May 1766: 'But in the mean time you have need of patience; and the more so, because you have a weak body. This, one may expect, will frequently press down the soul, especially till you are strong in faith. But how soon may that be, seeing it is the gift, yea and the free gift, of God! Therefore it is never far off! The word is nigh thee! "Only believe!" Look unto Jesus! Be thou saved! Receive out of His fullness grace upon grace; mercy, and grace to keep mercy.'
178. *Letters,* V, 219, London, 24th January 1771: 'From the first hour that I entered the kingdom it was a sacred rule with me never to preach on any controverted point—at least *not in a controversial way.*' (italics original).
179. Ibid.; *Letters,* V, 226–7, London, 26th February 1771; *Letters,* V, 304–5, London, 8th February 1772; with special emphasis in *Letters,* VIII, 95, London, 30th September 1788: 'Would it be right for me to propagate a doctrine when I believe to be false? particularly if it were not only false but dangerous to the souls of men, frequently hindering their growth in grace, stopping their pursuits of holiness? And is it right in you to do this? You believe the doctrine of Absolute Predestination is false. Is it, then, right for you to propagate this doctrine in any kind or degree, particularly as it is not only false but a very dangerous doctrine, as we have seen a thousand times? Does it not hinder the work of God in the soul, feed all evil and weaken all good tempers, turn many quite out of the way of life and drive them back to perdition?

'Is not Calvinism the very antidote of Methodism, the most deadly and successful enemy which it ever had? "But my friend desired that I would propagate it, and lodged money with me for this very purpose." What then? May I destroy souls because my friend desired it? Ought you not rather to throw that money into the sea? O let not any money or any friend move you to propagate a lie, to strike at the root of Methodism, to grieve the holiest of your friends, and to endanger your own soul!'
180. *Letters,* V, 130, London, 3rd March 1769.
181. Ibid.
182. *Letters,* VII, 392–3, Dublin, 4th July 1787; cf. also *Letters,* VIII, 83, London, 8th August 1788.

183. *Letters,* I, 251, note 1: 'Charles Wesley endorsed this letter [Utphe, 7th July 1738], "Panegyric on Germans".' In this letter (ibid., 250–1) John had described the life of the Brethren in Marienborn-Büdingen: 'The spirit of the Brethren is beyond our highest expectations. Young and old, they breathe nothing but faith and love at all times and in all places.' Further tensions arose between the two brothers because of the matter-of-fact way in which John had taken over, one might say usurped leadership of the student circle in Oxford and especially because of John's wedding plans both with regard to Grace Murray and Mary Vazeille (see below). Manifestly Charles felt himself to be the one who always played second fiddle and repeatedly wanted to assert himself. In doing so, he understandably seized upon John's personal affairs, where the Achilles' heel of his eminent brother was exposed. It is, however, indicative of the deep, indestructible bond between the two brothers that immediately after Charles had died John began to write his biography. Cf. *Journal,* VII, 432 (Diary), 3rd September 1788. In addition, it is worthy of note that when he designated himself the head of the Methodist movement, he called Charles its heart: *Letters,* IV, 322, Lewisham, 28th February 1766, to Charles.

184. Cf. his highly significant letter to Samuel Walker in Truro written from Bristol, 21st August 1756, which was published by Albert F. Hall, 'Charles Wesley and Lay-Preaching', *Proc. W.H.S.,* XV, (Sept., 1925), pp. 71–2. 'Lay-preaching it must be allowed is a Partial separation and may, but *need* not end in a Total one. The Probability of it, has made me tremble for years past; and kept me from leaving the Methodists. I stay not so much to do good, as to prevent evil. I stand in the way of my Brother's violent Counsellors, the object both of their Fear and Hate' (italics original). It is noteworthy how critical of the movement Charles was here, and one must give him great credit for remaining on the whole steadfastly loyal to it at such a critical juncture. [Translator's note: see also F. Baker, *Charles Wesley As Revealed by His Letters* (London, 1948), esp. ch. 8.]

185. *Letters,* I, 322–3, Bristol, 23rd June 1739.

186. *Letters,* I, 353–4, London, 21st April 1741.

187. *Letters,* II, 107–9, Beercrocomb, 31st July 1747; *Letters,* V, 316, Perth, 26th April 1772; *Letters,* V, 345, Colchester, 4th November 1772.

188. *Letters,* V, 269–70, Kingswood, 3rd August 1771, in conjunction with V, 264–5.

189. *Letters,* III, 129–31, London, 20th June 1755; III, 131, London, 23rd June 1755; III, 132–3, London, 28th June 1755; III, 135–6,

London, 16th July 1755; IV, 162, London, 8th September 1761; V, 88, Edinburgh, 14th May 1768; VII, 284, from Plymouth Dock, 19th August 1785.

190. *Letters*, II, 107–9, Beercrocomb, 31st July 1747: 'justifying faith'; IV, 187–8, September 1762: 'Christian perfection'; cf. also V, 20. Stockton, 9th July 1766; V, 38–9, London, 27th January 1766.

191. *Letters*, V, 40–1, London, 12th February 1767; V, 93, Norton near Stockton, 14th June 1768.

192. *Letters*, VII, 284–5, London, Plymouth Dock, 19th August 1785. This demonstrates yet again the pre-eminence ascribed to doctrine. [Translator's note: On Charles' position, see F. Baker, *Charles Wesley* (as in note 184) esp. ch. 11.]

193. *Letters*, III, 112, London, 20th October 1753; III, 113–4, London, 31st October 1753; IV, 245, Haddington, 25th May 1764; V, 15, Whitehaven, 27th June 1766.

194. *Letters*, VII, 327, Leeds, 3rd May 1786.

195. *Letters*, III, 77, London, 4th December 1751.

196. *Letters*, III, 96–7, Athlone, 8th August 1752.

197. *Letters*, III, 77, London, 4th December 1751.

198. *Letters*, III, 135–6, London, 16th July 1755.

199. *Letters*, I, 197–9, Savannah, 22nd March 1736.

200. *Letters*, II, 5–6, London, 31st July 1742.

201. *Letters*, V, 15–6, Whitehaven, 27th June 1766.

202. *Letters*, IV, 322, Lewisham, 28th February 1766; cf. also V, 76, London, 15th January 1768, where he refers with pride to his Nonconformist lineage as evidence of the preaching of the pure Gospel in one and the same family through four generations and as an obligation imposed upon the sons of his brother Charles. On this, cf. A. Skevington Wood, 'John Wesley's reversion to type. The Influence of his Nonconformist Ancestry', *Proc. W.H.S.*, XXXV, (December, 1965) 4, pp. 88–93. [Translator's note: cf. also F. Baker, 'Wesley's Puritan Ancestry', *LQHR*, 187 (1962), pp. 180–6; R. C. Monk, *John Wesley : His Puritan Heritage,* London, 1966, pp. 17–22.]

203. *Letters*, V, 88, Edinburgh, 14th May, 1768.

204. *Letters*, VI, 6, Shoreham, 15th December 1772.

205. *Letters*, VI, 82, Whitehaven, 6th May 1774.

206. *Letters*, VII, 70, Thirsk, 27th June 1781.

207. Letters, VIII, 46, Bristol, 17th March 1788. (The actual date is 1785. Telford printed the letter twice: 17th March 1785, *Letters*, VII, 261–2 and 17th March 1788, VIII, 45–6).

208. *Letters*, VII, 392, Dublin, 4th July 1787.

209. *Letters*, V, 117, London, 17th December 1768.

210. See supra, pp. 108–10. On Fletcher, see Luke Tyerman, *John Wesley's designated Successor* (1882); F. W. Macdonald, *Fletcher of Madeley* (1885); J. Marrat, *John Fletcher, Scholar and Saint* (London, n.d.); idem., *The Vicar of Madeley* (1902); C. N. Impeta, *De Leer van de Heiliging en Volmaking bij Wesley en Fletcher* (1913), pp. 290–393; John L. Nuelsen, *John William Fletcher* (1929).

211. *Letters*, VII, 93, London, 24th November 1781.

212. *Letters*, V, 82–5, Birmingham, 20th March 1768, to J. W. Fletcher; ibid, 231, Parkgate, 22nd March 1771, to J. W. Fletcher.

213. *Letters*, VI, 221, Newcastle-upon-Tyne, 1st June 1776.

214. *Letters*, VII, 263, Manchester, 3rd April 1785; *Letters*, VII, 375, Bristol, 10th March 1787, to Joseph Benson. Mary Fletcher, *née* Bosanquet, was to publish her husband's 'Letters to Priestley' after his death.

215. *Letters*, VI, 75, London, 26th February 1774; *Letters*, VI, 145–6, Northwich, 22nd March 1775.

216. *Letters*, VI, 10–2, Shoreham, (15th) January 1773.

217. *Letters*, V, 3–4, London, 28th February 1766: 'Unity and holiness are the two things I want among the Methodists.'

218. This is even clearer in the second letter on this subject, which culminates in the repeated phrase: 'just now!' *Letters*, VI, 33–4, Lewisham, 21st July 1773.

219. *Letters*, IV, 204, London, 6th March 1763.

220. Cf. John S. Simon, *John Wesley and the Advance of Methodism*, London, 1925, pp. 190–8.

221. Cf. J. Augustin Leger, *John Wesley's Last Love* (1910), which reproduces the manuscript material from the British Museum, London, and has thereby laid an incontrovertible foundation; J. S. Simon, op. cit. (see previous note), pp. 107–14.

222. *Letters*, III, 15–8, Newcastle-upon-Tyne, 10th October 1749, to John Bennet; *Letters*, III, 20–1, Newcastle, 10th October 1749, to J. Bennet (eirenically); *Letters*, III, 22–4, Kingswood, 3rd November 1749; *Letters*, III, 29, London, 23rd January 1750, to John Bennet.

223. *Journal*, III, 439, 3rd and 5th October 1749 (Diary).

224. Nonetheless, it lasted for several days: *Letters*, III, 24, Kingswood, 3rd November 1749, to John Bennet: 'Your marriage has actually had that effect which it was supposed would follow from me. My brother does not preach at all. Neither hath he spoken to me since Sunday.' *Letters*, III; 19, prefatory note.

225. This happened in the week of the end of March and the beginning of April 1752, and while he was visiting one of her sons in London in 1788.

226. Cf. his moving letter in *Letters*, III, 22–3, Kingswood, 3rd November 1749, to John Bennet: 'I felt no resentment, though deep concern. Yet I judged it my bounden duty to answer for myself, and give them the true account of what had been so strangely misrepresented. The account I gave of my former friend was such that they cried out one and all, "You are blinded in her still!" with many other words which I care not to repeat. It was in hope of softening Sister Procter that I afterwards told her of our weeping over each other. But I never said that she "repented of her former romancing"; nor one word which was unkind or untrue. Nay, it was my speaking so tenderly which made Sister Procter cry out, "Oh how has she used *you*!" And how do you use *her*!

'They who know the whole affair know that I have been the greatest sufferer, but not the greatest sinner. Not that I can clear myself neither. I loved you both too well. Forgive me this wrong. Both you and she go the right way to clear me of this fault. A few more pangs, and my heart will be at liberty.

'Upon reflection I find I have done you wrong in another instance also. I have not spoke plainly to you. I have not delivered my own soul. Indeed, I had not power to speak. But I might have wrote. And so I did on September 7 from Newcastle; and again from White-haven (a copy of which I sent to Mr. Perronet for his judgement): but both these letters were stopped. If you desire it now, you should have it, with Mr. P.'s answer.

'Once for all I must speak, for my heart is full; although, alas! what avails it now? I loved you as my own soul. I left with you my dearest friend, one who was as necessary to me as a right hand, as dear as a right eye; one whom I looked upon then (and not on slight grounds) as contracted to myself. But suppose I say only, one I loved above all on earth and fully designed for my wife. To this woman you proposed marriage without either my knowledge or consent. Was this well done? God warned you the same night that I had *took* her first (but I could not take her unless she *took* me too). You wrote me word you would take no farther step without my consent. Nevertheless, not only without my consent, but with a thousand circumstances of aggravation, you tore her from me, whether I would or no; when all I desired was to refer the whole to impartial men! And all the blame lies upon me! And you have acted with a clear conscience to this day! I think not. I think you have done me the deepest wrong which I could receive on this side the grave. But I spare you. 'Tis but for a little time, and I shall be where the weary are at rest.' Mr. P. is his friend Perronet.

227. *Letters*, III, 19–20, Leeds, 7th October 1749, to Thomas Bigg.
228. On 1st June 1751 he resigned from all his privileges in a Latin letter to the Rector and the Fellows of Lincoln College: '*sponte ac libere resigno*' (*Letters*, III, 68–9).
229. *Journal*, III, 393, Saturday, 8th April 1749.
230. *Journal*, III, 513, 18th February 1751, note 1. [Translator's note: on this whole sad affair, see also F. Baker, *Charles Wesley* (as in note 184 above), ch. 6.
231. *Letters*, III, 61–2, Bristol, 5th March 1751.
232. *Letters*, III, 63, prefatory note; *Letters*, VI, 90, Newcastle-upon-Tyne, 10th June 1774, to his wife (high praise).
233. See above, note 230.
234. *Journal*, III, 517, Wednesday, 27th March 1751.
235. *Letters*, III, 64–5, Tetsworth, 42 miles from London, 27th March 1751.
236. *Letters*, III, 65–6, Evesham, 30th March 1751.
237. *Letters*, III, 91–2, Newcastle-upon-Tyne, 22nd May 1752.
238. *Letters*, III, 154, Lewisham, 7th January 1756; *Letters*, III, 179–80, Limerick, 18th June 1756 (very cursory and formal); *Letters*, III, 176–8, Waterford, 7th May 1756.
239. *Letters*, III, 213–4, Liverpool, 24th April 1757.
240. *Letters*, IV, 36–7, Colchester, 27th October 1758.
241. *Letters*, IV, 4–5, London, 27th January 1758, to Mrs Ryan.
242. *Letters*, IV, 49–50, Norwich, 23rd December 1758.
243. *Letters*, IV, 61–2, Grimsby, 9th April 1759. For J. Wesley's correspondence with Ebenezer Blackwell, see *Letters*, IV, 52–3, Everton, 2nd March 1759, and for Blackwell's reply, see *Letters*, IV, 53–4, March 1759.
244. *Letters*, IV, 75–8, Coleford, 23rd October 1759.
245. *Letters*, IV, 79–80, Bedford, 24th November 1759.
246. *Letters*, IV, 89, Liverpool, 23rd March 1760.
247. *Letters*, IV, 101–2, Ennis, near Limerick, 12th July 1760.
248. *Letters*, IV, 152–3, Whitehaven, 24th April 1761.
249. *Letters*, V, 105, Newlyn, 5th September 1768.
250. *Letters*, III, 125–6, Manchester, 9th April 1755, to Ebenezer Blackwell; *Letters*, III, 127, Keighley near Leeds, 29th April 1755, to the same. Cf. *The Journal of Charles Wesley*, ed. Thomas Jackson, 1849, II, 201–2.
251. *Journal*, V, 399–400, 23rd January 1771.
252. *Letters*, VI, 115, Bristol, 26th September 1774, to Sarah Crosby.
253. *Letters*, VI, 98–102, York, 15th July 1774.
254. *Letters*, VI, 101–2. With reservation; more forcibly in his letter of

1st September 1777; *Letters*, VI, 273–4. This came to a full crescendo in his cruel, final parting letter of 2nd October 1778; *Letters*, VIII, 273–4, Bristol.

255. *Letters*, V, 329–30, Dewsbury, 10th July 1772, to his brother Charles.

256. *Letters*, VI, 273–4, Gwennap, 1st September 1771.

257. *Letters*, VIII, 273–4, Bristol, 2nd October 1778. The last-ditch attempt at reconciliation made by his wife's son-in-law, William Smith of Newcastle-upon-Tyne, at the Methodist Conference held in London, in August 1779, also came to nothing. Smith wrote to Joseph Benson about this; *Journal*, VI, 246, note 4: 'I talked freely to both parties, and did all in my power to lay a foundation for future union; but alas! all my attempts proved unsuccessful. I had to leave matters no better than I found them. It is, indeed, a melancholy affair, and, I am afraid, productive of bad consequences' (MS. Life of Benson).

258. Gertrud von Le Fort, *Die ewige Frau* (1934), [19th edn, 1960], pp. 107ff.

259. *Journal*, VI, 337, 12th October 1781.

260. *Letters*, III, 23, Kingswood, 3rd November 1749. See note 226.

261. *Letters*, VI, 91–2, Newcastle-upon-Tyne, 22nd May 1752: 'I rejoice for your sake (sc. over the praise being bestowed on her in Newcastle); but I condemn myself. I have not made such use of the time we have been together as I might have done. The thing which I feared has come upon me. I have not conversed with you so seriously as I ought. I ought always to speak seriously and weightily with you as I would with my guardian angel.'

262. *Letters*, VI, 273, Gwennap, 1st September 1777: 'But upon reflection I see I was too hasty.'

263. Especially clear in this respect in his letter to James Morgan (*Letters*, V, 103–5, St Just, 3rd September 1768), in which he attacks as unscriptural the teaching that a penitent sinner is already in a state of grace by virtue of remorse itself. Specific examples of the expulsion of preachers: James Wheatley in Bradford-upon-Avon because of sexual misdemeanours (*Letters*, III, 69, Bristol, 25th June 1751); and Thomas Wride's exclusion on account of unseemly talk (*Letters*, VI, 161, Dublin, 22nd July 1775, to Thomas Wride).

264. *Letters*, V, 15–7, Whitehaven, 27th June 1766.

265. Wesley expressly used the *terminus technicus* from the Acts of the Apostles for this group (φοβούμενοι τὸν θεον) in the original Greek (Acts 10², ²², ³⁵; 13¹⁶ and ²⁶).

266. Here, too, he is using the Greek word: φερόυμενος. Here there is no precise paradigm from the New Testament, but for the substance one

would think of Acts 27$^{15, 17}$ (in the derivative sense) and of Hebrews 6$^1$ and 2 Peter 1$^{21}$ (in the literal sense).

His use of New Testament Greek is illuminating and calls to mind the greatest prayer manual of the Anglican Church, Lancelot Andrewes' (1555–1626) *Preces Privatae,* which he wrote out by hand in the original languages of the Bible for purely personal use. Best edition: *The Greek Devotions of Lancelot Andrewes . . . from the manuscript given by him to William Laud, afterwards Archbishop of Canterbury and recently discovered,* ed. Peter Goldsmith Medd, London, S.P.C.K., 1892.

267. *Letters,* IV, 322, Lewisham, 28th February 1766, to Charles.

268. *Letters,* V, 314, Congleton, 25th March 1772, to Charles: 'Oh what a thing it is to have curam animarum! You and I are called to this, to save souls from death, to watch over them as those that must give account! If our office implied no more than preaching a few times in a week, I could play with it; so might you. But how small a part of our duty (yours as well as mine) is this! God says to you as well as me: "Do all thou canst, be it more or less to save the souls for whom My Son had died". Let this voice be ever sounding in our ears; then shall we give up our account with joy.' Here again the use of the classical expression *cura animarum* in the original language is highly significant. Cf. *Letters,* V, 316, Perth, 26th April 1772, to Charles: 'Your business as well as mine is to save souls. When we took priests' orders, we undertook to make it our one business. I think every day lost which is not (mainly at least) employed in this thing. Sum totus in illo.' Cf. also *Letters,* IV, 322, Lewisham, 28th February 1766, to Charles.

269. *Letters,* V, 175, London, 15th January 1770, to Mary Bosanquet: 'It is not strange if the leading of one soul be very different from that of another. The same spirit worketh in everyone; and yet worketh several ways, according to His own will. It concerns us to follow our own light, seeing we are not to be judged by another's conscience.' Cf. *Letters,* V, 255, Castlebar, 31st May 1771, to Miss March: 'The dealings of God with man are infinitely varied, and cannot be confined to any general rule; both in justification and sanctification He often acts in a manner we cannot account for.'

270. E.g. *Letters,* III, 41, Birr, 28th June 1750, to Joshua Strangman; *Letters,* III, 118, Bristol, 21st September 1754, to Samuel Furly; *Letters,* III, 229, St Austell (Cornwall), 25th September 1757, to Dorothy Furly; *Letters,* III, 302, London, December 1751, to Bishop Lavington; *Letters,* IV, 11, Dublin, 5th April 1758, to Elizabeth Hardy; *Letters,* IV, 270, Norwich, 13th October 1764, to Miss

March; *Letters,* IV, 312, Kingswood, 5th October 1765, to Sarah Crosby: 'What an admirable teacher is experience!'; *Letters,* V, 92, Newcastle-upon-Tyne, 7th June 1768, to Ann Bolton; *Letters,* V, 129, London, 3rd March 1769, to Lady Maxwell; *Letters,* V, 214, London, 28th December 1770, to Joseph Benson; *Letters,* V, 216, London, 29th December 1770, to Ann Foard; *Letters,* V, 316, Perth, 26th April 1772, to Charles; *Letters,* V, 317, Aberdeen, 1st May 1772, to Mary Stokes; *Letters,* VI, 45, Bristol, 29th September 1773, to Philothea Briggs; *Letters,* VI, 69, London, 20th January 1774, to Ann Bolton; *Letters,* VI, 72, London, 17th February 1774, to Ann Bolton; *Letters,* VI, 87, Edinburgh, 3rd June 1774, to Sarah Crosby; *Letters,* VI, 88, Newcastle-upon-Tyne, 3rd June 1774, to Miss March; *Letters,* VI, 125, Shoreham, 29th November 1774, to Elizabeth Ritchie; *Letters,* VI, 129, Reigate, 30th November 1774, to Miss March; *Letters,* VI, 129, Reigate, 30th November 1774, to Miss March; *Letters,* VI, 132, London, 27th December 1774, to Miss March; *Letters,* VI, 153, Charlemont, 9th June 1775, to Miss March; *Letters,* VI, 222–3, Newcastle-upon-Tyne, 2nd June 1776, to Hester Ann Roe; *Letters,* VII, 24, Epworth, 22nd June 1780, to Ann Bolton; *Letters,* VII, 75, near Leeds, 17th July 1781, to his niece Sarah Wesley; *Letters,* VII, 392, Dublin, 4th July 1787, to Lady Maxwell.

271. He mentions the life of Count de Renty in *Letters,* I, 112, 3rd October 1731, to Ann Granville; *Letters,* IV, 184, Cork, 18th June 1762, to Jenny Lee; *Letters,* IV, 293, Liverpool, 9th April 1765, to John Newton. These references show how conversant he was with it. He recommended it sometimes explicitly, sometimes indirectly; *Letters,* IV, 264, Bristol, 22nd September 1764, to Lady Maxwell; V, 129, London, 3rd March 1769, to Lady Maxwell; V, 267, Dublin, 13th July 1771, to Miss March; V, 271, Kingswood, 3rd August 1771, to Miss March; V, 320, Sunderland, 30th May 1772, to Hannah Ball; V, 338, Bristol, 31st August 1772, to Philothea Briggs; VI, 125–6, Shoreham, 29th November 1774, to Elizabeth Ritchie; VI, 166, Leeds, 28th July 1775, to Hannah Ball; VI, 200, London, 26th December 1775, to Francis Wolfe; VI, 207, London, 7th February 1776, to Miss March; VI, 222–3, Newcastle, 2nd June 1776, to Hester Ann Roe; VI, 270, Bristol, 2nd August 1777, to Elizabeth Ritchie; VI, 373, London, 14th January 1780, to Ann Bolton; VII, 66, Douglas (Isle of Man), 10th June 1781, to Ann Loxdale; VII, 127, Darlington, 25th June 1782, to Hester Ann Roe; VIII, 83, London, 8th August 1788, to Lady Maxwell; VIII, 171, near Bristol, 16th September 1789, to his nephew Samuel Wesley; VIII, 253, London,

3rd January 1791, to Adam Clarke. He made a significant confession about himself, citing de Renty in support, in a letter to Hannah Ball (*Letters,* VI, 381, Dorking, 17th February 1780), in which he extolls death as a liberator from the limitations of separate individual existence.

272. Significant from this point of view is his letter to the Swedish court chaplain and canon, Dr Carl Magnus Wrangel in Sala (see Vol. II, Part 1, p. 91), to whom he felt compelled to issue urgent warning as to the dangers of a privileged position in Church and State. In doing so, he emphasized that he felt this to be his pressing and bounden duty, even though they only knew one another slightly. Cf. *Letters,* V, 180–1, London, 30th January 1770. An earlier instance is his letter of 20th March 1759, to Miss Johnson (?): *Letters,* IV, 59–60, Colchester.

273. Cf. Vol. II, Part 1, pp. 30, 36 and 129–31. A notable instance on the other side is his letter to an Irish lady, whom he rebuked for deserting the Methodists. Here he was a model of supreme courtesy. Cf. *Letters,* V, 139–41, Tullamore, 27th June 1769.

# Chapter 9: John Wesley as Educationalist

1. '*An die Ratsherren aller Städte deutschen Landes, dass sie christliche Schulen aufrichten und halten sollen*' (1524). W.A. 15, 27–53. ('*To the corporations of all towns of the German nation, that they should establish and support Christian schools*'.)

2. An Account of the Religious Society begin (sic) in Epworth, in the Isle of Axholm, Lincolnshire, 1st February (later stated to be 7th February) 1701–02 (written by Samuel Wesley in diary form). Manuscript in the Archives of the S.P.C.K. (now a publishing house) in London: Wanley MSS., pp. 186–94. P. 190: 'There are I believe 30 or 40 other sober persons in the town who should be glad to enter the Society: But we are not hasty in admitting 'em till we have very well acquainted with 'em. These will make a considerable Body, and are most of 'em Just entring the Scene of life: besides the Society we could get a Charity-School erected amongst us, it would I believe go a great way toward the securing two Generations.' On the educational policy of the Religious Societies, cf. W. K. Lowther Clarke, *A History of the S.P.C.K.,* 1959, pp. 19–58, where comparatively little is said about the lessons and the internal organization and more about the administrative basis. For Wesley, cf. Alfred H. Body, *John Wesley*

*and Education*, London, 1936 *(passim)*. [Translator's note: see also
F. C. Pritchard, *Methodist Secondary Education* (London, 1949), in
which it is maintained that Wesley's plan for Kingswood school was
at least partly modelled on the Dissenting Academies (pp. 64–5);
and R. G. Ives, *Kingswood School in Wesley's day and since* (London,
1970).]

3. The letters and reports are in manuscript in the same archives, *Misc.
Letters* I (6th June 1735–13th January 1736, cN 2/1), p. 13, to Dr
Waterland, Master of Magdalen College, Cambridge, 5th July 1735,
and to Gotthilf August Francke in Halle, 27th June 1735.

4. *Letters*, I, 302, Bristol, 30th April 1739, to James Hutton; *Journal*,
II, 168–71, note (from George Whitefield's Journal). For Whitefield
as the pioneer, cf. *Letters*, I, 356, London, 27th April 1741, to George
Whitefield.

5. *Journal*, II, 203, 21st May 1735 (Diary); *Letters*, I, 305, Bristol,
7th May 1739, to James Hutton; I, 313, Bristol, 28th May 1739, to
the same.

6. *Journal*, II, 322–3, 27th November 1739; in slightly altered form,
*Letters*, I, 338–40, Bristol, 6th December 1739, to Nathaniel Price.

7. *Journal*, II, 521, 11th January 1742. Snowde's pardon: *Journal*, II,
336, 12th February 1740.

8. *Letters*, I, 356; *Journal*, III, 125, 15th March 1744.

9. *Letters*, I, 355–8, London, 27th April 1741, to George Whitefield.

10. *Journal*, III, 125, 15th March 1744.

11. Viney's Diary, Part V, in *Proc. W.H.S.*, XIV. (1923), p. 19 (19th
February 1744).

12. Viney's Diary, Part XIV, in *Proc. W.H.S.*, XV. (1926), pp. 192–3:
'My Thoughts as above brought me to think on my own Call, and I
cannot help thinking it is to Labour in some shape among Children
for their Good, an y$^e$ Good of posterity. But how shall I do to come
into the way of my Call? The Bre$^n$ have excluded me their Communion, and beside, some of their Methods with Children I cannot
approve. Mr. Westley would employ me this way, but we are not of
one Mind in Doctrines, nor does his Aim in having a school appear
to me extensive enough, he purposing to take only justified Children
(as he speaks).' An echo of this is to be heard in Wesley's publication
written late in life, *Remarks on the State of Kingswood School* (1738):
*Works* [3rd edn, 1831], XIII, p. 268: 'My design in building the
house at Kingswood was, to have therein a Christian family; every
member whereof, children, excepted, should be alive to God, and a
pattern of all holiness.

'Here it was that I proposed to educate a few children according to the accuracy of the Christian model. And almost as soon as we began, God gave us a token for good: *four of the children receiving a clear sense of pardin.*' (italics mine).

13. *Journal*, III, 238, 7th April 1746.

14. E.g. Ann Clowney: *Journal,* III, 339, 10th April 1746, in London.

15. The text of the Authorized Version (King James' Bible) comes closer in its imperative form to the original text than Luther's German translation. The spacious grounds are mentioned in *A Plain Account of Kingswood School*, 1781, *Works* [3rd edn, 1831], XIII, p. 259.

16. On Stolte, the most informative person is Johann Albrecht Bengel, who in 1713 was in close contact with him in Jena for six weeks. Cf. Karl Hermann, *Johann Albrecht Bengel, Der Klosterpräzeptor von Denkendorf*, Vol. I, 1937, pp. 197–8; in addition, J. Wesley's *Journal*, II, 58–61, 21st August 1738. He reports accurately on every minute detail of the school rules, including the unique practice that the authority to punish rested with four teachers who were attached to no one school—an astonishing insight into the educational value of impartiality (*Journal*, II, 60).

17. Cf. Gerhard Reichel, *August Gottlieb Spangenberg*, 1906, pp. 18–20. Cf. also Erich Beyreuther, *Zinzendorf und die sich allhier beisammen finden*, 1959, pp. 254–5, 263–7.

18. *Journal*, II, 60.

19. *Remarks on the State of Kingswood School* (1783), *Works* [3rd edn, 1831], XIII, p. 268 (reproduced in note 12). He himself has confirmed that he did not expressly formulate this idea until this late stage. Cf. *A Plain Account of Kingswood School* (1781), *Works* [3rd edn, 1831], XIII, pp. 255–6: He took for granted what was not self-evident to others. The family idea receives insufficient attention in Body (see note 2); he emphasizes social responsibility.

20. *A Plain Account* (as in note 19), p. 259.

21. *A Short Account of the School in Kingswood, near Bristol* (1768), *Works* [3rd edn, 1831], XIII, p. 251.

22. *A Plain Account* (as in note 19), *Works* [3rd edn, 1831], XIII, p. 260.

23. *A Short Account* (as in note 21), p. 251: 'It is our particular desire, that all who are educated here may be brought up in the fear of God.' Cf. *A Plain Account* (as in note 19), p. 259: 'Our first point was, to answer the design of Christian education, by forming their minds, through the help of God, to wisdom and holiness, by instilling the principles of true religion, speculative and practical, and training them up in the ancient way, that they might be rational, scriptural Christians.' Cf. also the passage given in note 12 from the *Remarks*

(1781). *Letters*, II, 128, Bristol, 12th February 1748, to Mrs Jones, of Fonmon Castle: 'At my return from Ireland, if not before, I believe the School in Kingswood will be opened. If your son comes there, you will probably hear complaints; for the discipline will be exact; it being our view not so much to teach Greek and Latin as to train up soldiers for Jesus Christ.' *Letters*, VI, 196–7, London, 23rd December 1775, to the Swedish 'Societas pro Fide et Christianismo': 'Although it is to be desired rather than expected that the general plan of modern education may be amended, yet a treatise on that subject, which was printed in England some years since, has not been without success. A few have dared to go out of the common road and to educate their children in a Christian manner; and some tutors of the University have trained up them under their care in a manner not unworthy of the primitive Christians.' Cf. also Body, op. cit. (see note 2), pp. 47ff., 84ff.

24. *A Plain Account* (as in note 19), p. 259.
25. Ibid., p. 260.
26. *Journal*, II, 60 (see note 15).
27. *A Short Account* (as in note 21), p. 251: . . . 'the rules will not be broken in favour of any person whatsoever.'
28. Ibid., pp. 250–1.
29. On this, cf. also the fact that one of the books belonging to the library of Kingswood School was *Experiments on Electricity*. Kingswood School's Library catalogue, 1782, in manuscript at Kingswood School, Bath.
30. *A Short Account* (as in note 21), p. 250.
31. *A Plain Account* (as in note 19), p. 259.
32. Espec. clear, ibid., p. 257.
33. Ibid., pp. 262–3, 264–5.
34. Ibid., p. 263.
35. Ibid., p. 258, p. 261.
36. Ibid., p. 262.
37. Ibid., pp. 256–7.
38. Ibid., p. 266.
39. Ibid., p. 267: 'Meantime I can only say, as a much greater man said, Hier stehe ich: Gott hilffe mich!' In modern German, this would read: 'Hier stehe ich: Gott helfe mir.'
40. Ibid.
41. *Remarks* . . . 1783 (see note 19), pp. 268–9.
42. *A Thought on the Manner of Educating Children*, 1783, *Works* [3rd edn, 1831], XIII, pp. 434–7; against Rousseau's *Émile*, pp. 434–5.

43. Ibid., p. 436.

44. It was also in this spirit that he exercised his sway over the school-mistresses in his movement, especially Mary Bishop. Cf. *Letters*, V, 153–4, Ipswich, 5th November 1769.

## Chapter 10: John Wesley: Take him for all in all

1. Otto Dibelius, *Ein Christ ist immer im Dienst. Erlebnisse und Er-fahrungen in einer Zeitenwende*, Stuttgart, 1961. [Translator's Note: In the original German this book is entitled, '*A Christian is always on duty*,' the reason for this choice of title being given on p. 8. The allusion is lost in the English translation, which is entitled *In the Service of the Lord*. (E. T., Mary Ilford, Faber, 1965).]

2. Cf. supra, pp. 9ff, 78f, 110–12, and his sermon on *The Catholic Spirit*, section I, paras 12–8: *Forty-Four Sermons on Several Occasions* by John Wesley (1944), [3rd imp, 1948], pp. 448–50. In this respect he diverged sharply from German Pietism, to which he was so greatly indebted. The personal experience of being a child of God by regeneration through faith guaranteed for the Pietists a closer and deeper fellowship than the confessionally based common membership in the one Church, resting as it did on uniformity of doctrine. As a particularly eloquent witness to this, cf. the statements of Spener's disciple Egid Günther Hellmund in *Der Enthusiast und Syncretist*, Frankfurt-am-Main and Leipzig, 1720, p. 58: 'And whether or no we may likewise recognize as our Church brethren those weak in faith in other Christian Churches, e.g. in the Roman Catholic, Greek and the like Churches, because they do not belong to our Church and are not in communion with us (Kirchengemein-schaft), nevertheless we may and must surely recognize as our brethren in faith those who with us are born of God and with us have a faith in Jesus Christ in their hearts, by the same token as I, alas, cannot recognize all those who are my brothers in the Church be-cause they have no true, lively faith in their hearts, nor evidence such faith by their deeds.' John Wesley's attitude to Roman Catholicism is not altogether easy to determine, because here several factors came into play. He himself was suspected by Lavington and also in other quarters of being a 'Papist' and so discredited in the eyes of the 'En-lightened' spirit of the age; politically, he was at times accused of being a supporter of the Stuarts, who had been exiled because of their Roman sympathies. He fully acknowledged the exemplary piety

of de Renty and of Gregory Lopez, and also of Armelle Nicholas; he had made both friendly and hostile contacts with Irish Catholics, was a staunch opponent of papal claims to supremacy, and also found Scholastic theology completely alien to him. Despite all his disagreement on matters of principle, he had a genuine admiration for the drive and inner consistency revealed in the life-work of Ignatius Loyola. His dissent was particularly provoked by the unquestioning identification of the honour of God with the interests of the Roman Church and the use of lying in the pursuit of these ends, which reminded him forcibly of Count Zinzendorf (*Journal*, III, 40, 16th August 1742). He incorporated into Methodist hymnody specific items from Loyola's *Spiritual Exercises*: cf. R. Ernest Ker, 'Loyola and the Wesley Hymns', in *Proc. W.H.S.*, XXX, (1955–56), pp. 62–4; Reginald Kissack, *Loyola and the Wesley Hymns*, ibid., XXX, (1955–56), p. 136. On the other hand, in 1768 he passed very adverse comment on the Jesuit mission in Paraguay at the time of the expulsion of the Jesuits by the Governor of Buenos Aires—when hostility to the Jesuits was at its height. Cf. *Letters*, V, 121–2, 1768, to Dr Brown.

Methodism was one with German Pietism in being classed for polemical purposes with the Jesuits. Cf. Christian Ernst Kleinfeld, *Öffentliche Entdeckung der Ursprache, um welcher willen er die Pietisten für Jesuiten halte*. Leiden, 1726, esp. p. 29: 'Accordingly I say that the design of the Pietists is first and formost to create confusion among the Protestants, then to bring about the eclipse of the sciences, next to throw off obedience to the secular authority, and finally by these means to put the yoke of anti-Christ, the yoke of the Papacy, over the necks of us Protestants again.'

3. This is why he refused to make salvation dependent on an abstractly conceived understanding of the doctrine of justification and knowledge of it. *Journal*, V, 243–4, 1st December 1767.

4. His physical appearance has been described by John Whitehead, who as a doctor was particularly qualified to do this. Cf. *The Life of John Wesley*, Vol. II, 1796, p. 484: 'The figure of Mr. Wesley was remarkable: his stature was low; his habit of body, in every period of life, the reverse of corpulent, and expressive of strict temperance, and continual exercise; and notwithstanding his small size, his step was firm, and his appearance, till within a few years of his death, vigorous and muscular. His face, for an old man, was one of the finest we have seen. A clear, smooth forehead, an aquiline nose, an eye the brightest and most piercing that can be conceived, and a freshness of complexion scarcely ever to be found at his years, and

impressive of the most perfect health, conspired to render him a venerable and interesting figure. Few have seen him without being struck with his appearance; and many who had been known to change their opinion the moment they were introduced to his presence. In his countenance and demeanour there was a cheerfulness mingled with gravity; a sprightliness, which was the natural result of an unusual flow of spirits, and yet was accompanied with every mark of the most serene tranquillity. His aspect, particularly in profile, had a strong character of acuteness and penetration.'

On his health, cf. Richard Butterworth, 'John Wesley's Health', *Proc. W.H.S.,* XIV (1924), pp. 162–5. Contrary to Wesley's optimistic judgement on his own physical fitness, Butterworth points out that between 1739 and 1790 he was ill 39 times and critically ill in November 1753, when he even composed his epitaph (*Journal*, IV, 90, 26th November 1753).

5. *Letters,* VII, 19, Newcastle, 11th May 1780, to Sarah Crosby.

6. Thomas Paine, *The Age of Reason*, Paris, 1793–95. An enthusiastic supporter of the French Revolution, Paine had hurried to Paris to further the cause and had become a French citizen. He wrote this book during the term of imprisonment which he had to serve as a Girondist and opponent of the execution of Louis XVI. In writing this book he wanted to refute atheism by using the Enlightenment's own forms of reasoning and to enthrone natural religion.

7. William Whiston (1667–1752) would be worthy of a monograph. On 18th December 1710 he provisionally resigned from the Society for Promoting Christian Knowledge of which he had been a founder member, with the following letter. This letter does full justice to his high principles. The high regard in which he himself was held by the Society is shown in turn by the fact that, departing from its previous practice, it directed that his letter be included verbatim in its extracts from correspondence: 'This comes to give our Society for Promoting Christian Knowledge the Reason of my absenting myself from their Meetings now I am come to reside in Town whereas I so seldom us'd to fail them when I was but occasionely there. I confess I am not able to enter into this Matter nor to absent myself from the Society without some concern and uneasiness.

'I have the same designs for advancing true genuine Christian knowledge and practice that the rest of the Society have. My heart is intirely with them in their brave and religious and charitable and Christian undertakings. I am still as willing and as ready as ever to assist and encourage and advise in any of their affairs. I own myself to receive no small benefit comfort and edification my self from their

Society, and I cannot without unwillingness and regret bear to be excluded or banished from them. Yet I do by no means think it prudent in me considering the circumstances I am at present under any longer to frequent their meetings, since there may such inconveniences thence arise as may hinder not only my self but the rest from doing that good which otherwise might be expected. Insomuch that the very same design of *Doing Good* which prompted the Society to choose me at first and me to accept the same and to frequent their Assemblies seems now to require my absenting my self from them; so long I mean as y$^e$ reason for such absenting shall stand good; and till those important things I have to propose to the Christian World be so thoroughly examined, that I may stand justifyed before all good men, and they may see it necessary to joyn my designs with those which are already engag'd in, in order to the through reformation of the Christian Church, and the hastening the coming of our Saviour's Kingdom of peace and holiness. This I verily believe will be found necessary in no very long time. But since it is not in that state at present and suspicions and jealousies may easily arise in the meane time; I do hereby take my leave of the Society, Begging of God to Bless them in all their religious undertakings, and to open the Eyes of the Christian world to see believe and practice exactly according to the revelation by his son and offering my hearty Service to y$^e$ Society and every Member of it in any such designs as in my present circumstances I may be assisting in, in a more private manner and hoping y$^e$ Almighty God will in this matter accept of my hearty good will for y$^e$ deed, and not excluding from all reward of those pious undertakings which I have hitherto been ready to promote by my own private endeavour and good wishes and prayers for their success and advancement in y$^e$ world.

I am S$^r$ y$^e$ Society's and yo$^r$ most humble Serv$^t$

Will: Whiston'

Handwritten in the Archives of the S.P.C.K., in *London Letters received by the Society and read abstracted*, vol. 2 (1709-10, Thursday, 5th January–Thursday, 31st May 1711.CR1/2, pp. 195-7, no. 2420). Italics original. [Translator's note: Whiston did in fact later form a (short-lived) Society for Promoting Primitive Christianity (cf. his Memoirs, London, 1749).]

8. This point merits special evaluation. Cf. John Wesley's autobiographical passage on this subject: 'I abridged Dr. Watt's pretty Treatise on the Passions. His hundred and seventy-seven pages will make a useful tract of four-and-twenty. Why do persons who treat the same subjects with me, write so much larger books? Of many

reasons, is not this the chief—we do not write with the same view? Their principal end is to get money; my only one to do good.' *Journal*, V, 300, 17th February 1769. Noteworthy here, too, is Wesley's neat use of contrast: 'principal' and 'only' end are placed in sharp contrast. Isaac Watts' book bore the title *Treatise on the Love of God; and on the Use and Abuse of the Passions*, London, 1729. Cf. also the *Arminian Magazine*, 1784, supplement to the October issue: 'Men wholly unawakened will not take the pains to read the Bible. They have no relish for it. But a small Tract may engage their attention for half an hour: and may, by blessing of God, prepare them for going forward.'

9. *Journal*, VII, 461, 5th January 1789, and note 2 in loc. According to Sir Joshua Reynolds' Diary, Wesley sat for him in March 1755. Considerable light is thrown on these matters by J. Wesley's correspondence with Walter Churchey about the latter's poetry and his English translation in 1788 of *Ars pingendi (The Art of Painting)*, a book written in Latin by the Frenchman Alphonse du Fresnoy. See *Letters*, VIII, 74, near London, 22nd July 1788; ibid., 81–2, London, 8th August 1788; ibid., 107, London, 8th December 1788. Cf. pp. 81–2: 'There are many good lines, and some very good both in the ode and the translation of The Art of Painting. And I really think you improve in versifying: you write a good deal better than you used to do, and appear to have greater variety of words as well as more strength. But there is nothing (to use the modern cant word) sentimental in either the old or the translation. There is nothing of tender or pathetic, nothing that touches the passions. Therefore no bookseller would venture to buy them, as knowing they will not sell. And they lie utterly out of the way of the Methodists, who do not care to buy or even to read (at least the generality of them) any but religious books. I do not believe all my influence would induce them to buy as many copies as would suffice to pay for the printing.' Similarly, ibid., p. 107: 'The Methodists in general have very little taste for any poems but those of a religious or a moral kind.' It becomes clear that John Wesley had real knowledge of, and opinions on, what was expected of the effective literature of his times, and had his own criteria for a good style. At the same time, however, he said in no uncertain terms that publications of this kind were irrelevant for the Methodist movement.

10. *Journal*, V, 296–7, December 1768: 'In the latter end of the month I took some pains in reading over Dr. Young's Night-Thoughts, leaving out the indifferent lines, correcting many of the rest, and explaining the hard words, in order to make that noble work more useful

to all, and more intelligible to ordinary readers.' In 1770 his abridgement was published in Bristol: *An Extract from Dr. Young's Night-
Thoughts on Life, Death and Immortality*, Bristol, 1770. (Richard
Green, *The Works of John and Charles Wesley* (Bibliography), 1896,
no. 269.) On Thomas Gray, cf. *Journal*, VI, 134, 5th December 1776:
'In the way (from Godmanchester to London), I read over Mr.
Gray's Works, and his Life wrote by Mr. Mason. He is an admirable
poet, not much inferior to either Prior or Pope; but he does not
appear, on the whole, to have been an amiable man. His picture, I
apprehend, expresses his character—sharp, sensible, ingenious, but,
at the same time, proud, morose, envious, passionate, and resentful.
I was quite shocked at the contempt with which he more than once
speaks of Mr. Mason, one full as ingenious as himself, yea, full as
good a poet (as even Elfrida shows, as much as Mr. Gray despises, or
affects to despise it), and, over and above, possessed of that modesty
and humanity wherein Mr. Gray was so greatly deficient.'
    William Mason (1725–97) was one of a great host of ministers
who wrote poems in the eighteenth century. (On this, cf. Herbert
Schöffler, *Protestantismus und Literatur*, 1923). He was a Fellow of
Pembroke Hall, Cambridge, and became chaplain to the king, but
was relieved of his appointment for espousing the American cause in
the War of Independence. Being of a classical bent, he introduced the
choruses of Greek drama into his poem *Elfrida* (1752).
    Wesley's judgement on Gray shows with commendable directness
the absolute precedence which he gave moral judgements over
aesthetic values.

11. *Journal*, IV, 282, 17th August 1758.
12. *Journal*, II, 297, 23rd October 1739, where in criticizing William
Law's book on *The New Birth or Regeneration* Wesley quotes loosely
from Shakespeare's *Julius Caesar*, Act III, Scene 2, line 195; similarly, *Letters*, VI, 300, London, 14th February 1778, to Mrs Johnston,
he quotes from *Othello*, Act III, Scene 3, line 258; *Letters*, III,
164, Marlborough, 1st March 1756, to Ebenezer Blackwell, he
alludes to Regan and Goneril in *King Lear*; *Journal*, IV, 374, 10th
April 1760, he quotes *Hamlet*, Act I, Scene 5, line 20; *Journal*, V, 431,
1st October 1771, Part II of *Henry VI*, Act III, Scene 3, lines 27–9;
*Journal*, VI, 69, 17th June 1775, *Twelfth Night*, Act II, Scene 4, line
116. He read Shakespeare with particular frequency between October
1783 and March 1784. Cf. *Journal*, VI, 454–81, (Diary), *passim*.
His quotations from Milton's *Paradise Lost* and *Paradise Regained*
are so frequent throughout his life that they cannot be specified here.
See *Journal*, VIII, Index, and *Letters*, VIII, Index. *Samson Agonistes*

also crops up again and again: for example, even when he was 86 (*Letters*, VIII, 126, 31st March 1789, to several people in Dublin).

13. *Journal*, IV, 157, 14th April 1756: 'I looked over a celebrated book, *The Fable of the Bees*. Till now I imagined there had never appeared in the world such a book as the works of Machiavel. But de Mandeville goes far beyond it. The Italian only recommends a few vices, as useful to some particular men and on some particular occasions. But the Englishman loves and cordially recommends vice of every kind; not only as useful now and then, but as absolutely necessary at all times for all communities! Surely Voltaire would hardly have said so much.' Basically the same is said in *Letters*, V, 373, December 1768, to a Friend. On the famous book itself, cf. the thorough, painstaking characterization of it by Walther Hübner, *Mandevilles Bienenfabel und die Begründung der praktischen Zweckethik in der englischen Aufklärung. Ein Beitrag zur Genealogie des englischen Geistes,* in *Grundformen der englischen Geistesgeschichte,* ed. Paul Meissner, Stuttgart, 1941, pp. 275–331.

14. *Journal,* III, 490, 15th August 1750; *Arminian Magazine*, 1785, pp. 35–6. The Methodists came to be suspected of being Montanists because of James Clark: *Montanus Redivivus: or Montanism Revived in the Principles and Discipline of the Methodists (Commonly called Swadlers)*, 1760.

15. Cf. e.g., *Journal*, II, 238, 6th July 1739: III, 234, 24th February 1746; V, 297, 17th January 1769 (Mr Spooner in Chesham): *Letters*, VIII, 252, City Road, 1st January 1791, to John Fry. To be sure, frequent debates took place between Wesley on the one hand and Baptists and Quakers on the other, in which Wesley consistently brought out the force of the standpoint of the Bible. On the Covenant Service, cf. Frederick Hunter, 'The Origins of Wesley's Covenant Service', *Proc. W.H.S.*, XXII (1939–40), pp. 126–31. [Translator's note: Cf. also David Tripp, *The Renewal of the Covenant in the Methodist Tradition*, London, Epworth, 1969, and the extensive Bibliography, pp. 163–73.]

16. *Journal,* IV, 89, 13th November 1753; IV, 90, 26th November 1753; IV, 97, 6th August 1754.

17. *Journal,* VIII, 143–4. An account of the last days of John Wesley's life by Elizabeth Ritchie.

18. On this, cf. especially John S. Simon, *John Wesley. The Last Phase* (1934), pp. 229–32; *Letters*, VII, 238–9, Bristol 10th September 1784, to 'Our Brethren in America'.

19. *The substance of a Sermon preached in Baltimore and Philadelphia on the 1st and 8th of May 1791 on the death of the Rev. John Wesley.* By

the Rev. T. Coke, L.L.D., London . . . sold by G. Whitefield, Chapel, City Road, and at the Methodist Preaching Houses in Town and Country, 1791, pp. 7ff.

20. Ibid., p. 9: 'His mind was exactly formed for the abstrusest studies. But he sacrificed the whole to the Will of God, and the insatiable desire of his soul for doing good.' John Wesley did in fact pine for the life at Oxford with its tranquility and predictableness: *Letters*, VI, 6, Shoreham, 15th December 1772, to his brother Charles.

21. Coke, op. cit. (as in note 19), p. 11: 'I can without hesitation declare that I never knew one, concerning whom I could form any mature judgment, that sacrificed ease, pleasure, profit, friends for the welfare of the Church of Christ, with so much readiness, with so much freedom as Mr. Wesley.'

22. Op. cit., p. 10: 'No one has borne so complete a testimony against the great sin of England—dissipation and ungodliness: no one has borne a more pointed testimony against the great sin of America—the slavery and oppression of the negroes, than he.' It is worth noting that Coke here uses the negative form of the classical Puritan word for piety (godliness). [Translator's note: on negro slavery in America, see D. G. Mathews, *Slavery and Methodism. A Chapter in American Methodist Morality, 1780–1845*. Princetown, 1965.]

23. Ibid., p. 16: 'We may say of him what was observed of Athanasius on another occasion *Wesley contra mundum*, Wesley against the world' (italics original).

24. Joseph Benson, *Sermons on Various Occasions, and most of them on the principal subjects of Genuine Christianity*, London, 1802, Sermon IX: On the Life and Labours of the late Rev. John Wesley preached before the Conference at Manchester, July 26 1791. At their first Annual Meeting after his death, pp. 193–220. P. 204: 'His life was *one continued good work, one constant labour* to do good to the bodies and souls of men'. . . . P. 207: 'I have only to speak of him in the character of a *Shepherd* and *Bishop* of Souls, in which he peculiarly shone, which was his *chief calling,* and his principal employment, and for which he was most admirably fitted by nature, and by grace. As probably no person has existed since the Apostles' days, who ever had so many souls under his care, so many to *feed* and *oversee,* so perhaps no one was ever better qualified for such a work'. . . . pp. 207–8: . . . as few or none of the clergy of the established church were willing to expose themselves to reproach, and engage heatily with him in the work; he had wisdom and courage enough to go out of the common track to take the Lord Jesus and his Apostles for his models' . . . P. 213: 'Almost every other branch of Christian doctrine

has advocates in abundance without us. But with regard to *faith working by love, and justification by faith,* together with *a new birth or a new creation,* manifesting itself by *universal holiness* of heart and life, the case is different:—To preach *these* is the proper office of a *Methodist preacher,* this being the very doctrine as we have seen in the former part of this discourse, which our late Reverend Father continually inculcated. And if it be our duty to *preach* it, surely it is equally or *more,* our duty to *experience* it. For certainly we would not wish to be *hypocrites,* going about and recommending to others what we have no experience of ourselves.' P. 214: 'It would be incredible that any one man should go thro' so much work, if we did not know it to be a fact that he went thro' it and that thro' the help of God, by attending to *one single circumstance,* and that is, to the *proper use of his time*' . . . P. 215: 'His whole life was one scene of serious business' (italics original). [Translator's note: In the event Benson did not take Anglican orders, though this had been his intention. On this point, see J. S. Simon, *John Wesley, the Master-Builder,* London, 1927, pp. 288–9.]

25. Ibid., pp. 219–20.

26. Ibid., p. 211.

27. Richard Rodda, *A Discourse Delivered at the Chapel in Oldham-Street, Manchester, March 13th, 1791, on occasion of the death of the Rev. John Wesley M.A.,* Manchester, 1791, pp. 9–12. P. 12: 'I am firmly persuaded that whoever will be at the pains to acquaint himself with the rise and progress of Methodism (so called) will scarce find any work of GOD which equals it since the Apostolic age.'

28. Ibid., pp. 12–26.

29. Ibid., p. 27.

30. Ibid., p. 13: 'GOD it is who justifies,
Only faith the blood applies;
Sanctifies and makes us whole,
Forms the Saviour in the Soul.'

31. Friedrich Schleiermacher, *Sämtl. Werke,* ed. L. Jonas, Vol. III: *Zur Philosophie,* Part 3 (1835), p. 83, in his funeral oration on Frederick II of Brandenburg and Prussia, delivered in the Academy on 24th January 1826: Über den Begriff des grossen Mannes ('On the notion of a great man').

32. Samuel Bradburn, *A Farther Account of the Rev. John Wesley M.A.,* London, n.d. (1791), p. 8.

33. Ibid., p. 11. As early as 1744 Richard Viney criticized him for preaching far too often every day. See *Proc. W.H.S.,* XIV (1924), p. 204.

34. Ibid., p. 11. On this, cf. the excerpt from the Diary of Johan Henrik
Liden (1741–93), who was Professor and Librarian at Lund, for
October/November 1769, reproduced in English translation in *Proc.
W.H.S.*, XVII. (1929–30). pp. 2–3 (Sunday, 15th October 1769):
'He preached today for an audience of more than 4,000 people (in
Spitalfield in London). His text was Luke 1: 68. The sermon was
short but eminently evangelical. He has not great oratorical gifts, no
outward appearance, but he speaks clear and pleasant. I was received
by him in his usual and friendly way. He is a small, thin old man,
with his own long strait hair, and looks as the worst country curate
in Sweden, but has learning as a Bishop and zeal for the glory of God
which is quite extraordinary. His talk is very agreeable, and his mild
face and pious manner secure him the love of all rightminded men.
He is the personification of piety, and he seems to me as a living
representation of the loving Apostle John.' P. 3 (2nd November): 'It
is unpardonable that during the blessed Passion Week it never is
preached a word about the Suffering of Jesus, but about entirely
other subjects. This is the real reason why Mr. Wesley created so
great attention by his sermons, because he spoke of a crucified
Saviour and faith in his merits—such the people never had heard.'
In a letter of 16th November 1769, John Wesley supplied information about Methodism to Liden, who was Professor of History:
*Letters*, V, 154–6.
    As will be clear, Liden's judgement differs slightly from that
expressed here by Bradburn, who was passing on a comment made in
Edinburgh, but agrees with him on the central point that he was not a
particularly gifted speaker in the technical sense, but that the effect
he had was based on the substance of what he said, the message itself.

35. Bradburn, ibid., pp. 12–4. The quotation is on p. 13. Joseph Benson
had also drawn special attention to the surprisingly sociable side of
Wesley's character: op. cit. (as in note 24), p. 205.

36. Bradburn, op. cit., p. 14.

37. Ibid., p. 16.

38. Ibid., p. 17.

39. Ibid., pp. 18–9.

40. Ibid., p. 19.

41. Ibid., pp. 20–1: 'He often said, "Cleanliness is next to Godliness".'
(p. 20).

42. Ibid., pp. 20–1: 'His modesty prevented his saying much of his own
experience. In public he very seldom, hardly ever, spoke of the state
of his own soul. . . . He told me, when with him in Yorkshire, in the

year 1781 that his Experience might almost any time, be found in the following lines—

> "O Thou who camest from above!
> The pure celestial fire to impart,
> Kindle a flame of sacred love
> On the mean altar of my heart!
> There let it for thy glory burn,
> With inextinguishable blaze,
> And trembling to its source return,
> In humble love, and fervent praise." '

P. 23: 'In the year 1783, I heard him say in Leeds Chapel (when preaching on: "I will take the cup of Salvation, and call upon the name of the Lord".) That, after all his travelling in the service of GOD, and all his preaching and praying, he saw nothing to depend upon, but, "God be merciful to me a sinner". The same I heard him repeat at Sheffield last summer.'

On his basically modest nature, cf. also his admission about himself in *Letters*, V, 163, The Foundery, 30th November 1769, to Professor John Liden of Lund: 'Never was there anything which I less desired or expected some years since than virum volitare per ora (Virgil's *Georgics*, III, 9), having from my infancy loved silence and obscurity.'

43. Bradburn, ibid., p. 24: 'In this imperfect memorial, I have endeavoured to shew my love to this venerable Saint.'

44. John Whitehead M.D., *A Discourse delivered at the New Chapel in City Road on the 9th of March 1791 at the Funeral of the late Rev. Mr. John Wesley*. London, 1791, p. 4.

45. *A Survey of the Wisdom of God in the Creation; or, A Compendium of Natural Philosophy*. In Two Volumes. Bristol, 1763. Ibid., In Three Volumes. Bristol, 1770. Ibid., in Five Volumes. London, 1777. This work was largely an English translation by Wesley of the second part of Johann Franz Buddeus' *Institutiones philosophiae eclecticae: Elementa philosophiae theoreticae*, Halle, 1703. The fact that Wesley selected precisely Buddeus (1667–1729), a German Lutheran divine, as an authority on natural philosophy remains noteworthy in view of the wealth of contemporary literature in England on these matters. Evidently the literature of his own country was to his mind too coloured by the Enlightenment. This whole question requires more thorough investigation. On this subject, cf. Frank W. Collier, *John Wesley among the Scientists*, New York, Abingdon Press, n.d. (1928), in which Wesley's scientific knowledgeability and principles are very

fully presented. [Translator's note: On Wesley and Buddeus, see J. Dillenberger, *Protestant Thought and Natural Science*, London, 1961, p. 157.]

46. Whitehead, op. cit (as in note 44), p. 5.
47. Ibid., pp. 6–10.
48. Ibid., pp. 12–4.
49. Ibid., pp. 15–8.
50. Ibid., pp. 19–20.
51. Ibid., pp. 20–2.
52. Ibid., pp. 23–7.
53. Ibid., pp. 27–30.
54. Ibid., pp. 31–44.
55. Ibid., pp. 44–50.
56. Ibid., pp. 50–7.
57. Ibid., p. 59.
58. Ibid., p. 60.
59. Ibid., p. 61.
60. Ibid., p. 63: 'Oh how happy a life to be spent in doing good, to have no attachment but to God and his work; to forsake all for it.' The phrase, 'doing good', also appears on p. 54.
61. *An Elegy on the much lamented death of the Rev. Mr. John Wesley*, no place or date, reprinted in *The Perkins School of Theology Journal*, Spring Number, 1956, pp. 3–5 (Southern Methodist University, Dallas, Texas) ed. David F. C. Coldwell under the title, 'An Unpublished Wesley Broadside'.
62. *An Elegiac Pastoral, occasioned by the death of the Reverend John Wesley who died March 2nd, 1791*, 14 pp.
63. *Journal*, VIII, 134 (John Wesley's Last Days. Account of Elizabeth Ritchie).
64. Cf. note 42 above, and *Letters*, VIII, 191–2, London, 26th December 1789, to John Dickins: 'Our insufficiency for every good work would discourage us, were we not convinced both by Scripture and experience that all our sufficiency is of God.'
65. Elizabeth Ritchie's Account (see note 63): *Journal*, VIII, 136, 137.
66. *Letters*, V, 15–6, Whitehaven, 27th June 1766.
67. With particular vigour in *Letters*, VIII, 60, Edinburgh, 20th May 1788, to Mrs Cock (Jane Bisson); VIII, 109, London, 27th December 1788, to the same; VIII, 128, Dublin, 7th April 1789, to the same; VIII; 159, Leeds, 3rd August 1789, to the same; VIII, 152, Dublin, 5th July 1789, to Rebecca Ingram. On Ann Bolton, see above p. 149.

68. His last letters particularly show this, as does the fact that even on his death-bed he expressed a desire that his sermon on the love of God might be widely circulated: *Journal*, VIII, 139. Cf. also his sermon on *The Spirit of Bondage and of Adoption* (Sermon IX in *Sermons on Several Occasions*, First Series: Forty-Four Sermons (1944) [3rd imp, 1948], pp. 96–110, esp. pp. 105ff.). Cf. also Bradburn, op. cit. (as in note 32), p. 15: 'in forgiving injuries, he evidenced to all who knew him, how much he lived under the power of Divine Love.'

This is confirmed by the first-hand accounts of personal experiences in letters and diaries of early Methodists which Wesley printed in his periodical, the *Arminian Magazine*. Cf. Rebecca Bennet to John Wesley, 13th August 1748: *Arm. Mag.* I (1778), pp. 581–4; Elizabeth Holmes to John Wesley, 28th August 1784: ibid., pp. 584–6; An Extract from the Diary of Mrs Bathsheba Hall: ibid., IV (1781), pp. 35–40, 94–7, 148–52, 195–8, 256, 309, 372, esp. p. 39 (1st March 1771), p. 95 (17th March 1771), p. 196 (10th July 1771), p. 197 (18th September 1771).

69. John Whitehead, op. cit. (as in note 44), p. 18; cf. above, p. 232 (Chapter 7, note 9).

70. This constantly recurring phrase shows the vigour with which John Wesley strove after pristine Christianity. He was not content to be numbered with the Apostles, but wanted to emulate the life of Jesus Christ Himself. Here Galatians 2$^{20}$ was taken with the utmost seriousness. Cf. the same lofty aim in Philipp Jakob Spener, *Erste geistliche Schriften*, 1699, pp. 108ff., where Luther is invoked.

71. The interpretation of the Sacrament in terms of the immediate presence of the Saviour and His saving grace, as put forward in Anglican theology, particularly by Richard Hooker (*The Laws of Ecclesiastical Polity*, 1594–98, Book V, Chapters 57–8: *Works*, ed. John Keble, 1839, vol. II, pp. 255ff.), then by Edward Reynolds (*Meditations on the Holy Sacrament of the Lord's Last Supper*, vol. II: *Works*, 1826 edn, vol III, pp. 7–9) and by John Cosin (*Works*, IV, in the *Library of Anglo-Catholic Theology*, 1851, pp. 155–7), is taken up by Wesley in his own individual way. This constitutes the legitimate element in the now popular Anglo-Catholic interpretation of his piety and is the reason for his admiration of such figures as Gaston Jean-Baptiste de Renty and Gregory Lopez.

72. Cf. my works: *Ursprung, Gehalt und Reichweite der Kirchengeschichte nach evangelischem Verständnis* (Inaugural Lecture on the occasion of entering upon the office of Rector of the Johannes Gutenberg University of Mainz, delivered on 6th December 1762): Mainzer Univer-

sitätsreden, no. 23, 1963, pp. 13ff.; prior to that, *Wort Gottes und Fremdlingschaft. Die Kirche vor dem Auswanderungsproblem des 19. Jahrhunderts,* 1953; and *Die Interpretation der neuzeitlichen Kirchengeschichte,* in Z.Th.K., 54 (1957), pp. 174–212.

# Bibliography

## A. PRIMARY SOURCES

### *1. Works by John Wesley*

BIBLIOGRAPHY: R. Green, *The Works of John and Charles Wesley*. London, 1896. (Addenda in *Proc. W.H.S.*, III, 1901/02, pp. 123–30; ibid. VIII, 1911/12, pp. 8–9; ibid. XXI, 1937/38, pp. 132–3, 155–8).

JOURNAL. *The Journal of the Rev. John Wesley* . . . Standard Edition ed. Nehemiah Curnock. 8 vols., London, 1909–16;
German selection: Frankfurt-am-Main, 1954 (Johannes Wesleys Tagebuch), (cf. F. M. Jackson, 'A Bibliographical Catalogue of Books Mentioned in J.W.'s Journals', *Proc. W.H.S.*, IV, 1903/04, pp. 17–9, 47–51, 74–81, 107–11, 134–40, 173–6, 203–10, 232–8).

LETTERS. *The Letters of John Wesley* ed. by John Telford. Standard Edition, 8 vols. London, 1931.

NOTES. *Explanatory Notes upon the New Testament*. Bristol, 1755 4th edn, 1765.

STANDARD SERMONS. *Wesley's Standard Sermons* edited and annotated by Edward H. Sugden. London, 1921.
German selection: Bremen/Zürich, 1938 (Wesley-Predigten).

SERMONS. *Sermons on Several Occasions*, London, 1944.

WORKS. *The Works of the Rev. John Wesley*. Bristol, 1771–74 (32 vols.). 3rd edn (with a preface by T. Jackson) London, 1829–31 (14 vols.). A new critical edition of John Wesley's Works is in preparation, under the general editorship of Joseph D. Quillian, published by the Oxford University Press (New York and London). The first volumes of the 30 expected were due to appear in 1968.
Charles and John Wesley, *The Poetical Works of* . . . Collected and arranged by C. Osborn. London, 1868–72 (13 vols.).

### *2. Periodicals*

Methodist History I–IV (1962–66).
*Proceedings of the Wesley Historical Society* I–XXXV (1897–1966).
Publications of the Wesley Historical Society
   1. John Bennet's Copy of the Minutes of the Conferences of 1744, 1745,

1747, and 1748; with Wesley's Copy of those for 1746. London 1896 (cf. Suppl. to Vol. IV of *Proc. W.H.S.*: Minutes of Conference for 1749, 1755, 1758 (Burnley, 1904) and: Minutes of the Methodist Conferences. London, 1802–64, 5 vols.).

3. Mrs. Wesley's Conference with her daughter. London, 1898.

4. Index to the Library Edition of Thomas Jackson's Life of Charles Wesley, London, 1899.

5. John Cennick: A Handlist of his Writings. London, 1958 (cf. *Proc. W.H.S.*, XXX, 1955/56, pp. 40–4, 50–8, 80–9, 104–7).

## 3. Manuscript Sources

Archives of the S.P.C.K. (Society for Promoting Christian Knowledge) London.

Methodist Archives, Wesley Research Library, London, Epworth House (City Road).

Archives of Francke's Institution at Halle.

(M. H. Jones, The Trevecka Letters . . . An Inventory of the letters with a digest of their contents. Caernarvon, 1932).

## 4. Contemporary Sources

*The Arminian Magazine*, Vol. I–XX, 1778–79 (cf. Suppl. to *Proc. W.H.S.*, VII: An Index to the Memoirs etc. . . . as contained in *The Arminian Magazine* . . . Burnley 1909/10).

*The Gentleman's Magazine and Historical Chronicle.* London, 1731ff.

Nikolaus Ludwig Graf von Zinzendorf and Pottendorf, περὶ Εαυτον. Das ist: Naturelle Reflexiones . . . n.p., n.d. (1746–49).

(by the same, anonymously), *Büdingische Sammlung. Büdingen, 1742–44* (3 vols.).

## 5. Works that influenced Wesley and by his Friends, Opponents and Contemporaries

BIBLIOGRAPHY: R. Green, *Anti-Methodist Publications.* London, 1902 (cf. the addenda in *Proc. W.H.S.*, IX, 1913/14, pp. 20–2; ibid. XI, 1917/18, pp. 70–2).

C. A. Federer, 'Methodist Anonyma'. *Proc. W.H.S.*, II, 1899/1900, pp. 80–7; ibid. V, 1905/06, pp. 134–6.

St. Pargellis and D. J. Medley, *Bibliography of British History: The 18th Century.* London, 1951.

Lancelot Andrewes, *Works,* Oxford, 1841–54 (11 Vols.).

Richard Baxter, *The Practical Works*. London, 1830 (Bibliography by A. G. Matthews, Oxford, 1932).

— *Autobiography, Being the Reliquiae Baxterianae* . . . London, 1925 (ed. J. M. L. Thomas).

Lewis Bayly, *Practice of Pietie*. London, 1613 (35th edn, 1635).

William Beveridge, *The Theological Works*. Oxford, 1842–48 (12 vols.).

Antoinette Bourignon, *Toutes les Oeuvres* (ed. P. Poiret), Amsterdam, 1686 (19 vols.).

John Bunyan, *The Whole Works* (ed. G. Offor). Glasgow, 1853 (3 vols.).

Joseph Butler, *The Works* (ed. W. E. Gladstone). Oxford, 1896 (3 vols.).

John William Fletcher, *The Works*. London, 1800–04 (9 vols.).

— *Posthumous Pieces*. London, 1794.

August Hermann Francke, 'Anfang und Fortgang meiner Bekehrung (1692)', in *L. Cordier : Der junge A. H. Francke*. Schwerin, 1927.

— *Segensvolle Fußstapfen* . . . Halle, 1709 (7 vols.).

— *Nicodemus oder Tractätlein von der Menschen-Furcht*. Halle, 3rd edn, 1707; E.T.: London, 1706.

John Gambold, *The Works*. Bath, 1789. Glasgow, 1822 (ed. T. Erskine).

Edmund Gibson, *Practical Tracts, Exhortations and Admonitions to the Public*. Dublin, n.d. (1778), 11 parts.

Jeanne Marie de Guyon, *Opuscules spirituelles* (ed. P. Poiret). Cologne, 1704.

James Hervey, *The Works* . . . Edinburgh, 1709 (with a bibliography).

Lord Peter King, *An Enquiry into the Constitution, Discipline, Unity and Worship . . . of the Primitive Church*, London, 1691.

George Lavington, *The Enthusiasm of Methodists and Papists compared*. I–III. London, 2nd edn, 1749–51.

— *The Moravians Compared and Detected*. London, 1755.

William Law, *The Works*. London, 1702 (9 vols.).

Francisco de Losa, *La vida que hizo el siervo de Dios G. Lopez en algunos lugares de la Nueva España*. Sevilla 1618. E.T. Paris, 1638.

John Milton, *Of Education,* to Mr. Samuel Hartlib, 1644.

Miguel de Molinos, *Guida spirituale*. Rome, 1681. E.T.: n.p. (London), 1688.

Pierre Poiret (Her.), *Recueil de divers traitez de théologie mystique*. Cologne, 1699 (I–II: *Mme Guyon*; III–IV: *Frere Laurent*).

— *La théologie réele* . . . Amsterdam, 1700.

— *La Vie de Demoiselle Antoinette Bourignon*. Amsterdam, 1683 (2 vols.).

— *La vie de Mme Guyon, écrite par elle-même*. Cologne, 1720. E.T.: Bristol, 1772 (2 vols.).

Jean Baptiste de Saint-Jure, *Le Chrétien réel ou la vie du Marquis de Renty* (1651). Cologne, 1701 (ed. P. Poiret), 2 tomes; E.T.: London, 1658.

Henry Scougal, *The Works*. Aberdeen, 1759 (2 vols.).

Ludovico Scupoli, *Pugna spiritualis*, 1657; Italian trans.: *Il Combattimento Spirituale*, Parigi, 1660; E.T. (of the version of Juan de Castaniza): *The Spiritual Conflict*. Paris, 1652.

Philipp Jacob Spener, *Hauptschriften* (ed. P. Grunberg), Gotha, 1889.

— *Pia Desideria* (ed. K. Aland). Berlin, 1940 (3rd edn. 1964).

Jeremy Taylor, *The Whole Works*. London, 1847–54 (10 vols.).

John Taylor (of Norwich), *The Scripture Doctrine of Original Sin Proposed to a Free and Candid Examination*. London, 1740 (4th edn, 1769).

Thomas à Kempis, *Opera omnia* (ed. M. J. Pohl). *Friburgi Brisigavorum* (Freiburg/Breisgau), 1902–22 (7 vols.).

E.T. of *Imitatio Christi* by G. Stanhope as *The Christian's Pattern*.

Josiah Tucker, *A Brief History of the Principles of Methodism*. Oxford/London, 1742.

William Warburton, *Works* (ed. R. Hurd). London, 1788–94 (7 vols.).

Charles Wesley, *The Journal* (ed. T. Jackson). London, 1849 (2 vols.).

— *The Early Journal* . . . (1736–39). London, 1909 (ed. J. Telford).

— *Sermons*. London, 1816.

George Whitefield, *The Works* (ed. J. Gillies). London, 1771–72 (6 vols.). (Bibliography by R. Austin: *Proc. W.H.S.*, X, 1915/16, pp. 169–84, 211–23).

— *Journals* (ed. I. Murray). London, 1960.

Edward Young, *Night Thoughts on Life, Death and Immortality*. London, 1742.

Nikolaus Ludwig von Zinzendorf, *Hauptschriften* in 6 Vols. (ed. E. Beyreuther und G. Meyer). Hildesheim, 1962/63.

9 Supplementary volumes to the original 6: Hildesheim, 1964ff.

# B. SELECT LIST OF SECONDARY LITERATURE

## *1. Biographical Literature on John Wesley*

BIBLIOGRAPHY: R. Green, 'A List of Published Biographies and Biographical Notices of John Wesley'. *Proc. W.H.S.*, II, 1901/02, pp. 217–36.

F. E. Maser, 'The Early Biographers of John Wesley'. *Meth. Hist.*, I, 1962/63, 2, pp. 29–42.

J. F. Butler, 'John Wesley's Defence before Bishop Butler'. *Proc. W.H.S.*, XX, 1935/36, pp. 63–7, 197–8.

R. Butterworth, 'John Wesley's Health'. *Proc. W.H.S.*, XIV, 1923/24, pp. 162–5.

— 'A Voyage to Georgia: Begun in the Year 1735'. Ibid., XI, 1917/18, pp. 108–11.

— 'Wesley as an Agent of the S.P.G.' Ibid., VII, 1909/10, pp. 99–102.

R. M. Cameron, 'John Wesley's Aldersgate Experience'. *Drew G*, XXV, 1955, pp. 210–9.

W. R. Cannon, 'John Wesley's Years in Georgia'. *Meth. Hist.*, I, 1962/63, 4 pp. 1–7.

A. Clarke, *Memoirs of the Wesley Family*. London, 1823.

Th. Coke and H. Moore, *Life of the Rev. John Wesley*. London, 1792.

M. L. Edwards, *Family Circle*. A Study of the Epworth Household. London, 1949.

— *Sons to Samuel*. London, 1961.

— *The astonishing Youth*. London, 1959.

F. C. Gill, *In the Steps of John Wesley*. London, 1962.

R. Green, *John Wesley*. London, n.d. (1882).

— *John Wesley, Evangelist*. London, 1905.

V. H. H. Green, *The Young Mr. Wesley*. London, 1961.

— *John Wesley*. London, 1964.

I. Haddal, *John Wesley*. A Biography. London, 1961.

R. Haire, *Wesley's One-and-Twenty Visits to Ireland*. London, 1947.

J. Hampson, *Memoirs of the late Rev. John Wesley* . . . Sunderland, 1791 (3 vols.).

G. E. Harrison, *Son to Susanna*. The Private Life of John Wesley. London, 1937.

F. M. Jackson, 'An Itinerary in which are traced the Rev. John Wesley's Journeys . . .' Revised by R. Green and H. J. Foster. Suppl. to Vol. VI of *Proc. W.H.S.* Burnley, 1907/08.

R. Kissack, 'Wesley's Conversion. Text, Psalm, and Homily'. *Proc. W.H.S.*, 1939/40, pp. 1–6.

U. Lee, *The Lord's Horseman*. New York/Nashville, 2nd edn, 1955.

A. Leger, *La Jeunesse de Wesley*. Paris, 1910.

M. Lelièvre, *John Wesley, sa Vie et son Oeuvre*. Paris, 1868.

F. J. McConnell, *John Wesley*, New York/Nashville 1939.

J. H. Martin, *John Wesley's London Chapels*. London, 1946. *W.H.S. Lect.* 12.

F. E. Maser, 'Preface to Victory; an analysis of John Wesley's mission to Georgia.' *RiL*, 25, pp. 280–93.

H. Moore, *The Life of the Rev. John Wesley*. In which are included the Life of the Rev. Charles Wesley . . . and Memories of the Wesley Family. London, 1824/25 (2 vols.).

E. K. Nottingham, *The Making of an Evangelist*. New York, 1938.

J. H. Overton, *John Wesley*. London, 1891.

R. Pyke, *John Wesley Came this Way*. London, 1938.

J. E. Rattenbury, *The Conversion of the Wesleys*. London, 1938.

J. H. Rigg, *The Living Wesley*. London, 2nd edn, 1891.

M. Schmidt, *John Wesleys Bekehrung*. Bremen, 1938. *BGM* 3.

W. C. Sheldon, 'Travelling in Wesley's Time.' *Proc. W.H.S.*, VII, 1909/10, pp. 2–8.

J. S. Simon, *John Wesley and the Religious Societies*. London, 1921.

— *John Wesley and the Methodist Societies*. London, 1923.

— *John Wesley and the Advance of Methodism*. London, 1925.

— *John Wesley, the Master-Builder*. London, 1927.

— *John Wesley, The Last Phase*. London, 1934.

R. Southey, *The Life of Wesley; and the Rise of Methodism*. London, 3rd edn, 1846 (with additional material by S. T. Coleridge and A. Knox); German trans., Hamburg, 1841.

G. Stevenson, *Memorials of the Wesley Family*. London, 1876.

E. H. Sugden, *John Wesley's London*. London, 1932.

I. Taylor, *Wesley and Methodism*. London, 1851.

J. Telford, *The Life of John Wesley*. London, 1886.

E. W. Thompson, *Wesley at Charterhouse*. London, 1938.

L. Tyerman, *The Life and Times of the Rev. John Wesley*. London, 1870–71. 3rd edn, 1876 (3 vols.).

R. D. Urlin, *The Churchman's Life of John Wesley*. London, 1880.

C. E. Vulliamy, *John Wesley*. London, 1931.

R. Watson, *The Life of the Rev. John Wesley*. London, 1831; French Trans. 1840.

J. Whitehead, *The Life of Rev. John Wesley* . . . with the Life of the Rev. Charles Wesley . . . London, 1793–96 (2 vols.).

## 2. On Theological Issues and Other Matters of Interest to John Wesley

F. Baker, 'John Wesley's Churchmanship'. *LQHR*, July 1960, pp. 210–5, October 1960, pp. 291–8.

— 'John Wesley on Christian Perfection'. *Proc. W.H.S.*, XXXIV, 1963/64, pp. 53–7.

F. L. Barber, *The Philosophy of John Wesley*. Toronto, 1923.

P. F. Blankenship, 'The Significance of John Wesley's Abridgement of the Thirty-Nine Articles'. *Meth. Hist.*, II, 1963/64, pp. 35–47.

A. H. Body, *John Wesley and Education*. London, 1936.

J. W. Bready, *Wesley and Democracy*. Toronto, 1939.

W. R. Cannon, *The Theology of John Wesley*. New York/Nashville, 1946.

H. Carter, *The Methodist Heritage*. London, 1951; German Trans.: *Das Erbe John Wesleys und die Ökumene*. Frankfurt-am-Main/Zürich, 1951.

G. C. Cell, *The Rediscovery of John Wesley*. New York, 1935.

R. L. Cole, *John Wesley's Journal*. London, 1938. *W.H.S. Lect.* 4.

F. W. Collier, *John Wesley Among the Scientists*. New York/Cincinnati/ Chicago, 1928.

L. G. Cox, *John Wesley's Concept of Perfection*. Kansas City, Mo., 1964.

C. H. Crookshank, 'Notes on Wesley's Journal'. *Proc. W.H.S.*, II, 1899/1900, pp. 33–5, 129–46; ibid. III, 1901/02, pp. 105–11, 140–8; ibid. VIII, 1911/12, pp. 103–4, 124–7, 170–2, 194–7.

T. Dearing, *Wesleyan and Tractarian Worship*. London, 1966.

J. Deschner, *Wesley's Christology*. Dallas, Texas, 1960.

S. G. Dimond, *The Psychology of the Methodist Revival*. London, 1926.

W. L. Doughty, *John Wesley: his conferences and his preachers*. London, 1944. *W.H.S. Lect.* 10.

— *John Wesley, Preacher*. London, 1955.

B. C. Drury, 'John Wesley, Hymnologist'. *Proc. W.H.S.*, XXXII, 1959/60, pp. 102–8, 132–5.

G. Eayrs, *John Wesley: Christian Philosopher and Church Founder*. London, 1926.

M. L. Edwards, *John Wesley and the Eighteenth Century*. London, 1933.

E. V. Eicken, *Rechtfertigung und Heiligung bei Wesley*. Diss. Heidelberg, 1934.

J. C. English, 'John Wesley and the Principle of Ministerial Succession'. *Meth. Hist.*, II, 1963/64, 2, pp. 31–6.

J. A. Faulkner, *Wesley as Sociologist, Theologian, Churchman*. New York/ Cincinnati, 1918.

R. N. Flew, *The Idea of Perfection in Christian Theology*. London, 1934.

C. L. Ford, 'An Examination of Quotations in the Journal of John Wesley'. *Proc. W.H.S.*, V, 1905/06, pp, 24–31, 47–53, 87–91, 110–21, 152–9; ibid. VII, 1909/10, pp. 33–9.

— 'An Examination of the Fragments of Devotional Verse Quoted in the Journal of John Wesley.' *Proc. W.H.S.*, V, 1905/06, pp. 174–84, 214–22.

S. B. Frost, *Die Autoritätslehre in den Werken John Wesleys*. München, 1938.

Th. Funk, *Die Aufänge der Laienmitarbeit im Methodismus*. Bremen, 1941. *BMG* 5.

B. J. N. Galliers, 'Baptism in the Writings of John Wesley'. *Proc. W.H.S.*, XXXII, 1959/60, pp. 121–4, 153–7.

A. R. George, 'Ordination in Methodism'. *LQHR*, 1951, pp. 150–69.

E. W. Gerdes, *John Wesleys Lehre von der Gottesebenbildlichkeit des Menschen*. Diss. Kiel, 1958.

E. Gounelle, *Wesley et ses Rapports avec les Français*. Nyons, 1898.

Michel Haemmerlin: *Essai dogmatique sur John Wesley d'après ses Sermons. Thèse presentée à la Faculté de Théologie Protestante de Strasbourg*. Colmar, 1857.

A. W. Harrison, 'The Greek Text of Wesley's Translation of the New Testament'. *Proc. W.H.S.*, IX, 1913/14, pp. 105–13.
— 'Wesley's Reading'. Ibid., XIII, 1921/22, pp. 25–9; ibid. XV, 1925/26, pp. 113, pp. 126–31.
G. C. Henry, 'John Wesley's Doctrine of Free Will'. *LQHR* 1960, pp. 200–205.
T. W. Herbert, *John Wesley as Editor and Author*. Princeton, 1940.
F. Hildebrandt, *From Luther to Wesley*. London, 1951.
— *Christianity According to the Wesleys*. London, 1956.
A. W. Hill, *John Wesley among the Physicians*. London, 1958. *W.H.S.* Lect 24.
B. G. Holland, *Baptism in Early Methodism*. London, 1971.
W. F. Howard, 'John Wesley in his Letters'. *Proc. W.H.S.*, XXIX, 1953/54, pp. 3–11.
F. Hunter, 'The Origin of Wesley's Covenant-Service'. LQHR, 1939, pp. 78–87.
— 'Sources of Wesley's Revision of the Prayer Book in 1784–88'. Proc. W.H.S., XXIII, 1941/42, pp. 123–33.
C. N. Impeta, *De Leer van de Hailiging en Volmaking bij Wesley en Fletcher*. Leiden, 1913.
F. Jeffery, 'John Wesley's *Primitive Physik*'. *Proc. W.H.S.*, XXI, 1937/38, pp. 60–7.
O. F. Kamm, *John Wesley and die englische Romantik*. Diss. Marburg, 1939.
A. B. Lawson, *John Wesley and the Christian Ministry*. London 1963.
J. Lawson, *Notes on Wesley's Forty-Four Sermons*. London, 1946.
G. Lawton, *John Wesley's English*. London, 1962.
M. Lelievre, *La Théologie de Wesley*. Paris, 1924.
D. Lerch, *Heil und Heilgung bei John Wesley*. Zürich, 1941.
H. Lindström, *Wesley and Sanctification*. Stockholm, 1946; German trans., *Wesley und die Heiligung*, Frankfurt-am-Main, 1961. *BGM* 6.
— 'The Message of John Wesley and the Modern Man'. *Drew G*, XXV, 1955, pp. 180–95.
T. F. Lockyer, *Paul : Luther : Wesley*. London, 1922.
K. W. MacArthur, *The Economic Ethics of John Wesley*. New York, 1936.
J. A. Macdonald, *Wesley's Revision of Shorter Catechism*. Edinburgh, 1906.
T. W. Madron, 'Some Economic Aspects of John Wesley's Thought Revisited'. *Meth. Hist.*, IV, 1965/66, 1, pp. 33–43.
C. L. Mitton, *A Clue to Wesley's Sermons*. London, 1951.
R. C. Monk, *John Wesley : His Puritan Heritage*. London, 1966.
N. W. Mumford, 'Organization of the Methodist Church in the Times of John Wesley'. *LQHR*, 1946, pp. 35–40, 128–35.
J. L. Nuelsen, *Die Ordination im Methodismus*. Bremen, 1935. *BGM* 2.

— *John Wesley und das deutsche Kirchenlied*. Bremen/Zürich, 1938. BGM 4.

J. Orcibal, *Les spirituels français et españols chez John Wesley et ses contemporains*. RHR, CXXXIX, 1951, 1, pp. 50–109.

— *L'originalité théologique de John Wesley et les spiritualités du continent*. Rev. Hist., CCXXII, 1959, pp. 51–80.

A. C. Outler, ed. *John Wesley*. New York, 1964.

J. R. Parris, *John Wesley's Doctrine of the Sacraments*. London, 1963.

M. Piette, *La Réaction de John Wesley dans l'évolution protestante*. Brussels, 1925; E.T.: London, 1937.

J. W. Prince, *Wesley on Religious Education*. New York/Cincinnati, 1926.

F. C. Pritchard, *Methodist Secondary Education*. London, 1949.

J. E. Rattenbury, *Wesley's Legacy to the World*. London, 1928.

— *The Eucharistic Hymns of John and Charles Wesley*. London, 1948.

J. H. Rigg, *The Relation of John Wesley . . . to the Church of England*. London, 1868.

— *The Churchmanship of John Wesley*. London, 1878.

W. E. Sangster, *The Path to Perfection*. London, 1943.

J. Schempp, *Seelsorge und Seelenführung bei John Wesley*. Stuttgart, 1949.

M. Schmidt, *Die Bedeutung Luthers für John Wesleys Bekehrung*. LuJ, XX, 1938, pp. 125–59.

— *Der Missionsgedanke des jungen Wesley auf dem Hintergrund seines Zeitalters*. Th Viat, I, 1948/49, pp. 80–97.

— *John Wesley und die Biographie des französischen Grafen Gaston Jean-Baptiste de Renty* (1611–49). Th Viat, V, 1953/54, pp. 194–252.

— *Der junge Wesley als Heidenmissionar und Missionstheologe*. Gütersloh, 1955.

— 'John Wesley als Organisator der methodistischen Bewegung', in *Für Kirche und Recht*. Festschrift für J. Heckel. Köln/Graz, 1959, pp. 313–50.

R. E. Schofield, 'John Wesley and Science in 18th-century England'. *Isis*, 44, 4, 1953, pp. 331–40.

P. Scott, *John Wesleys Lehre von der Heiligung*. Berlin, 1939.

D. C. Shipley, 'Wesley and some Calvinistic Controversies'. *Drew G*, XXV, 4, 1955, pp. 195–210.

F. Sigg, 'John Wesley und die "Christliche Bibliothek". *SzEv*, 1953, pp. 381–5.

J. S. Simon, 'Mr. Wesley's Notes upon the New Testament'. *Proc. W.H.S.*, IX, 1913/14, pp. 97–105.

— 'Wesley's Ordinations'. Ibid., pp. 145–54.

W. J. Sparrow Simpson, *John Wesley and the Church of England*. London, 1934.

J. W. E. Sommer, 'John Wesley und die soziale Frage'. Bremen, 1930. *BGM 1.*

L. M. Starkey jr., *The Work of the Holy Spirit.* Nashville, 1962.

R. Stevenson, 'John Wesley's first hymnbook'. *Review of Religion*, 14, 1950, pp. 140–60.

W. Strawson, 'Wesley and the Doctrine of the Last Things'. *LQHR*, 1959, pp. 240–9.

E. W. Thompson, *Wesley: Apostolic Man.* London, 1957.

J. M. Todd, *John Wesley and the Catholic Church.* London, 1958.

D. Tripp, *The Renewal of the Covenant in the Methodist Tradition.* London, 1969.

W. J. Turrell, *John Wesley, physician and electrotherapist.* Oxford, 1938.

R. D. Urlin, *John Wesley's Place in Church History.* London, 1870.

G. H. Vallins, *The Wesleys and the English Language.* London, 1957.

G. S. Wakefield, *The Spiritual Life in the Methodist Tradition.* London, 1966.

J. Wedgwood, *John Wesley and the Evangelical Reaction.* London, 1870.

Wesley Studies. By Various Writers. London, 1903.

G. W. Williams, *John Wesley's Theology Today.* London, 1960.

A. S. Wood, 'John Wesley's Reversion to Type'. *Proc. W.H.S.*, XXXV, 1965/66, pp. 88–93.

A. S. Yates, *The Doctrine of Assurance.* London, 1952.

## 3. On England in the 18th Century

C. J. Abbey and J. H. Overton, *The English Church and its Bishops in the Eighteenth Century.* London, 1878.

T. S. Ashton, *An Economic History of England : The 18th Century.* London, 1955.

S. C. Carpenter, *Eighteenth-century Church and People.* London, 1959.

G. R. Cragg, *Reason and Authority in the Eighteenth Century.* Cambridge Univ. Press, 1964.

J. M. Creed and J. S. Boys-Smith, *Religious Thought in the Eighteenth Century.* Cambridge, 1934.

J. Hunt, *Religious Thought in England From the Reformation to the End of Last Century.* London, 3 vols., 1870–73.

W. E. H. Lecky, *A History of England in the 18th Century.* London, 3rd edn, 1883–87 ( 8 vols.).

J. T. Lightwood, 'Tune Books of the 18th Century'. *Proc. W.H.S.*, II, 1899/1900, pp. 147–60; ibid., III, 1901/02, pp. 237–40; ibid. V, 1905/06, pp. 101–8.

H. Maclachlan, *English Education under the Test Acts.* Manchester, 1931.

F. E. Manuel, *Eighteenth Century confronts the Gods*. Cambridge, Mass., 1959.

D. Marshall, *Eighteenth-Century England*. London, 1962.

J. H. Overton, *The Evangelical Revival in the Eighteenth Century*. London, 1886.

J. H. Plumb, *England in the 18th Century*. Harmondsworth, 1950. Pelican Books A 231.

H. Schöffler, *Protestantismus und Literatur*. Göttingen, 2nd edn, 1958.

T. B. Shepherd, *Methodism and the Literature of the 18th Century*. London, 1940.

J. S. Simon, *The Revival of Religion in England in the 18th Century*. London, n.d. (1907).

L. Stephen, *A History of English Thought in the 18th Century*. 2 vols., London, 1876–80.

— *English Literature and Society in the 18th Century*. London, 1904.

N. Sykes, *Church and State in England in the 18th Century*. Cambridge, 1934.

G. M. Trevelyan, *English Social History*. London 1944. (German Trans. Hamburg, 1948).

R. F. Wearmouth, *Methodism and the Common People of the 18th Century*. London, 1945.

J. H. Whiteley, *Wesley's England*. London, 1938.

A. S. Wood, *The Inextinguishable Blaze*. Spiritual Renewal and Advance in the Eighteenth Century. London, 1960.

## 4. On German Pietism and its Influence in England and North America

M. Schmidt/W. Jannasch (edd.), *Das Zeitalter des Pietismus*. Bremen, 1965 (extensive bibliography, pp. 417–29).

W. G. Addison, *The Renewed Church of the Brethren 1722–1930*. London, 1932.

K. Aland, Spener-Studien. Berlin, 1943.

P. Althaus, 'Die Bekegrung in reformatorischer und pietistischer Sicht'. *NZSTh*, I, 1959, pp. 3–25.

C. F. Arnold, 'Die Salzburger in Amerika'. *JGPrÖ*, 25, 1904, pp. 222–61.

D. Benham, *Life and Labours of the Rev. John Gambold*. London, 1865.

— *Memoirs of James Hutton*. London, 1856.

H. Beyreuther, *August Hermann Francke—Zeuge des Lebendigen Gottes*. Marburg, 1956.

— *August Hermann Francke und die Anfänge der ökumenischen Bewegung*. Hamburg-Bergstedt, 1957.

BIBLIOGRAPHY

— 'Der hallische Pietismus und die Diaspora der Welt'. *Die evangelische Diaspora*, 30, 1959, pp. 1–29.

— *Zinzendorf*. Marburg, 1957–61 (3 vols.).

— *Studien zur Theologie Zinzendorfs*. Neukirchen-Vluyn, 1962.

W. Bettermann, *Theologie und Sprache bei Zinzendorf*. Gotha, 1935.

H. Bornkamm, *Mystik, Spiritualismus und die Anfänge des Pietismus im Luthertum*. Giessen, 1926.

S. Eberhard, Kreuzes-Theologie. *Das reformatorische Anliegen in Zinzendorfs Verkündigung*. München, 1937.

A. L. Fries, *The Moravians in Georgia*. Winston-Salem, N.C., 1905.

P. Grunberg, *Philipp Jakob Spener*. Göttingen, 1893–1906 (3 vols.).

F. W. Kantzenbach, 'Das Bild des Grafen. Ein Literaturbericht zur Zinzendorf-Forschung'. *Lutherische Monatshefte*, 1, 1962, pp. 384–91.

G. Knuth, *August Hermann Franckes Mitarbeiter*. Halle, 1898.

G. Kramer, *August Hermann Francke*. Halle, 1880–82 (2 vols.).

A. Lang, *Puritanismus und Pietismus*. Neukirchen/Vluyn, 1941.

E. Langton, *History of the Moravian Church*. London, 1956.

H. Leube, *Die Reformideen in der deutschen lutherischen Kirche zur Zeit der Orthodoxie*. Leipzig, 1924.

J. P. Lockwood, *Memorials of the Life of Peter Böhler*. London, 1868.

J. Th. Müller, *Geschichte der böhmischen Brüder*. Herrnhut, 1922–32 (3 vols.).

A. W. Nagler, *Pietism and Methodism*. Nashville, Tenn., 1918.

J. W. Nayler, *Charles Delamotte*. London, 1938.

E. Peschke, *Studien zur Theologie August Hermann Francke*. I. Berlin, 1964.

H. Plitt, *Zinzendorfs Theologie*. Gotha, 1869–74 (3 vols.).

G. Reichel, *August Gottlieb Spangenberg*. Tübingen, 1906.

A. Ritschl, *Geschichte des Pietismus*. Bonn, 1880–86 (3 vols.).

H. Schmid, *Die Geschichte des Pietismus*. Nördlingen, 1863.

G. Schmidt, 'Die Banden oder Gesellschaften im alten Herrnhut'. *ZBG*, III, 1909, pp. 145–207.

M. Schmidt, *Gesammelte Aufsätze zum Pietismus* (1967?).

— 'Die Anfänge der Kirchenbildung bei den Salzburgern in Georgia'; in *Lutherische Kirche in Bewegung*. Festschrift für F. Ulmer. Erlangen, 1937, pp. 21–40.

— Das hallische Waisenhaus und England im 18 Jahrhundert'. *ThZ*, 7, 1951, pp. 38–55.

— 'Speners Pia Desideria'. *ThViat*, III, 1951, pp. 70–112.

— 'England und der deutsche Pietismus'. *EvTh*, 13, 1953, pp. 205–24.

— 'Das Bild Zinzendorfs in der neueren Forschung.' *ELKZ*, 7, 1953, pp. 365–9.

— 'Teilnahme an der göttlichen Natur: 2 Pt. 1, 4 in der theologischen Exegese des mystischen Spiritualismus, des Pietismus und der lutherischen Orthodoxie': in *Dank an Paul Althaus*. Gütersloh, 1958, pp. 171–201.

I. C.Frh. v. Schrautenbach, *Der Graf von Zinzendorf*. Gnadau, 1851.

K. Schuster, 'Gruppe, Gemeinschaft, Kirche, Gruppenbildung bei Zinzendorf.' *ThExNF*, 85.

C. W. Towlson, *Moravian and Methodist*. London, 1957.

O. Uttendörfer, *Zinzendorfs religiöse Grundgedanken*. Herrnhut, 1935.

— *Zinzendorf und die Mystik*. Berlin, 1950.

J. G. Walch, *Historische und Theologische Einleitung in die Religionsstreitigkeiten der evangelisch-lutherischen Kirche*. Jena, 1730–39 (5 vols.).

G. A. Wauer, *Die Anfänge der Brüderkirche in England*. Leipzig, 1900.

## 5. On People and Books that Influenced Wesley; on his Friends, Opponents and Contemporaries

*Dictionary of National Biography (DNB)*. 63 vols. (ed. L. Stephen). London, 1885–90. Suppl. I, 1901; Suppl. II, 1912 (3 vols. in each). Twentieth Century, 1912–50 (4 vols.).

*Dictionnaire de Théologie Catholique (DThC)*. Paris, 1899–1950 (ed. J. M. A. Vacant), 15 tomes.

*Enciclopedia Cattolica*. Vatican, 1949–54 (12 vols.).

*A Dictionary of Hymnology*. London, 1892 (ed. J. Julian).

*Realencyklopadie für protestantische Theologie und Kirche (RE)* 3rd edn, 21 vols., Leipzig, 1896–1908 (ed. A. Hauck). Index Vol., 1909. 2 Supplementary volumes, 1913.

*Die Religion in Geschichte und Gegenwart (RGG)*. 3rd edn, 6 vols. Tübingen, 1957–62 (ed. K. Galling). Index Volume, 1965.

T. Armstrong, *The Wesleys—Evangelists and Musicians*. London, 1958.

F. Baker, *Charles Wesley as Revealed by his Letters*. London, 1948, *W.H.S.* Lect. 14.

— *Charles Wesley's Verse*. London, 1964.

W. Beal, *The Fathers of the Wesley Family*. London, 1833.

M. R. Brailsford, *Susanna Wesley*. London, 1910.

T. E. Brigden, 'Samuel Wesley junior . . . and his cycle'. *Proc. W.H.S.*, XI, 1917/18, pp. 25–31, 74–81, 97–102, 121–9, 145–153.

E. Clarke, *Susanna Wesley*. London, 1886.

W. Crook, *The Ancestry of the Wesleys*. London, 1938.

A. Dallimore, *George Whitefield*. (Vol. I.). London, 1970.

H. J. Foster, 'Mrs. W.—'. *Proc. W.H.S.*, VII, 1909/10, pp. 73–8.

A. G. Ives, *Kingswood School in Wesley's day and since*. London, 1970.

T. Jackson, *The Life of the Rev. Charles Wesley*. London, 1841.

J. Kirk, *The Mother of the Wesleys*. London, n.d. (1864).

J. T. Lightwood, *Samuel Wesley, Musician*. London, 1937.

F. H. Mills, 'Wesley's Wife in Wesley's Letters'. *Proc. W.H.S.*, XXI, 1937/38, pp. 120–7.

J. E. Rattenbury, *The Evangelical Doctrines of Charles Wesley's Hymns*. London, 1941.

W. F. Swift, 'Portraits and Biographies of Charles Wesley.' *Proc. W.H.S.*, XXXI, 1955/56, pp. 86–92.

J. Telford, *The Life of the Rev. Charles Wesley*. London, n.d. (1886).

L. Tyerman, *The Life and Times of the Rev. Samuel Wesley*. London, 1866.

F. L. Wiseman, *Charles Wesley*. London, 1933.

E. Aegerter, *Madame Guyon, une aventurière mystique*. Paris, 1941.

E. W. Baker, A *Herald of the Evangelical Revival* (W. Law). London, 1948.

F. Baker, 'Bishop Lavington and the Methodists'. *Proc. W.H.S.*, XXXIV, 1963/64, pp. 37–42.

S. Baring-Gould, *The Evangelical Revival*. London, 1920.

A. D. Belden, *George Whitefield*. London, 1930.

J. Benson, *The Life of the Rev. John W. de la Fléchère*. London, 1805.

H. Bremond, *Histoire littéraire du sentiment religieux en France*. Paris, 1916–33 (11 vols.).

F. F. Bretherton, *The Countess of Huntingdon*. London, 1940. *W.H.S. Lect.* 6.

D. Butler, *Henry Scougal and the Oxford Methodists*. Edinburgh and London, 1899.

— *John Wesley and George Whitefield in Scotland*. London, 1898.

E. Carpenter, *Thomas Sherlock*. London, 1936.

L. F. Church, *The Early Methodist People*. London, 1948.

— *More about the Early Methodist People*. London, 1949.

H. Chattingius, *Bishops and Societies*: A Study of Anglican Colonial and Missionary Expansion, 1698–1850. London, 1955.

G. R. Cragg, *From Puritanism to the Age of Reason*. Cambridge, 1950.

C. H. Crookshank, 'The Oxford Methodists, William and Richard Morgan'. *Proc. W.H.S.*, III, 1901/02, pp. 47–50.

S. Drew, *The Life of the Rev. Thomas Coke*. New York, 1818.

L. E. Elliott-Binns, *The Early Evangelicals*. London, 1954.

A. W. Evans, *Warburton and the Warburtonians*. London, 1932.

F. C. Gill, *The Romantic Movement and Methodism*. London, 1937.

W. E. Gladstone, *Studies Subsidiary to the Works of Bishop Butler*. London, 1896.

J. B. Green, *John Wesley and William Law*. London, 1945.

J. Guibert, *Theologia spiritualis ascetica et mystica*. Rome, 1946.

W. Haller, *The Rise of Puritanism.* New York, 1938.

A. W. Harrison, 'An Early Woman Preacher—Sarah Crosby'. *Proc. W.H.S.,* XIV, 1923/24, pp. 104–9.

— *Arminianism.* London, 1937.

H. Heppe, *Geschichte der quietistischen Mystik.* Berlin, 1875.

E. Hoole, *Oglethorpe and the Wesleys in America.* London, 1863.

— *Byron and the Wesleys.* London, 1864.

I. Jeremias, *Richard Baxter's Catholic Theology.* Diss. Göttingen, 1956.

M. H. Jones, 'Attempts to Re-establish Union Between Howell Harris, English and Welsh Methodists, and the Moravians'. *Proc. W.H.S.,* XVI, 1927/28, pp. 113–7.

D. Knowles, *The English mystical tradition.* London, 1927.

R. A. Knox, *Enthusiasm.* London, 1951; German trans. Olten, 1957.

G. Lawton, *Shropshire Saint.* A Study in the Ministry and Spirituality of Fletcher of Madeley. London, 1960. *W.H.S. Lect.* 26.

G. V. Lechler, *Geschichte des englischen Deismus.* Stuttgart und Tübingen, 1841.

J. Leland, *A View of the Principal Deistical Writers.* London, 1754–56 (3 vols.).

A. J. Lewis, *Zinzendorf.* Philadelphia, 1962.

A. V. D. Linde, *Antoinette Bourignon, das Licht der Welt.* Leiden, 1895.

M. L. Loane, *Cambridge and the Evangelical Succession.* London, 1952.

— *Oxford and the Evangelical Succession.* London, 1950.

A. M. Lyles, *Methodism Mocked.* London, 1960.

B. L. Manning, *The Hymns of Wesley and Watts.* London, 1942.

K. Minkner, *Die Stufenfolge des mystischen Erlebnisses bei William Law.* München, 1939.

W. F. Mitchell, *English Pulpit Oratory from Andrewes to Tillotson.* London, 1932.

E. C. Mossner, *Bishop Butler and the Age of Reason.* New York, 1936.

J. A. Newton, *Methodism and the Puritans,* London, 1964.

— *Susanna Wesley and the Puritan Tradition in Methodism.* London, 1969.

W. Nigg, *Grosse Heilige.* Zürich, 1946.

J. H. Overton, *William Law, Nonjuror and Mystic.* London, 1881.

— *The Nonjurors.* London, 1902.

E. A. Peers, *Studies of the Spanish Mystics.* London, 1927–30 (2 vols.).

F. J. Powicke, *Life of the Rev. Richard Baxter.* London, 1924–27 (2 vols.).

G. T. Roberts, *Howell Harris.* London, 1951. *W.H.S. Lect.* 17.

M. Schmidt, 'Das Erbauungsbuch, The Whole Duty of Man und seine Bedeutung für das Christentum in England.' *Th Viat,* VIII, 1961/62, pp. 232–77.

— 'Die Problematik des Puritanismus im Lichte seiner Erforschung.' *ZKG*, LX, 1941, pp. 207–54.

— 'The Ecumenical Movement in Continental Europe during the 17th and 18th Century', in: *A History of Ecumenical Movement*. London, 1954.

L. L. Schücking, *Die Familie im Puritanismus*. Leipzig, 1928.

(A. C. H. Seymour), *The Life and Times of Selina Countess of Huntingdon*. London, 1839/40 (2 vols.). (Cf. Suppl. to *Proc. W.H.S.*, V. An Index . . . Burnley, 1905/06.)

D. Shipley, *Methodist Arminianism in the Theology of Fletcher*. Diss. Yale, 1942.

C. E. Sommer, 'John William Fletcher' . . . in: *'Basileia'*, Walter Freytag zum 60. Geburtstag. Stuttgart, 1958, pp. 437–53.

C. J. Stranks, *The Life and Writings of Jeremy Taylor*. London, 1952.

N. Sykes, *Edmund Gibson, Bishop of London*. London, 1926.

N. Thune, *The Behmenists and the Philadelphians*. Uppsala, 1948.

L. Tyerman, *The Oxford Methodists*. New York, 1873.

— *The Life of the Rev. George Whitefield*. London, 1876.

— *John Wesley's designated Successor* (Fletcher) . . . London, 1882.

J. A. Vickers, *Thomas Coke and the Origins of World Methodism*. London, 1964. *W.H.S. Lect.* 30.

— *Thomas Coke, Apostle of Methodism*. London, 1970.

J. S. Watson, *Life of William Warburton*. London, 1863.

G. S. Wakefield, *Puritan Devotion*. London, 1957.

P. A. Welsby, *Lancelot Andrewes (1555–1626)*. London, 1958.

J. H. Whiteley, *Wesley's Anglican Contemporaries*. London, 1939. *W.H.S. Lect.* 5.

M. Wieser, *Peter Poiret*. München, 1932.

D. Dunn Wilson, 'John Wesley, Gregory Lopez and the Marquis de Renty'. *Proc. W.H.S.*, XXV (1966), pp. 181–4.

J. Woodward, *An Account of the Rise and Progress of the Religious Societies*. London, 1698 (4th edn, 1712).

## 6. General Literature on the History of Methodism.

F. A. Norwood, 'Methodist Historical Studies 1930–1959' (Bibliography). *Ch. Hist.*, 28, 1959, pp. 391–417; ibid. 29, 1960, pp. 74–88.

G. Stampe, 'A List of local Histories', *Proc. W.H.S.*, I. 1897/98, pp. 3–14. (A Supplementary List, ibid., VI, 1907/08, pp. 70–4).

F. Baker, *A Charge to Keep*. London, 1947.

— *John Wesley and the Church of England*. London, 1970.

W. C. Barclay, *History of Methodist Missions*. New York, 1949ff. (6 vols.). (Part One: *Early American Methodism*. New York, 1949/50, 2 vols.).

H. Bett, *The Spirit of Methodism*. London, 1937.

J. C. Bowmer, *The Sacrament of the Lord's Supper in Early Methodism*. London, 1951.

E. S. Bucke (Gen. Ed.), *The History of American Methodism*. In Three Volumes. New York/Nashville, 1964 (Vol. I: 1736–1844).

R. M. Cameron, *Methodism and Society in Historical Perspective*. New York/Nashville, 1961 (Vol. I: *Methodism and Society*).

D. Creamer, *Methodist Hymnology*. New York, 1848.

R. E. Davies, *Methodism*. Harmondsworth, 1963 (Pelican Book A 591).

R. E. Davies/G. Rupp (Gen. Ed.), *A history of the Methodist Church in Great Britain*. London, 1965ff. (4 vols.). Vol. I: *Methodism within the lifetime of John Wesley*. 1965.

J. R. Gregory, *A History of Methodism*. London, 1921 (2 vols.).

A. W. Harrison, *The Separation of Methodism from the Church of England*. London, 1945. *W.H.S. Lect* 11.

J. F. Hurst, *The History of Methodism*, New York, 1902–04 (7 vols.). (Vols. I–III: *British Methodism*).

T. Jackson (Ed.), *The Lives of Early Methodist Preachers*, Chiefly Written by Themselves. London, 1837 (3 vols.); 3rd edn, 1865, (6 vols.). (New edn in 7 volumes, 'Wesley's Veterans' by J. Telford. London, 1911–14.)

J. L. Nuelsen, *Kurzgefasste Geschichte des Methodismus*. Bremen, 1920; 2nd edn, 1929 (revised and enlarged).

G. Smith, *History of Wesleyan Methodism*. London, 1857–61 (3 vols.).

C. E. Sommer (Ed.), *Der Methodismus*. Stuttgart, 1968.

A. Stevens, *The History of the Religious Movement in the Eighteenth Century, Called Methodism . . .* New York, 1858–61 (3 vols.).

W. J. Townsend/H. B. Workman/G. Eayrs (Edd.), *A New History of Methodism*. London, 1909.

H. Wheeler, *History and Exposition of the Twenty-five Articles of Religion of the Methodist Episcopal Church*. New York/Cincinnati, 1908.

## 7. General Literature on English Church History

S.L. Ollard/G. Crosse (Edd.), *A Dictionary of English Church History*. Oxford, 1912.

E. J. Backnell, A *Theological Introduction to the Thirty-Nine Articles*. London, 3rd edn, 1955.

S. C. Carpenter, *The Church in England, 597–1688*. London, 1954.

J. Hunt, *Religious Thought in England*. London, 1870–73 (3 vols.).

W. F. Hook, *Lives of the Archbishops of Canterbury*. London, 1860–76 (12 vols.).

J. R. H. Moorman, *A History of the Church in England*. London, 1953.

M. Schmidt, 'Kirche und Christentum in Grossbritannien', in: *England-kunde, 12 Beiträge*... Frankfurt/Berlin/Bonn, 3rd edn, 1955, pp. 194–228.

H. Smith, *The Thirty-Nine Articles of Religion*. London, 1930.

W. R. W. Stephen/W. Hunt (Edd.), *A History of the English Church*. London, 1899–1910 (9 vols.). (Vol. VII: 1714–1800).

N. Sykes, *The English Religious Tradition*. London, 1953.

H. O. Wakeman, *An Introduction to the History of the Church of England*. London, 5th edn, 1898.

# Abbreviations

| | |
|---|---|
| *ARG* | Archiv für Reformationsgeschichte |
| *BGM* | Beiträge zur Geschichte des Methodismus |
| *Ch. Hist.* | Church History |
| *DrewG* | The Drew Gateway |
| *ELKZ* | Evangelische Theologie |
| *Isis* | Isis, an International Review Devoted to the History of Science and its Cultural Influences |
| *JGPrÖ* | Jahrbuch der Gesellschaft für die Geschichte des Protestantismus in Österreich |
| *LQHR* | London Quarterly and Holborn Review |
| *LuJ* | Luther-Jahrbuch |
| *Meth. Hist.* | Methodist History, Association of Methodist Historical Societies. Lake Junaluska, N.C. |
| *NZSTh* | Neue Zeitschrift für Systematische Theologie |
| *Proc. W.H.S.* | Proceedings of the Wesley Historical Society |
| *Publ. W.H.S.* | Publications of the Wesley Historical Society |
| *Rev. Hist.* | Revue Historique |
| *RHR* | Revue de l'Histoire des Religions |
| *RiL* | Religion in Life |
| *Sz Ev* | Schweizer Evangelist |
| *Th Ex NF* | Theologische Existenz heute, Neue Folge |
| *Th Viat* | Theologia Viatorum, Jahrbuch der Kirchlichen Hochschule, Berlin |
| *ThZ* | Theologische Zeitschrift |
| *W.H.S. Lect.* | The Wesley Historical Society (Annual) Lecture |
| *ZBG* | Zeitschrift für Brüdergeschichte |
| *ZThK* | Zeitschrift für Theologie und Kirche |

# Index